Russian Intellectual Antisemitism in the Post-Communist Era

Studies in Antisemitism

Russian Intellectual Antisemitism in the Post-Communist Era

Vadim Rossman

Foreword by Sidney Monas

Published by The University of Nebraska Press, Lincoln and London
for The Vidal Sassoon International Center for the Study of Antisemitism (SICSA),
The Hebrew University of Jerusalem

Library of Congress Control Number: 2001096328

"N"

Manufactured and distributed by the University of Nebraska Press for
The Vidal Sassoon International Center for the Study of Antisemitism (SICSA)
The Hebrew University of Jerusalem
Mount Scopus
91905 Jerusalem
Israel

Contents

Foreword

Vadim Rossman has an almost uncanny gift for locating the central idea of what might otherwise seem a tangled ideological network. He has in addition the ability to take it seriously without being swayed by it; to engage it, not so much in polemic as in a steady clarification that goes a long way toward refuting it. His book on the history of intellectual antisemitism in Russia does not purport to analyze the current political situation there, but provides a lucid account of a background that cannot but bring considerable weight to bear on any political situation that might arise there. He depicts the philosophical-psychological-historical basis for the idea of Russianness formed in a country where national self-identification has long been exceptionally problematic.

The continuous thread that weaves its way through the diverse chapters of this substantial book is the all but indispensable negative role that Jews have played in the history of what is now generally called, both by its critics and its adherents, the Russian Idea. This is the idea of Russian uniqueness and even superiority to other nations, especially those belonging to the west. It is a messianic idea and implies a special mission imposed on Russia by the course of world history, a mission based in turn on the persistence of religious feeling and a feeling for the sacred in Russia that has survived the rationalism and secularization of western thought.

If Russian national self-identity was deeply rooted in Eastern Orthodox Christianity, as the nineteenth-century Russian Slavophiles maintained, it was deeply shaken by the Bolshevik Revolution and the creation of the Soviet Union. The Bolshevik attempt to substitute a "Soviet" identity for the Russian, however, never quite "took," and, with the economic and political disintegration and collapse of the Soviet Union, shattered into fragments. A neo-Slavophilism of the twentieth century that called itself "Eurasianism" and tended to see Bolshevism and the Soviet Union as a necessary but passing phase in the historical development of the Russian Idea, originated abroad in émigré circles, encouraged by Stalin's turning to the Church and to traditions of Russian nationalism when he felt the Soviet Union under threat in the 1930s. Although Eurasian hopes in Stalin were bitterly disappointed, a kind of neo-Eurasianism had great intellectual vogue in the postwar Soviet Union.

It would be unjust, as Rossman points out, to assume that either the Slavophile or Eurasian traditions throughout their history were fundamentally or wholly or even preponderantly antisemitic. Indeed, some of their foremost thinkers were staunch defenders of the Jews and even semitophiles. Vladimir Soloviev, for instance, not only fought courageously for Jewish emancipation, but was a profound student of Jewish religious tradition. Even he, however, as Rossman points out, with all his genuine love for Jews and Judaica, tended to see Judaism as primarily a chapter in the history of Christianity rather than as an autonomous and separate religion.

Throughout these ideologies there is a deep-seated and perhaps inevitable ambivalence with regard to Jews and Judaism. Vassily Rozanov both loved and hated the Jews. Fedor Dostoevsky, like many Russian Christian intellectuals, made a sharp semantic distinction between "Evrei" — the Hebrews who prefigured Christianity and into whose midst Christ came and lived — and "zhidy," the "yids" who were his own contemporaries. In his publicistic tirades against Jews, Dostoevsky kept repeating the charge over and over again that not only did Jews "hate" Russians, but that it was inevitable, they being Jews, that they should hate Russians. It is curious, and of course not accidental, that the most recent charge by neo-Eurasians and other Russian nationalists against the Jews is that they are virtually inevitable "Russophobes."

Rossman does not satirize the Russian Idea or its ideologies. he does not confuse them with mob patriotism or mass antisemitism. He takes them seriously as thinkers, with whom it is possible to argue — sometimes on quite a high level — and whose mistaken ideas it is at least possible to refute. He takes serious measure of great, highly original, important writers like Dostoevsky and Rozanov. He introduces us to the now almost forgotten but extremely interesting French convert to Islam, René Guenon, who has had a second wave of influence in recent Russian translations of his "traditionalist" works. He introduces us to the volatile and often irresponsible, but wide ranging and sometimes remarkably intelligent Aleksandr Dugin, the main force of whose influence may well have passed, but who continues to write and to change in interesting and unpredictable ways. He tells us about the brilliant Aleksandr Kozhevnikov, who wrote a doctoral dissertation on Soloviev under Karl Jaspers in Germany, and later, under the name Kojève, established his own rather Marxist interpretation of Hegel on a whole generation of French intellectuals, and also served as economic minister to Premiere Giscard d'Estaing, but whose intellectual roots were in Russian messianism, and who actually wept, like many patriotic Russians, at news of the death of Stalin. He makes significant connections between the thinking of his Russian ideologues and similar tendencies in France and Germany.

Antisemitism has had a long and complex history in Russian intellectual life. There is certainly more to it than simply the rivalry of two conceptions of a "chosen people." Although the threat of imminent violence against the Jews in Russian that sent so many of them into emigration to Israel from the 1960s on seems to have receded if it has not entirely disappeared, the roots of antisemitism, and especially of an intellectual antisemitism connected to the Russian Idea are broad and deep, and popular antisemitism, though it is volatile and comes and goes, has not disappeared either. It is certainly not Rossman's purpose to relate his careful and serious study of antisemitic ideas to the imminent danger of renewed pogroms. It would be a mistake, however, to regard Rossman's restraint and avoidance of political hysteria as a sign of his work's contemporary political irrelevance. If one wants to understand the deep crisis of Russian national self-identification, or the problems of self-identification inflicted on Russian Jews, especially those who rightly consider themselves thoroughly Russian by culture, both those who have remained in Russia and those who have emigrated to Israel, then Rossman's book is essential and invigorating reading.

Sidney Monas
University of Texas at Austin

Preface

The concepts and ideas developed in this book — the work was done mainly between 1992 and 1997 — emerged in the course of several years of my research, teaching, and communication with a number of people in the United States, Israel, and Russia. While credit is due to many people, a few stand out.

I am grateful to David Braybrook for his advice and critical remarks. In addition, I wish to thank the Philosophy Department of the University of Texas at Austin for providing a congenial atmosphere in which to work. Seth Wolitz of the University of Texas at Austin and Zvi Gitelman of the University of Michigan Ann Arbor read the manuscript and shared with me some valuable ideas. Leon Volovici of the Hebrew University of Jerusalem provided much good advice concerning both formal and substantive aspects of this research.

I am especially grateful to Professor Sidney Monas, University of Texas, for his encouragement, help, and friendship. Our numerous conversations on Russian intellectual history were always very stimulating and helped me to shape some ideas. Very special thanks go to Alifa Saadya for her kind help with editing and preparation of the manuscript. I highly appreciate her sensitivity, experience, and advice which went far beyond the purely editorial aspects of the research.

I am also grateful for the financial support given by the Vidal Sassoon International Center for the Study of Antisemitism at the Hebrew University of Jerusalem.

I also want to express my gratitude to Anna Rakitiansky for her valuable advice with the bibliographical support for this book and help in obtaining some hard-to-find émigré and current Russian monographs and periodicals.

Very special thanks go to my wife, Janna Rossman, and to my parents, Iosif Rossman and Nadezhda Nikolaeva, for their constant support, patience and understanding.

Vadim Rossman
Austin, Texas

Introduction

This study examines the nature and meaning of Russian antisemitism of the perestroika and post-perestroika periods. The significance of antisemitism in Russian political and social life is widely recognized. The occurrence of antisemitic manifestations and incidents (vandalism, desecration of cemeteries and synagogues, attacks on Jewish property, graffiti inscriptions) are monitored and reported by newspapers and magazines, while a number of sociological surveys have studied the mechanisms of ethnic stereotyping and popular attitudes to the Jews.[1] In addition, there have been many works devoted to the study of political antisemitism both in Russia and in the Soviet Union.[2] The focus of this study, however, is not "grass-roots" antisemitism, nor political antisemitism, but intellectual antisemitism, that is, the views and arguments advanced to back up antisemitic positions. My primary focus will be the ways in which the Russian ideologists of antisemitism articulate their ideas. Intellectual antisemitism, that often fuels and animates all the various manifestations given above, has so far received scant attention among scholars. The student of antisemitism can find only some passing remarks and a few individual sections in general monographs on the ideology of Russian nationalism.[3] No systematic study of post-communist ideological antisemitism has been undertaken.

Moreover, reports in magazines and newspapers have created some persistent stereotypes about Russian antisemitism. These reports often suggest that antisemitism is a syndrome common to the lowbrow public, that antisemitic propaganda circulates mainly or almost exclusively among the undereducated strata of the population, and that Judeophobia meets almost unanimous opposition from intellectuals. The works of some social scientists have reinforced this stereotype.[4] Some observers even discuss the "appeal" of ultra-nationalism to intellectuals, as if it were something outside or separate from, the intellectual's activity. The notion that antisemitism is a syndrome of the lowbrow public, and the preoccupation with "grass-roots" antisemitism led to the corollary that the ideas of ultra-nationalists do not demand any serious response. This simplistic presumption governs many discussions on the ideology of Russian nationalism. It has been suggested in several studies that contemporary Russian antisemitism is nothing more than a relic of a "medieval" mentality, and that the arguments of antisemites can be easily dismissed as intellectually insignificant and outlandish. It is rarely recalled that in the interwar period the intellectual elite of one of the most culturally advanced countries of Western Europe was not immune to very similar "ridiculous" and "medieval" ideas.

Admittedly, the biases of the sociologists and journalists are derive from the very nature of the material with which they most often deal, namely, cheap or freely-distributed pieces of antisemitic propaganda like newspapers and leaflets, but this bias of selection can be avoided. In fact, the audience and the sources of antisemitic messages are more diverse than is often realized. To an appalling extent, antisemitic ideas and stereotypes are shaped and propagated by academics and those who see themselves as intellectuals. I shall specifically focus on the ideas of sociologists, historians, philosophers, theologians, political analysts, ethnologists, anthropologists, and literary critics who help to fix antisemitic prejudices in the minds of those exposed to their ideology. My account will also suggest that the arguments of Russian antisemites are quite sophisticated. In contrast to many scholars of antisemitism, who choose not to dignify with a response the ideologists of militant xenophobia, I shall address some of the false lines of argument that are sufficiently complicated as to mislead even an intelligent reader who may not be well-versed in the subtleties of political philosophy and the details of the view of world history invoked by antisemites.

In the course of my research I found useful the methods of the various social sciences, including sociology, history, political science, social psychology, and literary criticism.[5]

The discussion of different types of antisemitic discourse and their ideological functions constitutes a sociological aspect of my study. In this, I will focus on the social functions of antisemitic ideology and their role in the "climate of opinion" in post-Soviet Russia. I will try to account for the genealogy of the social forces that may have had an effect on the preoccupation with the "Jewish Question." The sociological part of my inquiry is descriptive. I quote many illustrative passages to demonstrate not only the content but also the tone of the discussions. In many cases, the actual language of the ideologists of nationalism is no less important than the content of their statements. These quotations are also necessary due to the fact that very few of the publications discussed are available in English translation. Some books and periodicals are not available even in the most extensive libraries. In my analysis of the antisemitic ideology I have tried to relate the immediate subject of my inquiry to the more serious problems that preoccupy social scientists and public discussion in post-communist Russia.

The revival of ideological antisemitism must be understood in the context of Russian intellectual history. A number of questions arise: why did the ghosts of antisemitism resurface in the post-communist period? What traditions do these "repressed contents" perpetuate? What continuities and discontinuities can be found in the intellectual attitudes of different trends? What new interpretations of the repressed contents are suggested? How do the old concepts affect current political and cultural debates? Which historical tendencies of intellectual and religious development have made the hostility toward the Jews so prominent?

The analysis and criticism of the normative — sometimes tacit — assumptions made by the ideologists of nationalism constitute another important dimension of my inquiry. I shall focus on their assumptions about the nature of human history, and those related to moral and political philosophy Many of their arguments are informed by the anti-liberal ideas of the communitarian political philosophy and draw upon some post-modern criticisms of the Enlightenment and modernity. Although these assumptions do not commit those who hold them to antisemitic beliefs, it is nevertheless the case that many antisemitic arguments depend upon these assumptions and can be invalidated once they are removed.

The recent debate between liberals and communitarians in Anglo-American political philosophy can help us to understand some facets of the anti-liberal stance of the nationalist ideologists. Central to the more respectable ideologies of nationalism is the idea of community. The preoccupation with the "Jewish Question" is a result of a difference in understanding the nature of the human community and the requirements for membership in that community. The nationalist critics of liberalism believe that market reforms and liberal political reforms destroyed the sense of community that was central to Russian civilization. The "Jew" functions as a metaphor for an alien who has lost his attachment to his race, a cosmopolitan, and the very symbol of the liberal transformation. Many communitarian critics of liberalism believe that those who discuss political philosophy from an objective and rational standpoint have, in fact, adopted a "Jewish" position. The ideologists of nationalism are thus interested not only in the concept of membership in the human community and the nature of the moral community, but in other normative questions about cultural and moral identity, the nature of citizenship, and the relationship between culture and the state.

Although it is quite difficult to preserve a non-partisan tone in discussing a topic as sensitive as antisemitism, I shall try to analyze objectively the flawed arguments and the manipulation of evidence so characteristic of the Russian ultra-nationalists, and in particular, to point to the perverse logic of their ideology.

My research is based on both academic works in the social sciences (sociology, historiography, psychology, economics, and anthropology) published in monographs and professional journals, and on the materials derived from public debate and published in various periodicals, magazines, and newspapers. The Anti-Defamation Committee of the Russian Jewish Congress, founded in 1996, classifies about 200 newspapers in Russia as openly antisemitic. Most of these are cheap newsletters with a small readership.[6] In this study, I will concentrate on the most prominent or widely-circulated sources.

In the sections that follow, I will outline the historical background for the development of the Russian nationalist ideology, and the major figures of this movement. I will then provide a classification of the various ideologies, followed by a discussion of the economic, political, and cultural forces that drive the nationalists.

RUSSIAN NATIONALISM IN THE CHANGING POLITICAL CONTEXT (1987–1997)

The political appeal of the nationalist parties and the history of their successes and failures is not the focus of my analysis. However, the political context of the formation of ideological antisemitism cannot be disregarded, since many concepts and theories of the ideologists of Russian nationalism have evolved in response to specific political circumstances. The ways in which the ideological concepts influence political actions and mobilize the agents of the historical process are also important for my study. Therefore, I shall discuss the most crucial episodes in the political history of Russia during the post-communist period, and identify the most conspicuous groups affiliated with the nationalist ideologists.

The history of post-communist antisemitism starts with the era of glasnost (candor). The politics of perestroika (restructuring) opened the floodgate of free political expression and set the stage for liberal social transformations and radical economic reforms. The still-dormant political forces began to recall the forgotten language of free political debate and to forge their new identities. The "philosophical" revolution, which according to Hegel paves the way for political revolution, was realized through a revolution in the periodicals. To a great extent, glasnost was an era of newspapers and magazines. Soviet history was reexamined in light of liberal doctrines and universal values. Questions about the political reconstruction of Russia turned out to be central to public discourse.

The era of political emancipation not only made possible the publication of formerly forbidden masterpieces of literature, along with open discussion of new ideas in the social sciences and history, but also paved the way for the revival of old xenophobic stereotypes and set the stage for the dissemination of extreme nationalist ideas. The proliferation of antisemitic propaganda turned out to be a very important manifestation of the ultra-nationalist mentality. The repressed mentality of antisemitism resurfaced and pervaded the nationalist discussions. The first years of glasnost have witnessed the vast proliferation of antisemitic periodicals, leaflets, caricatures, and other artifacts of the antisemitic subculture.

Even the massive emigration of Jews in the late 1980s and early 1990s did not lead to a decrease in the production and dissemination of antisemitic texts and xenophobic outbursts. Rather, the increased Jewish emigration has coincided with the new tide of antisemitism reported by sociologists. Pollsters from the All-Union Center for the Study of Public Opinion ironically summarized the results of their sociological survey in the laconic title of their report, "The fewer Jews there are in Russia, the more they talk about them."[7] The physical presence of Jews in the country is not a necessary prerequisite for the increase of antisemitic propaganda.

It is not difficult to find the "ancestors" of the major figures of post-communist antisemitism in the Soviet era. The two Soviet sources of antisemitism include the official anti-Zionist campaigns and the nationalist opposition to the communist regime. It is widely known that the Soviet Union supported antisemitic political campaigns. The exposure of the "murderers in white coats" (the "Doctors' Plot"), the struggle against "bourgeois Jewish nationalism," "rootless cosmopolitans," and the late Soviet anti-Zionist ideological campaigns are deceptive slogans of the antisemitic campaigns initiated and sponsored by the Soviet state. The anti-Zionist campaigns were especially persistent, lasting for about twenty-five years.[8]

There was also an antisemitism that emanated from the scores of underground and semi-official nationalist groups. These groups opposed the communist rule and blamed the Jews for fomenting the Bolshevik revolution.[9] They published their materials in *samizdat* and abroad. These groups mushroomed from the early 1960s, and survived in the perestroika period.

After the collapse of communism, both the Soviet anti-Zionist crusaders and the anti-communist nationalists joined the newly-shaped antisemitic parties. Two distinct antisemitic groups were especially visible on the political scene in the first years of glasnost — village prose writers and the group Pamyat.

Pamyat became the most famous of the ultra-nationalist groups.[10] Originally it was a loosely-organized "memorial" society dedicated to the restoration and preservation of historical buildings and churches. Pamyat took an extremely antisemitic political stance following the ascension to its leadership of Dmitry Vasiliev, an engaging and demagogic speaker who pressed for the destruction of Jewish-designed monuments in Moscow. The statements and megalomaniac excesses of Pamyat leaders were so outlandish that many modest nationalists suspected the KGB was using it in an attempt to discredit the growing nationalist movement.

Intensive press coverage of Pamyat activities made the organization quite famous both in Russia and abroad.[11] However, the nature of its popularity and the sources of its fame should be properly understood. Pamyat was the first organization to embrace the ideology of the Black Hundreds and ideas about a Jewish conspiracy against Russia.[12] This shocked public consciousness, and it should be observed that the image of Pamyat was damaged even in the eyes of staunch nationalists. This group was unable to formulate a consistent and serious antisemitic ideology. It appealed almost exclusively to the fringes of society, and the more prominent ideologists of Russian nationalism always tried to stay away from this odious and unpredictable group.[13] Moreover, media preoccupation with Pamyat created a mistaken impression that antisemitism appeals and finds its audience only in lunatic fringe and that it is a marginal phenomenon. Walter Laqueur, a well-known student of Russian nationalism, aptly points out that

> The early years of glasnost belonged to the sectarians and extremists. They were the first to appear on the political scene; they were certainly the shrillest and loudest. But their ideas were usually too bizarre, their activities too outlandish to be taken seriously.... Thus political initiative passed to the "respectable" right.... [By 1991] the new wave of patriotic organizations regarded Pamyat as a political embarrassment; the very name "Pamyat" was to be eschewed because it had negative connotations.[14]

Some members of the "respectable" right were associated with the group of "village prose writers" *(pisateli-dereven'schiki)*. They and the literary critics associated with them argued that political and social reforms could not succeed without a revival of traditional moral values and the restoration of the traditional community. This group included the well-known Russian novelists, Valentin Rasputin, Vasily Belov, and Viktor Astafiev. Their concern for the village community and the environment was coupled with accusations against the Jews for the destruction of the community in the course of the revolution of 1917, and for much of the damage done to the environment. The village writers were emblematic figures in the nationalist movement but their ideological position was not sufficiently articulated. They were unable to develop serious proposals for practical ways to carry out the reconstruction of Russia. It is no coincidence that by 1991 both Pamyat and the village writers faded from the center of attention. However, their message and their public appearance was crucial for the establishment of newer politically viable and more pragmatic nationalist groups.

The collapse of the USSR was perceived by nationalists as a disaster equal to or even worse than the Bolshevik Revolution, and it kicked the movement into high gear. In the years since the coup the trend on the right has been toward coalition-building rather than splintering into special-interest factions. Various nationalist groups united in opposition to Yeltsin. The founding of the weekly newspaper *Den'* was one significant landmark in the coalition-making process. The editors of the newspaper tried to formulate a common ideology for political opposition to the liberal political reforms and market economy. The nationalists also formed various associations to coordinate the activities of individual groups. In 1992 they established the National Salvation Front, which encompassed virtually all nationalist groups, and the Russian National Council *(Russkii Natsionalnii Sobor)*. These organizations staged emotional rallies and united under their banners the most diverse political forces in opposition to the reforms, — monarchists, Orthodox fundamentalists, Slavophiles, and neo-Stalinists. In addition to the disenchantment with the liberal reforms and a concern for the preservation of the empire all these groups shared xenophobic attitudes — anti-Western, anti-American, and antisemitic. Samuel Kassow has aptly pointed out that antisemitism served as a "glue" which could effectively bind the different anti-liberal forces.[15]

Whereas in the coup of 1991 the nationalists could only join the neo-communist keynote conspirators, in the later coup attempt of October 1993 they played the key role. This coup was ideologically inspired by "patriotic" propaganda of the anti-liberal media. The defense of the constitution that was used as a pretext for the coup was played out by the nationalist slogans that set its tone. Many leaders of Russian nationalist groups and parties took an active part in the fights near the White House. The crowd yelled such slogans as: "Yankee, go home!" "Strangers, get out from Russia!" "Disclose the origins of those who work in the Russian media!" and "We are Russians! God is with us!"[16]

Afterwards, Yeltsin tried to ban the most radical newspapers, the mouthpieces of organizations that had supported the coup. However, this measure was not very effective. The publishers of *Den'* simply changed the title of the newspaper and began publishing again a few weeks later. Other ultra-nationalist periodicals followed in their footsteps.

Vladimir Zhirinovsky did not support the coup, and this helped him to emerge after 1993 as the most visible political figure on the Right. The strong showing of his party in the parliamentary elections surprised both his opponents and supporters. It is remarkable that Zhirinovsky frequently uses antisemitic slogans in his political propaganda. His scurrilous remarks about the Jews and his general distaste for them are widely known and well-documented.[17] In public rallies and in print Zhirinovsky and his fellow travelers continuously denounce Zionism as the sinister force striving for the world domination and economic supremacy. The governments of the United States, France, and Great Britain, as well as international organizations are said to be controlled by the Zionists.[18] Abroad, Zhirinovsky and Liberal Democratic Party seek to build connections through an international anti-Zionist alliance.[19] The anti-Zionist rhetoric of Zhirinovsky often turns into wild antisemitic statements. Thus, he claims that Russia needs to deal with its national minorities as Nazi Germany did with the Jews and Gypsies.

Zhirinovsky does not belong to the club of nationalist high intellectuals, who tend to dismiss him both as a demagogue and a Jew.[20] They disavow his excesses and try to dissociate him from the mainstream patriotic movement. Some even suggest that Zhirinovsky is a "second edition" of Pamyat, designed by the liberals to discredit the very idea of nationalism.[21] Nevertheless, Zhirinivsky is, in practical terms, the most successful nationalist leader, and one of the few who can get a hearing for his antisemitic ideas in the parliament. His political standing and charisma thus force the highbrow nationalists to take seriously his position and actions.

The alliance of various groups of Russian nationalists turned out to be quite fragile. The conflict with Liberal Democratic Party is only one among many other conflicts and ideological disagreements within the nationalist movement. Coalition-making endeavors often fail because of the radical differences in the programs of different factions. The Chechen war and the discussion of the future of Russia within or outside of the "Eurasian Union" evoked a number of serious ideological conflicts within the nationalist establishment. The attitude to the "Jewish Question" is one of the few areas of agreement. The "glue" of antisemitism makes it especially valuable and attractive for coalition-minded nationalist leaders. However, even this area of agreement is unstable. Differing trends within the nationalist movement provide a variety of explanations for hatred of the Jews, and these cannot be reduced to one common ground.

Before discussing the varieties of the ideological antisemitism, it should be noted that the development of the nationalist movement exhibits one striking tendency: the grass-roots expression of xenophobia and antisemitism and the ideologically "blind" and inarticulate manifestations of social protest gradually gave way to the full-fledged antisemitic ideologies and the development of specific ideological languages. While at the early stages of political and economic reforms, scores of nationalists have been steeped in emotion, expressing quite low interest in the articulation of their ideas, at the later stages they have focused on the intellectual elaborations of their positive programs and critical positions. The age of blind resistance to the new "liberal despotism" gave a way for the new "age of ideologists" who tried to exploit the frustration of the people as a result of the reforms. These ideologists created specific "ideolects" for each nationalist faction who wrote the manifestos and monographs that have taken the place of newspaper articles.

The Varieties of Antisemitic Ideologies

Some social scientists have assumed that post-communist antisemitism is a homogeneous phenomenon, although closer attention to the phenomenon reveals a variety of perspectives among the nationalist groups. The factions differ in the importance they give to the "Jewish Question," and in the type of resolution they suggest. Identifying differences among the nationalist ideologists turned out to be rather a complicated task for social scientists. I shall cite several attempts to classify Russian nationalist ideologies, and will suggest a classification of my own.

Two Russian sociologists, Leonid Gudkov and Alexander Levinson, have distinguished three basic types of antisemitism in the former Soviet Union:

The *xenophobes* make no distinction between Jews and other foreigners and outsiders. Xenophobia is identical with tribal or ethnic hostility.

The advocates of *instrumental antisemitism* hold the Jews responsible for the negative consequences of modernity. The Jews are portrayed as the classical bearers of liberal and modern values, and are believed to subvert the values and virtues of traditional society.

Ideological antisemitism or antisemitism proper. In contrast to xenophobia and instrumental antisemitism, ideological antisemitism articulates its position in theoretical arguments.[22]

Such a classification may be useful for a sociological survey, but is less so for understanding antisemitism as an ideological phenomenon.

An alternative was suggested by Theodore Friedgut in his paper "Antisemitism and its Opponents: Reflections in the Russian Press." He distinguishes four different trends:

Antisemitism that dwells on the issue of "Russophobia" in the belief that Jews have "an immanent national character" alien to Russian life and values.

The representatives of *instrumental antisemitism* are concerned with the devastating effects of the economic and political reforms and oppose the Jews for supporting individual economic activity.

Anti-Zionists define Zionism as a world conspiracy for universal Jewish domination.

The representatives of *"zoological antisemitism"* believe that the Jew is "an instrument of satanic forces." Friedgut believes that this type "needs little elaboration" and is "an offshoot of Christian theological antisemitism."[23]

Friedgut's classification is problematic, however, since the categories often overlap among the various nationalist groups. Anti-Zionism is taken up by several groups, while zoological antisemitism is not the only type of antisemitic thinking that can be said to have originated in Christian theology.

Another alternative is to distinguish trends of nationalist ideology on the basis of the periodicals with which they are associated, or on the basis of particular interest groups. However, the arguments of the various contributors to the same periodicals may differ. Some of the periodicals introduce themselves as forums that give everybody an opportunity to voice his perspective (e.g., *Zavtra*). Thus the second option would not work for the same reason. Members of the many associations and groups could disagree on many problems including the "Jewish Question." Some nationalist groups were originally and deliberately instituted as coalitions that united people with quite different ideological positions (e.g., different members of Pamyat or the National Salvation Front could believe in Russian identity in quite different ways).

The classifications on the basis of ideological principles seem to be more helpful. John Dunlop distinguishes three kinds of nationalism: liberal, conservative, and lumpen While antisemitic ideas are very prominent in the conservative and lumpen nationalism, liberal nationalism does not presuppose hostility to the Jews.[24] Today it is clear that the antisemitic ideologies of post-communist age are more diverse than suggested by the picture drawn in this classification. It also does not discuss the specific ways in which the hostility to the Jews is articulated.

The classification of nationalist ideologies which best fits this study was devised by Vladimir Solovei in his lucid and instructive review of the Russian "national patriotic movement." He distinguishes five types of "national patriotic parties": National Marxists, Traditionalists (a combination of Orthodoxy, autocracy, and populism), National Liberals, Paganists, and eclectic ideological groups.[25] This classification could be complemented by the introduction of the concept of an "enemy," and adjusted to the context of the discussion of antisemitism.

The simplest and most effective way to handle the problem is to distinguish the antisemitic ideologies from one another on the basis of the main targets of their criticism (Judaism, Zionism, the Jewish "race," Jews as promoters of modernity, etc). The targets can be identified by examining the different programs for social and political transformation suggested within the different trends of Russian nationalism. These programs are based in turn on different philosophies of history. Each type of nationalist ideology has its own historical vision and concept of Russia's future. Russia's identity as the agent of a world historical process embedded in a "grand historical narrative" determines the "choice of enemies." The metaphysical enemy (Jewry) is perceived as interfering in the "natural course" of Russian history and obstructing the realization of Russia's historic mission.

On the basis of these different philosophies of history I distinguish five types of antisemitic ideology. Each vision of history corresponds to a special type of authentic community.

The Jew as Cultural Foe

Neo-Slavophilism is the oldest trend in Russian nationalism. Neo-Slavophiles believe that culture is the most important ingredient of Russian identity. The Jew, a rootless and homeless cosmopolitan, is an enemy of Russian culture and of culture in general. The Jew is opposed to the Russian peasant world and the vernacular that have given rise to the authentic expressions of Russian culture. A Jew is also associated with the forces of modernity.

The Jew as Religious Foe

The representatives of *National Orthodoxy* believe that the primary identity of Russians is religious. Russian Orthodox consider themselves to be the most authentic Christians. Therefore, Jews are seen as projecting a hatred of Christians upon Russians. National Orthodoxy is a philosophy of anti-Judaism.

The Jew as Social Foe

National Bolsheviks believe that Russian identity is socialist (cf. the common Soviet idiom "we are socialist by origin"). National Bolsheviks to a great extent follows the line of argument evolved by the ideologists of Soviet anti-Zionist campaigns. They focus on the Jewish bourgeoisie, economic monopolies, political lobbies, and the ties between American Jewry and Israeli Zionists. Jews are usually described by them as arch-capitalists and economic manipulators, the natural enemies of Russian socialists. National Bolshevism appears as anti-capitalism and anti-Zionism.

The Jew as Racial Foe

Racism is not very popular among contemporary Russian nationalist intellectuals. It is predominantly the phenomenon of a lowbrow public. Many articles published in the racist periodicals are reminiscent of Nazi propaganda sheets like *Der Stürmer*. Some are not only antisemitic but also anti-Christian. Jews are portrayed as the enemies of the Aryan race in the metaphysical setting of a racial war.

The Jew as Geopolitical Foe

Neo-Eurasianism is a geopolitical nationalism that proclaims the Jews to be the geopolitical enemies of the continental civilizations and of Eurasia in particular. At the same time it represents an attempt to reconcile and synthesize the antisemitic positions of all other groups of antisemites. Culture, race, social orientation, and religion are described as functions of the geopolitical orientation of Eurasia. The Jews are alien to Eurasian ethnicities in all these different aspects.

Before discussing these five trends, let me make some observations about the peculiarities and advantages of this classification. Although it does not pretend to be exhaustive, it does attempt to be comprehensive, encompassing the most significant trends in Russian nationalism and the types of antisemitism associated with them. Needless to say, that the boundaries between these five trends are quite flexible and that confusion can easily arise.

However, the advantages of this classification are fourfold:

It allows us to compare different trends in terms of their arguments, to isolate their peculiarities and to put the phenomenon of Russian antisemitism into the context of wider intellectual debates in Russian society;

It allows the student of Russian antisemitism to understand the appeal of different nationalist discourses chronologically and to identify the reasons for their prominence. Different ideological justifications of antisemitism correspond to different stages in Russian history after glasnost. For example, the first stages of perestroika were dominated by the anti-communist antisemitism of the Neo-Slavophiles, while the neo-Eurasian type of nationalism and antisemitism came to dominate the nationalist camp after the collapse of the USSR. The crisis in economic expectations and widespread economic collapse allowed neo-Bolshevism to enter the nationalist discourse.

Thematic classification is already implied by the classification by trends. It is easier and more natural for some trends to thematize certain topics than for others, due to the difference in their agendas. Different trends in antisemitic discourse are associated primarily with specific disciplines. National Bolsheviks focus on economic issues. The concerns of neo-Slavophiles extend to, but are not limited by, the philosophy of culture and literary criticism. The racists take up issues in anthropology, medicine, the biological sciences, and are engaged in pseudo-historical inquiries. Geopolitics and history are especially prominent in neo-Eurasianism. Finally national Orthodoxy is preoccupied with theological speculation and the history of religion. In practical terms it means that the proponents of National Bolshevism rather than the ideologists of racism would be more prone to discuss "Jewish Mammonism"; a discussion of deicide might be expected from the National Orthodox, but not from the neo-Eurasians. Of course, some "wandering topics" can be found in all these trends and across the political spectrum. However, my classification allows us to emphasize the peculiarities of discussion by each particular trend.

It allows us to understand particular attitudes and ethnic stereotypes in the context of different narrative structures. This can give a more qualified picture of these attitudes, since the particular stereotype could be a part of quite different narrative structures, which govern the perception of the social world. Identification of the narratives can contribute to better design for sociological questionnaires.

Some authors have argued that antisemitic concerns occasionally haunt the liberal media in Russia. For instance, some liberal media were preoccupied with the supposed Jewish origins of conspicuous figures in Russian social and political life (Zhirinovsky, Berezovsky). I believe that there is nothing specific to the liberals in such preoccupations and that the source of the antisemitic messages of the liberal media should be found outside the liberal discourse.[26]

Another trend that might be suspected of harboring serious antisemitic components is that of the statists *(gosudarstvenniki)*. I believe that in spite of the statists' affiliation with the more radical trends of nationalism they are not the exponents of antisemitism. Generally speaking, nationalists do not need to be obsessed with the "Jewish question." Statism is a good example of non-antisemitic nationalism.[27]

It is important to observe that each type of nationalism is associated with the idea of a specific type of community (the community of Eurasian ethnic groups, the community of socialist nations, the mystical community of Russian culture, the community of members of the Aryan race).[28] In his ingenious inquiry into the origins of modern nationalism, Benedict Anderson in *Imagined Communities* has suggested that it emerged in response to the dissolution of traditional community and the loss of legitimating power by the European dynasties (the collapse of the sacred language–sacred monarch–sacred time syndrome). The collapse of the USSR, followed by the rise of contemporary Russian nationalism has reproduced the same logic in the form of a "farce" that followed the original "tragedy" as described by Anderson. What is especially important for our study is that the "imagined community" of Russian nationalists is "imagined" in such a way that Jews are excluded from membership. In addition, they are said to be the most serious enemies of these communities, endangering their very existence. I consider the eruption of ideological antisemitism a by-product of the preoccupation and "imagining" of the perfect community.

SOURCES OF CONTEMPORARY RUSSIAN ANTISEMITISM: POLITICAL, ECONOMIC AND CULTURAL

Discussion of the sources of contemporary antisemitism is not my focus, but nevertheless, a hypothesis about the sources — political, economic, and cultural — of ideological antisemitism is quite important. Political and social sources play a primary role in the formation of antisemitism. They are fueled and exacerbated by the economic and cultural forces.

Political and Social Sources

The rise of Russian nationalism and the concomitant growth of xenophobia were triggered by the collapse of the USSR. The collapse of the Soviet empire precipitated a crisis of national identity. The "community of the Soviet people" collapsed and disintegrated. It was quite natural for people to compensate for this lost identity through the articulation of ethnic and religious affiliations. The idea which runs through the whole of my study is that the eruption of antisemitism — especially striking in the case of ideological antisemitism — was closely connected with the search for a new identity and for more authentic and stable community ties.

The new identity is shaped through the articulation of the defining features of the out-group. The Jews had already functioned as an out-group both in the traditional religious consciousness and in Soviet ideology. Rediscovery of the old antisemitic stereotypes and the creation of a new antisemitic ideology helped to re-forge and sustain the new identity and "imagine" the new community. These stereotypes maintain the borders of the "imagined community" and prevent it from disintegrating.

The type of political culture and the alienation of the population from political life is another significant consideration. The widespread belief in the inability of ordinary people to influence political decisions is conducive to the development of the "paranoic style" in politics. In the course of perestroika, the pattern of popular political engagement was changed, but the underlying type of political culture turned out to be more persistent. The political problems of the country — the absence of political elites experienced in self-government; the lack of an established civic culture; the low level of institutional political activity (e.g., the low participation in the presidential elections of 1993 and 1996) — contributed to the paranoic style. This special type of political culture creates a breeding ground for the proliferation of conspiracy theories and the belief in the "clandestine forces" of history (Jews, Masons, and Zionists). This political culture experiences difficulties in accommodating itself to the age of pragmatic political calculations and pragmatic decisions.[29]

Economic Background

The general atmosphere engendered by rapid economic decline and drastic social change also contributes to the development of nationalism and xenophobia. Economic expectations for many were not met in the course of perestroika and liberalization. While many initially believed that the social and economic transformations of perestroika would promote Russia to the ranks of the affluent countries of the West, the course of economic reform betrayed these expectations and suggested quite a different place for Russia in the new world economic order. The dream of membership in the European community of technologically developed countries was supplanted by the reality of a third world country supplying the world market with cheap natural resources. Personal incomes have fallen, the crime rate has soared, and the public health system and cultural infrastructure have disintegrated. The gap between the richest and poorest segments has grown continually. The results of the reforms were especially devastating for professionals working for the state and for scientists and scholars in academic institutions. The conversion of the military industry, the disruption of economic ties with countries of the former Soviet Union, and the reconstruction of outmoded industries created considerable unemployment and undermined professional identities. Hyperinflation and voucher privatization, coupled with political instability have significantly intensified the search for scapegoats.[30] Economic turmoil has contributed to the supposition of a plot to "demote" Russia and destroy its industry, culture, and educational system. The social and political situation in post-communist Russia invites comparison with Weimar Germany. It is no accident that the metaphor of Weimar Germany often governs reports and discussions about the rise of Russian nationalism.[31]

Cultural Sources

The rise of antisemitic sentiment and the development of antisemitic ideology exhibit historical continuity with centuries-old traditions. It is noteworthy that from the eighteenth century on, anti-liberalism was a mainstream tradition in Russian political philosophy. In the period of perestroika, the remarkable anti-liberal and antisemitic legacy of Russian culture, which was repressed under the Soviet regime, was rediscovered. Quite often the ultra-nationalists rely upon the "classics" of "home-made" antisemitic thought. First of all, one may mention the notorious forgery, the *Protocols of the Elders of Zion*. The Vitiaz publishing house continued this tradition with its special collection of booklets, *A Home-Library for the Russian Patriot*. In addition to foreign "classics" like *The International Jew* by Henry Ford, the collection included such "masterpieces" of antisemitism as *What We Do Not Like About Them?* by Vasily Shulgin, *The Jewish Question* by Feodor Dostoyevsky, *The Wars of the Dark Forces* by Nikolai Markov, *The Masonry and Russian Revolution* by Grigorii Bostunich,[32] *The Jews in Russia* by Alexander Selianinov, *Equal Rights and the Jewish Question* by Alexander Liprandi, and *De-Zionization* by Vladimir Yemelianov.[33] The ultra-nationalists also rediscovered some works by Russian religious philosophers[34] (to be discussed in detail in due course), and other conspicuous figures of Russian cultural life of the pre-revolutionary period (e.g., the writings of a lexicogapher Vladimir Dahl on ritual murder and infanticide; the reports to the government of the Russian poet Gabriel Derzhavin; the memoirs of poet Alexandr Blok; and the essays of Andrei Belyi among many other pieces of "enlightened" antisemitism). The ultranationalists claim to be the only rightful heirs of the grand tradition of Russian culture and emphasize the continuity in antisemitic preoccupations among the best representatives of this culture. Many of them debunk the liberal myth of the incompatibility of antisemitism with true intelligence and high Russian moral standards.

Another cultural reason for the proliferation of antisemitic stereotypes, often overlooked, is simply ignorance of Jewish history and culture. It is widely known that during the Soviet era, universities and colleges never included Jewish studies in their curricula; Jewish history and culture were neglected and oppressed as academic disciplines. I know many Jews in the former Soviet Union whose first lessons in Jewish history came from reading between the lines of anti-Zionist propaganda. However, it would be wrong to associate the lack of serious knowledge about Jewish culture and religion only with Soviet oppression. Many Russian intellectuals of the Silver Age (1900–1925), not to mention the intellectuals of the nineteenth century, who often discussed Jewish subjects in their writings (e.g. Rozanov, Shulgin, and Shmakov) demonstrated a surprising ignorance of the basic ideas of Jewish culture. Surprisingly, even the study of the Old Testament was inadequate for a Christian country. The Orthodox Church never elaborated anything comparable to the German schools of biblical criticism, the French school of Oriental studies, or British "Hebraism" (Matthew Arnold's term). Russians and Russian intellectuals have lived "next door" to Jews for a long time, yet in many cases their knowledge of the Jewish culture, its customs and holidays, was less accurate than their studies of exotic and remote cultures like the Chinese. The legacy of "Hellenism," another important ingredient of European culture, was always much more respectful.[35] Thus, some allegations of Russian antisemites actually exhibit ignorance of Jewish culture more than ill intentions.

This work is divided into six chapters. Two chapters deal with Eurasian antisemitism. The other four chapters discuss the four other trends in nationalist ideology. In the concluding section I will provide a brief summary, and discuss the philosophical normative assumptions of the ideologists of antisemitism. Each chapter begins with a general background on the historical context, social groupings, periodicals, and names associated with each particular trend of nationalist ideology, in order to provide a full understanding of subsequent sections.

NOTES

1. Robert Brym claims that in the past six years nearly a dozen surveys on the subject have been conducted. See L. Gudkov and A. Levinson, "Otnoshenie naseleniia SSSR k evreiam," *Vestnik Evreiskogo universiteta v Moskve,* no.1, 1992; idem, "Izmeneniia v otnoshenii k evreiiam naseleniia respublik na territorii bivshego SSSR," *Vestnik Evreiskogo universiteta v Moskve,* 4 (1993); A. Brym, and A. Degtyarev, "Antisemitism in Moscow: Results of an October 1992 Survey," *Slavic Review* 52 (1993); A. Brym, "Russian Attitudes towards Jews: An Update," *East European Jewish Affairs* 26, no. 1 (1996). See the selected bibliography for the

English translations of titles that were primary sources; English translation of the titles of other documentation (mostly newspaper articles) are not provided.

2. See W. Korey, *The Soviet Cage: Anti-Semitism in Russia* (New York 1973); B. Pinkus, *The Soviet Government and the Jews* (Cambridge, England 1984); G. Kostyrchenko, *Out of the Red Shadows: Anti-Semitism in Stalin's Russia* (New York 1995).

3. A. Yanov, The Russian Idea and the Year 2000 (Oxford 1987); M. Agursky, The Third Rome: National Bolshevism in the USSR (Boulder, Colo. 1987); S. Carter, Russian Nationalism: Yesterday, Today and Tomorrow (New York 1990); W. Laqueur, The Black Hundred (New York 1994).

4. For instance, American sociologist James Gibson suggests and tries to demonstrate in his survey that the relatively powerless groups of society with the lowest education level is almost the only social niche where antisemitism is disseminated and has a chance of survival. See J. Gibson, "Misunderstanding of Anti-Semitism in Russia: An Analysis of the Politics of Anti-Jewish Attitudes," *Slavic Review* 53 (1994). In a similar vein, the Russian social scientist V. Solovei, argues in his very instructive review of the Russian nationalist parties and groups that "all the social strata of the Soviet society are represented in the national patriotic movement except the top strata of intelligentsia," V. Solovei, "Russkaia ideiia segodnia: analiticheskii obzor russkogo natsionalno-patrioticheskogo dvizheniia," in *Rossiia v XX veke* (Moscow 1994), 702.

5. See D. Braybrooke, *Philosophy of Social Sciences* (Englewood Cliffs, N.J. 1987).

6. See A. Stanley, "Success May Be Bad for Jews As Old Russian Bias Surfaces," *New York Times*, 15 April 1997. It is interesting to trace the dynamics of growth in the volume of antisemitic periodicals. In 1992 Tankred Golenpolsky, editor-in-chief of *Evreiskaia gazeta* (Jewish Gazette) and currently a leader of the Anti-Defamation Committee, reported fifty-six Russian periodicals as antisemitic. By spring 1994 there were 157 periodicals of antisemitic orientation. "Generalnaiia prokuratura Rossii — posobnik fashistov," Russkaia misl' 4032 (1994). Even if the criteria of Leonid Pudovkin (in *Russkaya misl'*) and Golenpolsky are different, these statistics are very impressive. In 1994 the antisemitic periodicals ranged from 10,000 to 300,000 printed copies and their total monthly circulation exceeded 1,000,000 copies.

7. "VZIOM. Chem men'she v Rossii evreev, tem bol'she o nikh govoryat," *Megapolis-Express,* 17 September 1992.

8. The anti-Zionist campaigns began in the mid-1960s. Walter Laqueur points out that between 1965 and 1985 some ten million copies of anti-Zionist books had been published. W. Laqueur, *Black Hundred,* 110. According to A. Naiman, the Soviet Union published 400 anti-Zionist titles during a 25-year span in about 15 million copies. A. Naiman, "Antisemitism — komu eto vigodno?" (Kiev 1991), 4.

9. Most conspicuous among these groups were Veche, and the All-Russian Social Christian Union of Liberation of the People (VSHSON); their ideology is discussed by A. Yanov, *The Russian Idea and the Year 2000* (Oxford 1987); M. Agursky, *Contemporary Russian Nationalism* (Jerusalem 1982); J. Dunlop, *The Faces of Contemporary Russian Nationalism* (Princeton, N.J. 1983).

10. Pamyat is a generic name for several nationalistic extremist groups. Although it arose in the early 1980s, very few people knew about its existence before 1987 and it was not a phenomenon of great social significance.

11. C. Bogert, "Russia's New Right," *Newsweek,* 12 February 1990; M. Deich and L. Zhuravlev, *Pamyat kak ona est* (Moscow 1991); S. Carter, *Russian Nationalism: Yesterday, Today and Tomorrow* (New York 1990), 103–117; H. Spier, "Pamyat: An Appeal to the Russian People," *Soviet Jewish Affairs* 18, no. 1 (1988); V. Krasnov, "Pamyat: A Force for Change?"; P. Midford, "Pamyat's Political Platform: Myth and Reality," *Nationalities Papers* 19, no. 2 (1991).

12. Black Hundred is a generic name for the reactionary, antirevolutionary, and antisemitic groups formed in Russia during and after the Revolution of 1905.

13. In the early years of perestroika both liberals and "respectable" nationalists believed that Pamyat was organized by KGB authorities. While liberals believed that it was organized in order to smear the democratic opposition, nationalists believed that it was created to discredit the nationalistic movement. The leader of the "Christian-Democratic" opposition to the liberal reforms claimed that the "KGB infiltrates Pamyat agents into the ranks of the opposition, creates bogus parties and provokes it to commit illigal actions." Y. Trigubova, "Otmezhevalis' ot Pamiati," *Nezavisimaia gazeta* 12 October 1992. Although the KGB might have supported Pamyat and favored its activity, the suspicions of both parties seem to be based on the misunderstanding of the grass-roots sources of antisemitism and the "initiative of the masses."

14. W. Laqueur, *Black Hundred,* 264, 220.

15. S. Kassow, "Should Soviet Jews Leave?," *Tikkun* 5, no. 5 (1990): 30.

16. "Miatezh." *Moskovskiye novosti,* 10 October 1993. 4–5.

17. In one of the interviews, Zhirinovsky said that Russian antisemitism is a defensive reaction to anti-Russian sentiments, which are disseminated by the Jews working on the editorial boards of newspapers, radio, and television. They always say that Russia is a barbaric country, he complains. "We just want a minimum proportionality to avoid the harmful psychological impact that can result in antisemitism." V. Pope, "A New Face of the Old Russia," *U.S. News and World Report,* 27 December 1993–3 January 1994, 33.

18. I. Minin, "Teoreticheskie osnovi natsional-sotsializma," *Sokol Zhirinovskogo* 2 (1992).

19. Gerhard Frey of the German People's Union is a personal friend of Zhirinovsky. He attended the Third Congress of the LDP. See G. Frey, "Ia liubl'u Zhirinovskogo i Rossiiu," *Kurier,* 17 February 1994. In 1991 Zhirinovsky met with Iraq's Saddam Hussein and praised his anti-Zionist policy. In the same year he met with National Front leader Jean-Marie Le Pen. In 1994 he paid a call on his friend Edwin Neuwirth, who has denied that Nazis used gas chambers to kill Jews during World War II and was proud to have served in the Waffen-SS. See K. Fedarko, *"Hello, I Must Be Going," Time,* 10 January 1994.

20. An American reporter working for the Associated Press and CNN unearthed a set of alleged family documents in Alma-Ata suggesting that Zhirinovsky's real father was Volf Isaakovich Edelstein. See also "Israelis say Zhirinovsky once sought visa," *New York Times,* 28 December 1993; S. Schmeman, "In Moscow Zhirinovsky is remembered as Jewish advocate," *New York Times,* 16 December 1993. Zhirinovsky never admits this fact inside Russia, claiming that such documents are forgeries and result from the intrigues of his political enemies. Nevertheless, when interview for the Israeli newspaper *Maariv* on 11 January 1994, he said that he never concealed the fact that his father was a Jew, that he is proud of it and that 90 percent of the members of his party are Jewish, cited in L. Navrozov, "Zhirinovsky," *Midstream* 40, no.4 (1993): 11.

21. The serious ideologists of intellectual antisemitism consider Zhirinovsky a danger to the Russian Idea and to the anti-liberal movement in general. Michael Nazarov argues that Zhirinovsky "makes his stand in the style of Hitler or Vladimir Jabotinsky and discredits the very idea of national power by his vulgar appearence and cynicism." M. Nazarov, "Istoriosofiia smutnogo vremeni," *Nash sovremennik* 6 (1992): 148. Some nationalists insist that during the parliamentary campaign Zhirinovsky was supported by Yeltsin and the liberals. They claim that the media created a very favorable image for him depicting him as a self-made man and an outstanding personality, who was supported by liberals because: (a) the threat of Zhirinovsky will suspend the opposition of the radical democrats to Yeltsin; (b) it will guarantee Yeltsin long-term support from the West, as the counterbalance to Russian fascism; the Zhirinovsky syndrome would justify the anti-Russian campaigns of the West and the arms race; (c) "Zhirinovsky syndrome" compromises the nationalist movement by caricaturing its slogans; (d) Zhirinovsky's rhetoric can fan the conflict with the former republics. Kasintsev argues that the true nationalists voted not for Zhirinovsky but for the Communists, the agrarian party, and the DPR. A. Kazintsev, "Na pereputie," *Nash sovremennik* 2 (1994): 121–24.

22. L. Gudkov and A. Levinson, "Evrei kak fenomen sovetskogo soznaniia (Problema antisemitizma v byvshem SSSR po materialam issledovanii Otdela teorii VZIOM)," *Teatr* 7 (1992): 147.

23. Th. Friedgut, "Antisemitism and its Opponents: Reflections in the Russian Press: From Perestroika until the Present," ACTA series, no.3 (Vidal Sassoon International Center for the Study of Antisemitism, Jerusalem, 1994), 6–9.

24. J. Dunlop, "The Return of Russian Nationalism," *Journal of Democracy* 1, no. 3 (1990): 114–15. J. Dunlop, "Russian Nationalism Today: Organizations and Programs," *Nationalities Papers* 19, no. 2 (1991): 149–51.

25. V. Solovei, "Russkaiia ideiia segodnia," *Rossiia v XX veke. Istoriki mira sporiat* (Moscow 1994), 700.

26. Some students of antisemitism (e.g., Arthur Herzberg and Zygmund Bauman) have suggested that the ideology of Enlightenment itself (and in particular, liberalism) has engendered a specific brand of antisemitism associated with the belief in the stubborn particularity of the Jews and their inability to embrace universal values and become fully rational. This is exemplified by some ideas of Enlightenment (for instance, in the writings of Karl Marx and the philosopher Otto Weininger, a student of Immanuel Kant who became famous in the fin-de-siècle because of his scandalous antisemitic book *Sex and Character*). Marx and Weininger believed that Jews should renounce their "Jewishness" in order to embrace universal culture. I found little evidence of the prominence of this type of antisemitism in Russian debates of the post-communist period. In addition, I would not identify this type of antisemitism with the liberal discourse that is properly understood.

27. Sergei Kurginyan is one of the conspicuous leaders of Russian statism. He opposes himself and his group to the fascist leanings of nationalistic ideology. He has criticized the doctrines of Russian racists and the tendency to give the idea of a "Jewish conspiracy" status on its agenda. The "demonology" of the statists is quite different. Their chief enemy is anti-national forces. Kurginyan claims that none of the individual ethnicities can be accused of anti-state and anti-national sentiments. He calls "self-alienation" the phenomenon of indifference or hostility towards one's state. The "self-alienated" people — those who refuse to identify themselves with the Russian state and Russian interests and accept foreign socio-cultural codes — could easily belong to any ethnicity. Kurginyan distinguishes three parts of the Jewish population: those who completely identify themselves with the Russian state and nation; those who are ready to participate in the construction of the Russian state as a part of a Russian- Jewish community; those who identify with Israel. This latter group should be allowed to emigrate to Israel and their decision should be respected by the state and the citizens. However, activity on behalf of international agencies at the expense of the state, which goes beyond the provisions of these three options, should be considered anti-constitutional. See S. Kurginyan, "Natsional'naiia doktrina," *Rossiia* 2 (1993): 21–24.

28. Benedict Anderson himself tried to dissociate racism from nationalism. He claimed that the concepts of racism are derived from the ideologies of class rather

than from the ideology of nation. However, this view is not sufficiently supported. I believe that racism is an aberration of nationalism and that it envisions a specific type of community alternative to other communities. B. Anderson, *Imagined Communities* (London 1983), 136.

29. According to the recent sociological survey, 17.8 percent of the respondents in Moscow agreed, or were inclined to agree, that a global Zionist plot against Russia exists. Nearly a quarter of the respondents said that they were "undecided" as to whether this conspiracy exists. See R. Brym, and A. Degtyrev, "Antisemitism in Moscow: Results of an October 1992 Survey," *Slavic Review* 52, no.1 (1994): 5.

30. Every citizen of Russia was entitled to receive "vouchers" representing his or her share of state property, in an attempt to expedite the transition to a market economy. Vouchers are roughly equivalent to stock that issued by the state, and could be used to purchase stock of different Russian plants, or sold on the free market.

31. See A. Yanov, Posle Yeltsina. Weimarskaiia Rossiia (Moscow 1995).

32. Nikolai Markov and Grigorii Bostunich were among the leaders of the Black Hundreds. During the Second World War both joined the Nazis, who propagated their antisemitic writings. Bostunich became a personal friend of Himmler and Heydrich. See W. Laqueur, *Russia and Germany: Hitler's Mentors* (Washington 1991), 158–67.

33. At least 18 of the 25 booklets in this set are preoccupied with the "Jewish Question" and Zionism.

34. V. Boykov, ed., Taina Israilia. Evreiskii vopros v russkoi religioznoi misli kontsa XIX — pervoi polovini XX veka, (St.Petersburg 1993); S. Bulgakov, "Sudbi mira, griaduschee," Nash sovremennik 7 (1993).

35. The term "Hellenism" is that of Matthew Arnold, for whom Hellenism and Hebraism are the two most important ingredients of European culture. It was common for Russians to trace their cultural origins back to Byzantium, the last stronghold of Hellenism.

CHAPTER 1

Neo-Eurasianism:
Leviathan, Behemoth, and the Jews

The Eurasian and neo-Eurasian perspective on the "Jewish Question" is an important component of contemporary Russian antisemitic ideology. Before embarking on an analysis of this, however, it is important to note the political contexts that led to the development of Eurasianism and neo-Eurasianism.

Eurasianism is a school of social thought and cultural criticism, which began in 1921 in Sofia as a Russian émigré movement that advocated a "turn to the East." The school was founded by a group of Russian intellectuals and scholars, Prince Nikolai Trubetskoi, a linguist; Georgii Florovsky, a theologian and philosopher; Pyotr Suvchinsky, an art critic; and Pyotr Savitsky, a geographer and economist. Eurasianism greatly influenced some trends in historiography (especially the thinking of George Vernadsky and Lev Gumiliov), linguistics (Nikolai Trubetskoi, Roman Jacobson, and Viacheslav Ivanov), music (Igor Stravinsky), and cultural studies. Many prominent Russian émigré intellectuals sympathized with Eurasianism and contributed to Eurasian periodicals. A remarkable example is Alexandre Kojève (Alexander Kozhevnikov), the prophet of the "end of history" and a teacher of many French post-modernists.

Originally, Eurasians were primarily concerned with denouncing European elements in Russian history and culture, and vitriolically rejected the "tyrannical yoke" of Romano-Germanic civilization. They focused on the innate spiritual ties — cultural, linguistic, and religious — with Russia's Asian brothers. By the late 1920s and early 1930s, the emphasis shifted toward the geopolitical construction of a future Russian-Eurasian state. What linked the various Eurasian theoreticians was the conviction that Russia, as a unique cultural area, was to remain separate from, and even in opposition to, Western Europe. Most Eurasians felt that Communist control was in their day a necessary evil that would eventually be replaced by a more suitable form of power (some of them supported the Bolsheviks for this reason). By 1935, however, the cohesion of this group of theoreticians fragmented to the point of complete disintegration.[1]

The advent of perestroika awoke Eurasianism from its graveyard slumber with a veritable flood of interest among Russia's post-Soviet intelligentsia. The Eurasian ideas and concepts became extremely popular and pervasive in the political language of the leaders of various movements of that period. The collapse of the USSR contributed to the popularity of its concepts and terminology in political debates and intensified academic discussions.

In my analysis, I will discuss only one of the neo-Eurasian groups, that of Russian nationalist intellectuals united around the newspaper *Den'* (Day) and the journal *Elements. Eurasian Review*. They develop the arguments found in early Eurasianism and reshape them to the context of present-day political debate and the needs of those shaken by Russia's lost status as a world superpower. The special section "Eurasia" in *Den'* became an intellectual forum for prolific writers such as Alexander Prokhanov (editor-in-chief of *Zavtra*), Alexander Dugin, Vadim Kozhinov, Shamil Sultanov, Vadim Shtepa, and Anatolii Glivakovsky. They denounced the attempts of "cosmopolitan forces" to integrate the doctrines of Eurasianism into their discourse, considering themselves to be the only legitimate successors of classical Eurasianism in contemporary Russia.[2]

Adoption of the Eurasian perspective marks a new stage in the development of nationalistic discourse, offering a number of advantages to the nationalists. First of all, it allows them to abandon the predominant anti-communist posture of the mainstream nationalistic discourse of the perestroika period. Thus, it enables the reconciliation of different ideological attitudes to the Soviet period, and the consolidation of diverse nationalistic trends. A common language can then be shaped for the anti-liberal opposition to the government. In particular, the Eurasian paradigm provides ideological justification for the alliance of Left-Right forces in their opposition to liberalism and Western-style democracy. Another important advantage of this ideology is that it appeals to Russians as well as to other national minorities of the former Soviet Union. The Eurasian perspective underpins the resistance to local separatist tendencies and permits escape from accusations of parochial Russian chauvinism. So the shift of emphasis from *Blut* (i.e., racial affiliation) to *Boden* (i.e., one's connection to one's land or region) permits extending the sphere of influence of nationalist ideology, both ethnically and socially.

At the same time, and perhaps most importantly, the Eurasian ideology offers consolation and provides a new identity to those who experienced a crisis of their identity and the sense of fragmentation that resulted from the collapse of the USSR. The Eurasian ideology is not only nostalgic but also forward-looking, since the ideology insists that the future belongs to the young Eurasian civilization — the pivotal area of history and Heartland of the world.[3]

It is important to observe that the ideology of neo-Eurasianism significantly differs from the original Eurasianism, in spite of the declarations of the movement's current representatives. Whereas classical Eurasianism set Russia in opposition to Western Europe and Romano-Germanic civilization, many neo-Eurasians now see "Eurasia" embracing not only Asia and Russia but all of Europe. In addition, they foresee a united continental power to oppose the foreign infiltration of the Atlantic (or American) states. The concept of a Eurasian empire stretching from Dublin to Vladivostok was elaborated by the late Jean Thiriart, a contemporary Belgian geopolitician and leader of the Jeune Europa movement. Thiriart visited Moscow in 1992 and established friendly relations with the editorial staff of *Den'*. Thiriart's most eccentric idea was to surrender Western Europe to the Soviet Army in order to deliver it from "American occupation" and political servitude to Israel.[4] This radically new geopolitical concept of Europe was accepted by at least some Russian neo-Eurasians.

While the original Eurasians feared Europeanization and the infiltration of Catholicism, "number one enemy" for today's neo-Eurasians is Americanization and "Judeo-Protestantism," including their offshoots: liberalism and the market economy. The anti-American thrust of the argument is especially important for understanding the neo-Eurasian perspective on the "Jewish question." Neo-Eurasians coined the term "Atlanticism," referring to all maritime or oceanic civilizations ("thalassocracies" — symbolized by the mythical biblical sea monster, Leviathan) as opposed to the continental Eurasian civilizations ("tellucracies" — symbolized by the biblical "Behemoth" of the book of Job; see note 6 for more on the use of these terms).[5] Atlanticist civilization is represented by Great Britain and the United States, while Russia and Germany represent the typical Eurasian land civilizations. Atlanticist civilizations are market-oriented, since their geographical location means they are better equipped to promote trade. Their concern with individual freedom and human rights is an outcome of their commercialism. The Eurasian states, on the other hand, are agricultural, authoritarian, and militarist. A strong state power and the maintenance of civil religion — a religion designed to conform to the needs of the state — are the major concerns of continental civilizations. Wars between these two kinds of civilization — "Leviathan" and "Behemoth,"[6] are natural, and the preservation and acquisition of living space —the "Great Space of the Soviet Empire" — is essential for the survival and normal functioning of great powers.[7] Such ideas are heavily indebted to the theories of Western European geopoliticians like Friedrich Ratzel, Rudolf Kjellen, Halford John Mackinder, and Karl Haushofer.[8]

Whereas the earlier Eurasians spoke of spiritual ties with their "Turanian brothers" (the Turkic and Finno-Ugric ethnicities living on the territory of the Russian Empire) neo-Eurasians consider the Arab and traditional Muslim world, especially Islamic fundamentalism, as Russia's natural allies in resistance to the sinister anti-continental powers, Americans and Zionists.

In contrast to classical Eurasianism, some neo-Eurasians believe that the conflict of Atlanticism and Eurasianism originated in confrontations in the ancient world. In neo-Eurasian discourse the distinction between Atlanticism and Eurasianism becomes pervasive to the point of obsession. The distinction is used to describe political history, the history of literature and the arts, and the history of philosophy (e.g., Thales is obviously an Atlanticist, while Heraclitus is a Eurasian).

Last but not least, while in classical Eurasianism the "Jewish Question" was marginal and mainstream Eurasianists condemned antisemitism, for neo-Eurasians antisemitic statements and concepts have become indispensable ingredients in their discourse. Neo-Eurasian antisemitism is not only an eclectic construction of different antisemitic arguments; it has shaped a new justification for antisemitism, which should not be confused with that of other nationalist trends, and which was not familiar to the founding fathers of classical Eurasianism. In the following two sections I will juxtapose and contrast the two interpretations of the "Jewish Question" articulated by early and contemporary Eurasians. An examination of the texts of classical Eurasians and neo-Eurasians demonstrate a discontinuity in the attitude to this problem.

THE "JEWISH QUESTION" IN CLASSICAL EURASIANISM

Although some of the early Eurasians did address the "Jewish Question," only a few of them did so using the terms and categories of Eurasianism. Let us look at the works of four representatives of the movement. First, we will examine an essay, *Racism* (1935) by one of the founders of the movement, Prince Nikolai Trubetskoi (1890–1938). The second essay, *Russia and the Jews* (1928), was written by Lev Karsavin (1882–1952), a prominent leader of the left-wing Eurasians. Another leader of the left-wing Eurasians, was the "Red Prince" — Dmitrii Sviatopolk-Mirsky, the author of *The Jews* (1929). Lastly, we have the paper *Jewish Easternism in the Past and in the Future* (1931)[9] by Jacob Bromberg, a minor figure in the movement. All four essays are crucial for the understanding of the early Eurasian perspective on Judaism and Jews. Jacob Bromberg's paper is particularly valuable as an example of the perception of Eurasianism by a Jewish member of the group pondering the peculiarities of the specific Russian-Jewish identity and experience, and advocating a new perspective of Russian Jewish history suggested by the Eurasian discourse. This essay could probably shed light on the personal hopes and expectations of those Russian Jewish intellectuals involved in the movement or sympathetic to it in different periods of post-October history (e.g., Sergei Efron, Artur Lurie, Roman Jacobson, Semeon Frank, and Lev Shestov). Lev Karsavin's ideas can help us get a better grasp of the implications of the "Jewish question" for the religious project advocated by some members of the movement.

Nikolai Trubetskoi's essay, *Racism,* appeared in 1935 when the Nazis were already in power in Germany and the Eurasian movement was already at low ebb. Trubetskoi denounced Nazism and condemned those Russian nationalists who chose to collaborate with Nazi Germany. The focus of his paper is an attempt to dissociate the Eurasian movement from antisemitic undercurrents.

Trubetskoi begins with the attempts of some Russian émigré antisemites to inveigle the Eurasianist movement into their cause, employing Eurasian ideas and concepts as a justification for their antisemitic instigations. Trubetskoi summarizes their argument that the indigenous population of the USSR consists of three races: Eastern European, Turanian, and Tungusic (according to von Eickstedt's classification), sharing similar traits due to mixed marriages and their common culture and psychology. The Jews, however, do not belong to any of these races and, consequently, their culture and psychology is alien to the natives of Russia-Eurasia, and the Jewish presence in Eurasia exerts a corrupting influence on the native population. Marriages with Jews, the argument goes, should be prevented, because racial features never completely disappear, and Jewish genes will affect the racial hybrids.

Trubetskoi disavows this "anthropological materialism" and condemns the misuse of Eurasian concepts by Russian antisemites. He does not deny the existence of the laws of heredity, but states that inheritance determines only morally neutral features like mental activity, an aptitude for music, mathematics, humor, and some other personal aspects. In the case of the Jews, Trubetskoi argues, one can talk about their inherited "quickness of wit, combinatorial talents ("pushiness," "resourcefulness") and passionate temper," that is, features that can be beneficial for the non-Jewish host.[10]

Trubetskoi, however, does believe that the Jews may be a corrupting influence, albeit not because of their race. It can be explained as a result of complex socio-psychological circumstances, the key to the "Jewish question" is a specific psychology of the Jews as "immigrants with a stable immigrant tradition of two thousand years." Trubetskoi contends that observation of the peculiarities of life of Russian immigrants in Western Europe and their moral standards could facilitate a proper understanding of the Jewish syndrome. Such phenomena as solidarity when confronted by strangers, cliquishness and cronyism, double standards of morality, are very characteristic as well for the communities of Russian immigrants in Western Europe. In this respect the Russian immigrants of the first generation had much in common with the shtetl Jews. The concept of identity and attitudes to the host culture by the young generation of Russian immigrants is more complex and ambiguous. On the one hand, they feel strong attraction to the host culture and wish to become like others. Sometimes they are even ashamed of their Russianness. On the other hand, they try to dissociate themselves from the host culture and even despise it. The psychological complexes of the young generation of Russian immigrants remind Trubetskoi of the attitude of the intelligent Jews to Russian culture. The major indicator of this "immigrant psychology" is the immigrants' objective approach to all national values and ideals.

> The young immigrant who adopted the culture of the host people and is a native speaker of its language, does not share the patriotic enthusiasm of this people and tends to look at everything dear to this people coldly, from the "objective point of view." This objective point of view exposes the absurdity and theatricality of everything strange which is not experienced from inside as one's own.... And this necessarily induces the irony, the vitriolic and corrupting irony which is so characteristic of the Jews. This irony is a revenge for the fact that "they" (foreigners, gentiles) have their own national enthusiasm and their own concrete sacred notion, the motherland.... This irony also functions as a mechanism of self-defense, since in the absence of this irony the immigrant would lose his identity and would be absorbed by the strange people.... The most typical Jews really enjoy the dismantling of all the ideals of the strangers and their substitution by the cynical and cold calculation of benefits. These Jews like to find vile motives behind the sublime and to express themselves in pure negation.[11]

Trubetskoi admits that in many cases the negation and skepticism could be counted as a productive step in the creative evolutionary process, but he remarks that in the majority of cases the Jewish irony goes far beyond constructive criticism and is not conducive to good results. Their corrupting activity is detrimental not only to the host people but also for the Jews themselves. It exposes a special neurosis that requires a special treatment.

Trubetskoi does not propose a possible treatment, but he makes clear that the racists' policies and their proposal to limit Jewish rights would not help eliminate the problem; he remarks that the civil emancipation of the Jews should be promoted and mixed marriages encouraged. He claims that the aloofness and particularism of the Jews are facilitated by their religious separation and by persecution, but he does not elaborate on these subjects. He deliberately avoids discussion of religious problems, since he considers Eurasianism a purely scientific doctrine. It does not take into consideration racial factors and does not presuppose any commitment to a particular creed or religious ideals. Nor does he suggest concrete ways of integrating the Jews into the Eurasian community, although he apparently favors a policy of assimilation.

For Lev Karsavin, a student of Western religious history, however, the religious dimension of Eurasianism and policies of the future Eurasian state toward the Jews are of great importance.

Karsavin distinguished three "ideal types" of the Jews on the basis of their behavioral patterns and their possible influence on the rest of the Eurasian community. The first, "religious-cultural Jewry," is a natural ally of Russian and other Eurasian peoples in the struggle against the destructive influence of the West. The second type is represented by Jews who are completely assimilated into Russian culture. "Jews at the cross-roads" constitute the third type, which he considers dangerous both for the Eurasian community and for the "authentic" Jews themselves, for it represents the assimilating "periphery of the Jewish people in the state of decay." This type consists of Jews who can neither accept the host culture or the cultural and religious tradition to which they were born. The perverse assimilation of this third type, Karsavin argued, is determined by the specific universalism of Judaism and by the reluctance of the assimilating Jews to exchange their chosenness for a "mess of pottage." These Jews do not accept any organic culture because of its particularity and believe in some international and abstract culture of all humanity. The ideals of these Jews are cosmopolitan, abstract, and lifeless. It is not surprising, then, that these denationalized Jews are especially susceptible to the destructive ideas of Marxism and other revolutionary international doctrines. The danger comes not from the skepticism, nihilism, and irony of the assimilated Jews, as Trubetskoi suggested, but from the universalist and cosmopolitan ideals and aspirations of modernity which the "periphery of the Jews" have adopted. These "Jews at the cross-roads" greatly contributed to the Europeanization of Eurasia and to the realization of the Bolshevik project, although he admits that the communist revolution cannot be explained solely by reference to the subversive influence of this third category of Jews. The Bolshevik coup was primarily a result of the decay of Russian culture itself, and the Jews only facilitated the destructive processes that took place in Russian society independently of them. Karsavin argued that the new Eurasian state should support a healthy and organic Jewish culture in its struggle against the "periphery of assimilating Jews." These "non-Jewish Jews," to use the term coined by Isaac Deutscher, a biographer of Trotsky,[12] are dangerous and harmful, both for the truly Jewish and truly Russian social life and culture.

Karsavin believed that the Jewish community should enjoy all the rights of other Eurasians and should become an "equal member of the Eurasian federation." The Jews do not need a territory within Russia-Eurasia, since they are united not by territory but by their religious and cultural tradition, especially by their "Law." The question of Jewish communal life outside Eurasia is especially challenging for Lev Karsavin. He resolves the problem by reference to different possible "incarnations" *(individuatsii)* or realizations of each culture:

> The Jewish people are a united and organic whole. But any organic whole is not homogeneous and is divided into united particular wholes. Jewry is not an exception. But its peculiarity and role in the history of mankind is that it is divided according to the internal propinquity of its parts to certain cultures. One part of Jewry is naturally kindred to the Romanic culture, while the other is kindred to German or Eurasian-Russian culture. Therefore, Russian Jewry, being the incarnation of Jewry, is also the incarnation of the Eurasian culture. The "correlation" and double nature of Russian Jewry could be determined empirically.[13]

Karsavin insisted that the Eurasian "incarnation" of Jewry does not presuppose the complete absorption and assimilation of the Jewish people. The Jewish religious tradition and particularity should remain intact.

Support for "religious-cultural Jewry," however, does not imply that the Eurasians are indifferent to the centuries-long tensions between Judaism and Christianity. Responding to Christian critics, Karsavin maintained that Orthodoxy is not compromised by the Eurasian ideology; indeed, the adoption of Eurasianism might well lead naturally to the voluntary conversion of Jews. Support for the local [Eurasian] Jewish community (as opposed to a call for general non-discrimination against Jews) would in the end facilitate the conversion of the Jewish people as a whole. Karsavin felt that conversion en masse would be less painful for the Jews than individual conversions. It should be observed that Karsavin believed in a special non-universal Christianity and claimed that the well-known statement of the

Apostle Paul — "There is neither Greek nor Jew.... But Christ is all, and in all" (Colossians 3:11) — is often misinterpreted. In Karsavin's view, Paul's words do not imply any kind of "Christian cosmopolitanism" and, consequently, conversion need not imply complete assimilation. Jews should enter the Orthodox Church as a specific Jewish congregation of Orthodoxy and not simply as individual "cosmopolitans."

It is not surprising, Karsavin argues, that Western Christianity was unable to convert the Jews. Russian Orthodoxy is better equipped to do so, because Russians and Jews — Orthodoxy and Judaism — have much in common despite of the incompatibility of many Christian and Judaic doctrines. In contrast to "universalistic" Catholicism, Orthodoxy preserves the ethnicity of its converts and is not aloof from national ideals and concerns — especially attractive for the Jews, who wish to preserve their national particularity. Neither Judaism nor Orthodoxy is interested in proselytizing and imposing its creed on others. For both groups, social ideals and morality are crucial elements. The idea of a historic mission permeates the consciousness of both Russians and Jews, and in addition, Russian religious philosophy has much in common with kabbalah and hasidism. It is no coincidence that the history of Russians and Jews is interwoven.[14]

The Red Prince Dmitrii Sviatopolk-Mirsky was a friend of Karsavin, and an ideologist of the extreme Left within the Eurasian movement. He was a member of the editorial staff of the newspaper *Evraziia,* published in Paris for only two years (1928–1929), and published a series of essays entitled *The Ethnicities of the USSR.* Unlike Karsavin and other Eurasians, Sviatopolk-Mirsky was unconcerned about Jewish participation in the Russian revolution, a matter which preoccupied other members of the Russian intelligentsia at the time. His central concern was the integration of the Jewish "extraterritorial ethnicity" into the Eurasian cultural zone. He did not believe that Zionism could resolve the problem of "extraterritoriality" and condemned the movement as the "most harmful type of retrospective romanticism." Zionism has involved small groups of Jews into the imperialist politics of Great Britain and the exploitation of the Palestinian Arabs.[15] Sviatopolk-Mirsky believed that the best way of integrating the Jews was their peasantification; "there are more Jewish peasants in the USSR than Jewish colonists in the Palestine."

> The peasantification of the Jews of Russia is not merely a demographic enterprise. The approximation of the class structure of Jewry to the normal structure of the neighboring ethnicities could help more than anything else to extirpate the real plague of Russian life, the endemic antisemitism. It is going to be an effective means, since it has

been already determined that in the areas of the old Jewish agricultural communities antisemitism is negligible.[16]

"Antisemitism is a very serious plague," he goes on to argue. "It is one of the first obligations of any conscientious Russian person and, in particular, of any Eurasian to fight against it."

It is interesting to note that Sviatopolk-Mirsky's ideas were congenial to some early Marxist Zionists. Ber Borokhov (1881–1917) one of the leaders of Poalei Zion, believed that settling the Jews in Palestine would help to accomplish the task of the class transformation of Jewish society — the Jews would become workers and peasants — and this would eventually eliminate antisemitism. The only difference between Borokhov and Mirsky is that Borokhov believed that Zionism would be most effective in achieving the class transformation, the latter thought that it could be best accomplished by the adoption of Eurasianism. The change of occupation would help the Jews to become a full-fledged member in the family of Eurasian ethnicities.

According to Sviatopolk-Mirsky, the prominence of Jewish leaders in the revolution and construction of the USSR was actually an important contribution to the Eurasian cause, not a crime against Eurasia and not a liability.

> The Jews were instrumental in the preservation of the unity of the political and economic organism and the overcoming of Russian chauvinism. The centrifugal aspirations of the Jews who have emancipated themselves both from provincial nationalism and chauvinism have greatly contributed to the establishment of the present supernational unity of the Soviet country. The "Jewish preponderance" is a compensation for the centuries in which the Jews were not admitted to the state and social construction.[17]

The historical and spiritual kinship of Russian Jews to Eurasia is a focus of Jakob Bromberg's paper that appears to have been much informed by his reading of Karsavin. Bromberg attacks the Jewish Westernizers, the proponents of Enlightenment and *Bildung,* which he believes had failed in providing the promised security and prosperity to the Jewish community. Emancipation in Western Europe did not bring about a blending of cultures, and was accompanied by the growth and intensification of nationalistic hostility and racist ideology. In Russia the destructive Bolshevik revolution caused a "territorial and economic defeat of the main ethnic base of Judaism, that is, the Eastern Jewish people of Russia." Westernized Jews themselves contributed to this defeat and to the collapse of the Russian-Eurasian state that had shaped their identity and spiritually sustained their cultural and religious development. The "Jewish Westernizers" broke off from the Eastern

Jewish tradition. Their intellectual development — namely, the contamination of Jewish religious enthusiasm with the alien form of destructive Western ideas — exemplifies the phenomenon called "pseudomorphosis" used by Oswald Spengler.[18] The Jewish Westernizers are opposed to the lower strata of the Jewish population that preserved Eastern Jewish traditions and the wisdom of generations who lived in the great territory of Eurasia. The crisis of Eastern Jewry and the persecution of Jewish religious and cultural life in Soviet Russia by the "Jewish section" of the Bolshevik party marks the spiritual bankruptcy of the "cause of Moses Mendelssohn" and the concomitant crisis of the "peripheral false culture" of Berlin Enlightenment which he produced.

> We witness the downfall of all the hopes of fanatic Jewish Westernism. We don't know yet whether the kingdom of reason and justice exist on the earth or have to come from somewhere else.[19]

Bromberg believed that the "Eastern Jewish people" *(vostoevreiskii narod)* is a separate entity, the product of Eurasian "place-development" *(mestorazvitie)*.[20] It is noteworthy that he disregards the word "European" from the standard Russian expression "Eastern European Jewry." His "Eastern Jewish people" is a Russian translation of the German term *Ostjude*. Bromberg suggests that Eurasian Jews need to look back and take seriously the "Oriental and Asian legacy of their culture," which "became a bugaboo for its enemies."[21] The Jews should be proud that they are "the only real Asiatics in Europe." The Eurasian project, which is sustained by "Jewish Easternism," should help the Eastern Jews to denounce the myths of Europocentric historiography and maintain their Oriental identity just as Eurasianism helps Russians to discover their cultural Asiatic roots.

The discourse of Westernism and the Enlightenment made the Eastern Jews blind to the congruity of Russian-Eurasian and Eastern Jewish cultures, especially as articulated by Oswald Spengler with his concept of a specific "Magian Culture" that encompassed Islam, Judaism, and Eastern Orthodoxy. Bromberg wrote:

> It is a time for the Eastern Jews to stop asking for equivocal compliments and half-recognitions from the enlightened West. They need to interpret their historical experience, especially the starting point of this experience...in Asia, in the Middle Eastern *oikumene* in a new light. The recognition of this fundamental fact immediately generates a sense of religious and cultural unity with the "host people." This "host people" also entered into the circle of Asian cultures after its reception of Byzantine Orthodoxy. Whatever our assessment of the differences between Orthodoxy and Judaism is, both

of them belong to one and the same Asian Magian culture, for the description of which we need to give credit to Oswald Spengler.[22]

The original congruity of two "Magian" cultures explains a number of congenial phenomena and parallels in development over the course of Eastern Jewish and Russian-Eurasian social and spiritual history. These phenomena are downplayed or completely ignored within the predominant discourse of Westernism adopted by the Jewish "pseudo-intelligentsia." The Westernist discourse is tendentiously preoccupied with Russian-Jewish confrontations and pogroms. The intellectual clichés and stereotypes of Westernized historiography do not permit an understanding of the phenomenon of Jewish-Russian constructive and creative interaction in history and the symbiotic relation between the two peoples. An adequate historical account of Russian-Jewish relations requires the introduction of the assumptions of Jewish Easternism, which Bromberg tries to spell out.

The kingdom (khanate) of Judaized Khazars, Bromberg argued, brought into being onto Russian territory the first true state. It was "a first draft of the state boundaries of the future Eurasian kingdoms: from the Carpathians to Tmutarakan." The khanate included all the elements to be seen in the entire history of Eurasia — the involvement of the Eastern Slavs with the nomads of Turanian and partly Semitic extraction within a single state. Religious tolerance in the Khazar kingdom anticipated the peaceful co-existence of Orthodoxy, Islam, and Judaism in Russia-Eurasia.[23] Bromberg pointed to important contributions made by people of Jewish extraction to Russian religious and political development. Luka Zhidiata, a bishop of Novgorod; an early Russian religious writer and preacher; Nikita Zatvornik; and Pyotr Shaphirov, the vice-chancellor of Peter the Great, became part of the glorious history of the Russian empire. The Judaizing heresy that arose within Orthodoxy in the second half of the fifteenth century had facilitated the development of Russian theological thought and contributed to the productive dialogue of two religious traditions. The response of the Orthodox tradition to this heresy was a precursor to the movement of Counter-Reformation in Europe. It was no accident that Russia was the motherland of hasidism, a Jewish religious movement. The mystical ascetic tradition of the *tzadikim* of the eighteenth century — Israel of Mezhibuzh (the Baal Shem Tov), Nahum of Chernobyl, Zalman Borukhov-Schneerson — have much in common with the traditions of Russian "elders," especially that of Tikhon Zadonsky. In particular, they share the idea of the special proximity of God to his creatures. The grace of a just man is beneficial for all the believers and it is expressed not only in the teachings but also in the behavior and activities of the laity. The "hasidic Easternist orientation," Bromberg contended, determined the loyalty of Russian Jews to the Russian Empire, and their heroism in the course of the Russian-French war of 1812. It is no coincidence that many Russian-Jewish intellectuals were prominent in the anti-rationalist and Easternist trends of Russian thought and criticized revolutionary activity.[24] In sum, the Eurasian narrative allows one to appreciate the examples of Russian-Jewish creative interaction and collaboration and to avoid the narrow-minded Westernized perspective of Jewish history.

Bromberg believed that the examination of Russian-Jewish history in the light of the new Eurasian perspective and the Jews' understanding of their Eastern identity, shaped by sharing the same "place-development" with Russians, could change the political and social position of Eastern Jewry.

> The spectacle of the ignominious dying of Western Jewry in the quagmire of egalitarian-democratic platitudes, and our own victims, should prompt us to make a firm and unequivocal choice. We need to turn our eyes again to the never-waning light from the East which glows today from the fire of the self-immolation of Russia.[25]

Bromberg obviously downplayed or passed over in silence a number of historical episodes that exposed the extreme hostility of Russian religious and state authorities to the Jews and the persistent antisemitic policies of various Russian governments. For instance, he seems to vindicate the Jewish massacres of the seventeenth century carried out by the Cossacks of Bogdan Chmielnicki, in which some 100,000 people were slaughtered. In his opinion, it was the collaboration of Jews with Catholic Poles, and the exploitation of Ukrainian peasants by Jewish stewards and tax farmers sufficed to explain the Cossack's "retaliation." With regard to the Judaizing heresy that arose in various forms in the fifteenth century and was suppressed by the Orthodox Church, he ignores the historical facts and claims that the suppression did not involve physical violence. He suggests that the Russian Church's reaction to the Judaizers was mild compared to the cruelty of the Inquisition in the West.[26] He ignores a basic fact that makes his attempt to contrast West and East meaningless: no Jewish community had been permitted to live in Russian lands before the Polish Partitions in the last quarter of the eighteenth century. In addition, he argued that European antisemitic attitudes and racial stereotypes were absent in Russian literature, which tried "to understand the Jew from within."[27] Perhaps all these generalized and historically inaccurate statements mark the price Bromberg paid for his loyalty to the Eurasian perspective on Russian history.

Bromberg's account of Eastern Jewish history can be better understood against the background of some undercurrents in the tradition of the German Jewish Enlightenment. Eastern European Jews were stigmatized as the archetypal "bad Jews" who failed to fit the Enlightenment ideals of individualism and rationality. For both Germans and German-Jewish partisans of Enlightenment, the East was a source of anxiety and a center of corruption. The "Talmudic" discourse of the superstitious and irrational *Ostjude* was opposed to the civilized rational language of the assimilated and enlightened Western Jew. In the language of the Haskalah, Eastern Jewry symbolized Asiatic, primitive, and even barbaric culture.[28] Thus, Bromberg is reacting against this stereotype of the Eastern Jew. For him, it is the Jewish Westernizers and the tradition of Haskalah with its excess of rationality and universality that are responsible for the Russian revolution and its extremes. The "Asiatic" and "primitive" culture of Eastern Jews is thus a victim of Western stereotyping rather than being itself a social and cultural disaster; its "irrationality" and mysticism are virtues rather than drawbacks. It is the Western Jews who have perverted Jewish culture and betrayed the original Magian essence of the true "Asian" Jewish culture. Bromberg's twist in evaluation proved congenial to such Western thinkers as Martin Buber, who helped renew interest in hasidism,, and other German-Jewish writers of the first part of the century like Arnold Zweig, Hans Kohn, and Bruno Bettelheim, all of whom saw the idealized healthy and culturally-integrated Eastern Jews as the opposite of the rootless, dissociated, and fragmented Jews of the West.[29]

Bromberg's perspective on Jewish-Russian-Eurasian congruity is not merely a curious episode in the intellectual history of the Russian emigration before the Second World War. One can find continuity in the early Eurasian quest for Russian-Jewish integration and the attempts of some contemporary authors to bring together and juxtapose the experiences of Jews and Russians. Some authors posit a special similarity and spiritual kinship between Russians and Jews today. Two examples will suffice: Vladimir Toporov, a well-known Russian linguist, has written about the positive experience of Russian-Jewish interaction. Although he is apparently unfamiliar with Bromberg's work, he focuses on same episodes of Russian-Jewish history as Bromberg did.[30] Lev Anninsky, a well-known literary critic and a champion of neo-Eurasianism, shares similar ideas.[31] These authors do not necessarily articulate the Eurasian aspects of the congruities in the historical and spiritual experiences of the two peoples but continuity with the thinking of JakoB Bromberg is clear.

In sum, discussion of the Jewish aspect by the four representatives of the Eurasian movement suggests different perspectives on the appropriate "Jewish" policies of the future Eurasian state. It is noteworthy that Nikolai

Trubetskoi points to an outside origin of racism and antisemitism in the Eurasian ideology. However, it seems that the very fact that such suggestions were being offered is hardly a coincidence. In the 1930s, Eurasianism was associated in the minds of many contemporaries with the ideologies and growth of fascist movements because of similarities in their programs, including anti-Westernism, anti-liberalism, the emphasis on economic autarchy, ideocracy, organic democracy (a term used by the fascist and Volkisch parties in Germany as opposed to the "mechanical democracy" of the parliament), and the preoccupation with geopolitics.[32] It is no accident that some sympathizers considered antisemitism to be compatible with Eurasianism; however, from the discussion by Trubetskoi, Karsavin, Sviatopolk-Mirsky, and Bromberg of Jewish aspects, it is clear that mainstream Eurasians did not share the racist assumptions of radical Russian chauvinism and steadfastly condemned antisemitic rhetoric.[33] Antisemitic tendencies in the original Eurasian movement were at most marginal. None of the classical Eurasian authors questioned the Eurasian identity of Russian Jews and all of them at least recognized the possibility of their successful integration into the Eurasian cultural zone.

None of the four Eurasian theoreticians considered the Zionist dream of restoring Jews to Palestine promising or politically feasible. This is surprising given their strong belief in the special bond between ethnicity and territory. Moreover, one has the impression that they perceived Zionism as something of a rival in that it might draw away potential Jewish supporters of the Eurasian movement. The classical Eurasian authors thought that, Zionists had overlooked or ignored the attachment of Eastern Jews to Eurasian "place-development" and their lack of interest in the building of independent state.[34]

Thus, all four theoreticians agreed that nothing should preclude the inclusion of Jews into the "Eurasian brotherhood." Even if Jews in general or some particular groups tended to fall prey to emigrant psychological complexes, extreme particularism, the temptations of Zionism, and the ideology of Westernism, they were still full-fledged members of the Eurasian cultural and geographical landscape, and the Eurasian state of the future should be concerned with their absorption and full accommodation. Many neo-Eurasians, however, have abandoned almost all these assumptions. Moreover, their version of geopolitical nationalism has created a new geopolitical justification for antisemitism.

THE JEWS IN ALEXANDER DUGIN'S NEO-EURASIANISM

It is expedient to preface an analysis of the reevaluation of the "Jewish Question" in neo-Eurasianism by introducing one of its most prominent theoreticians who has shaped its conceptual language and outlined the new context of the discussion of the "Jewish Question". Alexander Dugin is the most prolific writer among contemporary Russian neo-Eurasians. Formerly a member of Pamyat, he left this organization in the late 1980s in order to establish his own group. Dugin introduces himself as a "metaphysician, conspirologist, and expert in sacred geography." He is editor-in-chief of three journals, *Milii Angel, Giperboreia,* and *Elementi.* He believes that Eurasianism exemplifies the broad ideology of an international movement of Conservative Revolution to which he feels allegiance.[35] It is a revolt against the predominant values of modern civilization corrupted by rationalism, liberal democracy, and materialism. Conservative Revolution is a trend of the counter-Enlightenment that supposedly transcends the conventional distinction between Right and Left, since it combines the conservative values of the Right and the revolutionary methods and spirit of political experimentation of the Left. The political movements of Italian Fascism, German National Socialism, the Romanian Iron Guard, and Spanish Falangists all contained elements of Conservative Revolution. The best formulation of the ideology can be found in the theories of the German "Young Conservatives" (Carl Schmitt, Arthur Moeller van den Bruck, Oswald Spengler, Ernst Jünger, Ludwig Klages, Martin Heidegger, and Werner Sombart),[36] and those of National Bolshevism (Henrich Laufenbach and Ernst Niekisch). Dugin contends that almost all Conservative Revolutionaries were Russophiles in varying degrees. The ideology found expression in the works of many other authors as well, such as the German Aryosophes (Guido von List, Jörg Lanz von Liebenfels, and Herman Wirth), the writings of Baron Julius Evola (a late Italian fascist), the poems of Ezra Pound, and the sociological insights of Vilfredo Pareto, Ferdinand Töennise, and Max Weber. Dugin is fascinated by the concepts of psychoanalyst Carl Gustav Jung, and the theories of French conspirologists, and he also makes frequent reference to the works of the Russian historiosophes and philosophers of culture, Konstantin Leontiev and Nikolai Danilevsky.[37] His critique of modernity draws upon the theories of French post-modernists, such as Jean Baudrillard, George Battaille, and Giles Deleuze. But Alexander Dugin's principal authority is undoubtedly René Guenon, a French Orientalist, metaphysician, and religious thinker.[38] Dugin has established personal contacts with representatives of the French *nouvelle droite* — Alain de Benoist, for example, is an associate editor and contributor to *Elementi* —

and other leaders of radical nationalist parties and movements of Western and Eastern Europe.[39] These contacts enable him to keep Russian nationalists informed about recent developments within Western European nationalism, to facilitate intellectual exchange between different groups of nationalists, and to coordinate their activity. Dugin's theories have been lambasted by virtually every group of Russian nationalists, mostly on account of their provocative apologetic for some Nazi leaders, as well as for their "contamination" of the authentic Russian movement by fascist and Germanophile ideas.[40] However, many of his concepts have nevertheless had a substantial impact on the doctrines of Russian nationalists and the political language of the Russian anti-liberal opposition.

Amicus and Hostis: Pax Euroasiatica and Its Mystical Antipode

The attitude to the "Jewish question" in neo-Eurasianism is determined by the specific concept of Russian nationalism and by a concomitant national myth. Following Carl Schmitt, Dugin claims that every political group or movement needs to define itself by its choice of friend *(amicus)* and enemy *(hostis)*.[41] The fundamental principles and orientation of Russian nationalism allows it to distinguish the Jews as a serious political and spiritual enemy. In his paper *Apology for Nationalism,* Dugin attempts to define the idiosyncratic features of Russian nationalist consciousness as opposed to nationalisms of other nations and ethnicities. Thus, he claims that for the American, nationalism is associated with pride in the achievements of liberal civilization and a market economy. French nationalism is concerned with cultural identity and loyalty to France. German nationalism is ethnic and racist, while the nationalism of Serbs and Romanians is Orthodox. Jewish nationalism is religious and messianic.

Russian nationalism, by contrast, has four distinctive features. It is (1) religious and messianic; (2) geopolitical; (3) imperial, and (4) communal.[42] These categories are not ranked in order of importance, although Dugin does suggest that the religious, messianic, imperial, and communal facets of Russian nationalism can never be properly understood without reference to its geopolitical foundation:

> Russian nationalism is inseparably linked with territory *(prostranstvo)*. Russians distinguish themselves not by blood, ethnicity, phenotype or culture. They are more sensitive to territory than any other people.... It is difficult to understand the origins of this "national intoxication" with Russian territory. Perhaps this unprecedented phenomenon and the religious metaphors of Russia — the "Last Kingdom," the "country as the world," the "Ark of

> Salvation" — can be explained by the combination of Slavic sensitivity and the nomadic instincts of the Turks in the steppe.... Russians regard territory as sacred. Their attitude to territory is anti-utilitarian. They never tried to exploit their land or to derive profits from it. They are guardians of territory, initiated into its mysteries, rather than its colonizers.... Therefore, in many cases Russians prefer non-Slavic people affiliated with Russian territory to other Slavs.[43]

The geopolitical foundations of Russian nationalism are reflected in the ideology of the Russian Orthodox Church. Politically, the special geopolitical status of Russia and the specific Russian sensitivity to territory requires that the society takes the form of a Eurasian empire.

Religious ideology is closely connected with the geopolitical identity of Russians, and legitimates this identity. For Russians, Orthodoxy is neither "a branch of Christianity" (like Protestantism) nor "universal" (like the Catholic Church). After the fall of Constantinople, Orthodox Russia became "the last shelter of Christ's truth in a world of apostasy" and "the last unspoiled bulwark of faith and sacredness in a world of evil." The notion of "Moscow — the Third Rome" expressed by the monk Philotheus, Dugin argues, presupposes that Russia is the Fourth Empire and the "restraining force" (the *katechon* referred to in II Thessalonians 2:7).[44] Russians are the eschatologically chosen people entrusted with the "mystery of grace" and empowered to prevent the appearance of the Man of Sin (antichrist).[45]

The form of empire is a condition sine qua non for the survival and preservation of Russian territory. Russians are "Eurasian Romans" who unite all other people and languages by their unique religio-territorial Weltanschauung. The imperial consciousness is tolerant of different ethnicities and creeds insofar as they remain loyal to the Eurasian entity and don't interfere with the construction of the empire.

The communal character of Russian nationalism presupposes that all social projects will appeal to its citizens. The individual cannot be dissociated from the nation even in theory.

> A person of Russian of origin who is detached from other Russians is erased from the sphere of interests of Russian nationalism. It is not surprising that a Russian Diaspora never existed in history.... Falling out of the social field of Russian people, a Russian ceases to be a bearer of Russian spirit.[46]

According to Dugin, Russian Jews do not belong to those non-Slavic people, allegiance to whom can "override the other Slavs," although they live on the same territory. Jewry is opposed to Russian nationalism in every respect. Its aspirations, attitudes, and allegiances expose them as the primary enemy *(hostis)* of the Russian-Eurasian project.

> For Russian nationalists a Jew is not only one stranger among others but the mystical antipode of their own nationalism. Their national self-consciousness stresses aspects that are directly opposite to those of Russian nationalism.[47]

(1) Jewish messianism and religious nationalism oppose the very foundations of Russian nationalism that is based on Byzantine Orthodoxy. Jewish eschatological messianism prevents them from seeing Byzantium as the "millennial kingdom" and recognizing Russia as the "restraining force" *(katechon)* and successor of Byzantium.[48] The Jews link the millennial kingdom with the future coming of Messiah, for to them, the millennial kingdom of Byzantium is associated with the humiliation and suffering of the Diaspora and their wandering among peoples who did not recognize their election and mission.

(2) Dugin goes on to theorize that the Jews deny the sacredness of territory because they did not accept the coming of Christ and, consequently, did not accept the idea of the redemption of the earth.

> For two thousand years the Jews did not have their own land, their national space. This fact has affected their ethnic psychology. They used to regard the environment as something strange, foreign, that is, purely functional, lifeless and decorative. The Jews don't understand and don't like space. They considered all the kingdoms in which they have lived "tref," that is, desacralized, corrupted and impure. It is only natural that Russians, being aware of this Jewish mentality, opposed it to their own concept of space and nature. In Russian consciousness the natural objects are the full-fledged living "citizens" of the Russian nation, the "baptized elements," which are permeated with the transforming force of Orthodox kingdom. It was a fundamental feeling of Russians that the redemptive sacrifice of the Son "rectified" the world of being.[49]

(3) The concept of empire also exposes the incompatibility of Russian and Jewish mentalities. The destruction of the Second Temple marked the end of Jewish statehood and the beginning of a new period — that of the Diaspora. Thus, in Jewish consciousness the coming of the messiah is associated with the restoration of the Temple and a Jewish state. In contrast, Russians associate the Temple with the mystical Body of Christ (Ephesians 4:4-13) and, in a broader sense, with the Orthodox Church. Whereas Russians felt the mystical presence of the Temple, the Jews could only sense the absence of

the longed-for Third Temple to be built in the future messianic age. Consequently, the Jews identify the "Eurasian Romans" with the "blasphemeous usurpers of their own national tradition."[50]

(4) In terms of the communal aspect of Russian nationalism, Russians are opposed to the particularism of the Jews. The Jews have their own "mystical self-identification," isolated and aloof from the life and values of the peoples with whom they temporarily have lived. Whereas Russians disappear in the absence of the communal *(sobornii)* unit, the Jewish "ego," on the other hand, is fostered by the absence of their kingdom and by the lack of involvement in a communal unity with other nations.

It is important to observe that Dugin's definition of Russian nationalism is normative rather than descriptive, for he wishes to encompass and integrate a variety of trends of Russian nationalism in a pragmatic way, consolidating religious, socialist, and Slavophilic trends. However, one should not be confused about the real nature of this synthesis. Dugin does not admit that his list presupposes a hierarchy of the different features of Russian nationalism. It is clear that the basis for his integration is the doctrine of Eurasianism, for the geopolitical aspect of Russian nationalism enjoys superiority over all other aspects. Furthermore, all other aspects make sense only by reference to, and in the context of, the geopolitical Eurasian axis of the whole construction. For Dugin, geopolitical terminology serves as a master language for the formulation of central religious and social problems. Geopolitical language is a mediator that unifies and combines the various "ideolects" of Russian nationalism. Dugin expresses different problems in terms of this geopolitical language: Russian Orthodoxy is only a religious justification of old historic Russian geopolitical ambitions.[51] Russian communitarianism is only a function of the Russian geopolitical essence. Needless to say, his interpretation of Orthodoxy and Russian communitarianism *(sobornost* and *obschinnost)* differ substantially from either the official view of the Russian Orthodox Church, or the conventional Slavophilic notion of community. Ultimately, Dugin is concerned with geo-politics, geo-culture, geo-religion, geo-tradition, and geo-community.

Given the prominence of the geopolitical argument, the explanation of the animus against the Jews is not difficult to understand. The supposed Jewish distaste for "space" is a key for understanding their alleged opposition to Russians and all other Eurasian or Indo-European ethnicities. The difference between the Eurasian and Jewish spiritual "styles" is an outcome of their different perceptions of space.

One can observe that Dugin's concept of the relation between the Jews and the original population of Eurasia is reminiscent of the position of the false friends of the Eurasian movement dismissed by Nikolai Trubetskoi as misinterpreting and misapplying the Eurasian doctrine.

Eurasianism versus "Atlanticism"

In the political thinking of the neo-Eurasians (governed by the dualistic categories of *amicus* and *hostis* with Jews as the enemy), we also find that the Jews have their own allies — the maritime "Atlanticist" civilization (i.e., those economically powerful countries like Britain and the United States), and "mondialists."

The term mondialism (French *monde,* world) was borrowed from the ideology of French right-wing intellectuals, and does not necessarily refer to the maritime civilizations, but rather emphasizes the unifying and globalizing tendencies of the contemporary world which have reached their climax at the present stage. Dugin defines mondialism as "the concept of integration of the planet under the rule of the West and laying the foundation for a World State ruled by one World Government in the future."[52] Trying to transform the world into a global "melting pot," the cosmopolitan and anti-national mondialistic civilization appeals to "universal values" and tries to instill these values in the national consciousness of all ethnic groups. Pretending to be universal, the mondialist philosophy actually conceals its partiality. The idea of a "new world order" and *Pax Americana* expresses the global ambitions of the mondialists, and it was the Jews who greatly contributed to the propaganda of universal values and human rights.[53] Dugin points to Jewish affiliation with subversive Leftist movements, which he considers a fifth column of mondialism. In the communist movement, for example, the mondialistic tendency is exemplified in the ideology of Leon Trotsky, who was preoccupied with the idea of a universal "permanent revolution" and considered Russia a springboard for the messianic communist revolution. Eurasian communists had quite different social visions: Lenin believed in the establishment of socialism in "one separate country," while Stalin believed in a "Eurasian Empire" of Soviet nations.[54]

Neo-Eurasians see a clear link between the goals of the Jews and the Atlanticists. It is no coincidence, they claim, that the expulsion of the Jews from Spain in 1492 coincided with the discovery of America, for Columbus took with him many Jews, whose "pernicious influence was unbearable to Catholic Spain."[55] The activities and ideology of many well-known Jewish leaders is governed and informed by the ideology of Atlanticism; the fact that the Jews wield political power in the United States and shape its foreign policies is often cited as evidence of their adherence to Atlanticism.[56] The origins of the spiritual bond between Western Atlanticism and the Jews can be found in the parallels in their histories, for both are heirs to the mythical civilization of Atlantis. Dugin also contends that the commercial maritime Atlanticist civilizations continue and enrich the nomadic tradition of the Semites.

> Maritime existence is the extreme development of nomadism which acquires a new quality at the moment of transition from land nomadism to floating in the continental seas and finally to the decisive moment of entry into the open Ocean.[57]

Dugin also observes that many of the American founding fathers and presidents directly identified America as a new incarnation of Israel. He contends that the notion of a special congruity between America and the Jews was shared by prominent Jews such as Edmond Wiseman, Simon Wiesenthal, and some early Zionist proposals to found a Jewish state in America.[58]

Both Americans and the Jews have a special proclivity for commercial activity. Historically, the maritime civilizations concentrated on the commercial sphere and were associated with specific branches of the Semitic race (Phoenicians, Carthaginians, and the Jews). The paradigmatic encounter of maritime Semites and continental Aryans in human history is the Punic war between Rome and Carthage — the incarnations of "Behemoth" and "Leviathan" mentioned above.[59] The proclivity for trade is completely alien to the very spirit of Eurasian (Indo-European) culture. Dugin draws upon the works of Georges Dumézil in which he argues that the caste of hucksters was unfamiliar to traditional Aryan society. Dugin believes that it is a fact of far reaching political significance:

> Within the Indo-European civilization the traders *(torgovtsi)* as a special caste or class emerged only at the late stages of development as foreign and racially alien components. In the Greek-Latin and in the Mediterranean area, the "Semites" and other representatives of the Levant were the bearers of the trade order.... Thus, capitalists and traders are the social "saboteurs," the social "strangers" *(inorodtsi)* within the economic systems of Indo-European white people.... Their civilization had introduced special laws which curtailed trade and debarred usury. It was the socio-economic manifestation of the white race and its social ethics.... Capitalism introduced not only economic but also racial and ethnic alienation.[60]

This idea is included in the political program of Dugin's political party of National Bolsheviks.

Dugin believes that the Punic war has never really ended. In the course of the Cold War, the eternal Carthage of maritime civilizations retaliated against the eternal Rome. Dugin believes that the Jews contributed to the defeat of the Behemoth of Soviet Eurasia.

Tradition and Counter-Tradition

The war of the continents, however, is only a projection of a more important and fateful conflict between two metaphysical forces in history — those of Tradition and counter-Tradition, Initiation and counter-Initiation expressed in the theories of René Guenon that have become part of the neo-Eurasian philosophy of history. "Initiation" is the process of the rediscovery of tradition, while counter-initiation is a process of alienation from tradition, in most cases at the conscious level.

According to Guenon, human history is cyclical. The current period is associated with the extreme degradation of the Primordial Tradition, which was universal until it split into a number of particular secondary religious traditions in the post-Babylonian period. Today, profane anti-traditional values ("the kingdom of quantity") have displaced even the traces of the Single Truth that once had been preserved in the secondary traditional forms. Two ideas are especially important with regard to the preservation of the Primordial Tradition.

(1) Some secondary traditions preserve the Truth of Primordial Tradition in varying degrees. Orthodox Christianity and Islam are the most traditionalist religions, while Catholicism and especially Protestantism have lost the original insights of the Tradition, having been poisoned by the humanistic values of mondialist civilization. Russia-Eurasia has a universal mission to denounce anti-traditional forces.

(2) In spite of the sharp conflicts between exoteric secondary traditions, the esoteric traditions of the same religions (Hermeticism and Gnosticism in Catholicism, Hesychasm in Orthodoxy, Sufism in Islam) have much in common and reproduce the logic of the Primordial Tradition. Orthodox forms of religion are superior to modernized, and consequently corrupted, forms.

René Guenon believed that kabbalah, the esoteric trend in Judaism, was also associated with the Primordial Tradition, and that negative and corrupting influences associated with the Jews arose from distorted versions of Judaism and from some secularized groups who fostered the forces of anti-Tradition and counter-Initiation. Dugin disagrees with Guenon, arguing that in fact, the basic principles of Jewish kabbalah are incompatible with other esoteric traditions. Dugin believes it is not the "secularized" or "profane" Jews who have subverted the esoteric tradition, but the "most Orthodox nucleus" of Jewry. He contends:

The Jews are the bearers of the religious culture, which is profoundly different from all historical manifestations of Indo-European spirituality, from the ancient Aryan pagan cults to Hinduism and Christianity.... In the Indo-European civilization the Judaic community was always perceived as something strange and foreign to the Indo-European mind-set and culture.[61]

Two elements preclude the identification of Indo-European esoteric tradition with its Jewish counterpart. First of all, the Jews insist on the particularity and superiority of Israel over all other people, a position incompatible with the doctrine of the Integral Tradition. Dugin describes the metaphysics of the *Zohar* as "a dreadful and radical xenophobic teaching."

Judaic esoteric eschatology suggests that the end of time is the upshot of the ancient struggle of the Jews against the gentiles.... In the eschatological situation, the Judaic religious impulse takes the form of an aggression against all forms of non-Jewish spirituality, which are identified with demonology.[62]

In addition, the Judaic concept of the cosmos has no analogies in the religious concepts of other ethnic groups:

The comparison of the Judaic metaphysics, on the one hand, and the diverse Indo-European traditions, which were united by one and the same "style," demonstrates that the interpretation of Cosmos constitutes a fundamental difference between the two. Judaism interprets the world as a Creation alienated from God. It sees the world as an exile, as a mechanical maze where the "chosen people" wander. The true mission of the "chosen people" is revealed not in the glorious victories of Joshua, the son of Nun, or the seer Ezra, but rather in the tragic *peripeteia* (wandering) of the Diaspora. The Diaspora correlates better than anything else with the spirit of classical Judaism which draws an insurmountable abyss between the Creator and the Creation.... The Cosmos of the Indo-Europeans is a living reality directly connected with God.... Even in the darkest periods of history...the nexus of the Creation and the Creator, the Cosmos and its inhabitants, with the Light of Original Cause is never broken. It continues either through the miracle of *eucharistia*... [i.e., the miraculous transformation of bread and wine into Christ's body and blood in the Eucharist], or through an heroic overcoming, or through a salutary, courageous asceticism. Indo-European consciousness is the consciousness of the autochthons par excellence. This consciousness is bound up with the soil, not with the Diaspora, with possession rather than loss, with connection, not with the gap in connection.... The orthodox Jews consider the Indo-Europeans "naive and infantile optimists" who have no idea about the dreadful mystery of the Abyss, about the theological drama of the cosmic Diaspora. The Indo-Europeans, on the other hand, believe that Jewish religious pessimism distorts the proportions of the sacred cosmos, deprives it of its solitary energies, de-sacralizes earth, space, time, and the unique fate of the autochthonous people.[63]

Dugin believes that the "most clear and most authentic Jewish doctrine" is found in the writings of the kabbalist Rabbi Isaac ben Solomon Luria (1534–1572) and his successors. It is here that one can best see the incompatibility of the esoteric Jewish tradition with the grand Primordial Tradition. Whereas the neo-Platonic philosophy described the process of creation as the emanation of the Principle into the exterior world and propounded the gradual incarnation of divine essences into sensible forms, Lurianic kabbalah describes the process of creation as the contraction (*tsimtsum*) of the divine essence and as exile from the original plentitude of divine potentialities. God withdrew into himself and concentrated his essence. The interpretation and functions of the *sefirot* (emanations) in Lurianic kabbalah also differs substantially from the neo-Platonic concept.

The primordial man — *Adam Kadmon* — an emanation of the creator aspect of God, poured light into ten "vessels." But the vessels that held these lights could not contain their power and shattered. As a result, the sefirot broke into myriad pieces (some flowing back, while others flowed into the void). Since that cataclysm, nothing in time, place, or order is where it is supposed to be. The Jewish cosmos lacks harmony and cannot function properly, because of the insurmountable distance separating it from God. This distance will never be bridged, even during the Great Sabbath after the coming of Messiah. Thus, in Judaic metaphysics Cosmos is identified with a Diaspora abandoned by God. "The creation is only the tragic symbol of Vanity without any hope for redemption."[64] The impossibility of theophany and the doctrine of absolute distance between the Creator and creation "communicates to the Jewish religious consciousness a skeptical attitude towards cosmology, mythology and all other aspects of Tradition which articulate the immanence and the absolute unity of the Principle."[65] In sum, Dugin declares that the Gnosis of Despair and absolute vanity of the universe are crucial elements of the kabbalistic and authentically Jewish worldview.[66]

Dugin claims that the Jewish tales about the *Golem* display the same logic as the myth of creation in Lurianic kabbalah, since the Golem is an image of man. In medieval Jewish folklore the Golem is an artificially created human endowed with life by supernatural means. The concept of Golem, Dugin contends, is the concept of "rough form animated by something essentially exterior to it."

> The Jew recognizes his own ego and his own people...in the grotesque image of the Golem, in the dismal human apparatus, which absorbs all the hopelessness of the abandoned world created once and forever.... The Jewish gnosis is the Gnosis of Despair, and therefore, the maxim of Ecclesiastes "he that increaseth knowledge increaseth sorrow" is related first of all to the Jewish knowledge about God and to the knowledge of the Jews about themselves.[67]

This Jewish vision of the universe and man, Dugin argues, goes against the basic intuitions of Indo-European religions, specifically against the concepts of Christianity, which he characterizes as a purely Indo-European religion. Dugin draws a line between historical Christianity and the "eternal *(nadvremennoe)* and pure" "super-religious Christianity." This "eternal Christianity" is a "primordial teaching" which "providentially appeals to the people of the North" and has a fundamentally anti-Judaic orientation.[68] There is historical continuity between Christianity and Judaism, but metaphysically the two religions have nothing in common. Dugin claims that "Judaism rejected not only the personality and mission of Jesus, but also the very principle of the immanent God."[69] Judeo-Christian Christianity is thus not the real "perennial Christianity" associated with the grand Tradition.[70]

Dugin claims that the basic concepts of the two religious traditions — centered on eschatology, Messiah, and demonology — have directly opposite meanings:

> In the Judaic consciousness the Messiah is not a Divine Hero who comes down from the Heaven of Principle to rectify the worn cosmos and to save the degraded human community, as it is for the Christians and for other non-Judaic eschatologies. The Messiah of the Judaic sources cannot be identified with the direct and triumphal revelation of the Transcendental.... Their Messiah will not bring anything new.... Judaists believe that both the saving and the saved are this-worldly and immanent.[71]

Judaism does not have the soteriological element common in all other religions; the Messiah of Judaists does not bring any "good news" (i.e., gospel) and does not promise a "return" to the original state. It is not surprising then that the Jewish Messiah is identified with the antichrist in "eternal Christianity" and other traditional religions.

The Jews and the Crisis of the Modern World

In the passage quoted above, Dugin claims that the orthodox and esoteric religious forms of Judaism are in opposition to Russian nationalism and Tradition. In addition, secularized and assimilated Jews also function as agents of counter-Tradition. The "sorrowful and mysterious face of Judaism" is revealed not only in Lurianic kabbalah, but also "in the novels of Kafka, the philosophy of Michelstaedter and in the scientific concepts of Einstein, a theoretician of the absolute Vanity of the material universe."[72] Moreover, sometimes the assimilated Jews — specifically Arthur Koestler, Otto Weininger, Carlo Michelstaedter, and Martin Buber — "reveal to the gentiles *(goyim)* the horrifying mysteries of the 'Judean war,' being ashamed of the dubious tactics of the Diaspora." Their writings demonstrate that the artificial cosmopolitan ideology can never reconcile Jewish metaphysics with the Indo-European, and that the "energies of our ethnicities, religions, theological and sacred instincts will inevitably burst through the old clothes of unnatural, unfounded and unrealistic doctrines."[73]

Dugin follows the conception of Carl Gustav Jung regarding a collective unconscious. The national consciousness is inferior to the collective unconscious in that it can fail to conceptualize the most profound intuitions and aspirations of a given ethnic group. Consciously or unconsciously, the Jews reveal counter-Traditional and counter-Initiation ideas as found in the logic and symbolism of kabbalah. Even assimilated Jews are therefore involved in the corrupting and subversive Atlanticist and mondialist projects of the contemporary world. Dugin identifies the theoreticians of "contemporary intellectual perversity" and advocates of destructive counter-Traditionalism as "children of darkness" and the "saints of Satan" of the Islamic tradition.

The destructive influences of the modern world are associated primarily with mondialism, liberal democracy, materialism, atheism, neo-spiritualism, effeminization, and the advent of a "bankocracy" which supplants the conventional capitalism of the "third estate." All these tendencies can supposedly be understood as secularized forms of Jewish esoteric doctrines.

(1) Dugin contends that mondialism in general, especially the mondialistic concept of the "end of history" is only a secularized version of the Jewish "kabbalistic eschatology" which lacks a soteriological dimension. The end of history means the end of ethnicities, religions, national states, isolated unique civilizations and ideologies, that is, the major agents of history. For Dugin, the most interesting and radical exponent of the theory of the "end of history" is not Francis Fukuyama (author of *The End of History and the Last Man* [1992]), but the Algerian Jew, Jacques Attali, a director of the European

Bank for Reconstruction and Development in London and special adviser to
the French government and to François Mitterand in 1981. Dugin claims that
Attali is well-versed in kabbalah and the Jewish esoteric tradition, and his
books, *1492* and *Lignes d'horizons*[74] perfectly illustrate René Guenon's
claims about the proclivity of assimilated Jews to anti-Traditional activities,
and substantiate the special dangers resulting from the Jews' "deflected
nomadism" *(nomadism devie)*. Jacques Attali proposes a new "Trade Order"
(or "Order of Money") in opposition to the "Order of the Sacred" (religious
order) and the "Order of Force" (military order) — previous ways of
controlling social violence. Attali suggests that the new economic order is
better equipped to prevent violence. The "Order of Money" is based upon the
new technologies of communication that utilize "nomadic objects" based on
microchips — the microprocessor, cellular telephone, personal computers,
video-disks, the Internet, etc. The pervasive employment of "nomadic
objects" in social practices will transform contemporary culture into a new
kind of "nomadic civilization" and render the spacial and territorial aspects of
human life less significant. Attali talks about the penetration of the nomadic
tendencies into different social spheres (labor, citizenship, the acquisition of
professions, etc.) and describes the new nomadism as the "highest form of the
Order of Money."

Neo-Eurasians thus associate Attali's predictions with the forces of anti-
Tradition. The "Trade Order" presupposes global unification and cannot
tolerate alternative forms of social organization. Neo-Eurasian champions of
Tradition fear that increased mobility in the material world, facilitated and
countenanced by the "new Trade Order," will inevitably be accompanied by a
loss of connection with the spiritual dimensions of the universe and will pave
the way for the complete degeneration of human civilization. The
universalism of mondialism is a parody of the true universalism of the
Traditional civilization. Dugin believes that the new de-territorialized "Trade
Order" is a prelude to the coming of the antichrist, the real master of the
materialistic world.[75]

(2) Dugin traces the roots of different political ideologies back to religious
or metaphysical doctrines, and claims that the structure of liberal democracy
reproduces the Jewish paradigm of Diaspora and exile. Despite the rhetoric of
human rights, the citizens of the liberal state are in fact completely alienated
from the process of decision-making and are deprived of full-fledged political
expression. An anonymous secret political elite manipulates the
consciousness of the people and presents its own decisions and policies as the
products of a collective process of decision-making. Liberal democracy is the
"society of spectacle."[76] The citizens of present-day liberal democracies are

just as alienated as the Diaspora Jews whom Dugin described before. The paradisical state is associated with organic democracy and the hierarchical social order, where the community is united around the same spiritual values and ideals and where there is no gap between the individuals and the state.[77]

Dugin describes the governing mondialistic cosmopolitan and anti-national elite — "the System" — as Jewish. "The ideal pattern of the 'System' is described by Franz Kafka in his famous novel *The Castle,* where the relations between the population of the village and the unapproachable Castle on the hill are grotesque, horrible and irrational." Dugin goes on to argue that the interpretation of the novel by Max Brod, "expert in Talmud and kabbalah," provides a new perspective for understanding the nature of the absolute and the irrational power of the contemporary political elite of the System.[78] In Brod's reading, the central point of the novel is:

> the allegory of the specifically Jewish, Judaist and even kabbalist interpretation of the Law (Torah), which reveals itself to the orthodox believer as a sophisticated design incomprehensible and absolutely alienated from the individual. Hence, the Castle is not a metaphor for the society of alienation but rather the very symbol of the Jewish Weltanschauung, of the Talmudic vision of the structure of the universe. This universe is absurd and lifeless because of its distance from the Creator, who reveals himself to his people only through a set of strict and incomprehensible prescriptions, which constitute the paradoxical maze of the Law.... If we take the Castle as a literary and symbolic image of the System, we can better understand the worldview of those representatives of the hidden elite who not only take advantage of the undemocratic model of the System but also justify it by reference to theological arguments.... If the people is healthy and if its spiritual tradition is different from that trend of Judaism which theologically justifies the Castle, then the People's Revolution should become the natural response to the despotism of alienation.[79]

Procedural democracy with its concomitant processes of alienation is opposed to the substantive democracy of traditional civilization By procedural democracy he means the forms of government focused on procedures (e.g., checks and balances, election system, etc.) which secure the institution of liberal democracy. "Substantive" democracy does not require any procedures: the leader can intuit the needs of the people and community without following any formal procedures.

(3) The de-sacralization of the cosmos in the Jewish esoteric tradition promotes materialism in modern science and philosophy. The "economic

materialism" of Karl Marx and the "psychiatric materialism" of Sigmund Freud exemplify the Jewish "intellectual perversity" that has contributed to the degradation of the modern world. Both theories explain the high and the superior by reference to the low and vile.

Dugin believes that Freud's psychoanalytical materialism is an important and dangerous ingredient of the liberal discourse. Psychoanalysis allows the mondialists to profanize the expressions of high spirituality and the values of traditional civilization and to reduce them to mere psychological sexual complexes. Dugin describes psychoanalysis in the terms used in Nazi propaganda, calling it a "Jewish science" based both on the intellectual constructions of Jews and on the experience of Jewish patients. He contends that the counter-Initiative nature of psychoanalysis suggests that the original source of this doctrine is the Jewish Masonic organization B'nai B'rith.

Freud reduced sacred, superhuman symbols into terms of individual sexual experience, to the primal and primitive drive for coitus, and disparaged the wholeness of psychic life and the highest archetypes of the unconscious. The practice of psychoanalysis is damaging for the unconscious of the patient. In Freud's psychoanalysis, the world of the unconscious is identified with the demonic and infernal world, which is inhabited by perverse and devilish images. Dugin draws a parallel between psychoanalysis and the doctrines of kabbalah.

> The Jewish kabbalah describes these spheres of vice as the world of *klipot*, a world of shells, where infernal entities violate all the religious proscriptions.... Psychoanalysis opens the door for the development of the inferior under-human forces.... Its contents have much in common with the dark rituals, which are associated with worship of the devil.[80]

(4) Freud's psychoanalysis is closely connected with another corrupting tendency of the modern world, that is, effeminization. Dugin argues that Freud's Eros is not the full-fledged and all-embracing cosmic Eros of the Indo-European tradition, but is exclusively feminine, the chaotic Eros of matriarchal cultures, ungoverned by high ideals and principles, without any particular organizing nomos; it is the blind libido of the kabbalistic demoness Lilith. "Freud insists that this Eros is supposedly oppressed by the patriarchal complex which is associated with consciousness and the ethical imperative. In other words, he simply does not recognize patriarchal and purely masculine sexuality, describing it in terms of 'oppression,' 'complex' and 'violence.'" The highest expressions of masculine Eros — heroism, contemplation, sacrifice, abstention — are not recognized by Freud as manifestations of eroticism. In reality, only the masculine eros can sanctify and illuminate the great energies of love.[81] Dugin believes that this

predominance of feminine Eros in psychoanalysis is due to the Jewish descent of its founding father. It was Otto Weininger who equated Jews with women in *Sex and Character* (1903), in the chapter entitled "Jewry." Following Weininger's concept of bisexuality, Dugin claims that the Jewish psyche is feminine and that the ideas of heroism and religious faith — the highest expressions of masculine eroticism — are incomprehensible to the Jews, and in particular to Sigmund Freud, who associated the ego and consciousness with Thanatos, the cosmic force directly opposite to Eros. Dugin believes that Jewish femininity is also expressed in a proclivity to masochism. In his review of the first Russian edition Leopold Sacher-Masoch's novel, *Venus in Fur*, Dugin argues that whereas the characters of the Marquis de Sade could be construed as caricatures of the Indo-European (Aryan) type of "hero" or "master" who attempts to destroy all obstacles in his way, the characters of Masoch are caricature of ever-suffering Jews, who find special pleasure and excitement in their own pain and suffering.[82] The heroes of Masoch and de Sade, Dugin argues, are the horizontal projections of two different types of eroticism, the Jewish and the Aryan.[83]

Dugin attributes significant political implications to the processes of effeminization. Political problems and conflicts are imbued with sexual connotations. The tendencies to effeminization are manifested in the ideology of human rights, pacifism, the ethics of non-violence, the rise of feminism and the recognition and acceptance of homosexuality, and in the all-absorbing liberal ideology of "soft" feminine oppression (i.e., a type of oppression that does not resort to physical force). In mondialism the totalizing reconciliation of all ideological and cultural movements is realized through a kind of castration of the most important elements of all traditions, that is, at the expense of the essential aspects of all specific and authentic ideologies. The eclipse of heroic and masculine values, Dugin argues, is manifested in the political and sexual orientation of the post-communist politicians. "The abundance of effeminized types among post-perestroika politicians, coupled with their specific ethnic extraction," Dugin argues, "exposes the process of de-nationalization and emasculation which accompanies the economic and political diversion of the West."[84] The Jews are trying to suppress the impulses and manifestations of Russian masculine sexuality evident in the construction of the Eurasian Empire.[85]

(5) The next destructive tendency of modern civilization is the rise of neo-spiritualistic movements and subversive Masonic organizations, both closely connected with the activity of the Jews. Dugin mentions the Beddarid brothers who founded the rite of Memphis-Mizraim; Max Teon, the Grand Master of "H.B. of L.", Samuel MacGregor Mathers, one of the founding

fathers of the Order of the Golden Dawn, Mira Alfassa, the "Mother" of Auroville, and the French philosopher Henri Bergson.[86] These neo-spiritualist trends are said to be even more dangerous than "pure profanism and agnosticism," because of their doctrines appear so similar to those of Tradition. In fact, they are only distortions and caricatures of authentic esoterism, for they adopt the concepts of progress and evolution, which indicate and manifest the corruption of modern civilization.

In sum, the abominable condition of modern civilization is associated with the "Judaization" of the world. The world of the "end of history," the world of mondialism and materialism, destitute of any manliness and spirit, indicates the provisional triumph of the Jewish principle. Dugin asks how the Jews could have acquired such incredible power, and thus, a theory of Jewish conspiracy comes into the picture.

The "Enlightened" Science of Conspirology

In his discussion of different theories of conspiracy, Dugin employs the concept of a collective unconscious. He tries to keep his distance from the vulgar Judeophobic concepts of conspiracy, but taken on a more sophisticated level, he finds these theories "interesting and plausible." He distinguishes five different concepts of conspiracy: Masonic, Jewish, a conspiracy of bankers, of the poor, and of the heterodox. In his descriptions, each of these theories have more or less pronounced antisemitic elements. Furthermore, the central and most basic conspiracy is that of the Jews:

> The idea of Jewish conspiracy, undoubtedly, corresponds to deep unconscious archetypes of very remote and diverse human communities. It is most likely that this theory is the activation of unconscious energies, which constitute the "conspirological instinct" at its source.[87]

The importance of a Jewish conspiracy in Dugin's theory may be fully appreciated in the context of his interpretation of the origins of the archetypes of the collective unconscious. For him, the archetypes constitute not only a specific "psychic reality," but are, first of all, the "remnants of a sacred Weltanschauung that are partly obliterated from the genetic memory of mankind."[88] The theory of a Jewish conspiracy, therefore, is part of the sacred outlook embedded in the deepest layers of the unconscious, and finds its realization in all antisemitic theories and ideologies. Antisemitic feelings and concepts are legitimated by the very structure of the sacred Weltanschauung. However ridiculous a particular interpretation or specific theory of Jewish conspiracy may sound, Dugin claims that it is justified because of the foundational "archetype" of which each concept of this sort is only an imperfect and distorted copy or reproduction. To paraphrase Hegel, everything unconscious for Dugin is real and everything real is unconscious.

> The idiosyncrasies of life, and, speaking of the Jews, their specific appearance and even their historically revealed proclivity for the subversive and destructive forms of "gescheft," are only the excuses for expression of a much more deep, sacred, and well-grounded mystical and theological hostility of Russian nationalism to Jewishness in all its manifestations.[89]

Nuremberg versus Auschwitz

Dugin does not suggest any concrete policy that should be adopted by the Eurasian Empire to handle the "Jewish Question"; rather, he resorts to very emotional and ambiguous language. At the end of one of his articles, Dugin talks about the inevitability of a "metaphysical battle" between Jews and Indo-Aryans and about the necessity of establishing "chivalrous rules" for this battle that might prevent the transformation of such a "profound metaphysical conflict" into "total war" involving "blind hatred and gloomy violence." He argues that

> The difference between metaphysical war and physical is that the first aims at the victory of a single Truth, while the second aims at the destruction of the enemy.... As it turned out, the German concentration camps could destroy Jews, but were unable to abolish Jewishness. By the same token, the Hasidic commissars were not able to slaughter the entire population of the "Russian tref kingdom" in bloody genocide.[90]

Dugin suggests that "metaphysical" antisemitism and calls for the physical annihilation of the Jews are really incompatible phenomena. In this manner, he blurs the obvious connection between Auschwitz and its ideological justification. Dugin stresses his claim that many members of the SS — specifically, intellectuals from the Waffen-SS *Deutsches Ahnenerbe* ("German Ancestral Heritage")[91] — did not share the Judeophobia of other National Socialists. Hitler, he argues, departed from the classic ideology of Conservative Revolution when it came to the "Jewish Question." The *Ahnenerbe,* unlike the mainstream Nazi ideologists, could be compared to a "medieval knightly order," with its high moral ideals, an "intellectual oasis within the framework of National Socialism," which "preserved and fostered the ideas of Conservative Revolution in their purity."[92] Russian nationalists could well use the ideas of the *Ahnenerbe.*[93]

Dugin, of course, glosses over the fact that Hermann Wirth, the founder of *Ahnenerbe,* was a notorious racist and one of the major contributors to the

Nordic theory. Wirth was involved in constructing racist theories based on serological studies of Jewish and Aryan blood types, and believed that the Jews were the mystical enemies of the Aryans. He was a great influence on Alfred Rosenberg, the ideologist who wrote *The Myth of the 20th Century*. In Wirth's major work *Palästina-Buch* he contended that Jews usurped Aryan knowledge, and that the Bible is derived from earlier Nordic texts, in particular from the *Ura-Linda Chronicle*, a notorious late nineteenth century forgery. The sole copy of the manuscript was said to have been stolen by members of the Jewish intelligence service.[94] In Dachau, Dr. Sigmund Rascher, under the aegis of the *Ahnenerbe*, conducted a number of medical experiments on inmates designed to discover the best method of reviving pilots who had been shot down in freezing water. Because of these activities Wolfram Sievers, who succeeded Wirth as head of the *Ahnenerbe*, was condemned to death by the Nuremberg trubunal.[95]

For Dugin, the phenomenon of Auschwitz is not a realization and logical completion of the illuminated "metaphysical" antisemitism of the Nazi ideologists, but merely an excess of National Socialism, and an unfortunate digression from the classical doctrine of Conservative Revolution. It is striking that he confers the same status on both the Nazi "Final Solution of the Jewish Question" and Jewish involvement in the Bolshevik revolution in Russia. The real tragedy evident at the defeat of the Axis countries was not Auschwitz, but rather the compromising of the doctrines of the Conservative Revolutionaries by Hitler's distortions. Dugin considered the Nuremberg tribunal a disaster, for it condemned and stigmatized the ideology of Conservative Revolution without qualification.

> The ideological map of the world after Yalta included only two poles.... Everything even slightly reminiscent of the ideology of the Third Way or Conservative Revolution was extirpated on the plea of total and universal "de-Nazification" on the global level. The Nuremberg tribunal was the first and unique trial in history which condemned not only people, but also ideas and intellectual doctrines.[96]

Dugin identifies the contemporary world as a "liberal Auschwitz," in which the mondialists "install into the brains of the population of mankind the computer chips of the fictitious multiplication of capital."[97] In terms of Dugin's "Tradition," this "liberal Auschwitz" is much more totalitarian and cruel than National Socialism.

In his use of the image of Auschwitz, Dugin clearly does not see the Holocaust as a radical foundational crisis of Western civilization. He claims that Auschwitz is only a liberal myth closely connected with the concept of the end of history. In liberal mythology Auschwitz functions as "the last immolation, the last sacrifice of history" which anticipates the messianic era. The annihilation of the Jews is a substitute for the second coming of Jesus, marking the end of history and the beginning of the "eternal Sabbath."[98]

In Dugin's "grand narrative" we live in the post-Nuremberg rather than the post-Auschwitz world. He not only disregards the question of the responsibility of German intellectuals for the Holocaust, but whitewashes the activities of the Nazis. At the same time, he stigmatizes their victims and charges them with even more serious crimes. The Nazis only "crime" was their insufficient loyalty to the ideas of the Conservative Revolution.

The Muslim World, Israel, and Conservative Revolution

According to American political analyst Samuel Huntington, the major conflicts of the contemporary world are due to the clash of civilizations rather than to ethnic (nineteenth century) or ideological (first half of the twentieth century) conflicts.[99] Civilizations are defined in terms of their specific historical and cultural traditions and religious foundations. Dugin, who accepts Huntington's analysis, claims that the Eurasian civilization is shaped by the religious traditions of Orthodoxy and Islam, whose traditional values are incompatible with those of mondialism and Atlanticism. The incompatibility rests on the fact that both Russian and Islamic civilizations hold that they themselves have a special mission in world history which is an alternative to that of European mondialist civilization. The Muslim world in general, and especially the most traditional and fundamentalist trends in Islam, are the natural allies of Russia-Eurasia in the struggle against the "new world order," oceanic civilizations, and mondialism. Orthodox Islam, Dugin believes, is actually closer to the Primordial Tradition than Orthodoxy, which has been distorted by Masonic and moralistic ideas in the course of the last two centuries. Orthodoxy and Russian traditionalism would greatly benefit from intensive intellectual and political contacts with the spiritual and political leaders of Islamic cultures. Dugin emphasizes that it is no coincidence that René Guenon and many of his successors converted to Islam. Dugin collaborates with the fundamentalist "Party of Islamic Renaissance" led by his friend and teacher Geidar Jemal. The journal *Den'* even features a special column, the "Slavonic-Islamic Academy," to discuss the spiritual and geopolitical connections between Orthodoxy and Islam.

Dugin claims that mondialists attempt to drive a wedge between the natural unity of Slavic-Russian and Islamic civilizations that oppose Atlanticist forces. He distinguishes two major groups — "hawks" and "doves" — among the mondialists. The right-wing hawks insist on the necessity of sustaining direct political and economic pressure on Russia. The "doves," on the other hand, use indirect pressure and are more perfidious. They are associated primarily with the American Jewish lobby that includes such figures as Armand Hammer, Henry Kissinger, Zbigniew Bzrezinsky, and at the present stage, the Jewish members of President Clinton's administration.[100] They purport to transform Eastern Europe rather than to defeat it, and ultimately plan to involve Russia in the realization of mondialistic objectives and projects, as well as involving that country in national and religious conflicts. The dream of the left-wing mondialists is to destroy the natural geopolitical and social ties between the Muslim East and Russia. Provoking conflict between Russia and the Muslim world is also vitally important for Israel.

> From now on, the foreign policy of the US will proceed from the necessity of struggle against antisemitism in Europe and Islamic fundamentalism. Clinton's lobby proposes to denounce the tactics of total destruction and elimination of Russia.... Big Bill is going to use Russia for the accomplishment of mondialistic policy against the Muslim South. The fundamental strategy of left mondialism towards Russia is based on the idea that Russia is not a "defeated enemy" but rather a "brainless instrument in our hands...." The Russian North can be easily involved in the conflict with the Muslim Central Asian South by some deliberate provocation. Sooner or later, Iran and Iraq, the main enemies of Israel, will be also implicated. This will draw blood from both the Russian and Muslim elite, and thus, two major enemies of the world government will start to destroy each other. This will make both Israel and the "civilized world" happy.[101]

The attitude towards Israel in neo-Eurasianism is quite ambivalent. On the one hand, the very establishment of Israel is an outcome of the strategy of England and Atlanticist civilization to sustain their political and economic influence in the Middle East.[102] In spite of its geographical position Israel is "the anti-continental formation begotten by Anglo-Saxon spies" and "the outpost of American influence in the region."[103] On the other hand, Israel is the only country in which the project of Conservative Revolution came to a fruition of the sorts, although this was overlooked in the West.

> Israel is the only country that has successfully realized in practice some aspects of the Conservative Revolution. In spite of striking ideological similarities [between Nazi Germany and Israel — V.R.] nobody dared to suspect or blame Israel for "fascism" and "Nazism" bearing in mind the great number of Jewish victims during the rule of Conservative Revolutionaries in Europe. The establishment of Israel was accompanied by the ideas of complete revival of the archaic

tradition, Judaic religion, ethnic and racial differentiation, socialist ideas in economy (in particular, of the system of kibbutzim) and the restoration of castes.[104]

Vladimir Zeev Jabotinsky, the founder of the revisionist movement of Zionism, is characterized by Dugin as one of the most prominent theoreticians and activists of Conservative Revolution.[105] Although the Israeli Conservative Revolution is opposed to the mondialistic principles of the global "melting pot," this does not mean that Israeli Jews are allies of the Eurasian cause, since their revived tradition is still incompatible and hostile to the Indo-European tradition. Whereas the project of the mondialists is identified with anti-Tradition, the Jewish "Conservative Revolution" probably can be described as Counter-Tradition. The Jewish Conservative Revolutionaries are better than mondialists only as partners in the "metaphysical" dialogue. However, their ideas are perfectly compatible with the fundamentally Atlanticist orientation of Israel. Dugin is saying that Israeli "Nazism" was privileged by the mondialists over all other nationalisms. In addition Dugin seems to praise the ideology of Naturei karta, an ultra-Orthodox Jewish religious sect that does not acknowledge the establishment of the State of Israel and lambastes Zionism. He seems to identify the doctrines of Naturei karta with the most traditional Judaism.[106] Thus, his ideas about Jewish traditionalism are quite ambivalent.

Neo-Eurasians accept the stereotype of Islamic and Arab anti-Zionism and Judeophobia. The Palestinian-Israeli conflict is described as a geopolitical conflict in which the Palestinians are fighting on the side of continental forces. Israel is, of course, an aggressive state committing genocide on the Palestinian population. Neo-Eurasians give moral support to the intifada and countenance the terrorist activities of the Palestinians and the religious fanaticism of the leaders of Islamic fundamentalist organizations, like Hamas and the Muslim Brotherhood. Shaaban Khafez Shaaban, Chairman of the "Palestinian government in exile," has had several opportunities to express his extreme anti-Zionist position in interviews and articles in *Den'*.[107] Shaaban is editor-in-chief of the ultra-antisemitic newspaper *Al-Quds,* edited and published in Moscow (where the headquarters of this government-in-exile are located).[108] *Al-Quds* is preoccupied with the occupation of Palestine by Israel, the Jewish-Masonic conspiracy, the influence of the Jews in politics and the media, and the heroic resistance of the Palestinians to the sinister powers of Zionism. Shaaban of course does not recognize the establishment of Israel, and insists that the full-fledged independence of the Palestinians can be achieved only by the destruction of the Zionist state. He opposes the Middle Eastern peace process and the government of Yasir

Arafat, whom he considers a puppet of the United States and Israel. It is noteworthy that some *Den'* contributors have also been published in *Al-Quds*. During the Gulf War in 1991 (in which Israel suffered missile attacks from Iraq), Saddam Hussein was seen as a hero by many Russian nationalist groups.

Neo-Eurasians discriminate between different Muslim countries and trends in Islam. Shia is seen as better than Sunni, since it combines conservative values with a revolutionary political strategy. The orthodox Shia of Iran and the thinking of Khomeini are especially congenial to the ideology of Conservative Revolution, since they presuppose both commitment to the grand Muslim tradition and the revolutionary resistance to modernity and mondialism. The "continental Islam" of Iran is opposed to the "ritualism and almost secularized ethics" of Saudi Arabia and Atlanticist and nationalist Turkey, which are seen as akin to Western Protestantism.[109] Turkey is regarded as a champion of mondialism in the region and Turanism and pan-Turkism is considered a great danger for Russia.

Dugin believes that the presence of a national myth is the only criterion by which to decide whether or not a nation has a historical mission. The "aesthetization of the political" — Walter Benjamin's expression — is one of the dangers of the new political consciousness propagated by Dugin. His valorization of the Russian psyche, and his cult of the unconscious and irrational, is quite conducive to physical violence [can lead directly to physical violence]. Dugin makes no attempt to conceal the violent implications of his political romanticism. For him, any activity of the Russian people is beyond good and evil: "We are the God-bearing people. That is why all our manifestations — high and vile, benevolent and terrifying — are sanctified by their other-worldly meanings, by the rays of the other City.... In the abundance of national grace, good and evil turn from one into another.... We are as incomprehensible as the Absolute."[110] Dugin admits that the nationalist myth can sound strange but sees this as no disadvantage. He deliberately appeals to the irrational driving forces of the psyche and to the mythic level of consciousness. His slogans are devised to affect and invigorate the political unconscious. Dugin believes that he has a special mission as an intellectual. "The true national elite," he claims, "does not have a right to leave its people without any ideology. This ideology should express not only what the people think and feel but rather what they do not think and feel, but what they have worshipped surreptitiously for centuries, even being unaware of it themselves."[111] It is evident from this passage that Dugin believed that he is uniquely qualified to interpret the unconscious of the Russian people.

One should acknowledge that Dugin was quite successful in the introduction of his concepts and images into the nationalistic discourse. Many of the discussions, both nationalist and liberal, are informed by his account of the geopolitical clash of civilizations and his abstruse visions of the "Jewish Question." This valorization of the irrational impulses, of the national unconscious, of spontaneity and the bellicose instincts, along with the disparagement of moral standards as irrelevant and a superficial means for evaluating the nation, makes Dugin's discourse especially dangerous, especially given the widespread dissatisfaction with the political and economic reforms.

I suggest a special name for the type of antisemitism advocated by Alexander Dugin and his fellow Eurasians: geopolitical antisemitism. Their account suggests that the Jews are prone to identify themselves with the Atlanticist geopolitical centers and that they play an important role among the Atlanticist forces.[112] Their account also suggests that within the confines of Eurasia the Jews should be treated as enemies and potential "geopolitical traitors" of the grand Eurasian community. It is also important to observe that the Jews are not simply the provisional allies of Atlanticism. They are described as eternal and metaphysical enemies of Eurasia.

NOTES

1. The most recent studies of Eurasianism include I. Isaev, *Puti Evrazii: Russkaiia intelligentsiia i sud'bi Rossii* (Moscow 1992); idem, "Geopoliticheskie korni avtoritarnogo mishleniia," *Druzhba narodov,* no. 11, 1993; L. Liuks, "Evraziistvo," *Voprosi filosofii,* no. 6 (1993); L. Ponomareova, ed., *Evrasiia. Istoricheskie vsgliadi russkikh emigrantov* (Moscow 1992); L. Novikova and I. Sizemskaia, eds., *Rossiia mezhdu evropoi i Asiei: evrasiiskii soblasn* (Moscow 1993); idem, eds., *Mir Rossii — Evraziia* (Moscow 1995); V. Kantor, A. Panarin, V. Senderov et al., "Evraziistvo: za i protiv (materiali kruglogo stola)", *Voprosi filosofii,* no. 6, 1995; *Evraziiskii proekt: realnosti, problemi, kontseptsii* (Moscow 1996); G. Sitniansky, "Problemi reintegratsii bivshego Sovetskogo Soiuza s tochki zreniia istoricheskogo naslediia Evrazii," *Acta Eurasica,* no. 2 (1996). Presumably, the paucity of research on Eurasianism in Western languages is due to the relatively insignificant role it played in Russian political ideology of the Soviet era. Eurasianism was perceived by Western scholars for the most part as a trend which characterized the peculiarities of the intellectual life of Russian emigrants.

2. A. Dugin, "Apologiia natsionalisma," *Den'.* no. 38 (1993).

3. Neo-Eurasians borrow the ideas of a "pivot state of Euro-Asia" and "Heartland" from the writings of Halford Mackinder, a British geopolitician, as expressed in his

short lecture, *The Geographical Pivot of History,* read in 1904 to the Royal Geographical Society of London.

4. See J. Thiriart, "Evropa do Vladivostoka," Den', no. 34 (1992); J. Thiriart, Y. Ligacheov, "Poka est' voini voina ne proigrana," *Den',* no. 37 (1992); J. Thiriart, "Evropa do Vladivostoka", *Russkii vestnik,* no. 30–31 (1992); A. Dugin, "Sumerki geroev. Pominalnoe slovo o Jean Thiriart," *Den',* no. 2 (1993).

5. The terms "thalassocraties" [Greek, sea] and "tellucracies" [Latin, earth] were introduced by Carl Schmitt in his book *Des Nomos der Erde* (Cologne 1950). See A. Dugin, "Carl Schmitt: 5 urokov dlia Rossii," *Konservativnaiia revolutsiia* (Moscow 1994), 63.

6. Leviathan and Behemoth are monsters mentioned in the book of Job (41:33–34) that came to be interpreted as apocalyptic beasts. Thomas Hobbes (1588–1679) was the first philosopher to employ these two images in a political sense. Whereas Leviathan symbolizes the strong peacekeeping state, Behemoth is a symbol for rebellion and civil war. Hence the title of his book *Leviathan* (1651) on the English civil war, where the rebellious forces of "Behemoth" are identified with the Anglican clergy and other centrifugal forces. Neo-Eurasians reinterpret the symbolism of Leviathan and Behemoth in terms of geopolitics, using Behemoth as a symbol of the "continental" powers, while Leviathan is a symbol of "maritime" civilizations. A. Dugin, "Begemot protiv Leviafana," *Elementi,* no. 7 (1996): 26. Carl Schmitt drew upon the original biblical source in which Behemoth is apparently a giant ox, hippopotamus, or elephant, while Leviathan is a sea beast ("king over all children of pride") whom Yahweh alone can control. In this context, the Jews are associated with Leviathan. Schmitt may have been familiar with Jewish sources for this association. In the Talmud, Leviathan is called the favorite fish of God (Baba Bathra, 74a–b). Norman Habel, a contemporary commentator on Job, distinguishes one special meaning of Behemoth as the "symbol of the mighty historical enemies of Israel." N. Habel, *The Book of Job: A Commentary* (Philadelphia 1985), 557–58.

7. A. Dugin, "Velikaiia voina kontinentov," *Den',* no. 4–7 (1992); A. Dugin, *Konspirologiia,* 92–94.

8. The theories of Karl Haushofer are especially important for neo-Eurasians, since he insisted on the necessity of the geopolitical unity of Russia and Germany. The Haushofer school formulated a theory of "great expanses," which directly influenced the 1939 German-Soviet Molotov-Ribbentrop Pact.

9. The term "Easternism" *(vostochnichestvo)* was coined by Bromberg as the opposite of "Westernism" *(zapadnichestvo).* Thus, Bromberg deconstructed the conventional distinction between "Slavophilism" and "Westernism." Slavophilism is only one type of "Easternism."

10. N. Trubetskoi, "O rasisme," *Neva,* no. 7 (1994), 261; E. von Eickstedt, *Rassekunde und Rassegeshchichte der Menscheit,* Vol. 8 (Stuttgart 1934).

11. Ibid., 260–61.

12. I. Deutscher, *The Non-Jewish Jew and Other Essays* (New York 1968).

13. L. Karsavin, "Rossiia i evreistvo," in idem, *Taina Israilia* (St. Petersburg 1993), 428–29.

14. Ibid., 423–24.

15. D. Sviatopolk-Mirsky, "Natsionalnosti SSSR. Evrei," *Evraziia,* no. 26 (1929).

16. Ibid.

17. Ibid.

18. Oswald Spengler borrowed the term "pseudo-morphosis" from geology. A pseudo-morph is a mineral which has replaced, or which appears in crystalline forms foreign to, its original formation. By the same token, some cultural forms, i.e., the religious enthusiasm of Jewish revolutionaries and Westernizers in Bromberg's example, are foreign to their original formation. For Spengler, Russian culture is also pseudo-morphic, since it adopts the foreign form of Byzantine Orthodoxy. The "pseudomorphic" origin makes the mineral's crystalline structure fragile. Spengler discusses this concept in the second volume of his *Decline of the West,* trans. C. Atkinson (New York 1980).

19. Y. Bromberg, "Evreiskoe vostochnichestvo v proshlom i buduschem," *Mir Rossiii — Evraziia,* eds. L. Novikova and I. Sizemskaiia (Moscow 1995), 201.

20. The term "place-development" was coined by Peotr Savitsky. It is a specific cultural center, closely connected with a specific geographical location.

21. Y. Bromberg, "Evreiskoe vostochnichestvo," 203.

22. Ibid, 203.

23. Ibid, 204–205.

24. Bromberg mentions Lev Shestov, Michael Gershenzon, Yulii Aikhenwald, Akim Volinsky, and the critics of Jewish involvement in the revolution — Landau, Pasmanik, and Bikerman. Lev Shestov (1866–1938) was a well-known Russian religious existentialist philosopher. Mikhail Gershenson (1869–1925) was a historian of Russian literature and social thought. Akim Volinsky (1863–1926) and Yulii Aikhenwald (1872-1928) became famous as literary and art critics. Bikerman, Landau and Pasmanik contributed papers to the book *Russia and the Jews,* ed. Bickerman et al (Paris 1978), first published in Berlin in 1923. They condemned Jewish participation and radicalism in the course of Russian revolution.

25. Y. Bromberg, "O neobkhodimom peresmotre evreiskogo voprosa," *Evrasiiskii sbornik* 6 (1929): 46.

26. The Church Council sentenced the Judaizers to death, with the major heretics being burned in wooden cages in Moscow in 1504. In the aftermath of the suppression of the heresy, Ivan the Terrible in the winter of 1563 drowned all the Jews of the occupied town of Polotsk who refused to be baptized with their wives and children.

27. Evidence is abundant of the hostile attitude in many works of Russian literature. Lev Vigotsky, a well-known Russian psychologist, has argued: "The future historian of the Jews in Russia will be puzzled by the attitude of Russian literature to the Jew *(zhid)*. It is both strange and incomprehensible that Russian literature being so much informed by the principles of humanity brought so little humanity to its portrayal of the Jews. The artists have never noticed a human being in a Jew. Hence, the lifeless mechanicism of the puppet, the ridiculous movements and gestures of which are supposed to make a reader laugh, the stamped cliché of a Jew, has replaced the artistic image. Hence, the similarity and even complete identity of the images of the Jews in the works of different writers.... The tradition downplays the peculiarities: a Jew is always and everywhere a reincarnation of the vile, dark, groveling, greediness, infamy, filthiness, the embodiment of human vices in general and the specific ethnic vices in particular (usury, spy, traitor)...." L. Vigotsky, "Lermontov," in *L. S. Vigotsky: Nachalo Puti,* ed. Joseph Feigenberg (Jerusalem 1996), 87. Bromberg refers to the writings of Nikolai Gogol, Feodor Dostoevsky, and Vasily Rosanov, among others. For a discussion of the antisemitic ideas of these writers see F. Dreizin, *The Russian Soul and the Jew. Essays in Literary Ethnocriticism* (New York 1990); D. Goldstein, *Dostoevsky and the Jews* (Austin, Texas and London 1981); D. Khanin, *A Modernist Conservative· Vasilii Rosanov's Aesthetics and Polemics* (in press).

28. See Z. Bauman, "Exit Visas and Entry Tickets: Paradoxes of Jewish Assimilation," *Telos* 88, no. 77 (1988): 50.

29. See M. Buber, "Der Geist des Orients und das Judentum," in idem, *Vom Geist des Judentums Reden und Geleitworte* (Leipzig 1916), 9–48; S. Gilman, *Jewish Self-Hatred: Anti-Semitism and the Hidden Language of the Jews* (Baltimore and London 1986), 273–305.

30. V. Toporov, "'Spor' ili "druzhba'?," in *Aequinox . Sbornik pamiati otza Alexandra Menia,* eds. E. Rabinovich and I. Vishnevetskii (Moscow 1991), 91–162.

31. L. Anninskii, "Prostivaiuschii sled Agosfera," *Zerkalo* (Tel Aviv), no. 105 (1993).

32. L. Liuks, "Evrasiistvo i konservativnaiia revoluitsiia. Soblasn antizapadnichest-va v Rossii i Germanii," *Voprosi filosofii,* no. 3 (1996).

33. Some articles in the Eurasian periodicals explicitly condemned antisemitism. See, for instance, the letter to the editor signed "Evrasietz" [Eurasian], "Emigrant Antisemitism," *Evrasiia,* no. 31 (1929).

34. L. Karsavin, "Rossiia i evreistvo," 428; Y. Bromberg, *Evreiskoe vostochnichestvo,* 202.

35. It is interesting to note that some scholars emphasize the Russian roots of the movement. Göran Dahl remarked that "the concept of 'conservative revolution' first appeared in the Berlin paper *Die Volksstimme* in 1848.... The first more frequent and serious use of the term, however, appeared among Russian writers, among them

Dostoyevsky, as a metaphor for what was to be done in the world where God had died.... However, it was Hugo Hoffmansthal — in a speech in 1927.... — who brought the concept wider attention. Von Hoffmansthal was expressing the widespread discontent with the Weimar Republic, arising from a tension between a modernizing society and a culture not ready to accept parliamentary democracy and industrial capitalism as an adequate environment." G. Dahl, "Will the Other God Fail Again? On the Possible Return of the Conservative Revolution," *Theory, Culture and Society* 13, no. 1 (1996): 26–27.

36. See A. Mohler, *Die Konservative Revolution in Deutschland 1918–1932: Ein Handbuch,* 3d ed. (Darmstadt 1989); K. von Klemperer, *Germany's New Conservatism: Its History and Dilemma in Twentieth Century* (Princeton 1968); K. Sontheimer, *Antidemocratisches Denken in der Weimarer Republik. Die politischen Ideen des deutschen Nationalismus zwischen 1918 und 1933* (Munich 1962); S. Breuer, *Anatomie der Konservativen Revolution* (Darmstadt 1993); F. Pflüger, *Deutschland driftet. Der Konservative Revolution entdeckt ihre Kinder* (Düsseldorf, Vienna, and New York 1994).

37. Nikolai Danilevsky's *Russia and Europe* (1871) is a prophecy that the Russian people's destiny is to lead Europe out of its social and spiritual anarchy by effecting a genuinely organic unity of religion, culture, politics, and social organization — the four main elements of civilization. Danilevsky anticipated some concepts of Spengler (in particular, that of specific "cultural types," and the cyclical pattern of their history).

38. René Guenon (1886–1951) was a French metaphysician and a historian of religions. His works were devoted for the most part to a critique of the modern world and discussing the significance of Eastern religious traditions in the process of the rediscovery of tradition in the West. His writings include *Orient et occident* (1924), *La crise du monde moderne* (1927), *La regne de la quantité et les signes des temps* (1945). Guenon emphasized the unity of truth and of traditional forms of religion, standing united in opposition to the modern world, which he saw as based upon the forgetting of the tradition. He believed that spiritual realization is impossible outside tradition and orthodox forms of religion. Guenon embraced Islam and moved to Cairo in 1930 where he spent the rest of his life. His ideas influenced not only his own students and successors but many well-known intellectuals, artists and politicians of Europe (in particular, the world-renowned historians of religion Mircea Eliade and Jacques Dumézil; the founder of the surrealist movement, André Breton; the novelist André Gide; and the ideologists of fascism Charles Maurras and Julius Evola).

39. Relevant Western European journals include: *Géopolitique* (France), *Krisis* (France), *Nouvelle École* (France), *Orion* (Italy), *Perspectives* (Great Britain), *Politica Hermetica* (France), and *Vouloir* (Belgium).

40. See S. Kurginian, "Esli khotim zhit," *Den'*, no. 1 (1993); A. Kazintsev, "Samoubiistvo pod kontrolem," *Nash sovremennik*, no. 3 (1993); Y. Bulichev, "V poiskakh gosudarstvennoi idei (razmishleniia nad raziskaniiami novikh pravikh)," *Moskva*, no. 5 (1993); K. Golovin, "Den' smeniaet noch," *Otechestvo*, no. 8 (1992). Sergei Kurginian believes that Dugin phenomenon testifies to the infiltration of fascist ideas into the Russian patriotic movement. this infiltration discredits the movement and therefore it is especially beneficial to the liberals. Other critics emphasize the anti-Christian connotations of Dugin's position and express their misgivings about his attitude to the Muslim East.

41. Schmitt introduced the friend-vs.-enemy distinction as a specific criterion of the political. See C. Schmitt, *The Concept of the Political* (New Brunswick, N.J. 1976), 26–27.

42. A. Dugin, "Apologiia natsionalisma," *Konservativnaiia revolutsiia* (Moscow 1994), 141–43.

43. Ibid., 142.

44. II Thess. 2:7: "For the mystery of iniquity doth already work: only he who now letteth will let, until he be taken out of the way."

45. Dugin refers to the theory of the Old Believers — schismatics who split from the Orthodox Church in the late seventeenth century. They believed (and still believe) that the antichrist has already come to the world, and often identified him with one or another of the Russian emperors.

46. A. Dugin, "Apologiia natsionalisma," 142.

47. Ibid.

48. It is important to emphasize that Dugin's appeal to the replacement theology suggested by the seventeenth-century schismatics was abandoned by the official Orthodox Church (the idea about realization of "millenarianism" in Byzantium). Dugin believes that the schismatics have preserved the most authentic aspects of Orthodox tradition. Russia had been bequeathed the "divine presence" from Byzantium.

49. A. Dugin, "Apologiia natsionalisma," 148.

50. Ibid, 148–49.

51. Dugin believes that the ancient pagan Aryan cults had the same ritual and symbolic paradigm as Christianity. In this ancient Aryan consciousness Russia-Eurasia was already associated with the "Residence of the gods," with the "Great Sweden." This "Great Sweden," the "white country of light" was the motherland of the most ancient Aryans, the ancestors of the Hindus. Dugin condemns the moralistic and sentimental ingredients of Christianity that entered from Protestantism, Masonry, and the intelligentsia. A. Dugin, *Kontinent Rossiia* (Moscow 1991), 52–53; idem, "Prorok zolotogo veka," in *Krisis sovremennogo mira* by R. Guenon (Moscow 1991), 148–49.

52. A. Dugin, "The Rest against the West," *Elementi*, no. 7 (1996), 40.

53. With his ideas about the congruity of Europocentrism and ancient Judeocentrism, Zakharov defends the old-fashioned version of Eurasianism. In his ideas about the congruity of Europocentrism and ancient Judeocentrism, however, he presents the reasoning of the Neo-Eurasians. since he spells out the neo-Eurasian reasoning. Zakharov contends that the Jewish philosophy of history is the historical prototype and the model for the Europocentric one. The Jewish philosophy of history is the first attempt to describe the history of all humanity and to discover one pattern in the development of mankind. "The universal human history has only one providential meaning, that is, the triumph of one people, Israel, over all mankind. It was the major point of their concept of world history...." Although the Europocentric philosophy of history is rational and cosmopolitan, while the Jewish one is theocratic and nationalistic, they have much in common. The "universal values" of European civilization are no more universal than that of Jewish "universal history." The Europocentric standards are only a product of development of the Romano-Germanic ethnicities, and they should not be imposed upon Eurasian historical development. V. Zakharov, "Izvraschenie velikorusskoi istorii," *Molodaiia gvardiia*, no. 9 (1992): 166–69.

54. A. Dugin, *Konspirologiia*, 99.

55. V. Prussakov, "Preodoletą Ameriku," *Zavtra*, no. 16 (1994). See also S. Putilov, "Taini 'Novoi Atlantidi' Becona," *Nash sovremennik*, no. 2 (1993). Some historians do believe that Christopher Columbus and some crew members were Jewish, and that the ultimate goal of the expedition was to find a new place for the Jews; from the beginning, Columbus never planned to go to India. See J. F. Amler, *Christopher Columbus's Jewish Roots* (New Jersey and London 1993).

56. See L. Okhotin, "Chego boitsia Bolshoi Bill," *Den'*, no. 9 (1993). Leonid Okhotin is a pen-name of Dugin. Dugin specifically mentions Armand Hammer, Henry Kissinger, and Jewish advisers of U.S. President Bill Clinton.

57. A. Dugin, "Apokalipsis stikhii," *Elementi*, no. 8 (1997): 56.

58. A. Dugin, "Misterii Evrasii" (Moscow 1996), 41–49.

59. See footnote 6 above.

60. According to Dumézil, traditional Indo-European society was composed of three castes: priests (spiritual leaders), warriors (kings, rulers, administrators) and producers (peasants, craftsmen). A. Dugin, *Tseli i zadachi nashei revolutsii* (Moscow 1995), 23.

61. A. Dugin, "Poniat' znachit pobedit," *Konservativnaiia revolutsiia*, 245.

62. A. Dugin, "Metafizika natsii v kabbale," *Konservativnaiia revolutsiia*, 281.

63. A. Dugin, "Poniat znachit pobedit," *Konservativnaiia revolutsiia*, 245–46.

64. A. Dugin, "Golem i evreiskaiia metafizika," 253.

65. Ibid, 252.

66. Dugin's interpretation of Lurianic kabbalah is inadequate and distorted. The kabbalist's interpretation of the story of creation does not end on the despairing note of *shvira*. The *tsimtsum* and the *shvira* were heavenly events in the past. *Tikkun* (return, rectification, mending) is redemption in the present and future and is in the hands of man. The *sefirot* continue to issue from Adam Kadmon and they do half of the work of the *tikkun*, and this leaves to humanity a vital part in the great restoration of wholeness.

67. A. Dugin, "Golem i evreiskaiia metafizika," 252.

68. A. Dugin, "Probuzhdenie stikhii," *Elementi*, no. 1 (1992): 4. Roughly speaking, the peoples of the North are identified with Aryans and are believed to be the original population of Eurasia. Following German Aryosophes, Dugin believes that the Nordic peoples *(Sonnenmenschen)* are creative and spiritual, while the "people of the South" *(Mondmenschen)* are mean, materialistic, and externally oriented. Dugin points out that the distinction between the people of the North and of the South is not purely geographical. The "Nordic spirit" can be found in Southern parts of the globe, while the primitive spirit of the South is present in the far North. Dugin explains this phenomenon by reference to the migrations of the descendants of Hyperboreya. See A. Dugin, "Ot sakral'noi geografii k geopolitike," *Elementi,* no. 4 (1993): 42–43. The Jewish tradition is said to be Western. In sacred geography, the West is the side of death, darkness, and decline, in opposition to the East, the side of life, bloom, and light. The West and the Jewish tradition are also associated with Atlantis, while the pure Primordial tradition is associated with the land of Hyperborea (the country in the far north whose inhabitants were renowned as pious adherents of the cult of Apollo). On the "Atlantic" origins of Jewish tradition see R. Guenon, "Mesto atlanticheskoi traditsii v Manvantare," *Milii Angel,* no. 1 (1991): 16–17.

69. A. Dugin, "Velikaiia metafizicheskaiia problema i Traditsiia," *Milii Angel,* no. 1 (1991): 24.

70. A. Dugin, Tseli i zadachi nashei revolutsii (Moscow 1995), 11.

71. A. Dugin, "Golem i evreiskaiia metafizika," *Konservativnaiia revolutsiia,* 257–58.

72. A. Dugin, "Golem i evreiskaiia metafizika," 256–57.

73. A. Dugin, "Poniat' znachit pobedit'," *Den'*, no. 18 (1992).

74. Its English translation was entitled title: *Millennium: Winners and Losers in the Coming World Order* (New York 1991).

75. A. Dugin, *Osnovi geopolitiki* (Moscow 1997), 128–30; C. Levalois, "Sochti chislo Zveria," *Elementi,* no. 2 (1993): 3–8; A. Dugin, "West Against the Rest," *Elementi,* no. 7 (1996): 40.

76. This term was introduced by Guy Debord, a French neo-Marxist sociologist and harsh critic of liberalism. G. Debord, *Society of the Spectacle* (London 1979). The term spectacle refers to the vast institutional and technical apparatus of late

capitalism, to all the means and methods power employs, outside of direct force, to obscure the nature of power.

77. A. Dugin, "Metafizicheskie korni politicheskikh ideologii," *Milii Angel,* no. 1 (1991): 89. Fascism is said to be derived from the Gnostic idea of the "Divine Subject" ("Angelic Leader," "Hero," "Sacred Emperor," etc.). Fascism, therefore, is the incarnation of the metaphysical immanence of Indo-European tradition.

78. Max Brod (1884–1968) was an Austrian writer and Zionist, a life-long friend of Franz Kafka. His interpretation of *The Castle* appeared first in the introduction to the first edition of the novel in German, and later in his biography of Franz Kafka. See M. Brod, *Franz Kafka. A Biography by Max Brod* (New York 1947).

79. A. Dugin, "Demokratiia protiv sistemi," *Elementi,* no. 5 (1995): 9–10.

80. L. Okhotin [Alexander Dugin], "Elevsinskie topi freidisma," *Elementi,* no. 6 (1995): 50–51.

81. Dugin's concept of eroticism is heavily indebted to the book of Julius Evola (1889–1974), *Metafisico del sesso* (Metaphysics of sex) (n.p, 1958), published by the Atanor Publishing House.

82. Leopold von Sacher-Masoch (1836–1895) was an Austrian novelist in whose stories many of the main characters take pleasure in having pain inflicted upon them. The term "masochism" is derived from his name. It is interesting to note that Sigmund Freud associated masochism with the Russian character: in his essay "Dostoevsky and Parricide" he discusses moral masochism as a phenomenon typical of the Russian psyche.

83. A. Dugin, "Ad Marginem. Sacher-Masoch" (Review), *Elementi,* no. 6 (1995): 64.

84. L. Okhotin [Alexander Dugin], "Elevsinskie topi freidisma," 154.

85. A. Dugin, "Erotism i imperiia," *Konservativnaiia revolutsiia* (Moscow 1995).

86. A. Dugin, *Konspirologiia* (Moscow 1993), 51. The Mizraim rite claims to trace its origin back to the Egyptian King Menes, or Misraim. Its foundations were laid at Milan in 1805 and it was introduced into France in 1814. In fact it was founded earlier by Count Cagliostro, and Jews were among the chief supporters of the rite. See A. Preuss, *A Dictionary of Secret and Other Societies* (London 1924); C. Hackethorn, *The Secret Societies of All Ages and Countries,* vol. 2 (London 1897). "H. B. of L." probably stands for "Hermetic Brotherhood of Luxor," Luxor being an ancient Egyptian place name. The Golden Dawn was a famous occult organization founded at the beginning of the twentieth century. Mira Richards (Alfassa, known as "the Mother") embraced the philosophy of the Hindu mystic Sri Aurobindo and took over the guidance of the ashram after his death in 1950. Auroville is a large religious city in India designed according to the teachings of Sri Aurobindo. Henri Bergson is mentioned in this context because his theory of spiritual evolution; his concept of *élan vital* greatly influenced many occultist movements. He also had personal connections with some conspicuous members of occult establishments (in particular, Samuel

Mathers, the founder of the Golden Dawn, was his brother-in-law). René Guenon claimed that Bergson "tried to de-rationalize the European consciousness and introduced into it some chaotic and infra-corporeal intuitions." Dugin suggests that all these organizations emphasized the horizontal materialist values, which are typical of Atlanticist organization. A. Dugin, *Konspirologiia,* 104.

87. A. Dugin, *Konspirologiia,* 20.

88. A. Dugin, "Khaos," *Den',* no. 26 (1993).

89. A. Dugin, "Apologiia natsionalisma," 149.

90. A. Dugin, "Poniat znachit pobedit'," *Konservativnaiia revolutsiia,* 247–48.

91. *Ahnenerbe* was founded in 1935 as a private research institute, with Himmler as director. By 1939 it had become a branch of Waffen-SS and a division of Himmler's personal staff. It financed and published research on ancient Aryan symbols, language, runes, mythological archeology, and folklore, projects initiated and inspired by Professor Hermann Wirth, a German-Flemish specialist in prehistory. The Ahnenerbe's pseudo-scientific work was intended to demonstrate the superiority of the German race in culture and history. Wirth's book *Aufgang der Menschheit* speaks of the roots of German culture in the ancient civilization of "North Atlantis."

92. A. Dugin, "Konservativnaiia revolutsiia. Tipologiia politicheskikh dvizhenii Tret'ego Puti," *Konservativnaiia revolutsiia,* 25.

93. Dugin extensively expounds the theories of Herman Wirth and the *Ahnenerbe* in his book *Giperboreiskaia teoriia* (Moscow 1993). Dugin worked with the archives of the *Ahnenerbe* captured by the Red Army and recently made available to the public. In 1993, he spoke several times on Russian television about the *Ahnenerbe* and German secret societies on the program *Mysteries of the 20th Century.*

94. Y. Vorobievsky, "Zvezda i svastika," *Novoe russkoe slovo,* 17 December 1993.

95. See J. Webb, *The Occult Establishment* (La Salle, Illinois 1976), 323.

96. A. Dugin, *Konservativnaiia revolutsiia,* 26.

97. A. Dugin, "Revolutsiia nevozmozhnaiia, neizbezhnaiia," *Elementi,* no. 7 (1996), 54.

98. See A. Dugin, *Misterii Evrazii* (Moscow 1996), 48.

99. See S. Huntington, "The Clash of Civilizations?," *Foreign Affairs,* no. 72 [1995], 22–49; idem, *The Clash of Civilization and the Remaking of World Order* (New York 1996).

100. Dugin suggests that the Jews were overrepresented in the Clinton administration. Yurii Begunov in his article claims that 57% of the Clinton administration were Jewish, and that 86% of American Jews voted for Clinton in the 1992 presidential election. Y. Begunov, "Evrei v pravitel'stve Klintona," *Russkoe delo,* no. 8 (1995). Begunov's article is based on the information published in the American racist newspaper *The Truth at Last,* no. 365 [n.d.].

101. L. Okhotin, "Chego boitsia Bolshoi Bill," *Den',* no. 9 (1993).

102. A. Dugin, "Konspirilogiia," 110.

103. A. Glivakovskii, "Stsenarii 'Atlantistov,'" *Den'*, no. 12 (1993).

104. A. Dugin, "Konservativnaiia revolutsiia. Kratkaiia istoriia ideologii tret'ego puti," 27.

105. Ibid., 15.

106. See the translations of the interviews with the rabbis, translated and with a preface by Dugin, in *Den'*, no. 18 (1992).

107. See "Palestinskoe soprotivlenie" (Interview of Shamil Sultanov with Shaaban), *Den'*, no. 31 (1992).

108. *Al-Quds* is the Arabic name of Jerusalem.

109. A. Dugin, "Geopoliticheskie problemi blizhnego zarubezhiia," *Elementi*, no. 3 (1993): 24–25; idem, "'Zaveschanie' Ayatolly Khomeini," *Elementi*, no. 4 (1993), 63.

110. A. Dugin, "Imia moe — topor. Dostoevskii i metafizika Peterburga," *Nezavisimaiia gazeta* 26 June 1996.

111. A. Dugin, "Carl Schmitt: piat' urokov dlia Rossii," *Nash sovremennik*, no. 8 (1992): 135.

112. In a number of articles published in the late 1990s — 'The Jews and Eurasia," "The Paradigm of the End," and "Irredeemable Israel" — Dugin expressed a much more favorable attitude toward Jews. In recent years, he has even gained some support in Israel. In some articles posted on the internet, Dugin refers to Bromberg, and fully accepts Bromberg's position. Dugin distinguishes between "Eurasian" Jews — the kabbalists, hasidim, and Bolsheviks — and opposes them to the "Atlanticist" Jews who follow concepts found in the Talmud, liberalism, and the Enlightenment. In his more recent works Dugin also praised Karl Marx and described Leon Trotsky as a Russian National Bolshevik. These recent works also show much less fondness for Islam and a kind of support for the Israelis in the conflict with the Palestinians. However, Dugin still believes that "Atlanticism" is the predominant theme among the Jews. Two websites that have posted some of Dugin's articles are: http://arctogaia.com and http:// www.crosswinds.net/~polarisrael/

CHAPTER 2

Antisemitism in Eurasian Historiography: The Case of Lev Gumilev

Lev Gumilev (1912–1992) is a prominent representative of Eurasian historiography and one of the most popular Russian historians of the post-Soviet era. In Russia he is often considered a philosopher of history of the rank of Johann Gottfried Herder, Oswald Spengler, and Arnold Toynbee. His research focused on the history of the ancient Turks and other nomadic peoples. Gumilev's publications during the Soviet period did not reveal his identification with Eurasianism, though his views were no secret. His central concepts were clearly inspired by Eurasian thinking: the idea that the "Tatar Yoke" was in fact a military union of Russians and Tatars against their enemies; his admiration for Genghis Khan; his ideas about the congruity of interest between the nomads of the Great Steppe and the Russians; and his dismissal of the "black myth" of the aggressive and wild temper of the nomadic peoples, whom he believed were peace-loving. After perestroika, Gumilev admitted the Eurasian presuppositions of his works, and admitted his links with the leaders of classical Eurasianism. Among other things, he had met and corresponded with the founder of Eurasianism, Pyotr Savitsky.[1]

His most important works were written in the Soviet period. However, his theories — and their antisemitic implications — acquired considerable social significance only after glasnost, when millions of copies of his books were published, and an avalanche of other publications about his theories appeared in Russian periodicals.

THE JEWS IN ETHNIC HISTORY

In *Ethnogenesis and the Biosphere of Earth,* Gumilev laid the foundation for his theory of ethnogenesis. This book could not be published until 1989 and the advent of perestroika, and had been circulated in *samizdat* before that.[2]

The reader of *Ethnogenesis* will find very few passing remarks on Jewish history or the place of Jews in society. However, the invisible presence of the Jewish element is extremely important for understanding the logic of the "ethnogenetic" theory and its antisemitic agenda.

Gumilev's central insight is that the landscape has a decisive influence on ethnicity. The course of ethnic history is determined by the relationship between the ethnic group and the landscape:

Ethnicities are always linked to the natural environment through their economic activity. This connection is manifested in two different ways, in the adaptation to the terrain and in the adaptation of the terrain to the ethnicity.... Gradually, the attachment to the landscape is formed. The denial of this type of connection amounts to the conclusion that people have no homeland....[3]

Gumilev believed that ethnicity is a biological, rather than social, phenomenon. Ethnicity is not simply influenced by geographical conditions; it is a part of the biosphere.[4] Particular ethnicities are attached to their areas just as animals are attached to their habitats. Any loss of connection with the terrain is detrimental both for the "species" and for the abandoned landscape.

The central characteristic of ethnicity, according to Gumilev, is the "stereotype of behavior." Ethnicity is not simply a racial phenomenon; it is manifested in deeds and in the interrelations of human beings. "The difference between ethnicities is determined...only by the stereotype of behavior, which is the highest form of active adaptation to the terrain."[5] Gumilev does not explain the mechanisms through which the landscape shapes the behavior stereotypes. He does suggest that the landscape determines the economic occupations of the residents, and that in turn determines the moral code and the behavior stereotype. In addition, he suggests a profound mystical connection between people and terrain.

The concept of *drive (passionarnost')* is another important component of the theory of ethnogenesis.[6] Drive is the energetic potential or vitality, and in the course of development, an ethnicity exhibits high or low drive, with important moral implications. Gumilev believed that a high level of drive promotes a specific sacrificial ethic — members of the "driven community" are ready to sacrifice their lives for moral ideals having unrelated to their private interests. This sacrificial ethic enables the communities with a high level of drive to conquer or achieve superiority over communities with a low level of drive. Moral goals

are more valuable to such people than their own lives. These goals lay the foundations to the anti-egoistic ethics in which the interests of the collective prevail over the craving for life and concern for one's offspring. While drive is penetrating the ethnicity, the development is creative. The degree of drive and the number of "driven" individuals determine the rise and decline of ethnicities.[7]

Mystical waves of drive push ethnogenesis through various phases. Evidence of a high level of drive is the prominence of individuals within a society who demonstrate the proclivity for the heroic ethic of self-immolation.

The heroic ethic is not merely one historical stage in the development of an ethnicity. In contradiction to his principle of historical development, Gumilev divides ethnicities into two groups: those nations that have a special proclivity for the heroic ethic, and those unable to embrace this norm. He borrows this distinction between nations of heroes and nations of tradesmen from Werner Sombart (1863–1941). the German economic and social theorist, one of the founding fathers of historical and cultural sociology. The Romans, Saxons and Franks are heroic; while Jews, Florentines, and Scots are the nations of tradesmen. In opposition to the "heroic nations," the "tradesmen" are inclined to a selfish and pragmatic utilitarian ethic.

Gumilev claims that the Jews changed the course of European history. He argues that before the twelfth century the Romano-Germanic ethnicities lived in small communities and exhibited their original stereotypes of behavior. Individuals could effectively carry out communal goals and did not pursue their own satisfaction at the expense of the community. "The 'craving for profit' was characteristic only for the Jews."[8] During the twelfth and thirteenth centuries the drive of the Romano-Germanic super-ethnicity gradually decreased, allowing the Jews to successfully impose on it their own commercial stereotype of behavior.

> The spirit of capitalism is a result of the scarcity of the original creative tension, which arises during the period of increased drive....
> The philistines [i.e., the "tradesmen"] are the by-products of the creative flight, from which they preserved only the "craving for profit."[9]

The historian describes this period as one of crisis in which the European ethnicities had lost their sense of morality and identity as a result of engaging in dishonest commercial activity. The "driven individuals" were displaced by "different types of tradesmen — money-changers, complaisant diplomats, intriguers, adventurers. These hucksters were complete strangers for the local ethnicities. They did not have any motherland. However, their lack of motherland satisfied the monarchs." Gumilev calls this the period of civilization. It was marked by vast waves of migration of the population from their organic communities and natural environments to urban centers. He observes that in the course of this development, the immigrants seize power in the civilized countries and they "enter into a reverse relationship with the aboriginal population. They teach them and introduce technical improvements." Such technological changes are often detrimental both for the natives and for the environment. Gumilev explained the downfall of Babylon as a result of the excessive melioration of the area introduced by the newly-arrived Jewish advisers of the king.[10]

Gumilev did not believe that contact between different ethnicities necessarily lead to the conflict, however, only some contacts might prove to be beneficial. As an ideologist of Eurasianism, he emphasized the natural (organic) character of the Russian-Turanian union. He distinguished three types of ethnic contact: "Xenia" is a peaceful type of ethnic encounter in which the "guest" feels at home in the landscape of the "host." The guest occupies his own ecological niche and does not try to influence the host's behavior stereotype. "Symbiosis" involves two ethnicities that harmoniously occupy the same geographical region. "Chimera" is the third type, in opposition to the first two: in this case, the guest's behavior stereotype perniciously supplants that of the host.[11]

Gumilev goes on to elaborate the concept of "complementarity," which can be "neutral," "positive," or "negative," depending on the nature of the ethnicities in contact with each other.[12] "Chimera" involves ethnicities with negative complementarity.

The chimeric type of contact occurs in periods of the influx of strangers, and Gumilev created an entire demonology of strangers. Immigrants in very different parts of the world are described as the very source of all evil, who treat the "[host] country with its nature and people" as "a mere field for their actions" which are always "egoistic and selfish."[13] Strangers are portrayed as devils who seduce the country into a commercial social order and eradicate the heroic ethic of the founding fathers. Gumilev's use of arresting demonic metaphors to strike terror into the heart of the reader is really incredible. Strangers are compared to "parasites," "vampires sucking human blood," a "cancerous tumor which devours healthy cells," and "tapeworms in the stomach of the animal."

> The super-ethnic system...is closely connected with the nature of its region. Each of its constituent parts and subsystems finds an ecological niche for itself.... But if a *new foreign ethnic entity* invades this system and could not find a safe ecological niche for itself, it is forced *to live at the expense of the inhabitants of the territory, not at the expense of the territory itself*. This is not simply a neighborhood, and not a symbiosis, but a chimera, i.e., a combination of two different, *incompatible systems* into one entity. In zoology the combination of an animal and a tapeworm in the intestine is called a chimeral construction.... Living in his body the parasite takes part in his life cycle, dictating a heightened need for food and altering the

organism's biochemistry by its own hormones, forcibly secreted into the blood or bile of the host or parasite carrier.... All the horrors of clashes at symbiotic level pale before the *poison of a chimera at the level of a super-ethnicity* [italics mine, V.R.].[14]

The same idea is conveyed in another passage, where strangers are compared to vampires:

The *parasitic ethnicity is like a vampire. It sucks out the drive* from the ethnic environment and brakes the pulse of ethnogenesis. Chimera...receives all it needs from the ethnicities in the bodies of which it nestles. Thus, chimera has no motherland. It is an *anti-ethnicity*. Chimera arises on the border of several original super-ethnicities and opposes itself to all of them. It denies any tradition and replaces them with permanently renovated "novelty" [italics mine, V.R.][15]

The behavior stereotype of the strangers undermines the traditional moral codes, notions of about good and bad, honest and dishonest actions, held by the given culture. The strangers' own moral code is not very demanding because they do not have any stable tradition behind themselves. It allows the "immigrants" to "adapt themselves very quickly to the changing circumstances."[16]

Strangers and immigrants are so dangerous that even their complete assimilation cannot save a country from the potential growth of chimeras. Gumilev claims that they are even unable to transform themselves in conformity with the behavior stereotype of the host ethnicity.

The subject of assimilation faces the following alternative. It needs to sacrifice his life or his conscience. It could avoid death by the price of repudiation of everything that was valuable to him and that converts him/her into a second-class person.... The latter [the host culture, V.R.] also gains little, since it acquires hypocritical and, as can be expected, inferior fellow-citizens. The motives of this behavior could never be controlled unlike its outward manifestations.[17]

Jews are never explicitly named in the discussion of different types of ethnic contact. However, they are present in the context of the discussion, and some particular remarks suggest that what was said about the sinister strangers and immigrants could just as well have been said about the Jews.

The next significant category in the theory of ethnogenesis is the concept of the "anti-system." The anti-system is a mechanism by virtue of which the chimera realizes its destructive potential.[18] The anti-system takes a negative attitude to this world and to nature, in opposition to the life-asserting attitude characteristic of the driven ethnicities. Moral relativism is an ingredient of anti-systems; those who share its ideology believe that the end justifies the means, so murder, betrayal, and dishonesty are turned into virtue. The idelogists of anti-systems celebrate reason and logical argument, unlike the healthy intuition of the life-asserting ethnicities.[19] Among the anti-systems, Gumilev names diverse intellectual movements such as Gnosticism, the Manichaeans, Ismaelism, the Cathars, and existentialists. He points out that the anti-system ideologies are especially popular in the cosmopolitan environments.

The ideology of anti-system can arise in two different ways. First, it can be generated by the synthesis of two completely different cultures. Different ethnicities can have different "rhythms" and their joint efforts can produce a cultural "cacophony." He cites the period of Hellenism as an example of the cacophonic cultural development of heterogeneous entities:

> Before the campaigns of Alexander the Great, Hellenes did not know about the Hebrews and Hebrews did not care about the Ionians.... Both ethnicities were talented and driven, but the contact of their ideologies gave birth to Gnosticism — a mighty anti-system.[20]

Second, the infiltration of an anti-system can result from deliberate subversive efforts by the strangers. These parasites often use an anti-system ideology in their political and ethnic struggle. The Eurasian historian identifies the "parasitic ethnicities" responsible for the propagation of the harmful anti-system ideas with the "Little People" *(malii narod)* — a euphemism for the Jews.[21]

The Jews are painted as the architects and universal agents of anti-systems, using them to eliminate the original ethno-cultural stereotypes and to pave the way for their own domination.[22] It is no accident when Gumilev asserts that many of the founders of anti-system ideologies are Jewish. Ubayd Allah, a founder of Ismailism, was a Jew. Jews created the Albigensian heresy and destroyed the original ideal of knighthood, as well as contributing to the development of Manichaeism.[23] The decline of European theology is also attributed to Jewish intellectual influence. Gumilev claims that in the ninth to eleventh centuries — a crucial period in the formation of Western European theology — many Jews were invited to teach various subjects in the religious academies, because Europeans did not have any serious "scholastic tradition" and lacked a sufficient number of competent teachers. Jewish professors took advantage of the situation and introduced their Christian students to various anti-system ideologies.[24] Gumilev points to the example of John Scotus Erigena, the Irish theologian, who was influenced by the Qarmatians (a heretical Islamic sect).[25] Spanish and Provençal Jews, aware of the destructive potential of such ideas, had introduced the theological academies to their thinking: "They did not share Qarmatian ideas, but they were glad to communicate these ideas to Christians in their own interpretation."[26]

> Judaists themselves were the antagonists of any teaching of anti-system. They loved in this world only themselves, their own deeds and their offspring. They resorted to secrecy and lies, the arms borrowed from their bitterest enemies, the Hellenic Gnostics to bring their ethnicity to triumph. But they used these arms only against Gentiles and akums (idolaters). Judaists knew perfectly well that Manichaeanism subverts any positive system. Because of that they preferred to see Manichaeans in other ethnicities, but not among themselves.[27]

I have already pointed out that the Jews are not mentioned explicitly in *Ethnogenesis;* most of the above quotations were taken from the later works of Gumilev, in which the antisemitic position is congenial to the very logic of his theory. However, it is interesting to note that Gumilev sometimes supports antisemitism even at the expense of the logic of his theory. Some critics of Gumilev have already pointed out the inconsistency in the belief in ethnogenesis as a process, alongside the belief in the stable and universal characteristics of some ethnicities. One has the impression from his works that the "Jewish stereotype of behavior" is not susceptible to change. It is unclear whether or not the Jews could ever experience an increase in their "drive" or whether Jewish history could assume the heroic path of development.[28] Whatever the answer to this question might be, both his theory and his "stories" are antisemitic. In the next section we shall see how he employs his theory of ethnogenesis in explaining concrete history and how his bias shaped the history of Eurasia that he recounted.

JUDEO-KHAZARIA:
"A DISASTER FOR THE ABORIGINALS OF EASTERN EUROPE"

Ancient Russia and the Great Steppe (1992) is the first of Gumilev's books in which the question of the historical influence of the Jews is addressed directly. He focuses on the historical interaction between the Turkic nomads and the Slavs, between the Forest and the Steppe of Eurasia. The thrust of the book is similar to his earlier publications and introduces little that is new. The "last Soviet Eurasian" repudiates the "black myths" of European historiography, which ascribes an aggressive and barbaric character to the nomadic people; and the accepted wisdom about the period in which the

Russians paid tribute to the Tatars — the Tatar Yoke (roughly 250 years in the 13th–15th centuries). In addition, Gumilev's observations and conclusions about the history of Khazaria go far beyond the short historical period and the geographical location as stated in the book's title. Russians and nomads, sharing a common experience on the same territory, along with economic and military cooperation, are perfectly "complementary." This complementarity is revealed, however, against the background of their opposition to the Jews, specifically, the Jews of Khazaria. While the behavior stereotypes of the nomads and the Slavs are similar, they had no common social bonds or similar values with the Jews, that could foster communication. Gumilev's only new contribution in *Ancient Russia* is the theme of opposition to the "enemy."

Khazaria was a medieval empire that occupied the southeast part of Russia ranging from the Caspian Sea and the Volga to the Dniepr. In the ninth century a large segment of the Khazars adopted the Jewish faith, having learned of it from the Jews who had fled the persecutions of Emperor Leo of Byzantium. The paucity of reliable data on Khazaria contributes to the popularity of the topic among Russian nationalists, and to the production of the most fantastic speculations about Khazar history.[29] Many of the nationalists credit Gumilev for the discovery of the topic and its "correct" interpretation.

Gumilev's academic credentials and expertise in the history of the Khazars set him apart from most other nationalists, however. He participated in archeological excavations of Khazar castles, and was a student of Mikhail Artamonov, a well-known historian of Khazaria. He also wrote a number of academic studies on the subject.[30] Nevertheless, his methodology and sweeping generalizations about very different historical epochs raise doubts about the validity of his claims. Gumilev "reconstructs" the history of Khazaria on the basis of his theory of ethnogenesis, and most of his "findings" cannot be verified by conventional historical documentation. Gumilev, in fact, disparages the available written sources and chronicles, and attempts to make his historical narrative fit his theory of ethnogenesis. In addition — and in spite claiming that his historical research is apolitical — Gumilev quite often projects contemporary realities onto the old days. His ideological purpose would be quite clear even to a person who is not very well versed in the subtleties of the medieval history of Russia and Eurasia.

Judaism in Relation to Christianity and Islam

Max Weber was interested in world religions because of the implications for their work ethic. Gumilev's interest derives from his belief that different religions foster certain behavior stereotypes. He believed that religion is a biological phenomenon, and an important manifestation of the ethnicity's unconscious and its genetic memory, reflecting the phase of ethnogenesis reached by a given ethnicity. Marx claimed that religious conflict is a disguised class conflict; Gumilev believed that religious conflict is essentially an ethnic conflict of behavior stereotypes.[31] The discussion of Judaism is based on these assumptions.

In his discussion of Judaism Gumilev draws on the centuries-old stereotypes of Christian antisemitism. He defines Judaism as "genotheistic" ethnic religion as opposed to monotheistic Christianity. He compiled an extensive list of crimes of this ethnic God, including the "persecution of innocent Egyptians, the cruel destruction of the original population of Palestine, including children"; he "favored the pogrom [*sic*! V.R.] of the Macedonians and other rivals of the Jews,[32] and supported the ideology of total destruction of the enemy. Talmudism, the post-exilic, modified form of Judaism assumed an even more aggressive and cruel character. Gumilev believed that xenophobia is a specific element of the Jewish behavior stereotype. The Talmud allegedly encourages Jews lie to Gentiles, and advocates the "teaching of predestination, which takes away human responsibility for any crimes and misdeeds." The historian alleges that all these cruel aspects of the Talmud are not widely known because it was originally a secret teaching of the rabbis.[33] Finally, it advocates the extermination of Christians, articulating anti-Christian principles absent from the original Judaic doctrine (Christianity is described by Gumilev as a "new young super-ethnicity").[34] He asserted that the Jews initiated a war against Christians, a conflict he defined as a war of behavior stereotypes. The Jews denounced Christians in Rome and the "Judaic fanatics of Bar-Kokhba" committed brutal murders and pogroms against Christians, torturing and stoning them.[35] The Romans did not distinguish between Jews and the Christians, and extended their negative attitude towards the Jews to the Christians.[36] Gumilev also makes the ridiculous claim that Judaism was "disseminated in Rome through women who had lost their traditional morals in the period of the Empire."

Gumilev argues that differences in dogma account for the different behavior stereotypes in the two "superethnicities." In particular, he focuses on the conception of Satan in the two religions: in the Old Testament, Satan is an associate of God, whereas in the New Testament, Satan is depicted as the enemy of Jesus.[37] To support his notion that the God of Judaism is the same as the Devil, Gumilev cites the biblical book of Job, in which God and Satan "take an experiment over the helpless and innocent Job,"[38] as well as the New Testament story of Christ's fasting in the desert (Matthew 4:1–13; Mark 1:13). Gumilev equates the choice of a believer as that between the Old Testament/Satan and the New Testament/God. He asserts that the Council of Nicaea's definition of the Trinity meant that Christians could no longer maintain their allegiance to the Old Testament scriptures, making reference to the teachings of Marcion, who similarly rejected the Jewish roots of Christianity.[39]

Gumilev considered it important to demonstrate the unity of the religious experiences of the Eurasian ethnicities. It is no accident that he draws many parallels between Christianity and Islam in their cultural traditions, customs, and social relations. He points to serious conflict between the Orthodox Muslim and Jewish cultures, and argues that "Jews were at odds with the Muslims more seriously than with Christians. They had conflicts with the Prophet himself...."[40] Gumilev focused on subversive activities of the Jews within early Muslim civilization. Abdulla Ibn-Saba, "a Jew converted to Islam," introduced Shia which led to a split in Islam, thereby creating the ideological basis for civil wars that led to the disintegration and collapse of the Caliphate.[41]

The theology of Orthodoxy and Islam have much in common, and are in opposition to Jewish theology.

> In the 10th century, the two Eastern religions, Orthodoxy and Islam, differed greatly in many of their tenets and ceremonies, but they were unanimous in that they contrasted God with the Devil and opposed their own positive principles to those of Judaism. It is not difficult to understand the difference. While Christians and Muslims prayed to one and the same God, although in a different way, the Judaists prayed to another God. This ruled out any confessional contacts with the Jews. Only business contacts with them remained possible.[42]

It is important to keep in mind that these assumptions about the relationship between the three religions is the foundation of Gumilev's history of Khazaria and many of his other narratives.

Judeo-Khazaria and Russia

In his history of Khazaria, Gumilev sets out to demonstrate the negative role of Judaism and the Jewish behavior stereotype in the medieval history of Eurasia: Judaism and the Jews have played an extremely negative role in the histories of Russia and the Turks of Khazaria. Jews are, in fact, the historic enemies of the Eurasian ethnicities. The focus of his approach is the behavior stereotype exhibited by the Jews in the course of their involvement in the Eurasian history — a type of behavior incompatible with the heroic ethos of the original Eurasian ethnicities, i.e., the Russians and nomads of the Great Steppe.

Gumilev considered the Khazars — one of the Turkic tribes which founded an empire between the Don and Volga rivers — the victim of the Jews. Their conversion to Judaism was the most crucial and tragic event in the whole of Khazar history. This conversion was facilitated by two waves of Jewish immigration to Khazaria. The first wave, in the fifth and sixth centuries was relatively harmless. The Jews came from Iran, where the Jews were persecuted for their participation in the "socialist" Mazdaq movement. These first Jewish arrivals did not bother the local population and took part in conventional economic activity (agriculture and cattle-breeding). The second wave arrived from Byzantium in the ninth century, having fled the persecution of Pope Leo III who attempted to convert them forcibly to Christianity.[43] Just as in the seventeenth century, the Jews persecuted in Spain found shelter in Holland, in the eighth century they enjoyed the hospitality of the Khazars and felt at home in the "Caspian Netherlands."[44]

Gumilev distinguished between the earlier wave of Jewish immigrants, who were Karaites (who rejected the Oral Tradition of Judaism), whereas the second wave was well-versed in the "misanthropic principles of the Talmud." The newcomers treated the earlier immigrants with contempt, despite the welcome they received and the help they were given in getting settled.[45]

Khazaria attracted the Jews first of all as an important trade center situated at the very center of international caravan routes. Jewish merchants played a crucial role in the rise of Khazaria; they were the so-called "Radhanites."[46] The "Jewish Radhanites," Gumilev contends, "constituted a super-ethnicity which preserved a very high level of drive. The dispersion did not bother them, since they lived at the expense of the anthropogenic terrains, i.e., the towns."[47] The historian painted the Jewish Radhanites as evil demons, remarking that in the middle ages trade did not benefit the populace, since the economy of natural exchange provided everything they needed. Commercial activity harmed the populations of both Khazaria and of the world outside:

> The trade was incredibly profitable, because it was not merchandise of wide consumption in which the "Radhanites" traded, but luxury goods. If one would render this into the categories of the twentieth century, this trade is comparable only to the foreign currency deals *(voliutnie operatsii)* and drug trafficking.[48]

Gumilev also blames the Radhanites for an underground trade involving the purchase of stolen goods from the Northmen.

Gumilev's most serious charge is that the Radhanites engaged in the slave trade, in particular, of Slavonian slaves, the most profitable business of the middle ages. Vikings and Hungarians supplied Khazaria with slaves and the merchants resold them to Muslim countries in Baghdad, Cordova, and Egyptian cities. Gumilev stresses that the pool of slaves for the most part were Slavs, Rus, and Guzes and that many of them were Christian. "Like Africa in the seventeenth–nineteenth centuries, Slavic lands became the main source of slaves for the Jews in the ninth and tenth centuries."[49] Gumilev's indignation is not so much for slavery itself, but rests in his claim that the Jews purchased and resold slaves of Slavic origin and Christians.[50] In addition, the Jews sold Khazarian idolaters, i.e., a people who gave them a shelter during the Jews' own hard times — which he offers as evidence of the lack of gratitude he claims is part of the Jewish behavior stereotype.[51]

As noted above, Gumilev attributes racist and xenophobic attitudes as part of the Jewish behavior stereotype. "In order to replace the Turkic nobility the Jews decided to use love as their weapon" and began to intermarry with Khazarian women.

> The Jews...received children from the Khazarian ethnicity either as full-fledged Jews, or as bastards. By doing this they impoverished the Khazarian ethnicity and impoverished their ethnic system.[52]

The Jews only fully accepted the sons of Jewish mothers and treated children from mixed marriages of Khazarian girls and Jewish men as aliens, following the "centuries-old xenophobic Jewish tradition." These rejected children were not allowed to study Talmud as full-fledged Jews; rather, they were "hidden" in Crimea, where they professed Karaism.[53]

There is a consensus among other historians that the Khazars adopted Judaism in order to safeguard its political independence from its powerful Christian and Muslim neighbors. Gumilev rejects this theory, and argues that Judaism was imposed upon the population of Khazaria in the course of a religious coup d'état. Obadia, an influential Jew, seized power, transformed the khanate into a puppet and introduced rabbinic Judaism as the state religion, with Jews occupying all the important positions within the state bureaucracy.[54] Thus, the Jewish ethnicity was transformed into a social strata of Khazaria. This "combination of the amorphous masses of subjects and the ruling class alien to the majority of the population by its blood and religion" paved the way for the formation of "chimera."[55] The accession to power of the new Jewish ruling elite marked the transformation of Khazaria into the "evil Empire."

> The period between the ninth and tenth centuries was a disaster for the aboriginals of Eastern Europe. It was the culmination of Judeo-Khazarian power. The aboriginals faced two alternatives: slavery or death.[56]

While other historians stress that Khazaria was one of the few countries in the middle ages in which pagans, Christians, Muslims, and Jews, could peacefully co-exist, Gumilev paints its history as being driven by the Jewish religious intolerance and their hostility toward Christianity and Islam. Gumilev claims that the Jewish political elite destroyed Christian church organization, oppressed the Muslims, and practiced savage reprisals on the religious dissenters. Judaism's religious intolerance and cruelty was manifested in the military administration of Khazaria. Failure to carry out a military task or order was punishable by death.[57] The Khazarian army consisted of mercenaries: "The chief of the Jewish community squeezed out the means from the Khazars for these mercenaries, which were supposed to suppress the same Khazars."[58]

Gumilev intimates that changes in Khazaria's international relations after the adoption of Judaism resulted from the Jewish behavior stereotype, specifically, Jewish perfidy and lack of moral consideration for the country's neighbors. International policy was determined by "considerations of profit and not by the considerations of faithfulness and prowess." Khazaria began to betray its former allies, the small nomadic ethnicities, and it established friendly relations with the despotic regimes of the medieval empires such as the Carolingians, Tan, Ottons, and Abbasids.[59] The alliance of the Vikings and the Jews, he contended, was especially dangerous for the original Eurasian ethnicities. "The two plunderers" divided their gains,[60] and the alliance allowed the Vikings to seize English and French cities, for the Jews helped them to acquire a navy, and supposedly opened the gates of besieged cities from the inside. In turn, the Vikings helped Jewish merchants to control the credit operations of English kings and their vassals. They also helped the Jews to establish and maintain the whole world market of the middle ages.[61]

Special emphasis is placed on the conflict between Khazaria and the Orthodox Christian tsardoms. Gumilev contends that Khazaria's rulers encouraged other countries to attack Byzantium, while Khazaria itself avoided open confrontations with that empire. The Varangian princedom of Kiev was a Khazar vassal, so the Jews had the opportunity of using Slavs in their campaigns against Byzantium and the Muslim countries. The Slavic people paid a "tribute of blood" to the khanate of Khazaria. The Varangians "sent their subordinate Slavo-Russes to die for the trade roads of the rakhdonites."[62] It is striking that Gumilev blames the Jews for the atrocities committed by the Slavs in Byzantium. The Khazarian tsar Joseph murdered some Christians and provoked a conflict with Byzantium. Then Pesakh, a Khazar military leader, went to Kiev and "urged Helga (Prince Oleg) to fight against Byzantium for the triumph of the commercial Jewish community."[63]

In the course of this war, Gumilev observes, Russian soldiers "committed atrocities which were horrible and unusual even for this historical period."

> Many of the Russian soldiers were already converted into Orthodoxy. However, they crucified the captives, hammered nails into the skulls, burned the churches and monasteries.... This war was very different from the wars typical of the tenth century. It seems that the Russian warriors had experienced and influential instructors [of warfare], and not only from Scandinavia.[64]

He intimates that only the Jews were capable of instructing the Russian warriors in this manner. The atrocities committed by the Slavs, he argues, were congenial to the principles of "total war" expounded in the Old Testament:

> The notion of total war was an unusual novelty for the early medieval period. It used to be a common convention that after the resistance of the enemy is broken, the victor imposes tribute and conscriptions.... But the total destruction of the population that did not take part in the military operations was a heritage of very ancient times. During the siege of Canaan by Joshua, son of Nun, it was prohibited to take captives and allow them to live. It was even prescribed to kill the domestic animals.... Obadiya, the ruler of Khazaria, revived this practice forgotten in antiquity.[65]

After the campaign against Byzantium, the rulers of Khazaria sent the soldiers to fight the Muslims. Gumilev alleged that Russian soldiers who were not killed in the battles were slaughtered by the Jews.

The reader can find the antisemitic sentiments of the "last Eurasian" in passing remarks such as the comment that commercialism and money-centeredness are specifically Jewish traits of character. In one of the episodes that he recounts, he suggests that the peasants killed prince Oleg because of his "Jewish psychology," that is, his greed in collecting tribute. Oleg ignored all contracts and agreements with his subjects. "This was a typical Jewish statement of a question, where the emotions of other party are not taken into consideration."[66] It is noteworthy that Gumilev exaggerated the amount of tribute the Russians were supposed to pay the Khazars, and even suggests a theory of a "Khazar Yoke" in Russia — a theory elaborated in more detail by some of his students.

Prince Svyatoslav demolished Khazaria in the second half of the tenth century, which Gumilev explains as resulting from the decline of Oriental trade and the rise of Orthodox Russia. He claims that for the ethnic Khazars and other local ethnicities it was an emancipation from an alien power. Those who remained of the Jews, Gumilev claimed, became relic ethnicities, the Crimean Karaites and the Caucasian Tats.

The historian laments that the destruction of Khazaria did not halt the subversive activity of the Jews against Russia. The Jewish community tried to monopolize commerce and handicrafts in Kiev and incited Russian princes to wage war against their neighbors. These wars created huge slave markets of captives and brought fabulous fortunes to the Jewish slave traders, especially active in Kiev and Chersoneses.[67] Gumilev even added new fuel to the ritual murder charge:

> They starved the captives. Just as in ancient times when the Jews had bought Hellenic and Christian slaves only to kill them. One monster of cruelty even crucified the monk of the Kiev-Pechersky Lavra on the cross.[68]

In Kiev, he claimed, such activities eventually led to pogroms as a response of the people to the Jews' subversive activities.

Unable to carry on their destructive activity in Russia, the Jews moved to Western Europe.

> The backbone of the Jews did not lose their will to victory. They found their shelter in Western Europe.... The descendants of Khazarian Jews forgot about the country where they lived and acted. It was only natural. The Lower Volga was not their motherland, but rather a stadium for their trial of strength.[69]

They found a "new Khazaria" in Spain. In Spain, the Jews had many privileges, including the right to settle in a ghetto where they had legal autonomy. Jews in the ghetto had immunity from punishment for their crimes against Christians, and Jewish scholars were free to introduce their anti-systems, which undermined Christian doctrine.[70] Jewish crimes — Gumilev refers to perpetual betrayals, anti-Christian activity, feigned conversions to Christianity, and the dissemination of the doctrines of the "anti-system." All these, Gumilev believed, were justifications for the atrocities perpetrated by the Spanish Inquisition.[71]

The Jews and the Nomads:
The Khazar Origins of the Eastern European Jews

The hypothesis of the supposed Khazar origin of Eastern European Jews was most recently advocated by the English writer Arthur Koestler.[72] Among other things, this theory has been utilized by some radical Palestinian hard-liners to delegitimize Jewish claims to the land of Israel.[73] Gumilev denounced the theory, however, this does not imply that he does advocate the rights of the Jews to the land of Israel. It is important to try to understand the intellectual origins and cultural context of his position. His opposition to the theory can be better understood against the background of the association between the nomads and the Jews in some trends of European culture.

Theories about the nomadic origins of Eastern European Jews and the "nomadic essence" of the Jewish mentality were prominent in Europe in the fin-de-siècle and interwar period. The French Hebraist Ernest Renan (1823–1892) wrote about the survival of "nomadic instincts" and the "nomadic nomos" of the Jews. René Guenon also wrote about the "perverse nomadism" of the Jews. Hélène Blavatsky, the founder of theosophy, suggested that the Jews have Turanian blood; she believed that the Jewish race is a mixture of the Mongol-Turanians and Indo-Europeans.[74] The symbols of the Russian Revolution represented by the Jews and the Mongols were quite prominent in the essays, poems and fiction of some Russian poets and intellectuals of the Silver Age. These combinations of images can be found in the works of the Russian symbolists and the group of intellectuals known as the Scythians (e.g., Alexander Blok and Andrei Belyi).[75] In the nineteenth century the theme of Jewish nomadism was especially articulated by the notorious German antisemite Adolf Wahrmund in his work *The Nomadic Way of Life and the Modern Domination of the Jews* (1887).[76] Wahrmund suggested that modernity is a modified type of a nomadic life and that the ubiquity of the Jews in the modern period and their success can be attributed to nomadic instincts they have preserved and which were in demand in modern societies. The nomadic conditions of modernity are natural and advantageous for the Jews, whereas those same conditions are disturbing and inconvenient for the Aryans, whose origins are agricultural. Since agriculture does not play a part in the life of the nomads, Wahrmund describes the nomadic ethos as parasitic, and spoke of the sordid moral qualities of the nomads.[77]

The association of the Jews with barbaric nomads was manifest not only in the works of obscure intellectuals. Alfred Rosenberg and other Nazi ideologists often described Bolshevik Revolution as a revolt of barbaric nomadic elements under the leadership of the Jews. Rosenberg compared the Jewish Bolsheviks with the Huns, Tatars, and other nomadic invaders of Europe in ancient and medieval times. He explained the popularity of Bolshevism in Russia as an overdose of Tatar blood in Russian veins.[78] Rosenberg was not alone in these beliefs. Rather, he reproduced some of the irrational fears present in European intellectual folklore and mythological constructions that haunted European minds.

Gumilev's theory can be construed as a response to this persistent association of the Jews with nomads. His goal was to save the nomads from the "canard" about their barbarism and wild temper and to stigmatize the Jews. In many of his works he suggests that the similarity between the nomadism of the Jews and that of true nomads is really superficial, for the attitudes of the nomads and the Jews to the landscape are very different. Whereas the nomads established a special relationship to the landscape, the Jews tried to escape any attachment to the land. They merely use the landscapes, but never get attached to them. The Jews are parasites; they consider the terrain only in pragmatic terms, and thus their attitude is directly opposite to that of true nomads. In contrast to the Jews, the nomads are not "rootless."[79]

In this sense, the Turanian nomads have much in common with traditional Russian farmers. The nomads have a "positive complementarity" with the Russian ethnicity and the Eurasian terrain. Farmer and nomad are perfectly compatible both in terms of their economic occupations and their behavior stereotypes. The Jews, on the other hand, could not peacefully cooperate and coexist with the aboriginal Eurasian ethnicities. Gumilev discounts the "black legend" of European historiography about the aggressive character and barbarism of the nomads. However, he reinforces another black legend — the legend of the "parasitic" Jews, which has even deeper roots in the European historiography than the legend of the barbaric hordes of the nomads.

To summarize Gumilev's views:

(1) The history of the Jewish ethnicity has assumed an abnormal course of development due to their detachment from their natural terrain. Unable to make use of resources that would have been available to them on their own natural territory, the Jews became a parasitic ethnicity that exploits other territories and those who dwell in them.

(2) The Jewish behavior stereotype includes disregard for the sacred norms of morality and tradition, a selfish in-group morality, a sense of ethnic superiority and exclusivity, and a willingness to betray. In Gumilev's writings the Jews appear as miserly, secretive, unscrupulous, mendacious, and perfidious. They are greedy and mercenary by instinct; they slip easily into crime, and are engaged in an immoral pursuit of wealth. They have no qualms about betraying those who have helped them. Hypocritical, secretive, and cruel, their perverse moral code makes them alien and hostile to other Eurasian ethnicities, and this explains the hatred of these groups for the Jews.

(3). The present state of the Western world is a result of the invasion of the Jewish behavior stereotype. It is important to observe that for Gumilev the Russian encounter with Khazaria is not merely a local historical episode, but part of the global historical narrative. The history of the confrontation with the Jews shapes the national myth of the role of Russia in the world historical process. The Eurasian identity of Russia was shaped in the course of its opposition to Khazaria. The Jewish behavior stereotype of the huckster is the reverse of Russian identity.[80] Gumilev's "narratives" have a Nietzschean flavor, with admiration for those who can commit violent acts and get away with them, and contemptuous of "hucksters" and the "nations of tradesmen" who are indisposed to violence.

Gumilev's position seems to have been clearly influenced by his teacher, Mikhail Artamonov, whose magnum opus is the *History of Khazaria*. Although it's a serious academic work, it contains a very biased characterization of Judaism. Some of its controversial ideas are certainly present in *Ancient Russia and the Great Steppe*, such as the exaggerated role assigned to the Khazars in Russian history, and the reference to the decline of Khazaria as a result of the conversion of its people to Judaism. Gumilev and Artamonov also share an extremely negative attitude towards commerce and trade (described as parasitic occupations), and the accusation that a Jewish ruling elite mismanaged Khazar government and alienated the main body of its non-Jewish citizens.[81]

THE RECEPTION OF GUMILEV'S THEORY BY RUSSIAN NATIONALISTS

Gumilev received a great deal of publicity in debates on historical and social issues in Russian periodicals. Liberal critics were unanimous in criticizing the historian for the misreading of the historical documentation, for the use of pseudo-scientific jargon, and for his racist and antisemitic leanings. Other historians accused him of fabricating data and of presenting an arbitrary interpretation of the documentation.[82]

The reaction of nationalist ideologists was much less uniform. Gumilev provoked a surprisingly mixed reaction in the circles of Russian nationalists. Many were fascinated by his writings.[83] Many nationalist leaders and ideologists began to use his theories as legitimization for their political agenda, using terminology from his theory of ethnogenesis, and even incorporating his pseudo-scientific language into their political programs. Others, however, dismissed his theories or found "Zionist leanings" in them.

The history of Khazaria received special attention from Russian nationalists, some of whom consider the political experience of Khazaria as a metaphor and symbolic anticipation of the "Jewish rule" of the early Soviet period. Thus, they speak of the early Soviet Khazaria that imposed its Jewish Bolshevik faith on the whole country and suppressed indigenous political expression. Yury Sedykh-Bondarenko, for example, juxtaposes Khazar, Tatar-Mongol, Nazi, and Judeo-Bolshevik Yokes of Russia. In the face of these foreign attacks, he argues, Russians were forced to choose totalitarian systems of rule.[84]

Other nationalist leaders go even further in their admiration of Gumilev. *The History of Russia and Russian Literature* by Vadim Kozhinov, a well-known Russian literary critic, is an elaboration and complement to the antisemitic insights of Gumilev, who was his teacher. The history of Khazaria occupies a very important place in his account of Russian literature. He claims that during the Soviet period, the Jews tried to instigate a conspiracy of silence on the study of Khazaria, and he alleges that Russian historians engaged in its study were persecuted by the Central Control Committee (TsKK) and the State Political Administration (GPU), where Jews held very powerful positions.[85] The Jews were afraid that general knowledge about their shameful past might become widely available, and so they attempted to conceal their history by any means possible. He credits Gumilev and other Soviet historians of Khazaria with the courage to study the subject, and Kozhinov himself set out to demonstrate the influence of the history of Khazar-Russian relations on the development of Russian literature. His discussion of Khazarian history follows the outline provided by Gumilev, and claims to be indispensable for understanding a particular stage in development of Russian literature. However, many passages of his history of literature look like an exercise in antisemitic hatred for the sake of the exercise.

Kozhinov's main thesis is that the Russian resistance to the Khazar invaders is the central theme of the epic stage in the development of Russian literature. The "Khazar Yoke" was thus more devastating and significant than the Tatar Yoke. He argues that the chronicles that describe the atrocities of the Tatars in fact may have described the atrocities of the Judeo-Khazars.[86] The notion of the "Khazar Yoke" in the epic stories is obviously an extrapolation of Gumilev's historical speculations placed in the sphere of literature. Kozhinov repeatedly concentrates on the "historical" episodes that demonstrate the gratuitous cruelty and ritual sadism of the Jews. Among other things, he suggests that the Jews bought Christian captives from Iran solely for the purpose of enjoying the sadistic pleasure of killing them.[87]

Kozhinov revises some parts of the story of Khazaria as presented by Gumilev and adds new "revolutionary" details. The Jews came to Khazaria, Kozhinov claims, from the Muslim East (Iran and Khoresm[88]), not from Byzantium. The Jewish community dominated Khoresm and had attempted to seize political power in the country. The plot was directed by the "local intelligentsia" (*habres,* derived from the Hebrew "comrades"), whom he identifies with Jewish scholars (rabbis).[89] He goes on to argue that in

Khoresm, the Judaists sustained the "ideology of a powerful rebellious social movement" similar to Bolshevism.[90] Kozhinov aligns the ideology of the Jewish intelligentsia of Khoresm with Mazdakism — "a socialist and communist movement in its inspiration," whose members "suggested the introduction of economic equality and socialization of property."[91] In the eighth century, the rulers of Khoresm called upon the Arabs to help them in their struggle against the Jewish rebels, and the Jews then moved to Khazaria after the suppression of their subversive activity. Kozhinov points out that the Jews did not themselves believe in Mazdakism, but were using it as a subversive ideological instrument in order to undermine the power of the state. It was no accident that they abandoned this "communist ideology" when they arrived in Khazaria.

Allusions to the political history of the twentieth century permeate Kozhinov's account of medieval Russian literature; he is even more interested in historical reconstructions and extrapolations than Gumilev, his mentor. He claims that Zionist ideology and practice "should help us to understand the distant historical realities of Khazar "kaganate" — the official name for the institution of power in Khazaria, a word that may be derived from the Hebrew "kohen." Mazdakites are described as rabid Bolsheviks and bigoted Zionists.[92] Kozhinov blames the medieval *habres* for treating other people as dust, just like modern Zionists toward Gentiles and non-Zionist Jews.

Kozhinov suggests that the historians have neglected a very important stage in the development of Russian literature. The only piece of folklore, however, which Kozhinov could find to substantiate this thesis is the *bylina* (epic tale) *Ilya Murometz and the Yid.*[93] Kozhinov intimates that Jewish literary critics have tried to conceal this masterpiece of Russian folklore from the public and dropped it from collections published during the Soviet period. The *bylina* describes how Ilya Murometz, an epic Russian hero *(bogatyr),* fought a strong Khazar warrior known only as "Yid," whom he defeated after a long struggle. Kozhinov sees a symbolic meaning in the manner in which Murometz finally defeats the Jew: in the course of the fight the Jew *(Zhidovin)* pins Ilya Murometz to the ground, but Murometz summons up new energy from the earth and overpowers the enemy. Kozhinov concludes:

> It is the awareness of the inseparable unity of Ilya with his native land
> that is epitomized in this Russian *bylina*. This unity is opposed to the
> "rootlessness" of his enemy.[94]

Paradoxically, some nationalists have criticized Gumilev's theory of ethnogenesis as Zionist-inspired. The central thesis, namely, the close connection between the ethnicity and its historic territory, is congenial to the tenets of Zionism, and it is true that the theory of ethnogenesis lends itself to this interpretation, although Gumilev could hardly have had it in mind. Some Russian nationalists do accept the idea of Zionism and consider it an ally in the struggle against the "inauthentic" Jews of the Diaspora. In an article published in *Den'*, Sergei Kosarenko, for example, claims that the establishment of Israel restored the Jews' lost connection with their native soil and transformed those Jews who moved to Palestine into a normal ethnicity. However, this means that from now on, Jews in the Diaspora fail the test of authenticity and should be condemned:

> In terms of ethnogenesis the Israelis constitute a normal ethnicity. However, the Jews of Diaspora during their two-thousand-year history turned into a unique group, which uses the territory already occupied by other ethnicities. With this, the Jews of the Diaspora regard the local population as...a certain kind of fauna. It is widely known, that the Jewish intelligentsia played a significant role in the formation of Russian revolutionary intelligentsia as the incubator and the backbone of the anti-system. But... [without the Jews — V.R.] this anti-system could not seriously affect the fate of Russia.... After the October upheaval the state officials refused to collaborate with the Bolsheviks, and positions in the state institutions were occupied by the Jews from the shtetls. This helped the government, but also gave birth to the ethnic chimera similar to the one in Judeo-Khazaria....[95]

It is not hard to guess that most other nationalists do not consider Zionism an ally. Apollon Kuzmin, a historian of Russia and the conspicuous representative of National Bolshevism, condemns both Zionism and Gumilev. In the first part of his article, he challenges the Eurasian ingredients in Gumilev's writings and the historical lapses derived from it.[96] In the second part he goes on to promote his own political agenda. Kuzmin points out that both Gumilev and Kozhinov misuse and misinterpret the credible historical documents. He also clearly indicates that many "facts" cited by Lev Gumilev are misrepresented. Kuzmin contends that the Eurasian historian downplayed the significance of the Tatar Yoke and exaggerated the role of Khazaria in Russian and world history. He also exaggerated the amount of the "Khazar's tribute," the Jewish presence in Khazaria, and the role of Judaism in the religious life of the kingdom. Kuzmin claims that the Khazars were Karaites, and therefore unfamiliar with the Talmud. He adds that Gumilev exaggerated the level of technical development in Khazaria. Kuzmin argues that Gumilev's Eurasian bias blinded him to the significance and effects of many historical events.

In the ideological section of his critique, Kuzmin points to some Zionist ingredients in Gumilev's theories and exposes his secret Jewish sympathies. The academic argumentation of the first part of his paper now give way to the inflammatory style one might expect in a Nazi pamphlet. Gumilev and Kozhinov, he claims, are obviously Zionists, as clearly indicated by their fantastic overstatement of the role of Khazaria and the importance of the Jews in world history, which can be found on almost every page of Gumilev's book. Such a view, Kuzmin writes, can only benefit the Zionists: "Gumilev's description of Jews as the people who have demonstrated inexhaustible drive for two thousand years fuels the pride of Zionist Nazis *(siono-natzisti)*."[97] In an ad hominem attack, Kuzmin goes on to claim that Gumilev himself has Jewish blood — his mother, the poet Anna Akhmatova, grew up in a Jewish milieu and her real surname was Arens.[98] Kuzmin offers his own explanation of the origin of Gumilev's antisemitism:

Where did the writer's [i.e., Gumilev] unexpected and unusual antisemitism, come from? Abrupt changes of attitude are very typical for the people of mixed origins. It was perfectly demonstrated by Grigorii Klimov, when he described "Hitler's Political Bureau," in which everybody was either of mixed origins, or converted to Christianity, or had Jewish wives. But in our case antisemitism is intentional and overt.... Apparently, the author is trying to catch on this "bait" potential critics from the anti-Zionist camp. The leaders of Zionism have proved more than once that antisemitism serves the purposes of Zionism.[99]

Kuzmin further explains that the popularity and media attention given to Gumilev's theories results from their "Zionist leanings." He argues that the concept of ethnicity — and specifically Gumilev's definition of the ethnicity in terms of the behavior stereotype — exposes the congeniality of these theories to the doctrine of Zionism. Theodor Herzl's definition of nationhood, he claims, is identical to that of Gumilev. Kuzmin disavows the very idea of a Jewish ethnicity:

Gumilev's concept of ethnicity can refer both to the nation and to the pseudo-ethnic mafia. Then, in conformity with this theory one is entitled to call the relation between the two inter-national conflict. Then one can start to advocate the "Little People" and its right to have their own way of being *(samobytnost')* and develop their culture against that of the Big People.[100]

In closing, I would like to make some observations about the link between neo-Eurasianism and the theories of Lev Gumilev. It should be acknowledged that the historian never addressed the problems of geopolitics explicitly, and did not employ conventional geopolitical distinctions, like that between Atlanticism and Eurasianism that figures so prominently in the works of Alexander Dugin. Except for some passing remarks about the Varangians, Gumilev did not discuss the sea and maritime civilizations, so in many respects his discourse is closer to the paradigm of classical Eurasianism. He opposes Eurasia to the Romano-Germanic world and gives little attention to the United States. It is the antisemitic component of his theories that makes his works so congenial to contemporary neo-Eurasians and to the ideological position of the "false friends" of Eurasianism described by Nikolai Trubetskoi in *Racism*.

Just like these false friends of the 1920s, Gumilev believed that the cosmopolitan Jews with their socially menacing behavior stereotype are the real enemies of Eurasia. Any peaceful and mutually beneficial co-existence between Russians and nomads with the Jews is hardly possible. Their relationship will always produce "chimeras" and will never achieve a productive "symbiosis" characteristic of organic cooperation. In contrast to classical Eurasians, Gumilev considered the Jews an extra-territorial ethnic entity. Jews are disqualified from membership in the grand Eurasian family of ethnicities due to their negative "complementarity" and their parasitic nature and perfidious habits. The Jews used the territory of Eurasia as a "mere field of action." Their behavior stereotype was odious to indigenous Eurasians. Gumilev did not appeal directly to racial criteria, but certainly in his discussion of the racial composition of Eurasians alongside his views about both "harmless" and "dangerous" ethnic contact could easily lend themselves to interpretation in the spirit of racist doctrines.

Gumilev's conclusions about the relations between Eurasian ethnicities are hardly convincing. What strikes the reader of his book is not the Jewish behavior stereotype, but Gumilev's own antisemitic stereotypes camouflaged in pseudo-scientific terminology and a quasi-academic tone. In fact, his "enlightened" position reinforces the most primitive antisemitic stereotypes.

The focus on Eurasia does not mean that its significance can be confined to only one trend of nationalist ideology. His historical speculations, and his image of the malicious Khazarian Jews have had an impact that should not be underestimated on many other trends of Russian nationalism, as we shall see in the following chapters.

NOTES

1. L. Gumilev, "Menia nazivaiiut evraziitsem," *Nash sovremennik,* no. 1 (1991); L. Gumilev, "Zapiski poslednego evraziitsa," *Ritmi Evrazii* (Moscow 1993), 33–66. Gumilev has had little influence on the Neo-Eurasians, although they do find some aspects, such as his interest in geopolitical distinctions, congenial to their thinking. Dugin is sympathetic to many of his concepts.

2. The book was deposited in the All-Union Scientific Institute of Technical Information in 1979. The first six chapters are available in English translation published by the Progress Publishing House. See L. Gumilev, *Ethnogenesis and the Biosphere,* English ed. (Moscow 1990). My account of Gumilev's theory of ethnogenesis in this chapter is based primarily on this early book, complemented by quotations from his later works, which better articulate points important to this study.

3. L. Gumilev, *Etnogenez i biosfera Zemli* (Leningrad 1989), 58.

4. Ibid., 41, 37.

5. Ibid., 42.

6. The translation of this term as "drive" was suggested by Gumilev himself. The Russian original is derived from the Latin word for passion.

7. L. Gumilev, *Tisiacheletie vokrug Kaspiia* (Moscow 1993), 5.

8. Ibid., 406.

9. L. Gumilev, *Etnogenez i biosfera Zemli,* 408.

10. Ibid., 413, 415.

11. Ibid., 143.

12. L. Gumilev, *Tisiacheletie vokrug Kaspiia,* 41.

13. L. Gumilev, *Drevniaia Rus' i Velikaya Step'* (Moscow 1989), 371.

14. L. Gumilev, *Etnogenez i biosfera Zemli,* 302.

15. L. Gumilev, *Tisiacheletie vokrug Kaspiia* (Moscow 1993), 41.

16. Ibid., 42.

17. L. Gumilev, *Etnogenez i biosfera Zemli,* 86.

18. The term "anti-system" became one of the key concepts of right-wing ideology. Some nationalist ideologists identify anti-system with perestroika, cosmopolitanism, and "Russophobia." See S. Kosarenko, "Antisistema," *Den',* no. 8–10, 1993.

19. L. Gumilev, *Etnogenez i biosfera Zemli,* 460–61.

20. Ibid., 458.

21. The concept of the "Little People" as opposed to the "Great People" was originally introduced by the conservative historian of the French Revolution, Augustine Cochin, and later on elaborated by Igor Shafarevich in his book *Russophobia.* Shafarevich used "Small People" as a euphemism for the Jews, who do not share the standards of the majority of population. See my discussion of

Russophobia in chapter 5 on Neo-Slavophilism; and L. Gumilev, *Drevniia Rus' i Velikaia Step'*, 249.

22. L. Gumilev, *Drevniia Rus' i Velikaia Step'*, 282.

23. Ibid., 460.

24. Ibid., 256, 354.

25. The Qarmatians (or Carmathians) were an Islamic sect, essentially Ismaili. See M. Stern, *Studies in Early Ismailism,* (Jerusalem and Leiden, 1983).

26. Ibid., 261.

27. Ibid., 150.

28. This contradiction "between the idea of ethnicity as a process and the belief in the invariable negative characteristics of some ethnicities" was noticed by Igor Diakonov, a well-known Russian historian. I. Diakonov, *Ognennii diavol,* 226.

29. The fantastic myths about Khazaria are well-known outside of Russia as well, and derive in part from the lack of reliable information about the real Khazar kingdom. The novel *Khazarian Diary* by the Serbian writer Milorad Pavic became an international bestseller. The most solid and fundamental studies are those of D. M. Dunlop, *History of the Jewish Khazars* (Princeton, N.J. 1954); and M. Artamonov, *The History of Khazars* (Leningrad 1962).

30. See L. Gumilev, *Otkritie Khazarii: Istoriko-etnograficheskii etuid* (Moscow 1966); idem, "Khazaria and Caspian (Landscape and Ethnos)", Part I, *Soviet Geography,* 1964, vol. 5, no. 6, 54–68; idem, "New Data on the History of the Khazars," *Acta Archaeologica Academiae Scientiarum Hungaricae,* 19 (1967): 61–103; idem, "Khazaria i Kaspii," *Vestnik LGU* 6 (1974): 83–95; idem, "Khazaria i Terek," *Vestnik LGU* 24 (1974): 14–26; idem, "Khazarskoe pogrebenie i mesto, gde stoial Itil," *Soobscheniia Gosudarstvennogo Ermitazha* (Leningrad 1962), vol. 22: 56–58; idem, "Pamiatniki khazarskoi kulturi v delte Volgi", *Soobscheniia Gosudarstvennogo Ermitazha* (Leningrad 1965), vol. 26: 49–51; idem, "Sosedi khazar," *Strani i narodi Vostoka,* no. 14 (1965): 127–42.

31. L. Gumilev, *Drevniia Rus' i velikaia step'*, 241, 104.

32. Ibid., 247, 96.

33. Ibid., 133, 141, 108–109.

34. Ibid., 96, 134.

35. Ibid., 98–99.

36. Ibid., 103.

37. Ibid., 256.

38. Ibid., 106, 227.

39 Ibid., 248, 105–106.

40. Ibid., 116.

41. Ibid.

42. Ibid., 248.

43. Ibid., 114–15, 117–18. Gumilev justified this persecution by claiming that the Jews had always betrayed the Greeks in their wars with Persians, and that they provoked social instability and iconoclasm.

44. Ibid., 118.

45. Ibid., 124.

46. The word *radhanit* is derived from the Persian *radh* (road), and *don* (to know).

47. Ibid., 216.

48. Ibid., 127–28.

49. Ibid., 221.

50. It is true that some Spanish Jews and Jewish Radhanite traders of Persia were involved in the Slavonian slave trade (some of the slaves were Christian), whom the caliphs of Andalusia purchased to form their bodyguards. However, It should be observed, however, that Jews treated their slaves better in many cases. The Church did not object to slave dealing by the Jews. It feared only that Jews would convert Christian slaves to Judaism. See I. Abrahams, *Jewish Life in the Middle Ages* (London 1932), 114–15.

51. Ibid., 130, 146, 153, 313.

52. Ibid., 139.

53. Ibid., 133.

54. Ibid., 136.

55. Ibid., 137, 141. Some contemporary historians believe that a large number of the Khazar people converted to Judaism, not just the rulers and nobility.

56. Ibid., 134.

57. Ibid., 143.

58. Ibid., 151.

59. Ibid., 165, 167.

60. Ibid., 171.

61. Ibid., 171.

62. Ibid., 187.

63. Ibid., 193.

64. Ibid., 195.

65. Ibid., 141.

66. Ibid., 203.

67. Ibid., 479, 314.

68. L. Gumilev, *Drevniia Rus' i Velikaiia Step'*, 315.

69. Ibid., 212–14.

70. Ibid., 354.

71. Ibid., 327.

72. The French historian Ernst Renan suggested in *Judaism as a Race and as a Religion* (1883) that Eastern European Jews were of Khazar origin, a hypothesis

supported by many other historians , including Tadeusz Czacki, Max Gumpilowicz, Isaac Levinsohn, Hugo von Kutschera. See, e.g., Hugo von Kutschera, *Die Chasaren: Historische Studie* (Vienna 1910). Before Renan, this idea was also expressed by Abraham Elijahu Harkavi, *O iazike evreev, zhivshikh v drevnee vremia na Rusi i o slavianskikh slovakh, vstrechaiuschikhsia u evreiskikh pisatelei* (St. Petersburg 1869). Most recently, the hypothesis was elaborated by Arthur Koestler, *The Thirteenth Tribe. The Khazar Empire and its Heritage* (London 1976), and supported by the contemporary historian Kevin Brook, *The Jews of Khazaria* (Northvale, N.J. 1999).

73. An interesting example of the antisemitic use of the hypothesis of the Eastern European Jews' Khazar origin is the article by Sergei Zhdanov, "What Is Zionism in Action?" Zhdanov, vice-president of the International Slavic Academy of Education, Arts, and Culture, resorts to the popular argument that the Jews cannot blame others for antisemitism, because they themselves are descended from the nomads and thus have no connection with the Semites.

"Russophobes like to blame everybody and talk everywhere about antisemitism.... Antisemitism is hostility towards Semitic peoples based exclusively on national features.... But is it really true that the Jews belong to the Semites? Of course not. In reality, Semitic peoples include only Arab nations and ethnicities.... Sefardi Jews did have some relation to the Semitic peoples because of a few mixed marriages.... But the other wave of Jews came to Europe from Russia. It was so-called Ashkenazi inhabitants of the steppe regions. They accepted Judaism as...a more profitable religion. They have nothing to do with the Semitic people.... Consequently, antisemitism is related only to the Arabs.... Unfortunately, this phenomenon exists and it is exemplified by the Jews' hatred of Arabs.... Therefore, Israel is both a Zionist and antisemitic country...." See S. Zhdanov, "Shto takoe sionist v deisvii," *Russkii puls* 42 (1993): 28–29. Shaaban Khafez Shaaban, chairman of the radical Palestinian government-in-exile, also advocates this theory. He insists that "the ethnic aspect of the 'Jewish question' has lost not only academic, but any possible sense because of the very recent appearance of Turko-Mongol 'Ashkenazim.'" See Y. Antonov and K. Shaaban, "Ne toropites v Izrail," *Al-Quds,* no. 11 (1993). The same line of argument can be found in an article by the Israeli journalist and Communist Party member Robert David. Jewish intellectuals, he claims, instigated a conspiracy of silence on all aspects of the Khazar theory because it deprives Zionists of the opportunity to misuse the argument of antisemitism — since Ashkenazi Jews are not really Semites. See Robert David, "Veschii Oleg i velikaiia step'," *Vestnik evreiskoi sovetskoi kulturi* no. 13 (1989).

74. E. Blavatskaiia, *Tainaiia doktrina* (Riga 1937), vol. 1, 393.

75. The "Scythians" became popular in the first two decades of the twentieth century; they viewed Russia as a purgative agent in a fading Europe and sought

renewal in the aboriginal. Some saw the Bolshevik Revolution as a force liberating the "barbaric" national essence.

76. A. Wahrmund, *Das Gesetz des Nomadentums und die Heutige Judenherrshaft* (Korisruhe and Leipzig 1887).

77. It is interesting to note that recently Wahrmund has been rediscovered by the German philosopher Reinhold Oberlechter. In his paper "The Farmers and the Nomads. The Anti-Neolithic Counter-Revolution as a Law of Modernity," he argued that "whatever the nomads call themselves, the Golden Horde or the Chosen People, their animality is obvious in all the spheres of life.... They transform everything into steppe and desert." His paper was translated into Russian and published by the Russian fascist magazine *Ataka* 72 (1995): 14–17.

78. This idea was especially articulated in A. Rosenberg, *Plague in Russia* (1922). See W. Laqueur, *Russia and Germany Hitler's Mentors* (Washington 1991), 112. I quote the Russian edition of this book.

79. See L. Gumilev, *Chernaiia legenda. Druziia i nedrugi Velikoi Stepi* (Moscow 1994), 305.

80. Ibid., 283: "Judean propaganda played the role of catalyst in the conversion of the Slavs into Orthodoxy."

81. See M. Artamonov, "Khazari i Rus," in *Mir L'va Gumileva. Arabeski istorii,* edited by A. Kurkchi (Moscow 1994), 334–36. Artamonov influenced other Soviet historians of Khazaria as well. Svetlana Pletneva, whose account of Khazar history is much better balanced, also blames the Khazars for the "speculative resale of goods," "commercial parasitism" and the domination of Jewish capital over the common people. See S. Pletneva, *Khazari* (Moscow 1986), 70–71.

82. See I. Mirovich, "Lev Gumilev i drugie," *Strana i mir,* no. 2 (1991); I. Diakonov et al., "Etika etnogenetiki" (Collection of articles), *Neva,* no. 4 (1992): 223–46; A. Yanov, "Uchenie L'va Gumileva," *Svobodnaiia misl,* no. 17 (1992).

83. See V. Kozhinov, "Istoriia Rusi i russkogo slova," *Nash sovremennik,* no. 10–12 (1992); idem, "Vot uzh deistvitel'no khazarskie strasti," *Molodaiia gvardiia,* no. 11–12 (1993); Metropolitan Ioann, "Torzhestvo pravoslaviia," *Nash sovremennik,* no. 4 (1993): 11–12.

84. Y. Sedych-Bondarenko, "Vidali, kto prishel," *Den',* no. 27 (1993).

85. V. Kozhinov, "Istoriia Rusi i russkogo slova," part 1, *Nash sovremennik,* no. 10 (1992): 167–69.

86. Ibid.

87. V. Kozhinov, "Istoriia Rusi i russkogo slova," part 2, *Nash sovremennik,* no. 11 (1992): 169.

88. Kharezm (Khwarezm) was ancient central Asian state (now Uzbekistan and Turkmenistan). Part of the empire of Cyrus the Great (6th cent. B.C.), Khorezm was conquered by the Arabs and converted to Islam in the 7th cent. A.D. Briefly

independent in the late 12th cent., it ruled from the Caspian Sea to Bukhara and Samarkand, but fell to Genghis Khan (1221), to Timur (late 14th cent.), and then to the Uzbeks (early 16th cent.), who called it the khanate of Khiva.

89. Kozhinov claims that according to the orientalist Bartold, the word *habr* is derived from the Hebrew *haver,* which is identical to the German *genosse* and Russian *tovarisch.* This *haber-tovarisch,* he contends, ran from the eighth through the twentieth centuries.

90. V. Kozhinov, "Istoriia Rusi i russkogo slova," *Nash sovremennik,* no. 11 (1992): 173.

91. Ibid.

92. V. Kozhinov, "Istoriia Rusi i russkogo slova," *Nash sovremennik,* no. 12 (1992): 176.

93. *Ilia Muromets i Zhidovin* in Russian. In colloquial Russian the word *Zhidovin (zhid)* has pronounced antisemitic implications (similar to the English *kike*). In old Slavonic languages, however, it did not necessarily have a pejorative meaning. It is believed that the word *Zhidovin* refers to the Khazar warrior.

94. Ibid., no. 12, 172.

95. S. Kosarenko, "Antisistema," *Den',* no. 8 (1993).

96. A. Kuzmin, "Khazarskie stradaniia," *Molodaiia gvardiia,* 5–6 (1993): 235, 245–50.

97. Ibid.

98. Ibid., 235–36.

99. Ibid., 251–52.

100. Ibid., 251.

CHAPTER 3

National Bolshevism:
The Secret Nature of Capitalism
and the Economic Reforms

The growth of the neo-communist movement in Russia was triggered by the disappointment felt by a large proportion of population with the general course of economic reform. The introduction of a market economy was associated in the eyes of many Russians with the violation of basic norms of social justice, for the reforms had produced rapid and sharp social stratification. The legal system and development of the institutional infrastructure of the new liberal state, including both economic and political institutions, did not make adequate provision against corruption and abuse of power by state officials. Political leaders ignored the welfare of those most vulnerable to the effects of the economic reforms, and even the liberal parties failed to address these issues adequately. These social processes paved the way for the formation of several new communist parties. Many old communist slogans and rhetoric were resurrected, for the unexpected difficulties of the period of transition to a market economy generated nostalgia for the lost Soviet past with its seeming stability and security. Such popular longings were quickly exploited by leaders of the new communist movements, and their concerns began to extend to some spheres traditionally associated exclusively with Russian nationalism — the traditional Russian community, the empire, and the glory of Russia. Gradually, slogans calling for restoration of the USSR have supplanted the strictly Marxist concerns. This ideological expansion has contributed to the overall popularity of the movement and to its integration with the nationalist opposition to the government.

The post-Soviet communist movements comprise various groups whose programs vary and who take a variety of attitudes toward Jewish matters. The largest is the Communist Party of the Russian Federation (KPRF) led by Gennadi Ziuganov, followed by the Russian Communist Worker's Party led by Victor Anpilov. Among the ideological publications we find *Glasnost, Molniia, Bumbarash, Kontrargumenty i kontrfakyi,* and *Narodnaia pravda.* My analysis in this chapter is based for the most part on articles in

Sovetskaiia Rossiia, Pravda, Molodaiia gvardiia, and *Al-Quds,* which reflect the official positions of the two largest communist parties. Reflecting the movement originating in the Soviet Union which survived in Russian ˈmigrˈ circles in the 1920s and 1930s, I will refer to these groups as "National Bolsheviks." The origins and ideology of these groups was delineated by the late Michael Agursky in *The Third Rome* (1987).[1] The discussion in this chapter will center on National Bolshevism in the post-Soviet period.[2]

The attitude to the Jews of the early leaders of the communist and socialist movements was quite ambivalent, although many leaders of the international communist movement were opposed to antisemitism.[3] However, it would be wrong to ignore the antisemitic ideas expressed by other leaders of the movement, whose inspiration was uniquely socialist.[4] The post-Soviet leaders of National Bolshevism reproduce and reinforce these ideas. Another source for their antisemitism lies in the Soviet anti-Zionist ideological campaign that peaked in the 1970s I will focus here on the original contribution of contemporary advocates of communism to antisemitic ideology. They show great creativity in applying old antisemitic socialist clichés and projecting the old stereotypes on current situations.

National Bolshevism can be best understood as a response to the discussion on the origins of Russian communism. Some Russian intellectuals consider communism to be absolutely alien to the traditional values of Russian society, while others have argued the opposite.[5] National Bolsheviks try to reconcile these two standpoints. They follow Berdiaev when they claim that communism is part and parcel of Russian traditional political thought, and that the Russian soul has a natural proclivity for socialist organization, as found in the traditional Russian village community. The ideal of equality (including an equitable distribution of wealth) pervades the communal morality of Russian peasants. National Bolsheviks see Russian communism in opposition to "Western communism." Some make use of ethnic categories in their criticism, saying, for example, that Jewish revolutionaries are representative of Western communism, and failed to understand the occult forces that drove the Russian Revolution. National Bolsheviks do not believe in the discontinuity of Russian history, as do the neo-Slavophiles. Moreover, the National Bolsheviks hold that Soviet civilization incarnated many values of traditional Russian civilization more adequately than did Russia under the tsars. To bridge the gap between the two periods they coined a special term: "Russian-Soviet civilization," and some of them identify the mystical Russian idea *(zagadochnaia russkaya dusha)* with socialism.[6] The true break in Russian history, they say, is the post-Soviet period of transition to liberal economic and political reforms, a time in which the country lost its crucial social identity. The economic reforms of Mikhail Gorbachev halted the natural course of development of Russian history.

This new concept of a socialist Russian core identity forced National Bolsheviks to introduce certain amendments to classical Marxist doctrine. National Bolsheviks believe the main class struggle today has moved away from relations between different classes inside the country to the international arena. The class struggle has assumed the character of an international opposition between affluent and poor nations. Some neo-communists invoke the theory of a "capitalist world-economy" elaborated by the American neo-Marxist, Immanuel Wallerstein and the Dutch economist André Frank.[7] According to their views, exploitation now operates through the system of imperialistic economic control by "world core" countries over those of the "periphery" and "semi-periphery." The imperialists have managed to suborn the proletariat of the West by using funds appropriated from the third and former second-world countries. They moved all non-profitable businesses overseas. Even before the "counter-revolution" in Russia, world capital misappropriated part of the surplus product of the socialist countries. Today the "world core" imposes upon Russia (and the third world) unequal distribution of labor and unequal trade exchange. Third world countries are merely a source of cheap raw materials. The political and economic reforms initiated by Mikhail Gorbachev and the liberals put Russia in the position of a third-world country, and enabled the "world core" countries to take advantage of the situation. This context of the discussion allows us to understand better the place of the Jewish aspect in National Bolshevik ideology.

The question of the role of the Jews in the world distribution of wealth and labor is quite prominent in the writings of National Bolsheviks, who, in contrast to the Russians, are described as paradigmatic capitalists and model representatives of the bourgeoisie.[8] The class conflict taking place today has a certain ethnic dimension, for many Russian neo-communists link the initiation of economic reform and liberal political changes with attempts by the Jews to promote their own economic and political interests. The collapse of the old communist regime is blamed on their subversive economic and intellectual efforts, prepared and directed by two forces controlled by the Jews — the powerful economic forces outside the country and the subversive dissident movement inside the USSR. These assumptions — although not all of them are clearly spelled out in their publications — govern the discourse of Neo-Bolsheviks.

Many antisemitic ideas of this sort are supported by the authority of Karl Marx. Russian Bolsheviks have rediscovered and given a new life to Marx's early essay "Zur Judenfrage." Marx's basic idea in this essay is quite simple: the Jews are the most adamant proponents of the pecuniary capitalist spirit, as well as the spirit of "haggling," "money-grubbing and gain."[9] This notion is frequently invoked and elaborated in the writings of the neo-communist leaders. Following Marx, for example, Viktor Tiulkin, first secretary of the Central Committee of the Russian Communist Workers' Party, in his *Pravda* article identified the spirit of usury with Jewishness.[10] The most extensive discussion of the relevance of the Marxian idea for the present-day economic situation can be found in Yurii Belov's article "Shylock and Kuzma," which will be discussed later on in this chapter.[11] Belov is a leader of the Communist Worker's Party.

National Bolsheviks are especially sensitive to the presence of international Jewish capital in Russia and the visible participation of some Jews in business activity during the perestroika period. Two main interrelated issues are brought into discussion: the "intervention" of international capital in Russian economic life and political impact of Zionists on Russian politics; and the role of Russian Jews in newly-established financial institutions.

"HOLDERS OF THE CONTROLLING SHARE OF WORLD STOCKS"

Many National Bolsheviks believe that capitalism is a "Jewish idea. On this point they diverge significantly from the classical Marxist thesis that the rise of capitalism resulted from technical progress, primarily after advances in the mode of production. Capitalism, the National Bolsheviks assert, is a by-product of the Judaized (Judeo-Christian) Western civilization that still pretends to be Christian. Sergei Kara-Murza, a prominent ideologist of the movement, contends that the central myth of the Judeo-Christian consciousness is the belief that it is the only "right" civilization, while others are backward and underdeveloped.[12] Western civilization is racist and elitist insofar as it does not treat the people of non-capitalist civilizations as equals. The ruling elite of this civilization believes that only one billion of the world population, the "golden billion," can enjoy a high standard of living due to the scarcity of natural resources.[13] In this context post-communist Russia is said to be especially important as a source of cheap labor and raw materials necessary for the lifestyle of the "golden billion" of the Judeo-Protestant West, that is, the new "Chosen People." The Jewish doctrine of "election," according to this argument, is a decisive ingredient of the "spirit of capitalism." Gennadii Ziuganov, Chairman of the Russian Communist Party, contends that from the nineteenth century on the Jewish Diaspora started to shape the Western world-view, culture and ideology and since that time its influence has constantly grown.... Western self-consciousness is shaped by the ideas of election, special calling and mission in the world, ideas which are so characteristic of the religious faith of the Judaists.[14]

The United States is a paradigmatic capitalist civilization. Quite naturally, it is described by National Bolsheviks as the purest embodiment of present day Jewish ideals and attitudes. Tatiana Glushkova, a poet and National Bolshevik publicist, contends that America borrowed its cult of the "golden calf" from the Jews.[15] In a similar vein, Gennadii Ziuganov claims that American "covenant theology" perfectly demonstrates the kinship between Jews and Americans:

> The Protestant immigrants identified themselves with the lawful heirs of the covenant, which was made between the forefather Abraham and God long before the birth of Jesus. According to this doctrine, America is the last link in the chain of the states and generations that can be traced back to Abraham. America is a contemporary New Israel populated with the "Chosen People." This is a central concept of the American national consciousness....[16]

According to Ziuganov, today there are many economically active groups that have inherited the Jewish ideology of "Chosen People" — British Protestants, Americans, non-Protestant Western Europeans — yet one can still easily distinguish Jewish financial and economic leaders as the most powerful in the world of capital. "As its market grows," Ziuganov argues, "the Jewish Diaspora which traditionally controlled the financial life of the continent, turns into the holder of the 'controlling share of stock' of the whole economic system of Western civilization."[17]

Gennadii Shimanov's notorious paper, "On the Secret Nature of Capitalism," is an extensive elaboration and articulation of the idea that the Jews are the "holders of the controlling share of world stocks."[18] His narrative of the genealogy of monopolistic capitalism integrates Marx's early reference to the "Jewish spirit of bourgeois society," Lenin's critique of imperialism as the highest stage in the development of capitalism, and the theory of a conspiracy of Jewish bankers.[19] The banking business, Shimanov argues, is the primary source of power and the heart of the whole structure of capitalist society. Jews traditionally have controlled the main flow of capital and were the dominating figures in the financial world of the European countries. "The superiority of the Jews over Christianity in the financial sphere was so overwhelming that even their formal lack of political rights could not deprive them of their actual power over their religious rivals."[20]

The transition from agriculture to money-lending and trade was not imposed upon the Jews by medieval persecution and their status as outcasts. Rather, it was determined by the Jewish spirit of money-grubbing and unlimited greed for gain inspired by the principles of their religion.

The aims the Jewish bankers, Shimanov argues, transcend the merely economic. Ultimately Jews are motivated not by the pure impulse of acquisition but by striving for world domination. Jewish financial power was magnified by mutual support and solidarity in deals made with gentiles. The principles and regulations of Jewish religious law as enunciated in Talmud specifically regulate economic activity with the gentile world. In particular, the Jewish *kahal* [community] is allowed to sell to a particular Jew a monopoly on trade with some particular gentile (the laws of *miropia* and *hazakah*). Price-fixing would then eliminate competition between the Jews in their deals with the gentile world, and would force the gentile customer to buy a particular product for a particular price.[21] The same religious laws, Shimanov alleges, also operate in the everyday business ethics of modern Jewish financiers: "In practice, usurers, traders, bankers and all other kinds of dealers constitute a titanic international cartel invisible to the outside world."[22] Bankers of Jewish descent act in concert, synchronizing and coordinating their policies with respect to currencies, interest rates, and the political climate in various countries. Consequently, they are invulnerable to the competition from gentiles.

It is not surprising that with the emergence of the modern banking system the Jews were better equipped than anyone to take it over. Shimanov points out that this takeover demonstrated the continuity of the Jews' financial domination and did not express a new trend. The only novelty, he argues, is the increased visibility of the real owners of world economic wealth. Modern banking started in the nineteenth century with the rise of the House of Rothschild. "In comparison with the Rothschilds," Shimanov claims, "all the kings of Europe looked like destitute beggars. The castles and palaces of the Rothschilds exceeded even the possessions of the kings of France and Queen Victoria."[23] The financial empire of the Rothschilds and other Jewish bankers greatly influenced the foreign and domestic policies of European countries. It has controlled the development of industry and has seized its most profitable branches. It determined styles and tastes in culture and art and manipulated public opinion through the press. However, this total control over the economic and socio-political life of Europe became too conspicuous and eventually the Jewish banking establishment realized that it must conceal its enormous financial and political clout and restructure its financial activity in such a way that its leadership and manipulation could become invisible. This was nothing new, only a realization of centuries-old dreams. "Jewry functioned for 2000 years as a semi-secret organization spread out all over the globe. It combined overt activity with secret activity."[24]

It was vitally important for the Jews to make their power anonymous. New tactics included the fabrication of firms with dummy owners and the transformation of Jewish-owned banking houses into joint-stock banks that were then given geographical names so as not to reveal their owners' names. This process created the impression that Jewish bankers had lost their power and control over the financial sphere. However, the change in the structure of financial power did not mean the end of Jewish financial domination. However, Jewish financial domination continued under this camouflage in an even more advanced stage.

Jewish capital was invested in the new apparently cosmopolitan banks, in which the share of particular Jewish bankers seemed negligible. Meanwhile, an individual banker's real power over the sum of the joint-stock was crucial due to his unknown union with the holder of the controlling share of stock. The benefits of the new system were spectacular, since it allowed Jewish bankers to control the capital of all stock-holders and investors and to rob them by means of fictitious bankruptcies.

The bankers also concealed their power by promoting Aryan financiers who had demonstrated loyalty to the Jewish cause. Many of these loyal Aryan financiers belonged to Masonic lodges where they were educated in the Jewish spirit. With such figures in highly-visible positions in the financial world, the Jewish financial elite popularized the American myth that claimed to offer fantastic social mobility in the new world and to instill the idea that prominent non-Jewish financiers and manufacturers obtained their power only by virtue of their own talent and effort. In reality the Aryan bankers served only as the tools of the all-powerful Jewish financial elite. For instance, the rise of the Rockefellers became possible only by virtue of political and financial support from the Jewish banking establishment. The economic boom in the United States, Shimanov goes on to argue, was brought about only by means of the enormous flow of European banking capital owned by the Jewish financial elite. It results from the nineteenth-century immigration of Jewish bankers from Europe to the United States, where the political climate was more favorable to their sinister activity. The banking houses of the Schiffs, Rothschilds, Warburgs, Guggenheims, Lehmans, Seligmans, Sachses, Kuhns, Loebs, and Levensons have determined the success, dynamics, and velocity of the American economy.[25] Shimanov contends that it is the Jewish banking families rather than the Rockefellers and other conspicuous false-fronts of Jewish capital that have transformed America into the "leading state of the capitalist world, which spreads its influence all over the globe."

Imperialism was defined by Shimanov as a non-commercial system within the secret power structure of the Jewish bankers. The institutions and practices of capitalist society in general are favorable for the Jewish elite, both in terms of the extent and range of power they have been able to acquire, and in terms of its secrecy. This is only natural, since they have shaped and structured these institutions themselves.

Of course, Shimanov heavily exaggerates the actual power of the Rothschilds and other European Jewish bankers during the nineteenth century; the "era of the Rothschilds" is a historical myth. In the course of the American industrial revolution and the rise of the American economy the "Jewish dukes" were hardly more important than the "robber barons." It is true that the large-scale production realized by the robber barons required financing from private banks, but the industrialists themselves controlled many banking houses.

Moreover, Protestant-owned banks were far more prominent than Jewish-owned banks, and the majority of those he mentions did not move to America from Europe but came into being in the United States. In Gerald Krefetz's study of the myth of Jewish financial domination, he points out that

> Jewish wealth was largely a result of the success of Jewish-German immigrants, who brought with them great ambitions, little capital, and few skills. Consequently, peddling and petty retailing were the start of Goldmans, Guggenheims, Lehmans, Loebs, Sachses, and Kuhns. Later, it became a point of pride and family honor whether one's ancestors "started with a wagon" or started on foot."[26]

Krefetz also remarks that in size and power the Jewish banking houses cannot compare with the Protestant banks like the J. P. Morgan, Drexel, Gould, Fisk, Harriman, and Hill.[27]

It is interesting to note that Max Weber, in his study of the rise of capitalism did not give great importance to Jewish commercial activity in its development. The industrial revolution itself generated the financial resources necessary for the development of modern banking, and in any case, industrial growth did not depend on financial resources to the degree suggested by Shimanov and other critics of Jewish financial power. Weber also emphasized the incompatibility of a "dualism of internal and external morality" with the spirit of capitalist business activity. Weber characterized this dualism of external and internal morality and the business practices it entailed — permission to accept interest from foreigners who did not belong to the community, tax farming, political financing of various kinds — as "irrational": "But all this was pariah capitalism, not rational capitalism such as developed in the West," he remarked. "Consequently, few Jews can be found among the creators of the modern economy, the large entrepreneurs; this type was Christian and only conceivable in Christianity."[28] Most of the robber barons, said by Shimanov to be fronts for the Jewish bankers, were in fact active Christians, and were the messengers of the "rational" capitalism that heralded a new type of civilization.

Clearly Shimanov is not offering an accurate depiction of the growth of the American economy, but is merely reinforcing well-known anti-Jewish stereotypes. A dualism of internal and external morality is hardly specific to Jewish commercial activity, and is not conducive to the development of rational capitalism in any case. Nor are Jews uniquely possessive and acquisitive.

While Shimanov's history of the rise of the American economy would not necessarily convince other proponents of National Bolshevism, many of them would share some of his assumptions, such as a belief in the secret nature of capitalism and the special Jewish contribution to its development. They would also agree that in the course of human history Jews have managed to seize world economic power and to camouflage this power. It is important to emphasize that Jewish bankers and industrialists are taken as the quintessential and archetypal capitalists, and it is natural for Jews to worship Mammon, the god of money. Stories of past and present Jewish "manipulators of wealth" — the Rothschilds, Schiffs, Poliakovs, Ginzburgs, Reichmans, Bronfmans, Gutniks — occupy an important place in their writings.[29] As the National Bolshevik Artemii Volokhov put it: "No wonder the working people hate the Jewish usurers: they have turned their tears, sweat and blood into gold."[30]

INTERNATIONAL JEWISH FINANCIAL SHARKS
IN THE TROUBLED WATERS OF PERESTROIKA

National Bolsheviks believe that post-communist Russia, socially and economically disorganized, and the main source of world reserves of raw materials, has become a new Klondike — an easy prey for the Jewish financial manipulators and transnational corporations. International economic and financial organizations — such as the International Monetary Fund (IMF), Trilateral Commission, Federal Reserve System, Bilderberg Club, European Bank of Development and Cooperation — are described in National Bolshevik publications as institutions completely controlled, or at least greatly influenced, by Jews. These organizations, especially its Jewish members, are blamed for the collapse of the USSR and for taking advantage of the drastic political changes brought about by perestroika. National Bolsheviks attack the prominent representatives of international business, political leaders, and intellectuals of Jewish origin who exert a visible (but greatly exaggerated) influence on Russian social and political life.

Examining the activities of those at the "top of world financial Zionism" who have supported perestroika and contributed to the development of the destructive forces associated with it, is an important item on the agenda of National Bolshevik periodicals.

George Soros, a legendary billionaire speculator, is an emblematic subversive Jewish figure whose name is most often invoked in this context. He became famous in the former Soviet Union and Eastern Europe as a philanthropist. In only three years (1991–1993) Soros contributed or committed around one billion dollars to support Russian scholars. Russian nationalists suspect that his activity in Russia is not disinterested, and in their publications, they emphasize the Soros's Jewish origins.[31] Some of these sources suggest that he is closely connected with Jewish and Zionist organizations and is an agent of the Israeli secret intelligence service, the Mossad, or alternatively, the American CIA. Supposedly, he had an important role in undermining the former communist regime, it is said that he subsidized the economic reforms of Mikhail Gorbachev and was an unofficial advisor to Boris Yeltsin. He also exercises influence over Russian politics through the IMF and Trilateral Commission. The secret international club, Magisterium, is described as an important channel of his influence.[32] Oleg Platonov, a "Masonologist," claims that Soros subsidized the "anti-Russian activities" of the perestroika leaders and the development of the "500 days" economic program that was designed to ruin the Soviet economy.[33] The chairman of the Security Committee of the Russian Duma, Ilukhin, claims that the special academic and educational programs supported by Soros are devised to indoctrinate and educate the Russian people in an anti-patriotic and cosmopolitan spirit.[34] Soros's intelligence activities include the collection of information about developments in Russian science. Ilukhin also claims that Soros personally was responsible for the sharp decrease in the exchange-value of the ruble in October 1994, and has taken full advantage of the policy of privatization.[35]

Robert Maxwell, a British publishing and media magnate, died in mysterious circumstances in November 1991.[36] Israel Shamir, *Pravda*'s reporter in Israel, claims that Maxwell was a Mossad agent, having become rich and powerful from the secret financial support of the Israeli intelligence agency. Maxwell's media empire, based in London, was supposedly a tool of the Mossad for controlling and manipulating public opinion in Great Britain and the rest of the world. Shamir contends that Maxwell — on instructions from the Israeli intelligence service — facilitated Gorbachev's popularity in the West through his newspaper empire. During the perestroika period, Gorbachev was especially important to the Jews as a subversive force in Russia. When the Mossad decided to put Yeltsin into office, Maxwell made every effort to dampen Gorbachev's popularity in "the most objective media of the world." Shamir believes that Mossad agents murdered Maxwell, who had wanted more money from the agency following his bankruptcy and had threatened to expose its role in Russian events.[37] Of course, Shamir's contention is neither plausible nor original. True, the world's tabloid press discussed Maxwell's supposed Mossad links along with dozens of other fantastic versions of his death. An article in the more reputable *Isvestiia* stated that Maxwell did have intensive contacts with the KGB, and Moscow suspected him of being a British double agent.[38] But there is no evidence that Maxwell was a Mossad agent. Shamir's eager reporting seems largely conditioned by his conception of the Mossad as "not an imaginary, but a real Soviet of the Elders of Zion."[39]

Jacques Attali, a director of the European Bank for Reconstruction and Development, is another important target for neo-Bolshevik attacks as a powerful European banker acting against Russian interests. In one newspaper article he is ironically characterized as a "well-known 'benefactor' of the Soviet Union whose name will stay in Russian history together with the names of such popular rascals of world usury as Armand Hammer[40] and George Soros."[41] Attali's offer of $50 million dollars to convert a military plant in Belorussia into a factory for making luxury diplomatic buses was seen as an attempt to undermine Russian military power.[42]

American theoreticians of a market economy and libertarianism are also considered enemies of Russia, whose economic disasters are blamed on the "precepts of a rabbi from Chicago" — the Nobel Laureate in Economics Milton Friedman — and the misleading and devastating advice of the "Learned Elders of Harvard."[43] Jeffrey Sachs, a professor of economics and director of the Center of Russian Studies at Harvard University, is one of the favorite villains in National Bolshevik publications. He is blamed for the theoretical justification of the "shock therapy" economic policy and "free pricing" carried out by the government of Yegor Gaidar. General Viktor Filatov, editor-in-chief of the *Journal of Military History,* has written that the "Zionist Mafia determines the course of economic reforms. Everybody knows that Russian economics is dominated by the American Jew Sachs."[44]

Zionist multimillionaires Rothschilds, Lazards, Guggenheims, Sachses and others using their protégés in the White House...forced the American government to acknowledge the state of Israel....[45] Sachs helped Zionists to seize power in the U.S. It is possible that our Sachs came from the same Sachs family. He is doing the same thing as they did, trying to turn Russia into the sheepdog of international Zionism.[46]

One typical caricature in a small fascist newspaper depicts two religious Jews holding an advertisement: "Welcome to the sale of Russia." The export of raw materials and natural resources to the West is often blamed on the Jewish beneficiaries of the "plunder of Russia."

In the past several years, the Russian media have discussed intensively the negotiations and potential agreements between Russian state institutions and private businesses and the Jews in the diamond industries of South Africa, Israel, and Great Britain, focusing on the diamond empire of Oppenheimer-Rothschild-Samuel.[47] One journalist spotlighted the sinister role of the De Beers company in the plunder of Russia, stating (correctly) that for more than thirty years, the London-based Central Selling Organization of De Beers served as a mediator in the trade of Russian rough diamonds. It sold Russian diamonds on the international market for significantly higher prices than the fixed prices paid to the major diamond producers. De Beers included large first-rate Russian diamonds in the mixture with other, less valuable, diamonds, allowing the company to raise prices for the whole. In accordance with their long-term contracts, Russians thus cannot sell diamonds independently on the world market. De Beers forces Russia to keep renewing this "colonialist contract" and takes advantage of the economic situation, relying on the corrupt officials of the Russian Diamonds and Gold Company.[48] Several articles in *Pravda* describe the negotiations between Russian officials, the Israeli diamond industry, and businessmen concerning the cutting of Russian diamonds and emeralds in Israel. The journalists claim that the deals are unfair, because the Israelis take an extremely high profit margin, while Russian diamond factories can hardly stay in business.[49]

The commodities and natural resources company, Siabeko, run by Boris Birnstein, an Israeli-Canadian businessmen and former Soviet citizen, is also charged with the depredation. Articles in the Russian media claimed that Birnstein bought raw materials at prices significantly lower than international norms, owing to his secret ties with top government officials.[50] He was also accused of laundering communist party money abroad, and not surprisingly, some National Bolsheviks claim that Birnstein is a Mossad agent. In a 1993 speech in the Duma, Iona Andronov expanded on this theme, asserting that Birnstein, on instruction by the Mossad, tried to destabilize the political situation in Russia by provoking serious conflicts within the political administration through fabricated documents intended to compromise some Russian patriots in the government.[51]

Concern over Western economic influence in Russia often narrows down to a focus on the presence of Jews in Western corporations who have expanded their operations to Russia. An article in *Al-Quds* is symptomatic. Entitled "McDonalds: The Evil Empire in Russia," it accuses "Cohen," the Canadian owner of the Russian chain of fast food restaurants, of attempting to "propagate food which does not square with Russian traditions and customs," a project only possible after perestroika. "Perestroika has collapsed," the author laments, "but McDonalds did not...." Supposedly, Cohen's Russian revenues equals dozens of years' income from McDonalds in Canada. "Russians let Cohen ravage its economy."[52] McDonalds is, of course, the very symbol of the global and homogenized culture of capitalism, while its Jewish owner is the very symbol of the forces that are taking over Russia.

The activities of Marc Rich are discussed in the same context. Rich was involved in international drug trafficking and arms smuggling; in 1983, he opened his first firm in Moscow, which consisted for the most part in the illegal export of raw materials, especially oil, and laundering money by investing it in Russian enterprises and stock companies. He contracted to sell oil recovered through the purification of waste from oil refineries. In reality, he did not purify any waste, but bribed officials and took oil directly from the pipes.[53] Not surprisingly, the article written by *Den*'s Analytic Center emphasized Rich's Jewish origins and claimed he, too, was a Mossad agent.[54]

Reporting on the doings of known Jewish bankers or villains might not seem particularly antisemitic to an outsider perusing the Russian press. However, the underlying meaning of such reportage can be understood only against the background and in the context of the philosophy of history found in National Bolshevik periodicals. Special attention to Jewish matters is neither a coincidence nor an objective reflection of social and ethnic realities. Nor do the authors need to articulate their antisemitic meaning or use abusive or denigrating language to convey the message. The very context of these periodicals clearly suggests an interpretation of, say, an article about the adventures of some "new businessmen" with a non-Russian last name.

The authors of these publications might think that in the way they frame their stories, they provide empirical support for speculative arguments made by some communist ideologists. However, the connection between the facts and theory is the reverse. The pattern of explanation and the narrative structure themselves guide the choice of the data and shape the social visions of the National Bolsheviks. Their ideological framework can easily accommodate certain types of ideological information (stories of greedy Russian Shylocks) and will exclude any evidence to the contrary. National Bolsheviks do not see much difference between the activities of George Soros and Jeffrey Sachs, on the one hand, and the criminal Marc Rich on the other. They do not distinguish between the types of activity in which these people are involved. Both activities symbolize for them the coming of the new capitalist Jewish order. The narrative of the class struggle, incarnated into the ethnic confrontation between Russians and Jews, makes the National Bolsheviks blind to the differences.

THE "NEW RUSSIANS" = JEWS

Today the term "New Russians" is widely used to designate the recently-created upper class of society that controls most enterprises and capital in the country. Apart from purely economic factors like the level of income, the characteristics of the new class include the special way it displays wealth and wastes money. Sociological polls suggest that the New Russians actually constitute an insignificant segment of the population.[55]

Many National Bolshevik ideologists believe the New Russians to be traitors to Soviet civilization, collaborating with foreign capitalists in the plunder of their own country. They are accused of indifference to their own countrymen and are said to have lost any sense of national identity.

The link between New Russians and Jews was the focus of an article by Yurii Belov of the Communist Workers' Party. Belov contends that any analysis of political and economic processes in contemporary Russia requires an understanding of "Jewhood." Karl Marx had demystified the phenomenon of Jewishness by distinguishing between the faith of the "hypocritical Jew of the Sabbath" and the "secular cult of the Jew." Marx also wrote: "The god of the Jews has been secularized and has become the god of the world." This Jewish god, Belov asserts, is money. Real emancipation is not the civil emancipation of the Jews, but rather the emancipation of society from Jewishness, — the "emancipation from haggling and money." Belov argues that this Marxist analysis allows one to conceptualize perestroika as a transplant of the "Judaized" Western model of capitalist societies to Russia. Yurii Belov clearly identifies the New Russians with the Jews:

> Jewry became a universal phenomenon in the bourgeois epoch marked
> by the formation of the egoistic man ruthless to his neighbors.... Any
> huckster is infected with Jewishness even if he belongs to other eth-

nicity and he likes to talk about his Russianness. "Jewishness"...has occupied Russia.[56]

This new capitalist spirit, Belov goes on to argue, is absolutely alien to Russian history and traditions. Socialism is a natural phenomenon in Russian national history where "the communal traditions, collectivism and the fight for social justice" always had a high currency. Belov laments that today the Jewish spirit of haggling permeates the whole fabric of Russian society, from economics and politics to everyday life. He believes that recent disasters of Russian history such as the economic reforms, the collapse of the USSR, the defamation of Russian history, and the appearance of leaders like Zhirinovskii are the result of the Jewish spirit of haggling in the attempts of new Russian leaders to make political capital by trading on and taking advantage of the pain and suffering of the Russian people.[57]

In a similar vein, Yurii Belov claims that xenophobia is alien to the Russian people and that "anti-Jewish sentiments express the natural reaction to the activity of the 'standard-bearers' of militant 'Jewry,' that is, to those who chose the line of Shylock."[58]

Sergei Kara-Murza, another National Bolshevik theoretician, similarly discusses the social significance of the new Russians, focusing on the implications of perestroika for moral consciousness.[59] The key to understanding the reforms, he contends, is through their relation to the Reformation. Perestroika sanctified the spirit of profit, usury, and other commercial activity. The Protestant Reformation in its day represented a turn away from the moral ideals of the Gospels to those of the Old Testament: the Protestant ethic praised by Max Weber is only a slight modification of the old Jewish ethic. Images and metaphors taken from the Old Testament for use by the champions of reform point to the serious shift in moral attitudes. Kara-Murza points to the use of "Masonic" construction terminology by the early reformers, and suggests that reformers went on to develop moral attitudes derived from the myths found in the biblical book of Exodus.[60]

The Exodus metaphor was originally applied to those Soviet Jews wishing to emigrate to Israel, but later on, the minority of Russians who perceived that the rest would be unable to adopt the reforms began to identify themselves with the Old Testament Jews:

> In the beginning, an analogy with the Biblical plot was meant quite literally and the slogan, "Let my people go!" seemed consistent as a demand for the right of emigration to Israel. Later on, however,... this metaphor was extended from the relations of the Soviet Jews to the USSR to the perestroika reform in general. Today it describes the conflict between those who want to return to the so-called "world

civilization" and those who represent our own ugly civilization ("Egypt") and the "Egyptians," that is, the masses of "inferior Soviet people." The chief rabbi of Moscow, Pinkhas Goldsmidt, made the following statement: "Gematria, the branch of Kabbalah which provides explanation for phenomena on the basis of the numerical meanings of the words, demonstrates that the sum of the numerical meanings of the words 'Mitsraim' (Egypt) and USSR are the same." Isn't this a challenge to the majority of the population? This statement is aimed at the consolidation of the "New Russians" before the horrifying march through the desert. They need to eliminate from their hearts any compassion towards "Egypt."[61]

Kara-Murza dislikes the use of metaphor in political debates but as such political exploitation is so common he believes it necessary to examine the real meaning of the whole story, and offers his own interpretation. According to Kara-Murza, the idea behind the plot is that it was a part of the original plan that God should "harden the heart of Pharaoh" and that the Jews would not leave Egypt peacefully. Therefore, the ten plagues were part of God's (actually, Moses') original plan regardless of Pharaoh's attitude toward the Jews and Moses' actions. Kara-Murza goes on to argue:

> In the case of the failure of the Reformation, the "New Russians" are going to make an Exodus; that is, make a break with living and dead "Egyptians," rob them and come through the desert to the Promised Land of the "market economy." But they should recall what were the circumstances under which this project took place and what happened to Egypt after all that. Everybody who accepts the idea of Exodus...makes his personal and irreversible choice. Either he rejects the whole idea of Exodus as a possible resolution of the Russian crisis and makes every effort to change this development, or he does agree to follow the new Moses, knowing beforehand that he leaves behind him rivers of blood.[62]

Kara-Murza accuses Jewish intellectuals — particularly the literary critic Lev Annenskii and the historian of the Middle Ages, Aron Gurevich — of doubting Russia's ability to become integrated into postindustrial civilization because of the "slave mentality" characteristic of the Russian people. Kara-Murza could have found similar statements made by purely Russian intellectuals. However, the major problem with Kara-Murza's accusation is that Gurevich and Annensky did not necessarily have Russian ethnicity in mind in their discussions: the context of their statements suggests that they were speaking of cultural rather than national characteristics, and refered to Russians in the sense of all its inhabitants regardless of ethnicity. This meaning of the word "Russian" is not unusual, and it is strange that Kara-Murza takes it in the narrow ethnic sense.

For Kara-Murza, the most striking feature of the Exodus story and its present-day application is that the divinity released the Jews from any responsibility and compassion toward the Egyptians.[63]

> They were not supposed to be grateful to the land of Egypt where the sons of Israel spent four hundred and thirty years and where they had been given the best territories. Their attitude was completely determined by the political situation of the rule of the last Pharaoh.... By the same token, the New Russians...leave behind themselves the scorched earth.[64]

Kara-Murza's reading of the book of Exodus not only ignores the historical context of the events, but misses the point. For Jews, the Passover is a holiday of freedom: the Jews were slaves in Egypt, and at stake was the liberation of the people, not their enrichment. It is no coincidence that Kara-Murza's article never explained who among the reformers had used the Exodus metaphor and in what context. Presumably he had in mind a Talmudic midrash (a traditional Jewish commentary) on the Exodus which several well-known liberals had used when discussing the current situation in Russia. The midrash questioned the necessity of having the Jewish people remain in the wilderness for forty years rather than having Moses lead them into the land of Israel immediately following their escape from Egypt. In the traditional commentary, it is said that the generation that had grown up as slaves in Egypt were allowed to die off, so that those entering the land had been born in freedom. By the same token, it would take time for Russia to get to liberate its society from the habits and mentality of the Communist regime. Thus, the Exodus metaphor actually identified Russians not with the Egyptians, but with the Hebrews going to the Promised Land! Certainly, some Russian-Jewish refusniks had identified Russia with Egypt, using the slogan "Let my people go!" but even this lacked the sinister implications suggested by Kara-Murza. Instead of offering a historical interpretation, Kara-Murza did exactly what he said he was trying to avoid — he used a charged biblical metaphor for his own political purpose.

For Kara-Murza, the New Russians are Jewish in a quite literal sense. In this, he is responding to a concept of Russian antisemitism formulated by Dmitrii Furman, a historian and head research fellow at the Institute of Europe, Russian Academy of Sciences.

In his examination of the results of one sociological survey, Furman points to the surprising "discrepancy between the very slight differences in the real content of Jewish culture and the culture of the ethnic majority, and the much greater differences in psychology and value orientations."[65] This discrepancy, Furman argues, is due to the specific phenomenon of "anti-Semitophobia":

> Their [the Jews', V.R.] perception of the threat of anti-Semitism is conditioned by their memories of the past, and the past of the Jews...is a continuous chain of persecution and humiliation. Hence the threat of anti-Semitism shapes the Jewish consciousness to a much greater degree than, perhaps, more realistic threats shape the consciousness of other national minorities.[66]

The fact that the cultural and economic role of the Jews is greater than their relative share of the population can be understood against the background of Jewish anti-Semitophobia, for this is conducive to social mobility. It also explains the tremendous drive for education and high social status that contributes to an increased sense of personal security, Furman argues. It is thus not surprising that when asked about parents' preferred profession for their children, 18.6 percent of Russians and 30 percent of Jews chose the occupation of businessman. The predominantly democratic orientation of Russian Jews and their support for the market-economy, Furman goes on to argue, does not originate from their democratic convictions but rather from the fear of antisemitism.

Kara-Murza laments that Furman failed to draw the appropriate conclusions from the evidence of the survey, which testifies to the business orientation of Russian Jews and their blind support for liberalism and a market economy. These Jewish attitudes should be understood first of all against the background of the perceptions of perestroika by the average Russian, and the discrepancy between the two groups' perceptions point to the opposition of their interests.

> In 1992 perestroika was already regarded as a disaster. The representatives of all ethnicities have rated perestroika as the least preferable period among fifteen other epochs [the "rule of the Peter the Great," "rule of Brezhnev," etc. — V.R.].[67] Only Jewish respondents have answered that perestroika is "the best era." The following question is on the mark. If one influential group considers good what is a disaster for the rest of the population and if it cultivates a "phobia" toward the majority of its compatriots on the basis of imagined malicious intentions, does this not aggravate social tension? Moreover, their prominent representatives make aggressive and offensive statements related to other peoples....[68]

Kara-Murza claims that against this background it becomes clear that Russia is "surprisingly resistant to the virus of antisemitism," unlike Western

Europe, where this phenomenon is typical. Dmitrii Furman's study, Kara-Murza argues, is only one example of the exaggeration of the real danger to the Jews and unfounded accusations of antisemitism logged against the Russians. Being preoccupied with Judeophobia, Russian Jews confuse antisemitism with other phenomena such as "children's ethnocentrism," "philosophical anti-Judaism" (i.e., the conflict of Russian and Jewish values) and the "hostility toward radical Jewish leaders." These three phenomena do exist in Russia but have nothing to do with antisemitism. Today Russia is undergoing a period of transition and it is only natural that under the circumstances, hostility toward radical Jewish leaders becomes especially salient. "Radical Jewish leaders" are taking power in Russian society, and this generates special tensions:

> One can observe it now as well as in 1917. But today it is not a Cheka official in a leather jacket with a revolver, but rather a banker, an expert, and an ideologist. Radical liberal politicians of Jewish descent function as a ram that is supposed to smash the "old regime." They are the most devoted champions of modernization and Westernization, the executors of a project which seem pernicious to the majority of Russians.[69]

Like Kara-Murza, Marina Belianchikova, another critic of Jewish capitalists, denies the presence of antisemitism in Russia. She argues that the prominence of Jews in high-level government jobs and business is the best evidence for the absence of antisemitism.[70] Belianchikova takes pains to identify members of the "radical" group and to subsume them under two categories — those who occupy important positions in Russian government and political parties, and those prominent in financial activity. A similar list was compiled by Leonid Radzikhovsky in his article "Jewish Happiness."[71] References to such lists are frequent in nationalist periodicals.

Nationalists often list the Jews among the most prominent Russian politicians associated with economic reform. Belianchikova names Alexander Lifshits, an assistant to the president on economic questions, and Yakov Urinson, a deputy minister of economics, both of whom are blamed in nationalist articles for the failure of the economic reforms, the recession in production, inflation, and lack of public reporting about politicians' discussions of Russia's economic problems.[72] Nationalist periodicals point to the Jewish origins of Boris Nemtsov, the former governor of Nizhni Novgorod who became a First Deputy Prime Minister in charge of economic reforms (1997). They also mention Grigorii Yavlinsky who elaborated the "500 Days" plan for transition to a market economy, considered a precursor to the "shock therapy," and the minister of economics, Evgenii Yasin.

Anatolii Chubais, one of the architects of the economic reform, is said to be half-Jewish. Evidence that Boris Berezovsky, a deputy chairman of the National Security Council of Russia, had received Israeli citizenship became a national scandal — one nationalist author even coined the term "Beresovschina" (cf. Bironovschina) to account for the current trend of corruption in Russian politics.[73] Russian politicians of Jewish origin also includes Yurii Baturin, the president's national security assistant, and Evgenii Primakov, head of the Russian intelligence service, and former prime minister.[74] Nationalists believe that Russian politics is also greatly influenced by the Jewish deputies in the Russian Duma (Victor Sheinis and Alla Gerber), the leaders of the government economic agencies (e.g., Bella Zlatkis, head of the securities and financial markets commission; and many members of other economic organizations and ministries), and political consultants for the Yeltsin government.[75] Among prominent Jewish leaders of Russian political parties, Belianchikova names Grigorii Yavlinsky (Apple — *Yabloko*), Anatolii Shabad (Democratic Choice of Russia — *Democraticheskii vibor Rossii*), and Konstantin Borovoi and Leonid Spigel (Party of Economic Liberty — *Partiya ekonomicheskoi svobodi*).[76] However, the overall influence of the abovementioned parties and their leaders on the current political situation is not very significant.

National Bolsheviks are interested even more in the New Russian bankers and industrialists of Jewish descent, "who chose the line of Shylock." Lev Weinberg (chairman of the board of directors of the Russian Bank for Reconstruction and Cooperation, a president of the Association of Joint Enterprises, and vice-president of the Union of Industrialists and Employers)[77]; Boris Berezovsky (head of the joint-stock company LogoVAZ and general director of the All-Russian Motor-Car Alliance); Roman Abramovitz (the owner and the member of the Board of directors of the Sibneft oil company); Michael Khodorkovsky (Menatep Bank); Pyotr Nakhmanovich (AutoVAS Bank); Leonid Roitman (International Investors Company); Mikhail Friedman and Alexander Rappoport (Alpha-group and Alphabank); Alexander Smolensky (Stolichnii Bank); Mark Massarsky (Russian Gold); Vitalii Malkin (Russian Credit); and Vladimir Resin, "the king of the Moscow construction companies."[78]

Two bankers — Vladimir Gusinsky and Boris Berezovsky — occupy a special place in the antisemitic folklore of the National Bolshevik newspapers. Gusinsky is a real estate, banking, and communications tycoon. In January 1996 he was elected president of the newly-established Russian Jewish Congress,[79] and is also head of the Most-bank, which is believed to handle all the major financial operations of the city of Moscow. The "richest

Russian Jew" as he was called by the newspaper *Zavtra* is believed to have very close ties with state officials, especially with Yurii Luzhkov, the mayor of Moscow. Russian nationalists believe that he used his political connections to promote his business, buy Moscow realty, and to lease plots for construction.

The other conspicuous figure on the list of Jewish bankers is Boris Berezovsky. His empire encompasses car dealership, banking, and real estate. He is the official dealer for Mercedes-Benz, General Motors, Volvo, and Honda. He also controls a substantial number of shares of the Russian airline, Aeroflot. The newspapers cite his special ties with government officials like Peotr Aven, the chair of the Ministry of Economic Affairs.[80] As mentioned above, reports that he held dual Israeli-Russian citizenship provoked a national scandal when he was appointed deputy chairman of the National Security Council.[81] Berezovsky also owns controlling shares of Russia's second largest Russian television channel, ORT (Russian Public Television),[82] and TV-6 (in which he owns 26% of the stock); the newspaper *Nezavisimaiia gazeta* and the magazine *Ogonyok*. Gusinsky owns additional stock in the newspaper *Segodnia,* in the journal *Itogi,* the television channel NTV (Nezavisimoe televidenie), and the central radio station Ekho Moskvi.[83]

The expansion of Jewish bankers into the print and broadcast media became a persistent topic of concern in nationalist newspapers, whose journalists made unequivocally antisemitic comments. "Anti-Russian propaganda on TV" was blamed on the Jewish tycoons. The Jewish origins of Gusinsky and Beresovsky are said to explain the biased agendas of television programs, specifically the propaganda of Russophobia, and the propagation of pornography. An editorial in *Zavtra* remarked:

> A united dozen bankers have sucked round Russia down to the boiled bones. Two of them are the most rapacious. They create constant torment. Gusinsky, the chairman of the Jewish Congress, and Berezovsky, a citizen of Israel, whose TV channels show to starving people their brethren eating caviar and turkey, and the mothers of soldiers their sons decapitated and mutilated in the Chechen morgues. And in the midst of weeping Russia, going mad with distress, they show constant ritualistic games played by the tireless jokers from Odessa.... [84]

Jewish bankers are portrayed as the source of Russian misfortunes in another *Zavtra* editorial:

> Citizens of the former Russian Federation,... you live under the jurisdiction of Jewish bankers whose wallets and scrota are protected by the giants of NTV and ORT.... The 13 banker-apostles created the

regime of "whip and honey-cake" in the country which has permitted the talented Jewish sufferers to take over power and to plunder Russian widows, old men and children.... Using their electronic clubs, they established a cruel dictate in the country in the midst of which they exterminate Russia.... Russia is raped and her eyes are gouged out; it is thrown under the "caterpillars" of NATO; it is losing the Caucasus and Volga region and has been cut off from its Belorussian brothers; it has been transformed into a slave market for Jewish and Chechen hucksters.[85]

It is noteworthy that in this example, Jews are associated with Chechens, a minority that draws even more negative responses in Russian society than the Jews, in the aftermath of the unsuccessful military campaign against Chechnya.

Another journalist describes "Russian TV" programs as a "malicious bacchanal" and "information war" waged against Russia.[86] He claims that the Jewish bankers acquired incredible power through their media empires that has allowed them to exercise a decisive influence on election campaigns and in shaping public opinion on central issues, including questions about the future of the Russian federation. In particular, he cites their crucial influence on the presidential elections and their attempts to prevent the restoration of the federation (Eurasian Union). The success of Boris Yeltsin in the 1996 presidential election was attributed to the "campaign of disinformation" organized by the Jewish bankers.[87] The activities of the Jewish bankers is said to be highly coordinated, and National Bolshevik writers see a continuity between the turn-of-the-century take-over of banking by the Jews and what has happened in post-Soviet Russia:

The whole of Russia is covered by a spider's web of foreign — in essence, Jewish — banks which loan money taken from the Russian people to Russian manufacturers. These high interest rates might well paralyze any industrial activity. The bankers capitalize on the depredation of the country and the people. They have a plenty of resources for the unbridled and obtrusive advertisement of their dubious services.[88]

Sergei Andreev in *Zavtra* links the bankers to the laundering of dirty money by Colombian drug dealers, the smuggling of weapons, and provoking war in Chechnya. He claims their control of the media tries to switch public concern from their own criminal activity to the less significant and more conventional criminal groups.[89] In a similar vein, Bratischev and Filimonov contend in their *Pravda* article that "the financial rulers of the West subordinate to themselves the financial sphere of Russia and to take hold of the national property of the country through the Russian commercial banks which are run by their dependents with Zionist convictions."[90]

The animus of the National Bolsheviks against the radical Jewish leaders often seems to be based on the assumption that any kind of business activity is intrinsically immoral. Thus, the only "radicalism" of the Jewish bankers and politicians is their involvement in business activities as such and in their promotion of liberal democracy. The negative attitude toward business is grounded in the ethos of a traditional agrarian society. In his study of Russian corporate capitalism, Thomas Owen attributes the failure of the economic reforms to a resentment of capitalism and the accumulation of wealth, as is evident in the antisemitic remarks of the National Bolsheviks.[91] They fail to draw a line between questionable business practices and legitimate ways of doing business, condemning any commercial activities without qualification. It may well be correct that Jews are represented in the corporate elite in numbers far out of proportion to their percentage of the general population. However, it is quite natural (for reasons that go beyond the compass of this study), given the historical prominence of the Jews in commercial activities.[92]

There is no doubt that some articles in the National Bolshevik press do provide adequate reporting, and ask legitimate questions about the practices of particular businessmen and politicians of Jewish origin.[93] It can also be agreed that certain statements of Russian-Jewish bankers are cynical and morally problematic.[94] However, one can scarcely conclude that "most" Jews are engaged in rapacious capitalism and fraudulent business transactions. Fraudulent business practices derive from the peculiar features of a wild Russian capitalism — perhaps any form of capitalism in its early stages of development — rather than to the moral principles of Judaism or the qualities of the Jewish character. Swindles, financial machinations, forgeries, corruption of officials, and a symbiotic relationship between business and government are very characteristic for the early stage of capitalism, and are quite independent of "Jewish greed or manipulative techniques."

The thesis about the coordinated activity of Jewish bankers is also problematic, for the "Jewish banks" and their owners are economic competitors for the same market segments. In many cases the bankers act in concert as a special interest group, but membership in this group is determined by economic interests, not ethnic identity.[95] National Bolsheviks disregard the obvious economic purposes of these groupings.

In any event, the prominence of Jews in business certainly does not imply the absence of Russians in the business life of the country. Jewish "overrepresentation" seems overwhelming in samplings taken by National Bolshevik periodicals, and in their imagination, than in actual business and political structures. Whatever the actual number of New Russian capitalists of Jewish origin might be, they are still a minority. Reports in the media about the "fifty wealthiest Russians" demonstrate that the majority of Russian banks and companies are owned by ethnic Russians.[96]

Social tension and conflict associated with the animus against the New Russians are understandable, given the continuing economic distress and hardship experienced by the population. However, focus on the "Jewish dimension" of the problem is artificial and inadequate. An examination of the real genealogy of the "New Russians" can help us better understand the preoccupation with Jewish tycoons. Many state and party officials played an important role in the process of privatization, turning it to their own individual advantage. State and party bureaucrats who formerly controlled the country's funds and resources were simply better equipped than anybody else to take advantage of the new opportunities, and many of them managed to exchange political power for property. The first "New Russians" had a Communist Party rather than Jewish pedigree. A survey of Russia's top 100 business people compiled by Moscow's Applied Politics Institute found that 61 percent of the country's new rich are former members of the *nomenklatura*.[97] The quick personal enrichment of these former Soviet officials was largely due to abuse of their powerful positions. Very few Russian Jews enjoyed membership among the privileged Soviet nomenklatura, thanks to state-sponsored antisemitism. Memory of corrupt party officials of the Brezhnev era is still alive in public consciousness. This background explains why it is so important for the new leaders of the communist party (many of whom could not take advantage of the process of privatization) to dissociate and distance themselves from the New Russians and to reinforce the old stereotypes of Jewish acquisitiveness and the "spirit of haggling." Identification of the mentality of the New Russians with that of the Jews, which became a commonplace in the publications of National Bolsheviks serves their political purposes. Their writings have an inflammatory effect on already present antisemitic sentiments, but scarcely contribute to any genuine understanding of the political situation.

REWRITING THE HISTORY OF THE CPSU: JEWS AND THE COMMUNIST IDEA

The Soviet period of Russian history occupies a special place in the ideology of National Bolshevism, who wish to defend the revolutionary deeds of the founding fathers against liberal "historical nihilism." However, in spite of their belief in the special Russian nature of Bolshevism, they have to face up to the prominence of Jews in the early revolutionary movement. Not wishing to appear tainted in the eyes of other nationalist groups, they have sought to revise the history of the communist movement.[98]

In fact, they quite simply explain away the Jewish involvement in Bolshevism by attributing all misdeeds and atrocities of the communist regime to Jewish "fellow-travelers" of authentic Russian Bolshevism. The general public, of course, only learned about Communist Party crimes in the aftermath of glasnost. National Bolsheviks therefore claim that leaders of the party either were insufficiently aware of the activities of Jewish communists — which were conducted surreptitiously — or else they were powerless to fight against such sabotage. Two lines of argument enable them to avoid embarrassment: criticism of Jewish communists for not being "true Leninists" but rather Trotskyites, and then claiming that Stalin's purges and other crimes was merely a matter of putting Trotsky's ideas into practice.

(1) "True Leninism" has different modifications, almost all arguments of which hinge upon the opposition between the Lenin line and the Trotsky line in the Bolshevik movement. National Bolsheviks thus continue the official Soviet history in which the CPSU accused Leon Trotsky of "double-dealing *(dvurushnichestvo)*. National Bolshevik ideologists often describe Trotskyism as a Jewish or Zionist trend in the Russian Bolshevik movement. They consider Lenin a Russian patriot who was going to build "socialism in one country," whereas Trotsky was the prophet of international communism and the ideologist of "permanent revolution." Other advocates of National Bolshevism explain the negative tendencies in Bolshevism as a result of penetration of the Party by members of other radical Left parties — Mensheviks, Socialist Revolutionaries, and Bundists — who joined the Bolshevik movement on the eve and shortly after the revolution. These Jewish revolutionaries changed the original spirit of Bolshevism and played the same role in the Bolshevik movement that the "Judaizing heresy" played in Orthodoxy.

One example of the "true Leninism" approach is found in V. Obukhov's history of the early CPSU. He contends that, contrary to common belief, Lenin characterized Zionism as a much more dangerous trend than antisemitism, but Soviet censors excluded Lenin's article on this from the collected works.[99] Obukhov argues that the historic tragedy of Bolshevism resulted from the admission of two Jewish groups into the party on the eve and shortly after the revolution — the so-called Interregional Group *(Mezhraiionnaia gruppa),* and the Poalei Zion (Jewish Communist Party [EKP]). The centrist Interregional group was led by Trotskyites and other Jewish revolutionaries, and tried to amalgamate the ideologies of the Bolsheviks and Mensheviks. Obukhov points out that Lenin did not approve the decision of the 6th Congress to admit these Jewish revolutionaries into the Party since he was out of the country at the time. The Jewish Communist Party joined the Bolsheviks in the early 1920s. Members of the Poalei Zion were required by the CPSU to suspend any Zionist activity and their contacts with the World Jewish Communist Union. However, in spite of their agreement to these stipulations, the "converts" did not abandon their Zionist past and smuggled the "tail of Bundism" into the party.[100] Members of these groups, Obukhov laments, infiltrated the party and set up a cliquish promotion policy, which paved the way for Jewish cronyism in the Party:

> In the first post-October years, the highest elite of Soviet authorities was disproportionately recruited from members of one ethnicity. In many departments this promotion policy was pervasive.... In many central and local institutions, Jewish clannishness became a powerful force. Its potency was due to its traditional character, the ability to adapt to circumstances and congruity with the petty-bourgeois spirit. Eventually the whole Soviet system was devastated by these clannish policies and by the "bureaucratic perversions," the dangers of which had been foreseen by Lenin.[101]

Obukhov attributes the crimes of the Communist Party — the violent suppression of "political deviants" *(ukloni)*, the purges, the broad-scale repression of the Russian people, and the punishments of members of the opposition — to the infiltration of Jews into the Bolshevik movement. Jews, he writes, were especially active in anti-Leninist trends within the Party. He also claims that Jews infiltrated the Soviet repressive institutions (OGPU, NKVD, and GULAG officials) in order "to exterminate honest Communists and to discredit the Soviet regime." However, the true Leninists — Stalin, Molotov, and Zhdanov — exposed these careerists.[102] They found that Jewish Communists "repressed members of the Party, hoping to get a promotion, and they issued a special decree which was directed against this irresponsible abuse of the prosecution process and repressive measures." Obukhov believes that the former "Bundists" fabricated documents, misinterpreted Soviet laws, and persecuted innocent members of the Party, thus drawing attention away from the real renegades. By the late 1930s, Obukhov goes on to argue, Stalin and other members of the Political Bureau identified the real criminals, although he admits that in the course of the Stalinist repressions "others have been ruined along with the Bundists and the Zionists." Stalin's policy, he assures his readers, had nothing to do with antisemitism. In contrast to the Bundists, who could never overcome their nationalism and propensity to usury and commerce, Stalin was guided by the class theory, without bias against the Jewish people.[103]

Some of the new "Leninists" blame Stalin for the purges and repressions, but many of them would trace the genealogy of these policies to Leon Trotsky, claiming that Stalin was only putting Trotsky's ideas into practice.

(2) Another response to the Jewish dilemma in interpreting Communist Party history places Stalin (who made the Soviet Union into one of the most powerful states in the twentieth century) in opposition to Lenin, Trotsky, and their followers. Here, the line of argument draws heavily on Stalin's infamous textbook, *The Course of History of the VKP (b)*.

Herman Nazarov's article, "Bolsheviks are Not Alike" is an example of the Stalinist argument.[104] Nazarov points to an important split over the Jewish question that occurred within Russian Marxism long before the Revolution. Georgii Plekhanov, the founding father of Russian Marxism, is credited with clearly foreseeing the danger of collaboration with the Bund and Jewish revolutionaries, while Lenin dismissed his warnings.[105] Moreover, Lenin broke with Plekhanov and began to work hand in hand with Jewish revolutionaries, and even went so far as to publish articles in the *Workers' Newspaper*, a mouthpiece of the Bund. Lenin's loyalty to the Jews was so deep that he opened Party membership to those in the Bund and Poalei Zion.

> The national Russian idea could have gained the victory, if Lenin had decided to stay with Plekhanov. But Lenin was a leader of the most reactionary left wing of the "internationalists".... The union of all nationalistic Jewish groups in RKP(b) laid the foundation for the punitive organization which built its own socialism. This socialism was the opposite of Russian socialism.[106]

Jewish Bolsheviks were awaiting the world proletarian revolution and regarded the Russian revolution as its dress rehearsal. It is remarkable that some National Bolsheviks go so far as to claim that Trotsky was the major "strategic figure" in the party, and Lenin merely a "tactical figure" who followed Trotsky's recommendations.

It was Stalin who challenged the Jewish fellow-travelers in the Bolshevik movement and gave new life to the ideas of Plekhanov. The politics of the "Great Retreat" (a term coined by the American-Russian historian Timasheff) put an end to Zionist and Bundist subversive activity within the communist movement. Aware of the difficulties of direct struggle against the perfidious Zionists in the party, Stalin incited a conflict between the two Zionist groups, the Trotskyites and the Leninists. In this, Stalin only utilized the name of Lenin for tactical purposes in his struggle against Trotsky. He targeted specifically the Trotskyites and Bundists, and had no intention of harming regular, innocent Party members. On the contrary, the Jewish fellow-travelers in the punitive institutions persecuted and terrorized both Party members and the population. The National Bolshevik advocates of Stalin suggest that even today, the ideologists of liberalism tend to downplay the importance of the repressions carried out by the Jewish revolutionaries, and they exaggerate the scope of Stalin's repression. Nazarov, however, did not choose to analyze Stalin's policies of "De-cossackification, de-peasantification, de-kulakification and mass shootings in Petrograd, Kiev, Kharkov, Odessa and Moscow in 1918–1922."[107] Nazarov explains the cruelty of the Stalinist period in the old Soviet way: supposedly, this cruelty was made necessary because of the persistence of the subversive activity of crypto-Trotskyites who had infiltrated into the Party, and whose clannishness and cohesiveness made their activities difficult to detect. Nazarov calls the Trotskyites "Zionist Bolsheviks." Similarly, Rumiantsev, the editor of *The Cause. Workers and Peasants Newspaper,* argues that the solidarity of the Trotskyites was determined by their lack of concern for Russia, their international connections and, more seriously, by their common ethnic background.[108] Some National Bolsheviks suggest that Stalin himself was murdered by the Jews in the infamous "Doctors' Plot."[109] Aleksei Baliev wrote:

> Joseph Stalin was murdered on March 2, 1953, on the night of the Judaic holiday Purim. They (the Jewish doctors — V.R.) tried to mislead the party, the people of the country, and the allies until March 6, by announcing the "sudden and serious illness of comrade Stalin."[110]

Herman Nazarov summarizes the struggle between the two lines in the Bolshevik Party:

> The Party which seized power in 1917 was controlled by Trotsky. In essence it was a party of Soviet Zionists. It is not surprising then that 80 percent of the communists with pre-revolutionary party background were arrested and 75 percent of the members of Central Committee elected by the 17th Congress of the Party were shut out. Stalin stopped the repressions against the people and the country started to live a creative life.... It is simply wrong to talk about the responsibility of the whole Party for the repressions and the terroristic wars.... In 1937, Russian Bolshevism gained victory over Trotskyism. Today, revived Trotskyism takes vengeance for its failure on Russian Bolsheviks and the Russian people.... Perestroika started with the criticism of Stalin: the former Zionist Communists were frightened most of all by Russian Bolshevism, by the workers and peasants who kicked the Bund out of the Party and gained victory.[111]

Another National Bolshevik, Ivan Shevtsov, seems in tune with this concept of Jewish engagement with the international socialist movement. He generalizes about the involvement of the Jews in international communist groups (mentioning in particular the Slansky affair in Czechoslovakia):

> Zionism...disguises its cosmopolitanism with the fig-leaf of internationalism. Under this pretext Zionists occupied leading positions in the socialist movement in order to compromise and profane socialist ideals. People of Jewish extraction have always occupied key offices in the socialist and communist parties of the West and they preferred the interests of Zion to the interests of the countries of which they were the citizens.[112]

Thus, National Bolsheviks have their cake and eat it too. They draw a line between the "benevolent" Russian Bolsheviks and the bad Jewish pseudo-socialists. The first group is vindicated and praised; the second, condemned. Since the old enemies of Russian Bolshevism — the Trotskyites and "Zionist communists" are still alive and led perestroika, the class struggle with its familiar ethnic overtones should be carried on.

"ZIONISM AND FASCISM ARE TWINS"

"Zionism" became a key term of the National Bolshevik ideology from the time of the Soviet anti-Zionist campaign. The Soviet propagandists heartily approved the passage of the United Nations resolution that defined Zionism as racism. At the end of the Cold War, when the resolution was rescinded, the Bolsheviks and other nationalists attributed the change to "Jewish influence." The ideologues of the Soviet anti-Zionist campaigns had gone much further than the United Nations definition: they claimed that Zionism is a global conspiracy of the Jewish financial elite that aims to establish Jewish world domination. Contemporary National Bolsheviks continue to draw on the outdated declarations of the Soviet-era crusaders.

Perhaps the most persistent idea is that Zionism equate with Nazism. Ivan Shevtsov calls Zionism an "international Nazi organization."[113] This idea crops up again and again in discussions of various topics.

Some writers, for example, suggest that Nazi ideologists merely elaborated the "racist" Jewish idea that Jews are a "chosen people." In addition, one finds a persistent trivialization of the Holocaust, applying its symbols to discussions of completely different phenomena. The economic situation in Russia, for example, is seen as amounting to a "Holocaust" — one attributed to Jewish bankers. It is quite common to identify the policies of Israel in the territories occupied at the time of the 1967 war with the Nazi policy of annihilation of the Jews of Europe. An article in *Al-Quds* was entitled "6 million victims of Israeli terror." "Reports" in *Al-Quds* include allegations that the Israeli army has used chemical weapons against the Palestinians; and that Palestinians have been the subject of Nazi-style "medical experiments" by Israeli doctors. *Al-Quds* accuses the Israeli military establishment of torturing Palestinian prisoners, and then covering up evidence of this by cremating the bodies.[114]

Zionists are also accused of perpetuating the "myth of Russian antisemitism." Extensive research on antisemitism during the Soviet period is motivated by the political agenda of the Zionists, and serves to distract the general public from becoming aware of the racist ideology and atrocities committed by Israel against the Palestinians. The Zionist myth of Russian antisemitism is used to encourage Jews to emigrate to Israel, thus providing settlers for the illegally occupied territories captured by Israel in 1967.

National Bolsheviks allege that Zionists themselves provoke and organize different manifestations of antisemitism. They supposedly benefit from disasters and political conflict in the former Soviet Union. "The atmosphere of chaos, instability and fear which has arisen in Russia after two and a half years of 'democratic reforms' is favorable only to the Zionists."[115] National Bolshevik periodicals publish articles in which Zionists are accused of collaborating with the Nazis, even in bringing about the Holocaust. The Nazis were attempting to clear the Jews out of Europe, while the Zionists wished to bring all ethnically "valuable" Jews to Palestine while allowing the Nazis to dispose of the "dead branches" of the Jewish family tree, including the Jewish elderly and poor. All these notions had previously circulated as part of the Soviet anti-Zionist campaigns. Nationalists reacted with glee over the "discovery" of the Jewish origins of many Nazi officers. An article in *Pravda* by Valentin Prussakov described the findings of Bryan Rigg, a young history student from Cambridge University, that "thousands of Jews had taken part in the Nazi movement and that many of them had managed to serve in the Nazi army during the Second World War," as reported by Russell Jenkins in the British *Daily Telegraph*.[116] Rigg had claimed that "thousand of soldiers with one Jewish parent or grandparent fought for the Nazis," some of them even occupying high-ranking positions. Prussakov took this "discovery" — at best a curiosity resulting from the peculiar Nazi definitions of race — as evidence of Jewish involvement in the annihilation of other Jews.[117]

Zionism is portrayed as an omnipotent worldwide force capable of penetrating any human activity in order to accomplish its goals. In the mythology of the National Bolsheviks, the Israeli intelligence services —the Mossad, Nativ, Shin-Bet, and AMAN) are the ultimate symbol of Zionist power.[118] Many of the nationalist articles about the Israeli intelligence services are based on accounts by Victor Ostrovsky, a former Mossad agent.[119] Robert David and Yurii Vlasov are two well-known authors who drew on Ostrovsky's exposé of the Mossad for their own articles.[120] Vlasov warns his compatriots that many Russian Jews are agents of international Zionist organizations, and those who are not agents themselves are ready to volunteer information related to national security to the numerous Zionist organizations, among which he includes the World Zionist Organization, B'nai B'rith, the United Jewish Appeal, Chabad, the National Congress for Soviet Jewry, Joint International, the Jewish Agency, and the Beitar, Bnei Akiva, and Maccabi youth organizations.

In sum, anti-Zionist sentiments are quite strong in the neo-Bolshevik periodicals and they change little compared with the old Soviet anti-Zionist crusades.

CONCLUSION

Clearly, the attitude of National Bolsheviks to Jewish matters reveals their betrayal of the cause of international communism and their denial of the narrative of universal emancipation that Marxism shared with ideologies of the Enlightenment. Quotations that they take from Marx's writings — even the reference to his early work on the *Judenfrage* — demonstrate their misreading of core Marxist doctrines. It is also striking that although the National Bolshevik parties touch upon vexing social issues — inflation, unemployment, violation of the basic rights of working people, etc. —their discourse differs substantially from traditional communist discussion of such topics. Their preoccupation with Jewish wealth and craving for power goes far beyond the Marxist condemnation of capitalism, for they allege that the Jews — both foreign and Russian citizens — engage in profiteering during economically hard times, are speculators and responsible for outrageously high prices, and thrive on the misery of others.

Michael Agursky's study of National Bolshevism, *The Third Rome,* suggests that the movement differs substantially from classical Marxism. Its eschatological spirit and the instinctive spontaneity of Russian socialism is quite unlike the "scientific doctrine" of Marxism as elaborated by Western communists. He traces Russian communism's origins to messianic sects and heterodox religious movements.[121] The National Bolsheviks continue the traditions of these radical sects and exhibit the same Gnostic hatred for this world and ardent yearning for the New Universe. Alexander Dugin, whose thought was examined in detail in the first chapter, defined the continuity between contemporary National Bolsheviks and the earlier religious sects as: "the Marxism of National Bolshevism is Marx minus Enlightenment."[122]

Thus, the National Bolsheviks are anti-liberal, and their conception of a "Jewish problem" in Russia escalates both class and ethnic hatred. They believe that the core values of the Russian community encompass a primitive equality, sense of solidarity, and equal distribution of goods, while Jewish social identity centers on the accumulation of wealth and exploitation of non-Jews. These capitalist "Jewish values" have disrupted the Russian moral community and bonds of solidarity. National Bolshevik slogans and declarations contain an explosive potential for violence, because they perceive themselves as waging war against the ethnic group that has so damaged the social fabric of Russia. The *Zavtra* editorial quoted earlier about Jewish bankers who created a "dictatorship" in Russia that "robbed widows, the elderly and children," ends with an open threat that evokes memories of the Nazi gas chambers:

The gentlemen from the Jewish congress,

The Russian apocalypse, to which you have brought us, will turn you into stinking smoke, and the devils in swastikas, who will dig in the hot ashes, will recognize your skeletons by the diamond cuff-links and the golden tooth-crowns.[123]

It is remarkable that the threat is addressed not to Jewish bankers, but to all of the members of the Jewish Congress.

NOTES

1. In 1920s the term "National Bolshevism" came to be the self-denomination of Russian émigré movement of "smenovekhovstvo" led by Nikolai Ustrialov. The name derives from its ideological manifesto, *Smena vekh* (Change of landmarks), compiled and published in Prague in 1921. The national communist party of Ernst Niekisch in Germany had much in common with Russian National Bolshevism; See L. Dupeux, *Nationalbolschewismus in Deutschland* (Munich 1985). Contemporary Russian National Bolsheviks have abandoned many beliefs of their older counterparts, being in many respects conservative rather than revolutionary. They could be better described as "national socialists," but since the term is so much associated with the German Nazis, I have chosen to use the term "National Bolshevism." M. Agursky, *The Third Rome: National Bolshevism in the USSR* (Boulder 1987). The Russian edition, *Ideologiia natsional-bolshevizma* was originally published in Paris in 1980.

2. In this chapter I will not discuss the ideology of the National Bolshevik Party led by Alexander Dugin and Eduard Limonov. National Bolshevism as conceived by Dugin differs substantially from my use of the term. Dugin defines National

Bolshevism as a combination of Left and Right ideologies. Elements of the Left are associated with radicalism, elitism, hatred of compromise, and the anti-liberalism of the Bolshevik party. Elements of the Right are associated with the emphasis on the irrational, mythological, anti-humanistic, and totalitarian. It is remarkable that Dugin identifies National Bolshevism with the mainstream Russian cultural tradition. Dugin contends that he does not subsume conservative circles of the CPSU under the category of National Bolshevism. Their link with the "authentic" National Bolsheviks of the 1920s and 1930s was never discussed by these conservative Bolsheviks. See A. Dugin, "Metafisika natsional-bolshevisma" in *Tamplieri proletariata* (Moscow 1997), 5–15. Thus, Dugin disqualifies from membership in National Bolshevism many of the groups that comprise the subject the present chapter. My account is based for the most part on the ideas of the former "conservative members of the CPSU." It can also be observed that Dugin's concept of Russian identity is geopolitical rather than social; according to him, social identity is only a product of geopolitical identity.

3. Many prominent communist leaders and ideologists (such as Friedrich Engels, Karl Kautsky, Edward Bernstein, and Vladimir Lenin) were known as uncompromising fighters against antisemitism; see, e.g., K. Kautsky, *Are the Jews a Race?* (Westport 1972). The phenomenon of antisemitism was described by the early communist leaders as a remnant of medieval prejudices exploited by the bourgeoisie to prevent class struggle, and intensified by the human relations typical of capitalism. Many communist ideologists held that capitalism is responsible for the instigation of national discord among peoples. The "Jewish question" could be settled only by the transition to a truly international communism. The first Soviet government was very much concerned about the spread of antisemitism and even issued the Decree of the Soviet of People's Commissars about the Suppression of Antisemitic Movements, adopted on 27 July 1918.

4. One can find the overt antisemitic statements or overtones in the works of such prominent leaders of socialist and communist movements of the nineteenth century as François Marie Fourier, Moses Hess, Mikhail Bakunin, Pierre Joseph Proudhon, Ferdinand Lassalle, and Karl Marx.

5. This idea was expressed by Nicholas Berdiaev, the Eurasian movement, and by representatives of Smenovekhovstvo. The best-known account is N. Berdiaev, *Origins of Russian Communism* (London 1955).

6. P. Romanov, "Russkaiia dusha propitana sotsializmom," *Pravda Rossii,* 4 May 1995; B. Khorev, "Russkaiia ideiia — eto sotsialism," *Pravda,* 29 September 1994.

7. The theories of Frank and Wallerstein are occasionally utilized by writers such as Boris Khorev in the nationalist periodicals. B. Khorev, "Russkaiia ideiia — eto sotsializm"; see also A. Chekalin, "Smogut li russkie v tretii raz nadut' Zapad?" *Pravda,* 15 February 1996. Wallerstein's paper appeared in *Zavtra:* I. Wallerstein, "Mir o treokh golovakh. Zatikhaushchee solo odinokoi Ameriki," *Zavtra,* no. 3 (1993).

8. One can trace this idea back to pre-Revolutionary nationalistic movements in Russia. It was also typical of the Soviet anti-Zionist campaigns, most explicit in the writings of Begun and Skurlatov: V. Begun, *Polzuchaiia kontrrevolutsiia* (Minsk 1974), 16–17; V. Skurlatov, *Sionism i aparteid* (Kiev 1975), 10–24.

9. Many liberal intellectuals consider Karl Marx's "On the Jewish Question" (1843) an antisemitic document. Whatever the intentions of its author, the essay inspired numerous antisemitic declarations. It is noteworthy that the essay was originally published in Soviet Russia with a preface by Anatoly Lunacharsky, the Minister of Education *(narkom prosvescheniia)* of the first Soviet government (this edition of Marx's essay was reprinted in 1906 and 1919). Lunacharsky wrote: "It seems to me that Marx's perspective on the Jewish question is absolutely right. Everybody who is able to admire the depth of thought and the strength of human intellect, undoubtedly, will take delight in reading his essay." A. Lunacharsky, "Predislovie k broshure Marksa," in *Sotsialism i evrei,* ed. A. Solzhenitsin (Paris and Moscow 1995), 190.

10. Cited in *Suschestvuet li v Rossii evreiskii vopros'?* (Moscow, 1994), 19.

11. Y. Belov, "Shylock and Kuzma. Evreistvo na fone russkikh problem," *Sovetskaiia Rossiia,* 21 October 1995.

12. S. Kara-Murza, "Po sledam Menelaiia," *Sovetskaiia Rossiia,* 26 January 1995.

13. This theory was introduced by the economist Anatolii Kuz'mich (b. 1933).

14. G. Ziuganov, *Za gorizontom* (Moscow 1995), 17–18.

15. T. Glushkova, "Zhestokii romans," *Zavtra,* no. 12 (1995).

16. G. Ziuganov, "Imperiia SShA: dvesti let amerikanskoi mechty," *Nash sovremennik,* no. 8 (1994).

17. Ziuganov, *Za gorizontom,* 17.

18. Gennadii Shimanov was a conspicuous figure in the nationalist movement in the 1970s and 1980s, who published many of his articles abroad. He contributed to the magazine *Veche* and edited his own miscellany *Mnogaiia leta.* Alexander Yanov devoted an entire chapter of his book *The Russian Idea and the Year 2000* to Shimanov's thinking. A. Yanov, "Russkaiia ideiia. Most cherez propast': nachalo chernosotennogo natsionalisma," *Neva,* no. 12 (1990): 163–71.

19. Shimanov criticizes Marx for downplaying the crucial role of banks in the development of capitalism and for his reluctance to emphasize the decisive impact of Jewish capital in the financial life of Europe in his later works (in particular, in *Das Kapital,* Marx "started his analysis from ascertaining the financial power of the Jewry," but gradually he "turned aside from the main line of the study of capitalism to the roadside and led the reader away to the discussion of secondary, not to say empty, questions in his voluminous maze. In a similar vein, Ivan Susanin brought the Poles to the dense forest." G. Shimanov, "Kto bolshe vsekh zainteresovan v mirazhakh i utopiiakh?" *Molodaiia gvardiia,* no. 4 (1994): 20.

20. G. Shimanov, "O tainoi prirode kapitalisma," *Molodaiia gvardiia,* no. 11–12 (1993): 167.

21. Shimanov refers to the *Book of kagal* (St. Petersburg 1888; originally published in Vilna in 1869), a well-known antisemitic work written by the baptized Jew, Jacob Brafman. Brafman worked as a censor of Jewish written works and adviser on Jewish affairs in the office of the governor of the Vilna district in the 1860s. In his book he alleged the existence of secret and illegal Jewish *kehillot* (communal boards) that governed the Jews of Russia, controlling not only Russian Jewish deals but also served as chapters of a worldwide Jewish government, whose center was the *Alliance Israélite Universelle* based in Paris.

22. Shimanov, *Book of kagal.*

23. Shimanov, "O tainoi prirode kapitalizma."

24. Ibid, 169.

25. These Jewish families of merchants and bankers immigrated to the United States from Germany in the mid-nineteenth century and became known in Jewish periodicals as the "Jewish Grand Dukes" of New York. See P. Birmingham, *Our Crowd. The Great Jewish Families of New York* (New York 1967). "Influential, conservative in life-style, but unorthodox in financial matters, and inbred (like the Rothschilds, their children married each other), Jewish bankers projected an image of concentrated power because they often acted in concert, collaborating on financial deals.... Because of their clannishness and presumed power, they were objects of scorn among the Populists at the end of the nineteenth century," quoted in G. Krefets, *Jews and Money: The Myth and the Reality* (New Haven and New York 1982), 47.

26. G. Krefetz, *Jews and Money,* 64.

27. Ibid, 47.

28. M. Weber, *Max Weber on Capitalism, Bureaucracy and Religion,* ed. Stanislav Andreski (London 1978), 131.

29. R. David, "Posle Raikhmana — kapitalism," *Den',* no. 36 (1992); A. Volokhov, "Zolotoiskateli ot sionisma," *Al-Quds,* no. 13 (1994); O. Platonov, "Evreiskii vopros v russkom gosudarstve, *Al-Quds,* no. 2 (1995); V. Prussakov, "Znakom'tes': Iosif Gutnik, milliarder," *Pravda,* 11 March 1997. Volokhov's examples of Jewish opulence are taken from the American Jewish historian Salo Baron, *Economic History of the Jews* (New York 1975).

30. A. Volokhov, "Zolotoiskateli ot sionizma," *Al-Quds,* no. 13 (1994).

31. V. Ilukhin, "Chei partner George Soros?," *Sovetskaia Rossiia,* 18 May 1995; S. Moskvitianin, "Tainaia diplomatiia Dzhorzha Sorosa," *Molodaiia gvardiia,* no. 2 (1994); "Dzh. Soros i ego sorosiata," *Sovetskaiia Rossiia,* 11 February 1995; A. Miroshnikov, "Udastsa li Sorosu zamenit' mozgi rossiianam?" *Novosti razvedki i kontrrasvedki,* no.1–2 (1995).

32. S. Moskvitianin, "Tainaia diplomatiia Dzhorzha Sorosa," *Molodaiia gvardiia,* no. 2 (1994).

33. O. Platonov, "Masonstvo v sovremennoi Rossii," *Al-Quds,* no. 5 (1995).

34. In his response to the anti-Soros articles Valerii Soifer, chairman of the international Soros educational program, stated that they do not have any requirements concerning the political orientation of the academic projects, "Novii zalp po Sorosu. Komu vigodno lishit Rossiiu realnoi pomoschi" *Isvestiia,* 30 May 1995. However, Soros admits that his programs are designed to promote his teacher Karl Popper's concept of an "open society." Soros's philosophy of history, articulated in his book *The Burden of Consciousness,* owes a great deal to Karl Popper. See M. Lewis, "The Speculator," *New Republic,* 10 and 17 January 1994.

35. V. Ilukhin, "Chei partner Dzhorzh Soros?" *Sovetskaiia Rossiia,* 18 May 1995; V. Viktorov, "Ruka Sorosa na elektrorubil'nike Rossii," *Zavtra,* no. 53 (1996).

36. Robert Maxwell (1923–1991) was born to a Jewish family in Czechoslovakia, and emigrated to Great Britain. During World War II, he won the British Military Cross. After the war, he entered the publishing business, and his holdings included such influential periodicals as the *Daily Mirror, People,* the *European,* the *Sunday Mirror,* the *Daily News,* and the Macmillan and Pergamon Press publishing houses. Many books by communist leaders of the Soviet Union were published by Pergamon Press.

37. I. Shamir, "Agent 'Mossad' rasskasivaet," *Pravda,* 18 October 1994. Another article on Maxwell of the same nature was published in the fascist newspaper *Russkii poriadok.* E. Sennikov, "'Pravda' o 'Mossad,'" *Russkii poriadok,* no. 1–2 (1995).

38. A. Shalnev, "Na skamie podsudimikh deti gazetnogo magnata," *Isvestiia,* 8 June 1995.

39. Ibid.

40. Armand Hammer (1898–1990) was an American millionaire businessman, art patron, and philanthropist of Jewish origin. He was chairman and chief executive of the Occidental Petroleum Company. He arrived in Moscow as a doctor in 1921 and became Lenin's friend. Lenin awarded him with business concessions intended to encourage other foreign capitalists to invest in the USSR. Hammer helped Lenin to organize new Soviet industries (mining and oil production). He retained access to Soviet leaders, who considered him a useful contact with the West, from the time of Lenin to that of Gorbachev. Russian neo-Bolsheviks often accuse him of plundering the Russian cultural heritage and its natural resources. See Y. Zhukov, *Operatsiia Ermitazh* (Moscow 1993). For a biography, see C. Blumey and H. Edwards, *The Dark Side of Power* (New York 1992). The underside Hammer's activities is discussed in Edward Epstein, *Dossier: The Secret History of Armand Hammer* (New York 1996), based on recently released Soviet archives and FBI documents.

41. B. Petrov, "Avtobus s tualetom Zhaka Attali," *Den',* no. 14 (1993).

42. Ibid.

43. A. Salutskii, "Vzorveotsia li finansovii Chernobil?," *Pravda*, 25 January 1996; N. Kreitor, "Razgovor s mudrimi lud'mi," *Zavtra*, no. 24 (1994).

44. V. Filatov, "Ni shagu nasad," *Den'*, no. 5 (1993).

45. Guggenheim, Sachs, and Lazards Frères are banking houses set up by Jewish immigrants from Germany and France between 1840 and 1880. Samuel and Harry Sachs were founding members of Goldman, Sachs, and Co.

46. V. Filatov, "Nasha krepost'," *Den'*, no. 21 (1993).

47. See Y. Byalii, "Almaznii klin" *Zavtra*, no. 49 (1995).

48. V. Zenkov, "Rossiiskie brillianti dlia diktaturi mirovogo kapitala," *Molodaiia gvardiia*, no. 6 (1995). Some experts point out that the Russian critics of De Beers ignore the fact that the company acts in the interest of all diamond producers and industries. De Beers spends 180 million dollars on advertising only and guarantees to purchase all rough diamonds from each producer at fixed quotas and firm prices. Some experts thus express misgivings about the possibility of creating an alternative market because of the expense involved, which Russia would not be able to afford. Y. Borovoi, "De Beers — Vacuuming Up the Diamonds in Russia," *New Times*, no. 8 (1995): 51.

49. V. Ershov, "Almaznii blesk rozhdaet suetu," *Pravda*, 6 March 1994; see I. Shamir, "A zarabotaet Izrail," *Pravda*, 2 March 1994; "Ziuganov ili Yeltzin," *Russkaiia gazeta*, no. 4 (1996).

50. I. Andronov, "O chem molchit uznik 'Krestov,'" *Zavtra*, no. 13 (1996).

51. I. Andronov, "O chem molchit uznik 'Krestov,'" *Zavtra*, nos. 14–15 (1996). See also Y. Vlasov, "Sionisti protiv evreev i russkikh," *Zavtra*, no. 36 (1995). None of these allegations were confirmed. The General Office of the Public Prosecutor announced that it has no information about illegal activity by Birnstein and his corporation in Russia or abroad. For more detail, see O. Kutasov, "Po sledam ischeznuvshei 'Siabeko," *Nezavisimaiia gazeta*, 1 March 1996.

52. "'MacDonalds': imperiia zla v Rossi," *Al-Quds*, no. 9 (1993).

53. Analiticheskii Tsentr Den', "Dollari, 'otmitie' v nefti, Atomnaiia bomba imeni Marka Richa," *Den'*, no. 13 (1993); S. Turchenko, "On vam znakom? Beglii amerikanets khoziainichaet v Rossii," *Sovetskaiia Rossiia*, 25 March 1993.

54. "Drug Burbulisa. Iz dosie na odnogo is krupneishikh prestupnikov mira," *Den'*, no. 13, 1993. Marc Rich fled the United States in 1983 to avoid charges of racketeering, tax evasion, and trading with an enemy (through the purchase of Iranian oil during the American hostage crisis).

55. It is difficult to come up with a precise number for the proportion of "New Russians" in the population because different social scientists use different criteria in defining the new class. In popular usage, the term can refer both to multimillionaires and to those who can afford to buy a foreign car.

56. Y. Belov, "Shylock i Kuz'ma," *Sovetskaiia Rossiia,* 21 October 1995.

57. Ibid.

58. Ibid.

59. Kara-Murza (b. 1939) is a professor of chemistry and specialist in the philosophy of science. From the beginning of perestroika he became a prolific political writer for the *Nash sovremennik, Pravda,* and *Sovetskaiia Rossiia.*

60. By "Masonic language" Kara-Murza is referring to the use of construction metaphors in the political slogans of perestroika leaders. Perestroika literally means "reconstruction" and expressions like "architect of perestroika," "work superintendent *(prorab)* of perestroika," and "construction site" were very common in the rhetoric of the reformers in the early stages. S. Kara-Murza, "'Novie russkie' i Iskhod," *Pravda,* 27 June 1994. New Testament ideals are significant for national Bolsheviks not because of their religious nature but because they are congenial to the communal spirit of Russian-Soviet civilization and socialist ideals.

61. Ibid.

62. Ibid.

63. Kara-Murza is apparently unaware of, or deliberately ignores the Jews' own traditions about Egypt and the Exodus: e.g., Jews remove ten drops of wine from the second full cup during the Passover Seder to signify that our joy cannot be "full" when we recall that Egyptians suffered the plagues; the Hallel Psalms are reduced in length; and stories in the Midrash clearly state the impropriety of rejoicing in the face of Egyptian death and suffering.

64. Ibid.

65. D. Furman, "The Mass Consciousness of Russian Jews and Anti-Semitism," *Russian Social Science Review,* 36, no. 5 (1996): 53. The paper "Massovoe soznanie rossiiskikh evreev i antisemitism" was originally published in *Svobodnaiia misl,* no. 4 (1994): 36–51.

66. Ibid., 156.

67. Kara-Murza refers to a sociological poll, but does not specify which one.

68. S. Kara-Murza, "Mifotvortsi," *Sovetskaiia Rossiia,* 6 January 1995.

69. Ibid.

70. M. Belianchikova, "Dostanetsia li zemlia faraonu?," *Nash sovremennik,* no. 4 (1995): 190. In the first years of perestroika, hunting for Jewish names in the Russian political and economic establishment involved ridiculous claims about the Jewish origins of prominent leaders and architects of perestroika: Alexander Yakovlev, Yuri Afanasief, Andrei Sakharov, and others. An article in *Den'* even suggested that Boris Yeltsin's surname was originally Eltsin, derived from the Jewish female name Eltsia; see "Eto interesno," *Den',* no. 32 (1992). Today, the mainstream mouthpieces of Russian nationalism are not particularly obsessed with crypto-Jews; the abundance of real Jews in positions of power have made such speculations redundant.

71. Published originally in *Novoe russkoe slovo* and later reprinted in *Zavtra*. See L. Radzikhovsky, "Evreiskoe schastie," *Novoe russkoe slovo*, 17 January 1996 and *Zavtra*, no. 29 (1996).

72. M. Belianchikova, "Dostanetsia li zemlia faraonu? Obzor pochti," *Nash sovremennik*, no. 4 (1995): 181–82.

73. "Berezovschina. Vnimaniiu Soveta Federatsii i Gosdumi," *Zavtra*, no. 50 (1996). "Berezovschina" is modeled after the term "Bironovschina," a short period in eighteenth-century Russian history and politics named after de Biron, the regent after the death of the empress Anna. This period is remembered as one of cruelty and corruption, and a symbol of foreign domination and exploitation.

74. The newspaper *Den'* also informed readers about the Jewish origins of the head of Russian Intelligence in "Tainaiia kariera Evgeniia Primakova," *Den'*, no. 28 (1992).

75. The political consultants include Emil Pain, a head of the Center for Ethno-Political and Regional Research of the President's Council, Victor Rubanov, a political consultant of the president ,and Mark Urnov, the head of the Analytic Center of the President's Administration. E. Fedorov, "Musornaiia," *Zavtra*, no. 5 (1996). Fedorov claims that Urnov is a Zionist and that he works on projects that aim to destroy psychologically the New Communist Party of Russia.

76. Belianchikova, "Dostanetsia li semlia faraonu? Obsor pochti," 188–89.

77. In 1994 some articles in some Russian periodicals accused Weinberg's Solev-Management company of misappropriation of gold under the guise of extracting precious metals from electronic scrap in foreign factories. In 1994 he was arrested and charged with bribing the inspector of the Main Customs Committee. However, from the very beginning of the investigation, there were lawyers and journalists who claimed that the charges were fabricated. The prosecutors described a birthday present of a gold necklace as a bribe. No evidence of misappropriation of gold was produced in the course of the trial. In 1996 the Ministry of the Interior announced that it had no claims against Weinberg's company and the court brought in a verdict of not guilty. Experts estimated the damage to the company as a result of these charges was some $2.5 million. See L. Nikitinskii, "Lev Weinberg nevinoven," *Moskovskie novosti*, 9–16 June 1996.

78. Belianchikova, "Dostanetsia li semlia faraonu? Obsor pochti," 187. *Zavtra* names "the famous representatives of the 'New Russians' among the founders of the Convention of the Russian Jewish Congress: Vladimir Gusinsky, Vitalii Malkin, Mikhail Friedman, el al. The Zionist movement in Russia has a new strong stimulus. The Convention was welcomed by Boris Yeltsin and Yurii Luzhkov. Vladimir Gusinsky was elected a Chair of the Congress. He also became a vice-president of the World Zionist Congress," "Tablo," *Zavtra*, no. 3 (1996).

79. A. Lvov, "Obrazovan Rossiiskii evreiskii kongress" *Russkaiia misl'*, no. 4109 (1996).

80. A. Chebuchenko, "Bankrot ego velichestva," *Zavtra,* no. 28 (1995).

81. The question of his dual citizenship was raised by *Izvestiia*'s well-known journalist, Golembiovsky. The information was confirmed by *Jerusalem Post* journalist Batsheva Tsur, "Top Russian Security Man an Israeli," reprinted in *Izvestiia,* 6 November 1996. See also M. Gokhman, "Bisnes i politika," *Russkaiia misl',* 7–13 November 1996.

82. The ORT television channel opened in 1995. Berezovsky owns a large share of the stock and is a vice-chairman of ORT's Board of Directors.

83. "Moskovskii tsar," *Sovetskaiia Rossiia,* 18 February 1995; N. Anisin, "Yurii Dlinnorukii," *Zavtra,* no. 10 (1994); V. Kucherenko, "Kniaz' grada sego," *Zavtra,* (June 1995); "Milliarder Gusinskii otnimaet u 'Zavtra' 100 millionov," *Zavtra,* no. 41 (1994); "Ten' Luzhkova nad Kremlem," *Zavtra,* no. 29 (1994).

84. "Komandir spetsnaza i detskaiia smertnost'," *Zavtra,* no. 4 (1997).

85. "Evreiskie bankiri i chechenskie granatometi," *Zavtra,* no. 48 (1996).

86. E. Rostikov, "Ot 'rossiiskogo' televideniia stradaet russkii narod," *Pravda,* 26 December 1996.

87. "Delo bankirov," *Zavtra,* no. 41 (1996).

88. N. Goriachev, "Vsio eto uzhe bilo," *Nashe Otechestvo,* no. 29 (1994).

89. S. Andreev, "Rasplata budet. Patrioticheskie spetzsluzhbi preduprezhdaiiut izmennikov," *Zavtra,* no. 28 (1995).

90. I. Bratischev, and P. Filimonov, "Keins i Roosvelt v chem-to bili pravi," *Pravda,* 8 February 1996.

91. See T. Owen, *Russian Corporate Capitalism from Peter the Great to Perestroika* (New York 1995).

92. Explanations vary about the supposed Jewish proclivity to commerce. Some attribute it to the principles of Judaism; some to restrictions on Jewish occupations (such as engaging in agriculture) enacted during the medieval period, and freedom from the prohibition of usury in Christendom; others attribute it to the psychology of strangers and the need of the host nation to depersonalize the exchange of goods; to the Jews' wide international connections; or to the racial qualities of the Jews or "Semites." Hillel Levine recently argued that the Jews developed a special mental attitude to economic value. They did not believe in any objective system of measurement of value for material objects of commodities. Economic value is purely a convention. H. Levine, *Economic Origins of Antisemitism* (New Haven and London 1991), 75–135.

93. Two adventurers of Jewish descent should be mentioned here: Dmitrii Yakubovsky is a young lawyer. Because of his connections with the highest officials of the Russian government, he took part in negotiations concerning the property of the Russian army in Germany, and received the rank of general. Later on he tried to compromise Alexander Rutskoy, a former Russian vice-president, alleging that

Rutskoy had secret illegal contacts with the Canadian company Siabeco. In 1995, Yakubovsky was charged with involvement in the theft of ancient manuscripts from the State National Library in St. Petersburg, together with six Israelis who were formerly citizens of Russia. A. Kerzhentsev, "'Shesterka' daet pokasaniia," *Trud,* 18 February 1995; "Kto pervim vistrelil v Rutskogo," *Zavtra,* no. 1 (1994). The other adventurer is Efim Zviagelskii, a former deputy prime minister of the Ukraine, who was appointed prime minister when he already had Israeli citizenship. He escaped from [left] his post after he had stolen $25 million from the national treasury. M. Odinets, "Nedogliadeli," *Pravda,* 15 July 1995; Belianchikova, "Dostanetsia li semlia faraonu? Obsor pochti," 186.

94. The self-revelations of "Jewish" bankers recorded in a special TV program in Israel are often quoted in nationalist periodicals; see V. Bondarenko, "...Pozhnut buriu," *Zavtra,* no. 51 (1996).

95. See, for instance, the open letter of a group of Russian bankers to the patriotic periodicals: B. Berezovsky, V. Gorodilov, V. Gusinsky, et al, "Viiti iz tupika," *Zavtra,* no. 18 (1996).

96. V. Trushkov, "Geroi kapitalisticheskogo truda," *Pravda,* 20 February 1996.

97. R. Frydman, K. Murphy, and A. Rapaczynski, "Capitalism With A Comrade's Face," *Transition,* 2, no. 2 (1996): 5–9. The authors report many remarkable cases of "simultaneous privatization" in Russia by the new "kleptoklatura," the newly rich with a Party background. Writing about the advantages of the new system for the kleptoklatura, they argue that the former party officials "gained title to the assets, and the new order gave them legal protection of their privileged status as property holders. By making them into owners of capital, privatization thus allowed them to preserve their hold on economic resources while also giving them the freedom that the old regime denied them," 5–6.

98. Some members of the Communist Party tried to dissociate themselves from the Jews on other occasions. André Gerrits points out that in the old days, the communist leadership did so, having realized that the conspicuous role of individuals of Jewish extraction negatively affected their national credentials and had an adverse effect on their attempts to establish a measure of legitimacy." A. Gerrits, "Antisemitism and Anti-Communism: The Myth of 'Judeo-Communism' in Eastern Europe," *Eastern European Jewish Affairs,* 25, no. 1 (1995): 71–72.

99. Lenin contended that "the danger of the Zionist movement is more serious for the development of the class organization of the proletariat than that of antisemitism." V. Lenin, *Sobranie sochinenii,* vol. 4 (Moscow 1924), 237.

100. V. Obukhov, "Sionizm kak mezhdunarodnii fashism," *Molodaiia gvardiia,* no. 8 (1994): 198, 200.

101. Ibid., 197.

102. Molotov was chairman of the Council of People's Commissars; Zhdanov was a secretary of the Central Committee of the Communist Party.

103. Obukhov, "Sionism kak mezhdunarodnii fashism," 202.

104. G. Nazarov, "Bolsheviki bolshevikam rozn'," *Molodaiia gvardiia*, no. 5–6 (1992).

105. Plekhanov wrote that "the members of the 'Bund' are inconsistent Zionists. They try to establish Zion not in Palestine but in the Russian state." G. Plekhanov, "Sobranie sochinenii," vol. 13 (Moscow 1926), 165.

106. G. Nazarov, "Bolsheviki bolshevikam rozn'," *Molodaiia gvardiia*, no. 5–6 (1992).

107. Ibid., 217.

108. A. Rumiantsev, "Vremia Stalina," *Molodaiia gvardiia*, no. 1 (1994): 81.

109. See N. Turoverov, "Vrachi-ubiitsi: pravda i vimisly," *Al-Quds*, no. 9 (1993).

110. A. Baliev, "V SShA zhdali ustraneniia Stalina," *Al-Quds*, no. 13 (1994).

111. G. Nazarov, "Bolsheviki bolshevikam rozn'," 220–21.

112. I. Shevtsov, "Fashism i sionizm — bliznetsy-bratiia," *Molodaiia gvardiia*, no. 9 (1995): 48.

113. Ibid.

114. "Kholokost v Palestine," *Al-Quds*, no. 13 (1994).

115. Y. Vlasov, "Sionisty protiv evreev i russkikh," *Zavtra*, no. 37 (1995).

116. R. Jenkins, "Germans confront role of Jews in Nazi war machine," *Daily Telegraph*, 2 December 1996.

117. V. Prussakov, "Tisiachi evreev sluzhili v fashistskoi armii," *Pravda*, 6 March 1997. In the *Daily Telegraph* article, Jenkins had claimed that "some historians aptly observed that the findings of Rigg presented nothing new" and that "serious historians have known really ever [sic]...that there were different categories of 'bastards'...who were treated differently."

118. Robert David [Israel Shamir] wrote a number of articles on the Israeli secret services. See R. David, "Tretiia sluzhba," *Zavtra*, no. 6 (1996); I. Shamir, "'Nativ' vivozit russkikh detei v Israil," *Pravda*, no. 32, 1996.

119. See V. Ostrovsky, *By Way of Deception* (New York 1990).

120. See Y. Vlasov, "Mi dolzhni verit' v Rodinu," *Zavtra*, no. 27 (1993); idem., "Ideiia narodnosti," *Zavtra*, no. 34–35 (1993); idem., "Sionisty protiv evreev i russkikh," *Zavtra*, no. 36–37 (1995); idem., "Kto zhe mi dlia Rossii," *Sovetskaiia Rossiia*, 3 April 1993.

121. M. Agursky, *The Third Rome.*

122. A. Dugin, "Metafizika natsional-bolshevizma," *Tamplieri proletariata* (Moscow 1997), 17.

123. "Evreiskie bankiri i chechenskie granatomeoti," *Zavtra*, no. 48 (1996).

CHAPTER 4

Neo-Slavophiles:
Trotsky, Rothschild, And the Soul of Russia

Slavophilism is the oldest trend in Russian nationalism. The post-communist ideology of neo-Slavophilism continues the tradition of nineteenth-century Slavophilism elaborated by the nationalist wing of the anti-communist dissident movement in the Soviet Union.[1] The magazine *Nash sovremennik* was the main voice for the movement during the first years of perestroika.

Before beginning an analysis of neo-Slavophilism, a few observations about the nature of its preoccupation with Jewish matters is in order.

First, it should be noted that all members of this group are exceptionally anti-communist, and hold that communism was completely alien to the course of Russian political and social history. Marxism and communism are seen as Western political phenomena that were imported into Russia. In its most articulate form, this position was advocated by Igor Shafarevich, who has identified communism with a persistent historical "death wish."[2] Neo-Slavophiles believe that the failure of Marxism in Russia was predetermined by the disparity and incongruity of the communist doctrine (which implies violence and cruelty) with traditional Russian social ideals and moral standards grounded in community life. It is no accident that during the first years of perestroika, when glasnost paved the way for criticism of the communist system, neo-Slavophilism was the most prominent trend in Russian nationalism. Many former leaders of the nationalist wing of the dissident movement in the USSR contributed to the ideology of neo-Slavophilism, including such well-known figures as Alexander Solzhenitsin, Igor Shafarevich, and Leonid Borodin — all of whom still feature prominently in neo-Slavophile publications.

Whereas other groups of nationalists emphasize religion, geopolitical affiliation, racial factors, or social orientation as distinctively Russian, neo-Slavophiles believe that culture, especially literature and the moral code of the traditional Russian community, are the core elements of Russian national identity. They believe in a specific Russian *Volksgeist (narodnii dukh)* — a concept borrowed from German Romanticism — which is best expressed in the non-discursive manifestations of the Russian spirit (e.g., literature and art). Not surprisingly, the movement's ideals and vision are often manifested in works of literary criticism. In the first years of glasnost, writers — specifically, the "village writers" *(pisateli-derevenschiki)* — were the most outspoken and conspicuous advocates of the neo-Slavophile position.

Neo-Slavophiles idealize the Russian peasants, romanticizing their lives, and promoting the idea that the peasantry represents the most authentic expression of Russian culture. Thus, the most serious crime of the communist regime was oppression of the peasant backbone of Russian society. The policy of de-peasantification was concomitantly a de-Russification of Russia. The organic, living world of the Russian peasant with its bonds between members of a moral community was displaced by a "technocratic," artificial, and "mechanical" society. The distinction between "organic" and "inorganic" development, community, etc., plays a decisive role in neo-Slavophile discourse that links the disruption of organic ties to the presence of the alien Jews.

Neo-Slavophile antisemitism centers on the following themes:

(1) The Russian communist movement, it is claimed, was predominantly Jewish: the prominence of Jews in Soviet government bodies and in the punitive organs of the Soviet state was far out of proportion to their numbers in the population. It is no accident that Jews carried out the socialist revolution that subverted the foundations of traditional Russian society.[3]

(2) Modernization and capitalist globalization devastated Russian society, particularly the agrarian sector. Russia's peasants constitute a unique and authentic estate, which alone preserved the Russian national spirit. This segment of society was victimized by the Jews who were the driving force behind modernization and capitalism.

(3) The cruelty of the modernization process, and modernity itself, is attributed by neo-Slavophile authors to Judaic moral principles. Its genealogy — exercised by both capitalists and commissars — can be traced back to the principles of the Old Testament, which they interpret as a cultural rather than purely religious document. It is noteworthy that the violence of capitalism is associated with Protestantism, which is often described as a mere branch of Judaism.

(4) Jewish commissars of the Soviet period persecuted the Russian intellectual and cultural elite more severely than any other segment of society. As a result of the revolution and the years of cosmopolitan communist rule, the authentic elements of Russian culture were displaced, and eventually corroded and dissolved. Jews dominated Russian culture and contaminated it with their own cultural forms — a spiritual invasion which was an extension of their political invasion. Literature, however, is the sacred

area in which the Russian spirit is preserved, and in spite of the devastation of the Soviet period, it remains strong and represents the last stronghold of Russian authenticity.

THE JEWISH COMMISSARS: THE MYTH OF THE JUDEO-BOLSHEVIK CONSPIRACY REVISED

The myth of a Jewish-Bolshevik conspiracy, especially popular in antisemitic ideologies found throughout Eastern Europe during the interwar period, has been characterized by André Gerrits as "one of the most potent myths in East European politics."[4] The myth was soon disseminated in Western Europe and on the American continent, and in the aftermath of perestroika, it was revived in new formulations in Russia. The sheer number of publications on this topic is so overwhelming that it is impossible to give a comprehensive account of the material. I shall focus, rather, on the most common features found in neo-Slavophile periodicals and emphasize the more intriguing tendencies in the interpretation of Jewish participation in the Bolshevik revolution, based on articles in the more conceptually articulate publications. In addition, we must take a look at the social role of this theory in the present political context.

The October Revolution is often described as a genocide against the Russian people. The ideology of Bolshevism and its internationalist rhetoric were only a pretext for the Jews to take power in the country. Neo-Slavophiles adduce what they believe to be "abundant evidence" for a Jewish-Bolshevik conspiracy.[5] Jewish-Bolshevik misdeeds can be summarized by the following list of predominant themes found in neo-Slavophile periodicals:

(1) Jews carried out the October Revolution, which led to the disintegration of the Russian state and society, and the destruction of its religion, culture, and literature. Jews also subverted the economy and caused its decline. These criticisms are often paired with an idealized picture of economic life in Russia (especially the rate of economic growth) under the tsars. Many periodicals publish details about the ethnic origins of prominent Bolshevik leaders as an indication of the nature of social transformation in this century. Trotsky, Zinoviev, Sverdlov, Kamenev, and others are held responsible for Soviet crimes. Some antisemites describe Vladimir Lenin as a Jew.[6] Jews in general are referred to as the "ruling class" of the Soviet state in its first thirty years.[7]

(2) The formation of collectives and suppression of the kulaks was devised by Jewish Bolsheviks specifically to annihilate the backbone of the Russian ethnicity. This policy of collectivization and de-peasantification was initiated

by Yakovlev — they cite his original name, Epstein — the People's Commissar of Agriculture *(narkom zemledeliia)* in Stalin's government. The Jewish members of the Soviet government are accused of deliberately provoking the famine of the early 1930s in order to annihilate the peasants.[8]

(3) Unlike the ideologists of National Orthodoxy, who see religion as the center of Russian life, neo-Slavophiles consider religion to be only one element of national life. Nevertheless, Jews are held responsible for the subversion of Russian religious life as well. Jewish involvement in the anti-religious (i.e., anti-Christian) campaign is epitomized by the activity of Yemelyan Yaroslavsky and Lazar Kaganovich. Yaroslavsky (his original name was Gubelman) was a chairman of the secret Antireligious Commission of the Central Committee of the Russian Communist Party. He was a prominent antireligious crusader and the author of a number of pieces of atheistic propaganda.[9] Kaganovich, the only Jewish member of Stalin's Politburo and first secretary of the Moscow Party Organization (1930–1935), was supposedly personally responsible for the order to destroy the Church of Christ the Savior, the very symbol of Orthodox Russia in Moscow (recently reconstructed under the auspices of the Moscow urban administration).[10]

(4) Many neo-Slavophiles claim that the concept of the Gulag was a Jewish invention; some go so far as to claim that it somehow balances or even outweighs Auschwitz in the type of atrocities and number of deaths. The large number of Jews in the NKVD and administration of the concentration camps *(Belomorkanal)* is taken as evidence of the ethnic basis for the torture of the victims. The "Jewish genealogy" of the camps, for example, is the primary focus of many of Sergei Naumov's writings:

> The first concentration camps were created during the civil war. Leo Trotsky (Leib Bronstein) initiated their establishment.... It was officially prescribed to isolate "class enemies" into concentration camps by special decree about the Red Terror which was suggested by Jeshua-Solomon Sverdlov. Katznelson, a member of ChKa, and Sangwill-Schmerling, a former Menshevik, were the directors of the first concentration camps.[11]

Neo-Slavophiles tend to focus on Bolshevik atrocities perpetrated in the earliest years of the Soviet regime. They believe that these crimes were later overshadowed by the Stalinist purges, and therefore, liberal critics of the Soviet regime deliberately downplay the persecutions in which Jews played a central role, and overemphasize the persecutions of the 1930s in which the Jews were victimized. Many neo-Slavophiles consider Stalin's purges and Party trials of the 1930s a kind of revenge for the atrocities committed by Jewish communists of the Lenin Guard *(Leninskaya gvardiia)*. The label "enemy of the people" — used by the Stalinist perpetrators to describe the accused — is in fact an accurate description of the Jews who were being tried.

(5) The Jewish Bolsheviks are also accused of attempting to eliminate the Cossacks — the military estate that for centuries had defended the fatherland against its enemies — by issuing a special decree calling for the "annihilation of the Cossacks as a class." Yakov Sverdlov, the first chairman of the Central Executive Committee of the Soviet Union, is held personally responsible for the persecution of the Cossacks.[12]

(6) Neo-Slavophiles often refer to the murder of Tsar Nicholas II and his family as a crime against the Russian people (a topic of great interest to the representatives of National Orthodoxy as well). The Jews claim to have acted on behalf of the proletariat and the peasants, but in reality they were pursuing only their own interests. Ultimately, it was the Jews, not the Bolsheviks, who took power.

The October Revolution and the period of communist rule is often described as a "holocaust" and they call for a discussion of the "historical sins of Jews before Russia."[13] An editorial that appeared in *Den'* is characteristic:

> The Bolshevik blow to Great Russia was delivered from the depth of Marxism, which is associated in the minds of Russian patriots with Jewish ideology, Jewish messianism and Jewish practice. This blow destroyed the Empire, smashed the foundations of Russian life, destroyed Orthodoxy, secular elite culture, popular traditions, morals, historic ideals. It provoked Russian bloodshed and annihilated several Russian estates — gentry, clergy, merchants, and peasantry. This is the main knot of contradictions in Russian-Jewish relations, in the deep layers of national consciousness. Jews did not acknowledge their role in the Russian revolution and tragedy and did not repent, being preoccupied with their own tragedy as victims in the Second World War. Russia does not have any debt to the Jews as conjured up by Jewish intellectuals. There is a historic debt of Jews to Russia but it is neither understood nor acknowledged. It intensifies the Russian-Jewish conflict. The Jews accuse Russians of antisemitism, label their movement Red-Brown and subject them to Russophobia...instead of making moral and intellectual efforts to atone.[14]

In a similar vein, Igor Shafarevich claims that in the Soviet period

> the Jews were emancipated from the Pale of Settlement, imposition of quotas, moved from the shtetls to the cities, for the most part to the big cities and have exceeded other ethnicities in their level of education

and in acquisition of academic degrees. Russian gentry and priests were destroyed, the villages ravaged, the birth rate dropped.[15]

The article in *Den'* claims that Israel and the Jews use a double standard when they attribute "national guilt" to Germans, Spaniards, Russians, and Ukrainians and refuse to acknowledge their own national guilt to Russians for the Bolshevik repression. Bondarenko refers to

> their excessive participation in the Bolshevik leadership, repressive politics,... the murder of Stolypin and Tsar Nicholas II, i.e., the events that changed the course of Russian history and caused a Russian Holocaust with its tens of millions of victims, which was much more horrifying than the Jewish one. Perhaps, international Jewish organizations should pay us their tribute, assuming their national responsibility?[16]

The disproportionate number of Jews who participated in the October Revolution and Communist and Left parties is not the only issue in the debate on Jewish involvement in the course of Russian history. Communism itself is considered by many to be a Jewish invention that reflects the peculiarities of the Jewish mentality. The fact that Karl Marx was of Jewish extraction is viewed as an indicator of the Jewish origin of Marxism, and it is claimed that there is an intimate connection between the doctrines of Judaism and communism.

Andrei Yudin's review of differing interpretations of Marx's essay "On the Jewish Question" is characteristic. He discusses the Marxian position against the background of the early nineteenth-century intellectual climate in Germany and the ideas that influenced Marx's arguments. Yudin agrees with Eugene Dühring and Arnold Toynbee about the specifically Jewish "origins" and background of Marxian doctrine, arguing that Marx advanced his theory to resolve his "personal psychological conflict" — the severe inferiority complex caused by his Jewish origins. Marx supposedly designed his theory to provoke and instigate the revolt of the cosmopolitan proletariat against traditional society (European feudalism, the aristocracy, the Russian community). The subversion of traditional society and the traditional national elites would benefit the Jews since it could wipe out their stigma. Thus, Marxism is interpreted as a psychological response by the Jews to their position in Christian societies. Yudin suggests that Jewish scholars like Erich Fromm, Isaiah Berlin, Julius Carlebach, and others worship Karl Marx as their "national saint" because of the hidden Jewish undercurrent in Marx's theories.[17]

Many neo-Slavophiles associate the principle of unitary and totalitarian power with Old Testament ideology, and believe that the social and political activity of the Jewish Bolsheviks were governed by these principles. Even Stalin was heir to the principles of the Oriental political despotism laid down in the Old Testament. Sergei Kuniaev, editor-in-chief of *Nash sovremennik*, eloquently expressed this idea in an article on the poetry of Osip Mandelstam. He argued that the Old Testament provides a conceptual key to understanding "the nature of the political regime" of the Soviet Union.

> It turned out that Stalin was the only educated man in the whole Soviet government. He did not need extensive knowledge of his European contemporaries and of the classics of Marxist tradition.... Stalin was guided by one book, the only one he seriously read. This book informed him about everything, about the law of being, about the mystery of power and about the secrets of government. This book was the Old Testament. Stalin did not waste his time in the Tiflis seminary. The most ancient part of the Bible came to be a handbook, a reference book and his guide to practical life.... Stalin learned from this book his most important lesson, the lesson about the power of the law. The law which everybody is supposed to obey for fear of severe punishment. His assistants were supposed to supervise observance of the law. It is not difficult to distinguish those places in the Pentateuch which have particularly impressed the supreme leader. Stalin had utilized and creatively transformed the commandments of Yahwe to Moses. "Ye shall make no idols..." (Lev. 26:1) When applied to the Levites and Stalin himself, it could be violated.... However, the commandment was to be obeyed rigorously with respect to the "other gods".... Churches were blown into the air all over the country.... It was a "godless five-year plan," the five-year plan of the struggle against the New Testament. Stalin inherited his hatred for Christ not from the ideology of the party but from the commandments of the Old Testament. "The illegal repressions"? Only ignorant people could think this way. Everything was countenanced by law. It was a law which everybody was supposed to obey.... The law was the divine revelation which was received by the leader....[18]

Other writers considered communism a modification of Old Testament principles. Alexander Kazintsev saw it reflected in the life of the ancient Jewish Essene sect:

> Collective labor and a system of public property are the distinctive features of the social practice of some radical sects in Judaism, not of Christianity. It was adopted by the Essenes, another name for the Qumranites.... Like any other group which tries to realize utopia in real life, the Qumranites confronted the fact that human nature is

imperfect and that it does not square well with the rationally planned "terrestrial paradise.".... The sect needed to suppress loyalty to the old customs and to change their social and individual psychology. The whole system was very similar to the concepts worked out by the "engineers of human souls" and the masters of social psychology after our revolution.... The Marxist utopia, which was accepted in our country, had the same qualities as the utopia of the Qumranites. The two thousand years which separate these two utopias did not make any difference. What a powerful spiritual tradition! The most intriguing fact about the whole thing is that contemporary Judaism acknowledges it and considers Marxism the collateral shoot of the fabulously ramified tree of Aaron.[19]

It is important to observe that neo-Slavophiles completely disavow the National Bolshevik theory, according to which the Russian Idea is identical to the social ideals of Communism and Bolshevism. Kazintsev wrote that many observers confused Jewish communism (epitomized by the Qumran community) with the traditional Russian ideal of communal life.

The Russian peasant community had followed the traditions of the early Christian associations. It was completely free of the dark inheritance of Judaism: from the rigid regimentation, impersonal collectivism, and strict hierarchy. Our peasant world had nothing in common with the communist community which followed the traditions of Judaism. In fact it was its exact opposite.[20]

Kasintsev and other neo-Slavophiles deny that the traditional peasant community was a natural foundation for the development of communism.[21] There is no continuity of experience between the Russian community and the Soviet *kolkhoz:*

The advocates of socialism often claim that not everything was wrong under the Soviets and point out that in Israel the kibbutzim, which are no different from our collective farms (*kolkhoz*), work perfectly well. It is true. But we need to keep in mind that kibbutzim fit very well to the Judaic tradition. The first kibbutzim were established at the beginning of the 20th century long before our collective farms. The latter were created according to foreign standards.[22]

In a similar vein, Yurii Borodai claims that the "system of communal socialism," with its bondage and egalitarianism was established very late, by the gentry in the seventeenth century, whereas the Russian people originally had a system of self-government.[23]

Thus, for neo-Slavophiles the link between communism and the Jews is threefold: the Jew Marx laid the foundations of communist doctrine; communist doctrine itself bears close similarity to the original principles of Judaism, in particular, in its emphasis on the law and totalitarian discipline; and the communist revolution in Russia was carried out mainly by Jews.

The morally problematic Neo-Slavophile arguments can be countered by a review of what is known by historians and social scientists about Jewish participation in the Revolution.[24]

Although the Neo-Slavophiles obviously exaggerate, it must be acknowledged that there was an extraordinarily high percentage of people of Jewish origin within the Left in general, including Bolshevism.[25] However, an awareness of the following factors enables a more balanced perspective:

(1) While Jews did occupy conspicuous positions in the communist movement, the overwhelming majority of Party members were of Russian or other ethnicity, as shown by the available data.[26]

(2) Jews who were communists remained a small minority within the Jewish community.

(3) The prominence of the Jews in the communist movement was conditioned by the socio-economic status of the Jews in Russian society. The oppression of the Jews in Russia and the lack of civil rights made communist ideals very appealing to a certain strata of the Jewish population. The communist utopia offered many Jews hope for social and political emancipation, social mobility, equality, and economic opportunity. Membership in the Communist Party meant the elimination of the stigma attached to being Jewish, and led to promotion to previously inaccessible ranks of society.

After the advent of communism, as Leon Volovici aptly points out,

> for the first time Jews began to appear in public functions, in politics, as high-ranking career officers in the military, and in the secret police — that is, in positions of power to which they had had no access before. The shock of Jewish visibility in such positions, even though it did not at all represent a Jewish collective body...seemed only to confirm all the fears and resentments of the populace.[27]

Only certain segments of the Jewish population became fascinated with political radicalism, while the majority associated their emancipation with the victory of the liberal parties or moderate socialist parties. Most often, Jewish interests were represented in the Russian parliament by the Constitutional Democratic Party (the Kadets).[28] Also noteworthy is that within the Russian Social Democratic Labor Party most Jews were members of the Menshevik faction and the Bund, since the communist revolution failed to address the economic interests of the Jewish majority.[29] The traditional Jewish occupations in Russia and the class structure of the Jewish population meant that the ideas about the redistribution of property were very unattractive for the majority of the Jewish population.[30]

If "revenge" played any role in their outlook, it was the social revenge of a subjugated people, relatively independent of their ethnicity, rather than the revenge of ethnicity as such seeking retaliation.

(4) Jews were fighting on both sides of the barricades and were affiliated with political factions across the whole political spectrum. A few individual Jews even joined the Black Hundreds.[31] Moses Uritsky, head of the Cheka[32] was assassinated by another Jew, Leonid Kannegiser; and Dorah Kaplan, a member of the Party of Socialist Revolutionaries, wounded Lenin. Even within the Communist Party, the Jews never acted as a coherent group. Many cases of opposition and deadly struggle between different members of the Communist Party of Jewish origin can be found in Arkadii Vaksberg's book, *Stalin Against the Jews*.[33]

(5) Jews within the Communist Party never represented Jewish culture; indeed, many leaders of the radical Left parties of Jewish extraction did not consider themselves Jewish. Trotsky and other Bolshevik leaders of Jewish origin not only denied any special treatment for members of the Jewish communities, but were often zealous in eradicating Jewish traces within the party and society. The historian Zvi Gitelman asserts that "there were very few Jewish Bolsheviks, and almost no Bolsheviks who were familiar with the Yiddish language or with Jewish life."[34] To use Isaac Deutscher's expression, they were "non-Jewish Jews."[35] No wonder that the traditional Jewish communities regarded Jewish members of the Party as renegades.

Those who believe in the "Judeo-communism" myth proceed from the unfounded assumption that Jewish identity is central for people of Jewish extraction and that they could easily sacrifice ideological convictions since that means less to them than their Jewishness. This assumption shapes the Neo-Slavophile story of the Russian revolution. However, it would be hardly possible for an impartial observer to find even one instance of a decision of the Soviet government induced or seriously affected by the Jewish origins of its members.[36]

The theory of a Jewish-Bolshevik conspiracy is one of the more primitive antisemitic concepts found in ultranationalist ideology. In the next section we shall see much more convoluted theories of the Jewish conspiracy, which try to demonstrate the confluence of the interests of the Jewish Bolsheviks and the Jewish bankers.

THE COMMISSARS AND THE BANKERS:
THE TROTSKY-ROTHSCHILD ALLIANCE

The notion that Jewish bankers and Jewish revolutionaries represented a united front is scarcely new. Mikhail Bakunin in the nineteenth century intimated this in some of his remarks about Karl Marx.[37] It was also elaborated in the *Protocols of the Elders of Zion*. During the Russian civil war it was disseminated by some in the White movement *(Beloe dvizhenie)*. Outside of Russia, it was espoused in Henry Ford's *The International Jew* (1922). Later on, the theory of a Plutocratic-Bolshevik conspiracy was borrowed and propagated by Nazi ideologists such as Alfred Rosenberg.[38] In the Soviet period, it cropped up in Alexander Solzhenitzin's historical novel *August 1914,* in which the character Alexander Israel Helphand (Parvus) — a banker, revolutionary, and Jew — appears.[39] Perhaps unconsciously, Solzhenitsin gives Parvus more responsibility for the October Revolution than Lenin and Trotsky together.[40] The idea was resurrected in the discourse of neo-Slavophiles in the post-perestroika period, the most important writers being Mikhail Nazarov, Alexander Kazintsev, and Yurii Borodai.[41]

The "Jewish war against Russia" is the central historiographic myth of the neo-Slavophiles. The Jewish establishment in the United States is accused of waging economic war against the Russian government as a response to discriminatory policies towards the Jews. In particular, the economic war represents revenge for the pogroms at the beginning of the century, the requirement that Jews live in the Pale, the special military conscriptions of Jews, and restrictions on the movement of American Jews in Russian territory. In order to subvert the tsar's regime, Jewish bankers subsidized the activity of revolutionaries, and exercised the same "stab in the back" strategy during the Russian-Japanese war and the First World War.[42] Nazarov explains:

> The money (1.5 million rubles) came from Felix Warburg.... He and his relative Jacob Schiff had subsidized Japan during the Russian-Japanese war of 1904–1905. He gave millions of yen for subversive propaganda among Russian captives in the Japanese camps and funded the revolution of 1905. Jacob Schiff spent 20 million dollars for the preparation of the Russian Revolution. Twelve million were spent before 1914. Trotsky and Alexander Parvus (Israel Gelfand) were also involved in this activity. It was not a coincidence that during the assassination of Stolypin, Trotsky was sitting in a cafe across the street, across from the theater.[43]

Nazarov cites the work of American historian Arthur Sutton, who pointed to the mutually beneficial collaboration of the Bolsheviks with the Jewish bankers. Wall Street bankers attempted to take advantage of the situation in Russia and expand to Russian markets, while the Bolsheviks were seeking access to new technologies for industrialization, financial support for their political and economic activities, and diplomatic recognition. The bankers' investment in the Soviet economy provided financial resources for the Russian government even though it was against the interests of the United States.[44]

What united the communists and the bankers above all, Nazarov claims, was the international cosmopolitan character of their ambitions. Both groups dreamed of a world government with a universal and homogeneous system of power. Both regarded Russia as an enemy, and no more than an instrument in the international struggle for power and world domination. Needless to say, Nazarov stresses the Jewish origins of the representatives of these two groups, and laments that Sutton downplayed this aspect, probably because he wanted "to avoid accusations of antisemitism."[45]

Nazarov observes that both the commissariats and Wall Street offices "were full of Jewish names." When the Bolsheviks launched the so-called New Economic Policy (NEP) in the early 1920s, the Bolsheviks received financial and technical support from the bankers, while the bankers took advantage of the "fabulous wealth collected during the entire history of Russia." Nazarov singles out Kuhn, Loeb, and Co., Armand Hammer and Nya Banken run by the "red banker" Olof Ashberg.[46] The bank owners acquired museum collections, works of art, Russian gold, Church property, and even royal treasures of the Russian empire. "So the money flowed now in the opposite direction but much more of it."[47] "This wealth helped the Soviet power gain victory in the war against its own people," Nazarov wrote.[48]

Yurii Borodai advances a more sophisticated explanation of the alliance between the revolutionaries and the bankers, presupposing a more intimate connection between the two parties. Borodai (b. 1934) is a senior fellow at the Institute of Philosophy of the Russian Academy of Sciences, who has published extensively on a variety of subjects ranging from the history of philosophy and epistemology to the history of Russian agricultural policies. His discussions of political and economic history, heavily tainted with antisemitism, will be the focus here. In papers and articles published in the 1990s, Borodai spells out many of the neo-Slavophile assumptions and suggests his own explanation for the Jewish involvement in Russian history. His central theme is that the union of the cosmopolitan forces crystallized in the social organizations of capitalism and socialism.

Borodai's analysis hinges upon a distinction between financial and industrial capital. He believes that a grasp of the heterogeneous character of capital is absolutely indispensable for understanding the social transformations of the twentieth century. Drawing on *The National Question and Social Democracy* by Otto Bauer (an Austrian social-democrat), and Rudolf Hilferding's *Das Finanzkapital,* Borodai associates industrial capital with Christianity and financial capital with Judaism, and predicts the final triumph of financial capital:

> It is inevitable that the cosmopolitan financial capital will win over the locally limited industrial one in all the industrially developed countries. This victory will be greatly facilitated by the activity of socialists and left radicals. These groups provoke strikes, social instability and other social tensions "when it is necessary." These activities increase the demand for banking credit; they strengthen financial capital and ruin the manufacturers.[49]

Paradoxically, the revolutionary movement and social instability are beneficial for the development of financial capital. Jewish financial capital is nomadic and mobile, while Christian industrial capital is vulnerable to workers' strikes and Bolshevik propaganda. The workers' movement can easily ruin industrial capital, while financial capital needs only to transfer its assets to another country. Thus, during the first Russian revolution of 1905–1906 the profits of commercial banks doubled. The bankers also took advantage of the situation in the course of the Depression of 1929 in the United States.[50] In this, Borodai's theory differs little from those of Nazi leaders who claimed that Jews enter into the workers' movement only to assume control over it and to channel the outrage of the masses against non-Jewish capital and thus safeguard their own financial interests.[51]

In general, Borodai accounts for the failure of the classical pattern of development of capitalism in Russia by referring to the disproportionate growth of financial capital at the expense of the industrial. Financial capital hampered the development of industrial capital and destroyed Stolypin's attempts to modernize the economy. For Borodai, the terms "financial capital" and "the Jews" are almost interchangeable.

The story of Plutocratic-Revolutionary cooperation began with the agrarian reform of 1861, when the traditional Russian village community received a large portion of land previously owned by the Russian gentry. However, the reform did not emancipate the serfs, who were supposed to pay off their debts to the gentry through their labor (corvée, quitrent). Some landowners did not want to receive the debt repayment via labor, and so the government paid them through bonds. The peasants were then obligated to pay their debt to the state treasury within fifty years. To prevent inflation the government artificially supported the value of the ruble on the foreign markets and introduced the gold standard. This artificial measure hampered the development of industrial capital and led to rapid the growth of financial capital. The peasants became clients of the omnipotent usurers.[52]

Borodai contends that Jewish financial capital came to be the main beneficiary of the reform of 1861. He mentions only Jewish banking houses — Poliakov, Alchevsky, Rubinstein, Brodsky — and claims that they were able to start their business activity only by virtue of the agrarian reform, eventually destroying Russia's industrial capital and gaining control over the economy at large.

> The accumulation of capital has allowed the newly established commercial banks to wage an attack on domestic industrialists. The bankers have expanded their control to a number of enterprises. They seized the most profitable railway concessions and penetrated into the administrative boards of many companies. Finally, they gained control over whole groups of corporations.[53]

Borodai discusses the careers of several prominent Jewish bankers as representative cases of the triumph of financial capital. The career of Baron Ginzburg, who emerged from an early career as a wine merchant and petty usurer to become one of the most prominent financiers, is paradigmatic. He made his fortune by speculating on Russian state bonds, buying them 20–40% below their face value. The famous gold mine Lenzoloto was among his holdings. Borodai accuses Ginzburg of provoking the bloody strike of 1912 that shook all of Russia. Another prominent Jewish banker, Simon Poliakov, monopolized coal production. He bought the Kursk-Kharkov-Azov railway, the chief channel for coal supply, and dictated coal prices.

Jewish financial capital also expanded into land-mortgage banking, Borodai claims, taking full advantage of the Russian agrarian reform and making their fortunes.

> After the reform the mortgage banks mushroomed in Russia like toadstools. Lazar and Rosalia Poliakov established the land bank of Moscow, Yaroslavl and Kostroma; the banking house of Ginzburg, controlled the land banks of Nizhnii Novgorod and Samara; Brodsky took control over the land bank of Kharkov, Bliokh — the land bank of Vilno, Kronenberg — the bank of Warsaw, Rafailovich — the Bessarabian land bank. These financiers derived their profits from Russian agrarian collectivism. They were vitally concerned in the conservation of Russian "communitarian socialism" which was an obstacle in the way of Russian industrial modernization.[54]

Pyotr Stolypin, the Russian minister of the interior until his assassination in 1911 and the constitutional premier (1906–1911), proposed an alternative to this dangerous path of development. He suggested creating a new independent class of farmers, thereby transforming traditional agrarian relations. Borodai believes that the reform suggested by Stolypin could have opened a "third way," neither capitalist nor socialist. Stolypin suggested that the government should abolish the redemption payments and give permission to the peasants to work both for the state and for private companies. Stolypin also suggested that the peasants should be able to leave the traditional village commune. He established a special Peasant Bank that was supposed to promote the reform and to lend money to the peasants at low interest rates. These interest rates were significantly lower than the ones offered by the Jewish mortgage banks. Borodai argues that the reforms were so successful that they promoted the establishment of "a free labour market, suspended the expansion of financial capital and allowed Russia to surpass all other countries in its rate of economic growth."[55]

The enormous success of Russian modernization, Borodai goes on to argue, unsettled the Jewish bankers and the revolutionary Left. Whereas the decline in the class struggle disappointed the Bolsheviks and other Left parties (Lenin coined a special term "agrarian bonapartism" to signify this phenomenon), the loss of profits from the dissolution of the village communes was very embarrassing for the Jewish mortgage bankers. Borodai then infers that the assassination of Stolypin in Kiev in 1911 by Dmitrii Bogrov, a baptized Jew, was arranged by the leaders of the Jewish bankers and the Bolsheviks.[56] The death of Stolypin, along with the two Russian revolutions prevented the implementation of the "system of agrarian Bonapartism" and the development of the ideology of a "third way" in Russia.

Borodai argues that the economic situation during the period of perestroika was reminiscent of the pre-revolutionary period. In particular, financial capitalism seriously hampered the development of industrial capital, and began to dominate the development of capitalism. This situation is really universal, since in the countries of the West as well, entrepreneurs no longer perform their old function as direct organizers of production and the epoch of business risk and free competition gave way to domination by monopolies. Business managers who have replaced entrepreneurs are not much different from state employees and wage workers. The "financial magicians" control not only the stock market but also extend their control to industry and state institutions. Borodai insists that the power of the financial magicians is identical with Jewish domination over the world.

Borodai's preconceived idea of an opposition between Christian industrial and Jewish financial capital blinds him to the known history. Many of the capitalists whom Borodai names — the Poliakov brothers, Alchevsky, and Brodsky — actually played an important role in the industrialization carried out by the government and guided by Minister of Finance Sergei Witte. The Poliakov brothers accumulated their capital by developing the railroads, which were the key element for industrialization. Borodai fails to acknowledge that the railroads constituted the largest single industry of the country, employing 400,000 workers in 1900. The capital invested in railroads can hardly be described as parasitic. Theodore von Laue, the historian of the first phase of Russian industrialization, points out that at this time railroads "increasingly determined the flow of goods and thereby the prosperity of every region of every branch of national economy."[57] Borodai claims that Poliakov invested in railroads in order to dictate coal prices. However, even privately owned railroads were regulated by the government (e.g., the government controlled the freight rates), and most railroads were gradually converted to state ownership.

As for the support of the Russian Revolution, the Bolsheviks received more financial resources from the "immobile Christian industrial capital" than from the "mobile Jewish capital." Financial contributions from the "Christian industrial capital" — supplied by Savva Morozov — are much better documented than the mythical "Jewish" contributions.[58]

Borodai claims that the government introduced the gold standard out of concern for the welfare of the gentry "wasting money in foreign resorts." The government supposedly feared that state bonds issued to compensate the gentry would drop in value as a result of inflation. However, the government had much more serious reasons to introduce the gold standard. It needed to maintain the country's credit in order to obtain more foreign investments. The emancipated peasants and decadent gentry were not the only clients of the "Jewish" investment banks. Moreover, Jewish bankers had no incentive for retarding the industrial development of the country because any economic decline undermined their own position. High interest rates would diminish the demand for the capital. Many Jewish bankers had a vested interest in Russian industry, construction projects, mining, and the railroads.

THE TOTALITARIAN BROTHERHOOD OF CAPITALISM AND SOCIALISM AND THEIR JEWISH ROOTS

Following the thinking of Hannah Arendt, publications of the perestroika period pointed out that fascism and Bolshevism had much in common, and both were totalitarian. Liberalism, it was believed, represented an ideology in complete opposition to all types of totalitarianism. Borodai, however, asserts that liberalism is in fact the breeding ground of totalitarianism, and is much more totalitarian than either fascism or communism. Borodai sets out to debunk the idea that the totalitarian spirit is a natural product of the Eastern mentality, claiming that its most horrifying forms have actually been generated in the liberal West. The purposive-rational forms of social organization cultivated in the liberal West result in the large-scale regimentation of labor on assembly lines, globalization, unification, the standardization of life, the leveling of personality, and hostility to everything original. Borodai believes that the liberal critics of the old Soviet system did not understand the real nature and roots of totalitarianism:

> Totalitarianism is a mortal disease of mankind. It starts with cosmopolitan atomization. Bolshevism and Fascism are the clearest manifestations of this international plague. But the successful democratic West is the constant source of the contagion.[59]

Borodai's primary contention is that the totalitarian spirit is triggered and nourished by the Jewish spirit and Judaic religious principles. Both capitalism and socialism are incarnations of the Judaism-inspired totalitarian spirit, and despite their apparent opposition, they are almost identical in terms of their social outcomes. Here, Borodai takes Judaism not so much as a religion but as a specific cultural moral code. Capitalism and socialism only rationalize and advance the concepts and impulses already present in ancient Judaism. Understanding this sheds light on the mystery of modern history.

> Two guiding stars help the Chosen People in their search for the ultimate end, the supremacy of the caste over the depersonalized human herd. The first star is a Star of Solomon, a Red Pentagram, while the second one is a Star of David, the Yellow Sexangle. In the age of Enlightenment, which came after the bloody slaughter of the Reformation, the Protestants, being the heirs of the covert wisdom of the Old Testament, managed to transform two astral mystical tendencies of ancient Oriental religion into rational doctrines. These two doctrines epitomize two different possible ways of socio-economic progress. All dissenters who disagreed with these doctrine were denigrated as retrogrades and obscurantists.[60]

Thus, capitalism and socialism merely represent two different ways to realize the same end — enslavement of the "depersonalized majority of people by the elitist Little People" and the drastic transformation of their consciousness. The only difference between socialism and capitalism is the type of enslavement. The socialist type utilizes direct coercion, epitomized in the concentration camps, centralized state planning, and the KGB; capitalist enslavement utilizes the free market system.[61] Borodai finds both types of enslavement in Russian history; he believes that the two types of social organization to which they are linked are alien to the authentic ideals of Russian society and were brought into Russia from outside.[62]

Some Neo-Slavophiles suggest a vision of Russian history of the last two century in the light of these two types of enslavement.

Borodai further explains the connection between totalitarian socialism and totalitarian capitalism through the figure of Rudolf Hilferding (1877-1941), an economist and ideologist of Austrian Marxism who "came from a religious Jewish family of merchants." He claims that Hilferding was the first person to use the term "totalitarianism" in a positive sense. Hilferding thought that monopolization and the concentration of capital facilitated the planning of production in all areas of the economy. "Organized capitalism" is also conducive for the regulation of prices. Moreover, monopolization strengthens state power and contributes to the regimentation of social life, which he saw as beneficial. Liberalism was good enough as the ideology for young capitalism, but advanced capitalism required quite different ideological justifications. Hilferding believed that liberalism could be exported by Western countries as a tool for subverting the political regimes of the enemy, although within capitalist countries themselves, the ideology was obsolete and almost useless. Hilferding believed that the victory of social democrats in the parliamentary struggle would change only the facade for the régime would have already been transformed by advanced capitalism.[63]

Not surprisingly, Borodai regards Hilferding's writings as self-revelatory testimony to the totalitarian nature of capitalist and socialist societies. The economist's Jewish origins reveal Judaism as the ultimate source of these totalitarian ideas. In order to demonstrate further the links between capitalism, socialism, and Jewishness, Borodai analyzed the theories of Karl Marx, Werner Sombart, Arnold Toynbee, and Max Weber. Although their accounts and assessment of the industrial revolution differ, Borodai argues that taken together, one finds a comprehensive picture of the rise of capitalism and modernization that allows one to see its Jewish background.

Borodai credits Karl Marx for his ingenious analysis of the process of clearing the estates, the rise of commodity production, and wage labor. Marx claimed that capitalist production required the supply of a new commodity, wage labor. Borodai contends that the Marxian analysis demonstrated that the agrarian revolution and the enclosure movement had nothing to do with the internal logic of commodity production. The enclosure movement was a result of political violence, exercised by a minority of the population. The peasantry, which had comprised the majority, was robbed by a small group of rapacious bourgeoisie. The struggle against "agrarian overpopulation" came to be an indispensable aspect of the expansion of capitalism. The clearing of estates in England became a universal pattern for the transition from traditional society to capitalism. This crime against the peasantry was the original sin of capitalist civilization.

Borodai also points to some flaws in the Marxian analysis. Marxian economic theory was blind to the non-economic motives of human behavior. This lack of sensitivity did not allow Marx to understand properly the social background of the clearing of estates and the propulsive forces behind the agrarian revolution. Borodai also blames Marx for categorizing the peasants as "petty bourgeoisie" in *Das Kapital*.[64] This misconception provided legitimacy for the repressive agrarian politics of the Soviet authorities. Like its counterpart in England, the Russian agrarian revolution carried out by the Bolsheviks ruined the "natural forms of human relations" and transformed the majority of population into a mere commodity. Borodai argues that the policy of "de-peasantification" *(raskrestyanivanie)* in Russia was realized in a punitive and predatory way similar to the classic pattern in Great Britain. The violence of Jewish Bolsheviks was only a projection and imitation of the original capitalist violence. Remarkably, Borodai claims that Stalin only materialized plans and policies suggested long before by Trotsky.[65]

Max Weber's works successfully bridged some gaps in Marxist theory, particularly in assessing the importance of religious beliefs in the generation of capitalism. Weber was the first to understand the crucial importance of Judaic principles in the development of capitalism, many of which were adopted by the Calvinists and laid down as the foundation of Protestant ethics, in the "spirit of capitalism." Weber used the metaphor "English Hebraism" to designate Puritanism. Borodai laments that Weber did not elaborate this important point and thus obscured the link between the spirit of capitalism and the Jews. Weber also failed to articulate the horrors of the agrarian revolution, due to his fascination with the virtues of the new class of the bourgeoisie and the potential of this class for establishing the new world order.

Borodai turned to the writings of Werner Sombart to explain both the Jewish roots of capitalism and the social nature of the agrarian revolution.

Sombart understood that the capitalist spirit was not necessarily Protestant, but rather the spirit of a cosmopolitan and uprooted people, untouched by the sentiments of the indigenous population. A cosmopolitan can better resolve problems of economic organization than someone with roots in the given culture, for the emotional attachments of the local people hamper their ability to cope with the rigid requirements of capitalist enterprise — parsimony, cold rationality, and utilitarian efficiency. The lack of any intimate personal ties with the native peoples of a country makes cosmopolitans less vulnerable and enables them to concentrate their energies on promoting their business interests. Sombart suggests that it is no accident that England became the fatherland of capitalism. Mass waves of immigrants from the continent made England especially suitable for the development of a market economy. The Huguenots (banished from France) and the Jews (banished from Spain) were among the first capitalists. In contrast to Weber, Sombart did not see a direct causal relationship between the rise of Protestantism and the development of capitalism. Protestantism facilitated the development of capitalism but could not initiate the process.[66] Borodai comments that the cosmopolitan Jewish pedigree of the first capitalists was more important than their religious background. Conversion to Protestantism did not seriously affect the Jews' success in business. Many of them preserved their faith, while making an impressive career.

Arnold Toynbee's *Industrial Revolution in England* sheds additional light on the last link in the story of capitalism. Since social status and political rights in England were the derived from land ownership, the acquisition of land, was crucial for the foreigners arriving from the continent. The demand for land rose, and as a result, the feudal laws of land ownership were revised and modern private property laws introduced. The purchase of land and concomitant acquisition of political rights by the immigrant *nouveau riche* explains both the enclosures and the ruthless attitude adopted toward the English peasants.

Borodai explains the modern, mainly Protestant, religious ideas as a function of immigrant psychology. Both Calvinism and Judaism are religions of homeless cosmopolitans. He acknowledges the differences between the two religions. Whereas for Calvinists the accumulation of capital is an end in itself, the Jews consume capital in a more or less traditional fashion (i.e., not constantly reinvested, but either consumed or hoarded). While the Jews hoard their capital, the Calvinists wished to invest their capital in new enterprises. Even so, Calvinism was nothing more than "a cosmopolitan Judaism open to the gentiles." It is Judaism "carried out to its logical end."[67] It is no coincidence, he observes, that many American synagogues were transformed into Judeo-Protestant temples.[68]

Borodai distinguishes three basic principles, all related to the psychology of strangers, which make the two religions congenial. Both advocate a theory of the Chosen People ("the theory of tribal arrogance") and the doctrine of predestination, according to which God has chosen some people for eternal life and left the rest to perish. God's choice for salvation or damnation is both arbitrary and final, and those not chosen are regarded as beasts devoid of any humanity. Second, both support cruel practices of social transformation. Third, both emphasize the principle of justice at the expense of mercy as found in the New Testament:

> One can learn from the dogmas of the Old Testament that sickness is a "sign of God's anger," "the seal of sin," "a just penalty".... The central idea of the Old Testament is the idea of justice, the idea of an equivalent exchange with God. This idea is incompatible with mercy.... If you are virtuous and obey the law, you will get a reward.... But if you violate the prohibition, you will be ruined. You could be punished by leprosy or ugliness. Thus, suffering is a sign of treason. By the same token, an epidemic indicates vice and shame. No wonder that [the Jews] used to evict sick people from their towns. They took them to the deserts and stoned them. There is evidence according to which some of them were even drowned in the Red Sea.... Judaists were not sensitive to suffering; since it was considered a sign of vice; they did not develop the virtue of compassion.[69]

Calvinists incorporated Old Testament cruelty in their ideology and practice of capitalism. He cites several striking examples. For instance, in the patterns of colonization of South and North America, the Catholic colonizers of Latin America married indigenous women, but among the Protestants in North America, this was forbidden. Murderers of American Indians were rewarded with special gifts, and it is noteworthy that Calvinists reestablished the system of slave labor. Vicious Calvinist ethics are also held responsible for the "slaughter of the Reformation" in Germany, which took the lives of two thirds of the population, and the unprecedented exploitation of children. The horrifying living conditions of the working class in the period of the original accumulation of capital is also attributed to the ideology of Old Testament "tribal arrogance" inherited by Calvinists.[70] Borodai asserts that Protestant countries continue the cruel practices of Calvinism; the liberal Protestant West supports the most authoritarian political regimes in the world. Despotic regimes in underdeveloped countries are now better equipped to pay their debts, thus these countries are even more exploited in order to increase the wealth of the Calvinist First World.[71] All these practices can be understood entirely and exclusively on the basis of the moral code prescribed by the Old Testament.

Borodai is opposed to liberalism as well, which he sees as a Jewish ideological tool that claims to be concerned with limiting state control of the private sphere and protecting human rights, but in fact is a kind of dynamite ready to explode the foundations of traditional community life and destroy its moral bonds. He holds responsible the Jewish philosophers Benedict Spinoza, Karl Popper, and Henri Bergson for the propagation of anti-traditional subversive liberal doctrines. The "open society," Borodai says, is amoral, and undermines the concept of self-sacrifice as conceived in traditional societies.

> In civil society *(Gesellschaft)* notions like duty and conscience turn into idle rhetoric, since they lose all their practical sense. The actual realization of the principle of the "freedom of conscience" leads to the loss of any conscience.[72]

Of Spinoza, Borodai writes:

> Asceticism, sacrifice, struggle with one's nature is the starting point of any transcendental system of beliefs. This system restricts the pursuit of carnal pleasures and desires, sometimes to the degree of complete self-abnegation.... Spinoza laid the foundations for the modern anti-spiritual moral outlook. He proclaimed the ideal of full self-expression and material satisfaction of the natural desires of one's ego as an end in itself.[73]

The "Jewish philosophers" Karl Popper and Henri Bergson have elaborated the liberal ideas of Spinoza and developed them into the famous theory of the "open society." Like Spinoza, both deified the sovereign individual at the expense of the community, and painted the closed traditional societies as sources of stagnation. In Bergson's most important work on political philosophy, *Two Sources of Morality and Religion,* he contends that the closed society is self-centered; religion and morality are static and absolutist, while conformity to the standards of the community becomes the prime duty of a citizen. The open society, on the other hand, requires freedom of expression and diversity and elimination of the dogmatism of the traditional religions. Bergson also believed that the multiplicity of closed societies was an obstacle to evolution. Borodai, by contrast, insists it is necessary to recreate traditional sacrificial virtues and the ethos that enables human beings to sacrifice their own interests to that of building strong communities.

Borodai believes that the advantages of life in an open society are largely exaggerated. The only alternative to the traditional morality of self-sacrifice in a closed society is administrative despotism and totalitarian functionalization. The social system of the open society offers benefits only to small minority groups — such as the Jews.

Borodai's argument is that moral norms stem from one's ethnic community, and are expressed in the unique terminology of the specific community. Arguments for the establishment of universal social codes and norms in an open society can only work to the advantage of the Jews. It is no accident that those whom Borodai refers to as the homeless "heirs of the Old Testament" were so conspicuous during the social transformations of the perestroika period.

The issue here is the value of the liberal social order and the significance of the transition to the new social order. Neo-Slavophiles clearly consider the projected new "open society" to be no better than the old Communist scheme for social change, both of which were tainted by Jewish involvement. The concept of a Jewish conspiracy governs their political discourse and historical visions.

Alexander Kazintsev, a prolific literary critic, expressed this clearly in an article in *Nash sovremennik,* claiming that "World Capital and the Communist International" have combined in a fight against Russia. The "Trotsky-Rothschild alliance" represents an "apocalyptic link":

> The whole century of Russian history turned into a fight between Trotsky and Rothschild. The century started with an assault on the stronghold of Capital and finished with the smashing of the socialist camp. First Lev Davidovich Trotsky, grinning in his beard, sends his victorious troops into battle. Then British Baron Rothschild, the "Judean King" as he was described by Dostoevsky, smiles crookedly and sends his detachments into battle. These two figures are rising over Russian fate like the monstrous giants Gog and Magog from the Old Testament. They smile because Russians punch, shoot and put each other into labour camps...for their fun and profit. Trotsky failed to exterminate the Russian people. They proved to be unusually tenacious.... Therefore, today they drive us back to Rothschild. But it is already clear that they are not going to build capitalism in Russia.... Before we arrive at the Baron, they will drive us back to Lev Davidovich...to keep us in this circle. It reminds one of the exhaustion of wild animals.[74]

Borodai and others have offered a complicated theory that involves the Jews in every evil, both ancient and modern, based on a misreading of the Old Testament, Enlightenment and post-Enlightenment philosophers, and even modern Russian history. His romanticization of "traditional Russian society" with its rosy view of peasant life cannot stand up to any serious scrutiny.

RUSSOPHOBIA, THE "LITTLE PEOPLE" AND THE
RUSSIAN-JEWISH INTELLIGENTSIA

We have already seen that many Neo-Slavophiles link the misfortunes of Russia in this century with uprootedness, disruption of community ties, and the advent of rule by outsiders. In this context the theory of the "Little People" advanced by Igor Shafarevich (b. 1923), a famous Russian mathematician, dissident, and an honorary member of the American Academy of Sciences until he was expelled, is especially important.[75] His key concepts were elaborated in *Russophobia*, a controversial antisemitic pamphlet that provoked intense debate in Russia during the perestroika period.[76]

Shafarevich claims that he discovered an intriguing syndrome in Russian cultural development that provides a key to understanding the course of Russian history in the twentieth century — the syndrome of the opposition of the "Little People" *(maliy narod)* to the "Great People" *(bolshoi narod),* that is, to the majority of the population.[77] The Little People despise the moral principles of the Great People, and disregards its traditions and culture. The values of the Great People appear to them as mere superstition and prejudice, and the Little People are completely lacking in mercy and compassion.

The phenomenon of the Little People is not uniquely Russian. Shafarevich drew on the observations of the conservative French historian, Augustin Cochin, whose concept of the Little People was advanced in his analysis of the forces behind the French Revolution.[78] According to Cochin, in the course of the eighteenth century a small minority — the Little People — gathering in the Academies and the Masonic lodges, became very hostile to the old traditions (religion and the monarchy). Although the Little People, educated to European standards, appeared to be quite civilized, Cochin saw them as "savages" like the exotic folk of Polynesia, quite unable to understand the animating force behind the traditions of the French people. The famous Declarations, supposedly made for the benefit of all French citizens, Cochin argued, in reality only provided rights for the Little People. Shafarevich went on to insist that the phenomenon was not confined to the era of French Revolution. The same pattern of relations between the Great and Little People can be found in England during the Puritan Revolution; in Germany of the early nineteenth century (where the attitudes of the Little People were exemplified by the Young Germany movement, and specifically in the poems of Heinrich Heine); in the Francophone world, the ideology of the Little People was manifest in the ideas of the Huguenots. In the Russian historical experience, Shafarevich believes, the opposition of Great and Little People is exhibited most vividly.

Shafarevich coined the term "Russophobia" to signify the attitude of hostility to the Russian people exhibited by the Little People. He finds Russophobic tendencies in many different spheres — in historiography, culture, politics, cultural criticism, and the mass media. The members of this "cohesive group" of Little People are quite diverse. Among historians, Shafarevich cites Richard Pipes of Harvard, Alexander Yanov of the University of California at Berkeley, and the late Russian historian, Andrey Amalrik. Russophobia is even more evident in Russian literature produced by the Little People. Shafarevich traces the origins of Russophobia back to the writers of the Odessa School — Isaac Babel, Eduard Bagritsky, Ilf and Petrov, and Haim Bialik. During the Second World War, Russophobia found its expression in the novels of Vasily Grossman and in the memoirs of Nadezhda Mandelstam, the widow of Osip Mandelstam. In the post-Stalin era, the mentality could be perceived in the songs of Alexander Galich, the poems of Iosif Brodsky, the writings of philosopher Grigorii Pomerantz, the writings of Boris Khazanov, and in the articles of the poet David Markish. Shafarevich provides extensive quotes from these figures to substantiate his claim that they are hostile to Russian social values.

The Western anti-communist crusade against the Soviet Union was in fact a disguised version of Russophobia. Russophobes have systematically defamed Russian history and the character of the Russian people. The following are the core myths found in Russophobic historiography and literature:

> The course of Russian history...was determined from its very early stages by some "archetypal" traits of the Russian character: slavish psychology, lack of a sense of human dignity, intolerance towards different opinions, the servile mixture of malice, envy and obedience to the foreign power. From very ancient times Russians learned to love strong and cruel power.... Simultaneously, Russians were haunted by the dream of a special role and mission of Russia in the world... [and] by the desire to save the world.... As a result, despotic regimes and bloody cataclysms have always accompanied Russian history.... However, Russians could not understand the real causes of their suffering. They are suspicious and hostile to everything foreign and blame for their misfortunes everybody — the Tatars, the Greeks, the Germans, the Jews...but not themselves.... The Revolution of 1917 is a natural outcome of the course of Russian history.... Some representatives of this trend express the standpoint of absolute pessimism and hopelessness and deny any meaningfulness to Russian history and existence....[79]

These "myths" of Russian historiography are deliberately forged by Russophobes and imposed on public opinion in Russia and abroad. Shafarevich believes the idea that Russia is a "nation of slaves (*narod rabov)* always bowing down before cruelty and groveling before a strong power" is the myth responsible for many other misconceptions. Russophobes articulate a widespread attitude that Russians are submissive toward authority, and throughout history have demonstrated self-defeating and self-destructive behavior. An examination of actual history and a comparison of the reactions of Russians and other, Western European ethnicities to similar historical situations exposes the ideological stereotypes of the Russophobes.[80]

Shafarevich further contends that universal human rights advocated by the leaders of the French revolution (and today by the Little People) are not really universal, but merely those desired by a small minority of the population.[81] The Little People, for instance, are preoccupied with the right of emigration for the Jewish minority, while many people (peasants) cannot move freely even within the country. The rights of the Great People do not concern the Little People.

Shafarevich attributes the anti-Russian stance of Russophobes to their Jewish background, specifically, to their "suspicious and inimical attitude to the world outside" and the "mentality of revenge upon the world." Russophobia is a product of "some powerful trend in Jewish nationalism" (or "some strata of Jewry"). "Jewish national sentiments," he claims, "are the most important propulsive force which drives the Little People."[82]

> The hatred of one ethnicity is closely connected with a special sensitivity to the people who belong to another [ethnicity].... There is only one ethnicity the concerns of which are discussed every day. The Jewish national emotions affect both our country and the world: they influence the negotiations about disarmament, the trade agreements and the international disputes of the scholars, evoke the demonstrations and strikes and come to the surface almost in every conversation. The "Jewish question" has a special power over minds; it overshadows the problems of the Ukrainians, Estonians, Armenians and the Crimean Tatars. The existence of the "Russian question" is not even acknowledged.[83]

Shafarevich is reluctant to identify the Little People with the Jews directly. He believes that the "Little People" syndrome could have different "incarnations" — not necessarily Jewish. However, Shafarevich emphasizes the fact that the religious principles of Judaism that shaped the Jewish mind for two thousand years [*sic*] are especially conducive to the formation of the mentality of the Little People. The extreme hostility of the Jews to all other ethnicities is well exposed in the Talmud and in the Old Testament. Shafarevich clarifies his position on the connection between the Jews and the Little People as follows:

> The Little People uses (for its incarnation) a certain group or stratum which has a tendency for self-isolation and which opposes itself to the Great People. It could be a religious group (Puritans in England), a social class (the third estate in France) or ethnic group (the trend of Jewish nationalism in our country). However, just as the nobility and the priests played an important role in the French revolution, many Russians and Ukrainians sometimes contribute to the ideology of the Little People. Openness gives more power to this ideology. Otherwise, the movement would be isolated and would not be able to exert a serious influence on the whole people.... Given the prominence of the standpoint of Jewish nationalism, it is only natural to think that the central nucleus, around which the Little People is centralized, is constituted by Jewish nationalists. Their role is the role of the ferment which expedites and directs the process of formation of the Little People. However, the very category of the Little People is broader. It could exist without this influence, although its activity and its role in the life of the country could be seriously diminished in their absence.[84]

This quotation indicates that Shafarevich takes the Jews as a synecdoche for the Little People; further, he suggests that the "Russian intelligentsia" is practically a code term for the Jews. The intelligentsia conceives itself as a small group that feels alienated from the majority of the population and from the beliefs of the Great People.[85] Furthermore, the intelligentsia impose their ideological convictions upon the Great People and control public opinion. The Little People shapes the public agenda and creates its own standards different from those of the majority. The mass media and other channels of intellectual education easily produce celebrities and forge public consciousness in the desired direction, because the Little People are very skillful at "brainwashing" techniques and in the "maintaining and fabrication of the authorities, which are based exclusively on the power of hypnosis."[86] Shafarevich contends that the overrated reputations of many Jews in twentieth-century culture were artificially created by Jewish journalists. "The influence of Freud as a scholar, the glory of Schoenberg as a composer and of Picasso as an artist, the fame of Kafka as a writer, and Brodsky as a poet, will be absolutely incomprehensible for future generations...."[87]

Identifying the intelligentsia with the Little People became quite popular in neo-Slavophile writings. Alexander Kazintsev, for example, believes that the Judaizing heresy of the fifteenth century shows the Jewish origins of the

Russian intelligentsia. In contrast to Orthodox nationalists, Kazintsev takes this heresy as a persistent social tendency rather than a religious heresy proper.

> [The] "Judaizing Heresy" is interesting to me as a symptom of sickness of spirit which came to be prominent not only in the 15th century but also in the later centuries. The rejection of faith and traditional beliefs is a visible manifestation of this sickness.... The "Judaizing heresy" demonstrated the spiritual detachment of the intellectuals from the unity of the people....[88]

The mentality of the intelligentsia, Kazintsev argues, is almost indistinguishable from that of the Judaizers, for both groups despise the common people and believe in their own exclusivity and special calling. Kazintsev describes Judaizers as liberal-minded intellectuals and individualists.

Both Judaizers and intelligentsia proclaim themselves independent of tradition and believe in the supremacy (or at least self-sufficiency) of reason over faith. This autonomy of reason was exemplified in both cases by their reading of the Holy Scriptures. Whereas traditionally the text was read in conformity with the interpretation of the religious authorities, the Judaizers interpreted the book according to their own understanding. They also attacked the traditions of Russian faith.

The Judaizers, who "managed to attract only the upper classes of several cities" were eventually defeated. Kazintsev admits that unfortunately, the authorities who fought the heresy were unfairly labeled "persecutors." The heresy managed to survive underground, and its destructive potential passed to the Russian intelligentsia. Kazintsev quotes *The Landmarks* — the manifesto of the Russian intelligentsia — to show its near-identity with the ideas of the Judaizers. The Bolsheviks and the liberal reformers of the perestroika period — groups that displayed the paradigmatic features of intelligentsia — became the Judaizers of the twentieth century.

In the first years of perestroika, Shafarevich's *Russophobia* was widely and intensively discussed in Russian periodicals. The author claims that his work elicited at least thirty essay-length responses in Russia and the West.[89] Many of the responses are quite interesting in and by themselves.[90] Looking at Shafarevich's work and the more serious responses to it, I shall elaborate some important social implications of his position and its impact on nationalist ideology.

Critics of Shafarevich quickly pointed out that the notion of a Russian "slave mentality" hardly originated with the "Jewish enemies" of Russia. Citations similar to or even more radical than those presented by Shafarevich can be found in the works of nineteenth-century Russian writers, including those of classical authors like Alexander Pushkin, Mikhail Lermontov, and Nikolai Gogol. Surprisingly, these kinds of statements are found not only in the writings of Russian Westernizers *(zapadniki),* but even in the classics of Slavophilism.

Second, not all such utterances should be characterized as expressions of Russophobia. The authors quoted by Shafarevich could just as well have had in mind the traditions of despotic and authoritative power evident throughout Russian political history, as discussed in the recent study by Daniel Rancour-Laferriere, *The Slave Soul of Russia.*[91] Traditions of self-immolation, self-abnegation, self-denunciation, and self-humiliation have been reported by even the most sympathetic observers of the Russian ethos and history. These characterizations can be found in the diaries or memoirs of the seventeenth-century travelers Adam Olearius and Giles Fletcher, and in *A Journey Through Eternal Russia* by the Marquis de Custine. These latter books have no connection with any Jewish "media war." It is bizarre that Shafarevich should associate Russophobia with the historiography inspired by Jewish nationalism.

It is also noteworthy that the "slave mentality" is discussed by the Russophobes not as a racial quality of Russians, but rather as the product of the long tradition of serfdom and political despotism. Serfdom was abolished only in 1861; and slavery existed in Russia until 1723. And in discussing the "Russians," the Russophobe authors cited by Shafarevich are referring to the nation, not the Russian ethnicity.

Some criticisms advanced by the "Russophobes" and cited by Shafarevich indeed sound defamatory and contemptuous. However, these statements do not provide any evidence for the membership of these authors in a single cohesive group. Even less could these quotations provide evidence for an ideological war against Russia supposedly being waged by the Jews. As many critics of *Russophobia* have already pointed out, many of these statements are taken out of their original contexts.

It would be hard to overestimate the role of *Russophobia* in the public debates in Russia during the perestroika and post-perestroika periods. Many of Shafarevich's terms and concepts were adapted by nationalist periodicals, including of course, the term "Russophobia" itself, and was widely used to counter the "myth" of Russian antisemitism. Russophobia even came to be a legal term, adopted by the courts as a special type of incrimination like antisemitism. Recently a court prosecuted Valeria Novodvorskaia, a radical leader of the movement for democratic reform, on a charge of Russophobia.[92]

Ultranationalists also adopted the term "Little People" as a euphemism for the Jews.

THE JEWISH-MASONIC CONSPIRACY REDISCOVERED

The supposed link between Masons and Jews is a subject of attention in several trends of Russian nationalism, but is especially prominent in Neo-Slavophilism and National Orthodoxy. The theory of a Jewish-Masonic conspiracy was advanced in the middle of the nineteenth century.[93] The idea has probably been spread most widely through the continuous re-publication of the *Protocols of the Elders of Zion*. Jews are accused of allying themselves with Masons to subvert Christian states from inside. Credence in the theory was revived in the perestroika period.[94]

Mikhail Nazarov, a prolific émigré Russian writer, was one of the prominent exponents of the theory's revival. He considers Jewry and Freemasonry as two distinct groups whose interests largely converged in the course of modern history. Nazarov draws heavily upon the works of the reputable historians Jacob Katz and Mikhail Gessen.[95] Gessen contended that the alliance of Freemasonry and Jewry — the key subversive forces of the nineteenth century — was quite natural, since both groups, according to Cochin's theory, were incarnations of the Little People. Nazarov points out that the Masonic lodges were the first institutions of European society to accept Jews as full members, and contributed their support to Jewish emancipation. Although Masonry did not accept Jewish particularism, since it contradicted the Masonic principles of "equality and fraternity," Jews were nevertheless admitted to the lodges, and greatly influenced the language and rituals of Masonry. Among the prominent nineteenth-century Masons, one finds Adolphe Crémieux (French Minister of Justice after the overthrow of Louis Philippe), Moses Montefiore (the English philanthropist), the Rothschilds in Germany, and Nathan in Italy.

Nazarov asserts that Jewry and Freemasonry tried to subvert the political institutions of the most conservative dynasties of Europe — the Hohenzollerns, the Habsburgs, and the Romanovs. Both Jews and Masons viewed these empires as their historic enemies, opposed to humanistic values and human rights. The Masons organized the assassination of Archduke Franz Ferdinand, and in the ensuing war, the Jews and the Masons were the only real victors.

Both Masonry and the Jews opposed the Church and traditional Christianity. The Jews opposed Christianity for theological reasons, but the Masons sought to "liberate" traditional Christianity and smuggle into it the humanistic ideas of the Enlightenment. The connection between the Jews and Masons can be seen in the fact that since the eighteenth century Masonry has adopted many Jewish elements, such as kabbalistic symbols and the laws of the "descendants of Noah" (the seven commandments that Jews considered to be obligatory on non-Jews as well) — at the expense of the Christian principles that originally inspired Masonry.

In addition, Nazarov dwells on the connection between Masons and Bolsheviks. He mentions a few Jews who belonged both to the Masons and the Communist Party. The Bolsheviks, he claims, adopted the Masonic Red Star (Star of Solomon), as a symbol of the Soviet state. Nazarov cites an entry in the diary of Leon Trotsky in which he recalls that during his imprisonment he learned about Masonry and, in particular, about the Red Star. Nazarov asserts that the Jewish financial elite (Jacob Schiff and the Warburgs) and Lord Milner (a Mason) funded the Russian Revolution. The Jewish financial elite also greatly influenced the decisions of the Provisional Government after the revolution of February 1917. However, after the October Revolution, the Jewish-Masonic alliance in Russia was suspended due to the special "religious dimension" of the Bolsheviks (many of whom saw their movement as a new religion), who no longer wished to maintain their contacts with the Masons and the Jewish financial elite.[96]

In Western Europe, on the other hand, the Jewish-Masonic alliance continued. By the end of the Second World War, the major historical goals of the Jews and the Masons were accomplished. The Balfour Declaration was realized through the establishment of Israel, while the establishment of various international organizations has undermined the principles of national autonomy and sovereignty.[97]

Nazarov concludes:

> The similarity between Jewry and Masonry and the confluence of their interests on different levels — social, political and worldview — have contributed to the generation of the theory of a "Jewish-Masonic conspiracy." It goes without saying that only some Jews and some Masons have taken part in the alliance. These people formed the active "nucleus" of a group which served as a prototype of the theory of conspiracy in question.[98]

Nazarov believes he has provided sufficient evidence to demonstrate a real basis for belief in a Jewish-Masonic conspiracy as expressed in the *Protocols of the Elders of Zion*. He distrusts the authenticity of the *Protocols,* but argues that the *Protocols* reflect in fictional form genuine tendencies of history. Nazarov categorizes this genre of fiction as "a sort of anti-utopia."[99]

Although Nazarov wants to give the impression that his only goal is to trace the convergence of interests of the Masons and the Jews, in fact he is much more ambitious. He is seeking historical justification for the irrational fear and anxiety induced by the Jews and Masons. Drawing on the research of a respected historian — Jacob Katz — he uses it to support his own version of the conspiracy theory. Katz's work did show a convergence of interests of Jews and Masons on the eve of the French Revolution and throughout the nineteenth century. Nazarov, however, considers this convergence so all-inclusive that he believes Jews and Masons were implicated in all the notable events of the past century.[100]

RUSSIAN WRITERS AND RUSSIAN-SPEAKING WRITERS: LINGUISTIC MYSTICISM

The Jewish role and contribution to Russian literature, and the question of the cultural identity of Russian-Jewish writers have been much discussed by literary critics.[101] As we saw, Igor Shafarevich singled out Russian writers of Jewish origin as a separate group. A primary focus of the critics is the myth of Jewish "contamination" of Russian culture and literature and the sources of that myth.

Ultra-nationalist Russian literary critics coined the term "Russian-speaking writers" *(russkoyazichnie pisateli)* to label and condemn Russian writers of Jewish origin, who by definition are alien to the "Russian spirit," yet pretend to express it in their works. The term does not refer specifically to Jews, but it is the Jews to whom they primarily refer.

The concept of the "Russian-speaking writer" is not new. Andrei Belyi, a well-known symbolist poet at the turn of the twentieth century, wrote an essay, "The Rubber-Stamp Culture" (1909), on the topic, recently reprinted in *Nash sovremennik.* Belyi contrasts the truly creative Russian national writers to cosmopolitan Jewish literary critics, who, he claims, are unable to understand and fully appreciate the power and ingenuity of Russian literature. Jewish critics tend to render this literature into the patterns of a "rubber-stamp" culture and accommodate it to mediocre international taste. Their discussion is primitive, and they tend to reduce it to standard, trivial things that could be understood by any average person, thus their interpretations are profane and superficial. A characteristic passage from the essay articulates the typical Neo-Slavophile view:

> Who are those mediators between the nation and its culture in the
> world of genius? Who is trying to separate the flesh of the nation from
> its spirit by international culture and modernist art in order to make

the flesh of the nation's spirit soulless and the nation's spirit impotent? Who are these emasculators? These people are strangers who are alien to the host nation and who are, unfortunately, deprived of their civil rights and, thus, cannot express themselves in other spheres. They greedily rush to the sphere that does not depend on the state and become the pioneers of culture (literary and musical critics and the managers of literary arrangements). The number of these literary critics and their influence grow. Most definitely they do not understand the depth of the people's spirit in its sound, color and verbal manifestations. The general mass of Jewish literary critics is absolutely alien to Russian art, writes in a jargon of Esperanto, and interferes with any attempt to deepen and enrich the Russian language.[102]

Belyi's comments have the virtue of clarity and brevity absent from the works of today's Neo-Slavophiles. Belyi's fling at the "Jewish" international language, Esperanto, was later taken up by the anti-Zionist writer, Yemelyanov. The Jews command only the international language, Esperanto, while the subtleties of the artistic use of natural language escape them.[103]

Interestingly, Andrei Belyi believes that giving Jews increased civil rights (including the possibility of fostering their own literary expression in "Jewish languages") could actually protect Russian literature from invasion and allow truly Russian writers to exercise a monopoly over the artistic use of the Russian language. Belyi advocates a new, figurative literary "Pale of Settlement" in order to protect the spiritual territory of Russia. Literature is a delicate and intimate aspect of Russian identity, and Russians must become more aware of the Jewish domination of literary criticism. The emancipation of Russian literature from the Jews (to paraphrase Marx) could be facilitated by promoting Jews in the state services, where their talents and diligence are more suited and could be better utilized. Belyi clearly articulates the concerns of many contemporary neo-Slavophiles, who would agree with him, except for the suggestion of promoting Jews in the civil service.

Nationalist writers, preoccupied with authentic Russian culture, identify several spheres of literature "taken over" and "judaized." They cite Russian-speaking writers associated with the canon of modern Russian literature, such as Joseph Brodsky, Osip Mandelstam, Boris Pasternak, and Isaac Babel, among others. In spite of their use of the Russian language, and paired with their attempts to camouflage their real identities under Russian surnames, their "Jewish essence" stands out in their works. Critics within the Writers Union have spoken out against the "crypto Jews" who falsely claim a Russian identity.[104] Suggested tests for authenticity and Russianness vary. Some neo-

Slavophile literary critics would require that writers have fully assimilated Russian cultural values; others would include only baptized Jews, such as Mandelstam and Pasternak. A more rigorous view would exclude any writer of Jewish extraction, even one who fully embraced Russian culture. For instance, Zderev argues that:

> one should not count Pasternak a Russian poet, although he was writing in Russian and it was his native tongue. Levitan was drawing pictures from Russian nature, yet we could not consider him a Russian artist. The same with Brodsky, Chagall and Rubinstein. Even less could this term be applied to Katz, Cohen, Kagan, Oistrakh, Frenkel, Blanter, Dunaevsky, Mravinsky, Shnitke....[105]

The "Odessa school" is blamed for having a disastrous influence on the Russian language and the development of Russian literature. Russian literature in the Soviet period reflects the clash between the indigenous tradition of "village writers" and the style of the Odessa school.[106] In Odessa school works, such as the novel *Twelve Chairs* by Ilf and Petrov, the traditional Russian estates and Russian types are derided. Neo-Slavophiles accuse Odessa school writers of vulgarity, and more importantly, of lacking a clear moral standard, thus betraying the grand tradition of Russian literature found among the "village writers." Any writer who shows an interest in the Odessa school is looked on as a traitor to the Russian spirit.

Among "authentic Russian writers" it is widely believed that Jews have undue prominence in the media, especially since perestroika, and are thus able to shape the literary tastes of the public. "Russian-speaking writers" are accused of having gotten support from organizations (such as the Soros Foundation), in order to propagate their own literary standards and inflate their reputations. Perhaps even worse, they are accused of having an undue influence in producing textbooks and educational materials, which fail to give sufficient attention to authentic Russian writers. Vladimir Lichutin, writing of educational programs sponsored by the Soros Foundation, writes:

> Soros propagates the ideology of the citizens of the world coupled by the complete detachment from the national culture and popular traditions. It also bears on the teaching of literature in schools and colleges. It is associated with the banishment of Russian classical literature, the presumptuous advertisement of literary impostors from among the Russian-speaking writers with double and triple citizenship.[107]

An anonymous writer, who signed himself "A.M.A.," complains that in the Soviet period, Jews infiltrated both the editorial boards of publishers of children's literature and centers for the production of cartoons: the publishing houses Detskaiia literatura and Malish were completely controlled by Jews. It is not surprising, A.M.A. argues, that the "Judaic storytellers" and cartoonists have educated Russian children in the spirit of Jewish stereotypes (i.e., images of the Jews in Russian culture as, e.g., heroes, actors, and so on, and Jewish views have come to dominate Russian culture).[108] He warns the post-perestroika public against the plague of Jewish "storytellers" who wish to maintain control over very important spheres of "spiritual production."

Clearly, the "authentic Russian writers" look upon Russian literature as a besieged castle whose defenders must be constantly on the alert against a pernicious Jewish influence. Kathleen Parthé, an American student of Soviet literature, points to the preoccupation with cultural borders:

> The obsession with borders and with saving the Russian writer as if he were an endangered species has brought forth the claim that the right wishes to turn Russian culture into one vast Pushkin National Park.[109]

It is important to understand the nature of the Neo-Slavophile obsession with the "purity" of Russian literature and its relation to their linguistic mysticism. Neo-Slavophiles believe in the primacy of aesthetic impulses over ideological and religious ones, and that literature is the key element of Russian cultural identity. Although Jews may be able to communicate in the Russian language, they cannot possibly express the spirituality and genuine Russian emotion of the language. For "Russian-speaking" writers, language is merely a tool, whereas "authentic" Russian poets and writers *live* in their language. They establish a special intimate and existential relationship with the word — a relationship impossible even for the most assimilated writers of Jewish origin. For the truly Russian writers, language is a matter of life and death: they are literally consumed by the language. Language is a kind of independent force that dominates them. Neo-Slavophiles identify the Russian language with the mysterious substance of the Russian soul. The fear that Jews might learn the "hidden codes" of the Russian language is a relic of the ancient belief in sympathetic magic. Access by Jews ("Russian-speaking writers") to the mysterious Russian soul should be regulated and limited, i.e., Jews should be unable to write Russian literature or criticism.

Kathleen Parthé discovered an intriguing syndrome in Russian literature that has a bearing on antisemitism. Literary biographies of Russian poets and writers often feature a particular "necromyth":

> In the narrative about the life of a Russian writer they emphasize his ethnic origins and the appropriate death.... [D]eath, which is inflicted by strangers and which is experienced as a suffering of a Russian for Russia. These origins and this kind of death legitimize the gift of the

author to influence Russia.... In this context the very narrative of the writers' life turns into a text in the "para-literal space." The conservatives construct the writers' biographies after the model of hagiographies.[110]

The death of the writer in Russian necromyths is often inflicted by a stranger — often a Jew. Even if the murderer is not Jewish, he is a member of cosmopolitan and Masonic organizations that are tools in Jewish hands. This persistent myth can be found in countless stories of Russian writers, and in revisions of the conventional accounts of their death produced in the period of perestroika on the basis of new "findings." Thus we are told that the Brik family killed Vladimir Mayakovsky; Sliafman killed the Russian poet and rock musician Igor Talkov and fled to Israel[111]; "mysterious forces" killed the economist Kuzmich; the same malicious forces poisoned Maxim Gorky, Vasily Shukshin[112] and Russian village poets. The famous Russian poet, Sergei Esenin did not commit suicide, but was killed by Volf Erlich in cooperation with other Jews, who hated everything Russian and wanted to deprive Russia of Esenin's poetry. The authors of these necromyths relish the details, which supposedly provide further evidence of the "ritual" character of the murders. They claim, for example, that Esenin was murdered a day before Christmas; the ink-spot on the manuscript of his last poem looks like a pig.[113] In his recent biography of Esenin, Sergei Kuniaev blames "Jewish Trotskyites" and the agents of Kamenev for the assassination of the Russian poet.[114]

A quasi-religious element enters into the necromyths, when Russian writers are said to have been "crucified" for Russia. Alexander Prokhanov refers to the poets as "Russian angels" who intercede for the Russian people before [the throne of] God. The tragic deaths enhance their status, and the overlay of Christian themes on their biographies (or rather, hagiographies) inevitably invites the addition of mysterious Jewish figures accused of their murders, just as the ancient Jews are accused of the death of Christ.

GEORGII GACHEV: THE ANATOMY OF THE JEWISH SOUL

Georgii Gachev, a member of the Writers Union, and author of a 16-volume study of "national images," is particularly interested in the structures of Jewish and Russian cultures.[115] He holds that a completely rational account of national cultures is hardly possible, and his work has centered on examining the root metaphors and central narratives of various cultures to determine their essential vision of the world around them. Gachev's study of the relationship of Jews and Russians, however, contains many popular antisemitic stereotypes which he claims are objective conclusions based on an analysis according to his universal culturological theory.

Gachev believes that any ethnic culture can be understood as a unity of three elements — cosmos, psyche, and logos. His hermeneutic method ("cosmosophy") and the subject of his studies ("cosmo-psycho-logos") are derived from these assumptions. A body of culture is defined by its relation to nature and earth (cosmos). The soul (psyche) of culture is identical with the national character and the typical emotional reactions of its members. The mentality and the way of thinking form the logos of the culture. All three elements are interdependent and constitute the secret language of the culture.

Jewish culture, according to Gachev, is abnormal, and two unique features of Jewish culture greatly influence the pattern of relations between Russians and Jews. First of all, the Jews relate to the world only through soul and spirit. A relationship to nature and ties to a specific region or country are absent for the Jews. Historically, he contends, Jewish culture could not establish a stable relation to nature and cosmos. Jewish culture in Israel is not authentically Jewish, for the true Jewish culture is represented only by that of the Diaspora.

> It is not a coincidence that the most rigorous rabbis believe that the establishment of the state of Israel was a mistake because it was founded before the coming of the Messiah and that the whole project of Zionism is an absolute betrayal of the Jewish essence. Therefore, the Holocaust was a kind of punishment for Zionism.... [Israel] gives the impression of something provisional.... Russian Jews especially suffer there because for generations they have absorbed the Russian fate. Of course, Russia needs the Jews, especially now, when their commercial, entrepreneurial and combinatorial skills could be very useful for the country.[116]

The relation to nature of non-Jewish cultures is evident in agriculture, the construction of cities, their architecture and monuments, and in military activity. The very structure of the Jewish culture did not allow them to develop all these spheres of activity. Jew also failed to develop the values and virtues associated with a specific relation to space and attachment to the land.

> It turned out that ancient Palestine, ancient Jewry, was only the starting point, a "runway" where they have created and shaped themselves. It was only a short period of time after which they could already keep their integrity and preserve themselves as a nation without any land, without any territory....[117]

Thus, Jewish culture lacks a crucial element present in all other cultures. This explains why the theory of relativity was developed by a Jew, Albert Einstein:

> All ethnicities are the slaves of cosmos, of the spatial-temporary relationship. In this respect the Jews could allow themselves unique freedom. The Jews do not have their own cosmos and they are not paralyzed by its influence. Thus, Einstein comes along and changes the conventional understanding.[118]

Lacking their own geographical space, the Jews compensated by becoming overly involved in spiritual and psychological activity. The Torah is the "territory of the Jews," Gachev claims. Since the normal "body" was absent (state, nature, territory), the Jews came to view the Jewish tribal aggregate as a kind of land substitute. Thus, according to Gachev, the second principle of the Jewish psyche is that of preservation of the "body of the people," according to the precepts of the Torah and Talmud. Gachev delineates two dimensions of self-preservation. First, he cites Jewish concern with "purity of blood": "No other ethnicity attributes the same role to ethnic purity as the Jews."[119] Second, is the obsession with preserving the life of each individual. Gachev suggests that the distinctively Jewish lack of heroism derives from their drive for physical survival at any price:

> It is the most important task of a Jew to survive. Russians like to talk about patriotism. They could die for their country and for the idea. The country will survive after your individual death. However, if a Jew dies it means that the national body which substitutes the national cosmos has lost its part. Hence, the cowardice and the weakness of the Jews.[120]

Gachev subscribes to Richard Wagner's belief that the Jews were not creative: creativity is a feature of "substantial nations, the French, the Germans, the Russians." Gachev's explanation sounds "favorable" to the Jews: since the Jews hold that the principles of the Torah represent eternal truth, they do not need to "reinvent the wheel." "The Jewish logos and intellect are concerned with "combinatrics," restructuring, interpretation and reinterpretation. The area of their activity is recombination, but not original creativity."[121]

The difficult relationship between Russians and Jews forms a persistent topic in the Gachev's writings. He lays out a metaphysical framework of Russian history that enables one to understand the specificity and importance of the Jewish-Russian encounter and interaction. He distinguishes three metaphysical agents of Russian history: the female principle (the motherland) and the two male principles (the People and the State). In Russian history there is one persistent theme, and the actors are always the same. The male actors — the State and the People — fight for the love of the Mother-Land. The State always wins. Remarkably, Gachev associates the Russian State with the power and influence of foreigners — Jews, Germans, and Caucasians. "The state was a catalyst of Russian history. It pushed the country to civilization using as its gauge and standard the countries of Western Europe." The state normally performs the function of the Husband, while the People is always subjugated and performs the function of a Son, in a land dominated by foreigners.[122] While some periods of Russian history were marked by the domination of the Germans, the October Revolution and the Left movements at the fin-de-siècle were predominantly Jewish:

> It is important to distinguish the attitude to the Jews of Russian people and the female Russia. Russia loves the Jews. In general it loves the foreigners; it has a lot of warmth and body. It is the sweetest thing for a Jew to marry a Russian woman, to become a part of a white substance. Jewry is a stepson of Russia, smart, energetic and business-oriented. This stepson realizes that the real son of the country is lazy and always needs supervision. By the beginning of the 20th century, the stepson has grown up and decided to become a husband to Russia. Russia is not his native mother and incest is not a real issue. After the October revolution the Jews took over the power in the country. The real son, the Russian people, is now the main adversary of the stepson. Hence, de-peasantification, the persecution of the kulaks and Russian substance.... The Jews did not have any special hostility but they tried to impose their own concepts.[123]

The tragedy of the Bolshevik revolution, according to Gachev, was that both agents were lacking in political experience:

> The Jews lived in Diaspora, while the Russians were infantile and did not have civic and political consciousness. The encounter of two underdeveloped ideologies generated the Talmudic ideology, Marxism-Leninism, which has prevented the formation of a civil society.[124]

So Gachev ends where other neo-Slavophiles begin, i.e., with the discussion of Jewish involvement in the revolution and blaming them for the violent changes they brought about in the course of Russian history.

Gachev is not necessarily an antisemite. However, his way of thinking and his theory of Jewish ethnicity easily lend themselves to antisemitic interpretations regardless of his own intent. He would never admit that he has antisemitic prejudices. His stereotypes of Russians and Russian history are hardly more favorable — he has even been accused of Russophobia. His arguments reflect the climate of opinion of the antisemitic intellectual subculture. The scholar of "national images" reproduced the most vulgar stereotypes about Jewish cowardice, lack of attachment to the soil, lack of consideration for Gentiles, and a tendency to be dogmatic — all standard constructions found in antisemitic writings. The theory of "national images" only served to reinforce these old xenophobic stereotypes and does not contribute to better understanding among ethnic groups. It is remarkable that Gachev speaks the same language as Russian neo-Slavophile nationalists and shares their mentality.

CONCLUSION

In sum, neo-Slavophile antisemitism is clearly anti-modern, proclaiming the primacy of natural "traditional" communal bonds over the "artificial" bonds of modern society and civilization. Neo-Slavophiles are hostile to cultural modernity with its urbanization, globalization, market economy, and liberalism. Modernity is associated with violence and coercion, and with the ubiquitous presence of Jews in the social environment.

The idea of cultural community permeates their discourse. Their criticism of liberal ideologists stems from their communitarian ideals, and their antisemitic posture can be better understood against the background of their communitarian position. Jews, they claim, cannot enter the traditional community because they are unable to accept the cultural norms and cultural myths of the community. Even if they came to understand these cultural norms, they would remain outsiders, since Jews can only relate to such norms in a rational and pragmatic way.

Neo-Slavophiles hold that a culture lives by its myths and prejudices embedded in its language, and in its cultural or social practices. Standards propagated by each particular culture provide the ultimate source of authority and the final court of appeal. Neo-Slavophiles deny that there is such a thing as a "universal" set of values: what is commonly held to be such is in reality, a "Jewish" value.

Liberalism is held to be Jewish model of society, and therefore cannot be considered "neutral" with regard to different cultures and value systems. The neo-Slavophile misconception of liberalism is so linked with their caricature of the materialistic, grasping Jew that it forms a full-fledged antisemitic ideology.

The Jews are held responsible for the contemporary crisis in Russian society in two quite different senses. In the psychological sense, they are accused of having introduced an attitude of indifference to community moral standards, and of having paved the way for a spirit of unbridled commercial activity. It is seen as very natural that the Jews feel contempt for agricultural labor and rural life, and they are responsible for making this the dominant attitude. Modern disenchantment is blamed on the cosmopolitan Jewish mind.

In the second sense, Jews are accused of having physically annihilated the traditional agricultural community, for they were prominent in both capitalist and socialist movements that challenged the moral attitudes associated with rural communal life. Here again, we see the distrust of "universal" moral standards. Neo-Slavophiles insist that there are no values independent of particular cultural norms. Jews, they argue, only use the concepts of rationality, neutrality, and universality, as a tool in their struggle against the authentic cultures of their enemies, and never apply the same standards of rationality to their own cultural myths.

The discourse of neo-Slavophiles is governed by two distinctions — that of organic versus inorganic community, and that of "authentic" versus "inauthentic" — both of which they relate to the Jews. The Jews embody the inauthentic, and their very presence makes the community inorganic. The Jews' experience of the Diaspora and their uprootedness makes them especially dangerous for the cohesiveness and the stability of any "organic" and "authentic" community. The Jew serves as a metaphor for the atomized individual as opposed to the person "rooted" through his community ties. Jewish "uprootedness" disqualifies them from even making proper use of another culture's language.

In passing, we may note that many neo-Slavophiles associate the Jews with the male principle and the exercise of violence, not only in overt statements, but in the language and metaphors used in discussing particular topics, such as modernization, urbanization, transformation and violence, and the principle of the Father.[125] Male Jewish violence is placed in opposition to the feminine cultural archetype of Russia. The intertwining of gender and race discourses is not unknown, however, it is remarkable that for neo-Slavophiles the gender/race association is the reverse of the other common trend which associates the Jew with the feminine principle. This latter association is prominent in neo-Eurasianism, where Jewry is linked with effeminization and opposes the masculine Aryan principle. We shall see in the following chapter on racist ideology, the idea of a feminine Jewish nature is well-articulated as an inferior condition.

NOTES

1. Russophilism is actually a more appropriate term for what I call here neo-Slavophilism, since the other Slavic ethnicities do not occupy a very important place in the writings of neo-Slavophiles. I use the term "neo-Slavophilism" to stress this trend's continuity with the Slavophile ideology of the nineteenth century.

2. See I. Shafarevich, "Sotzialism kak iavlenie mirovoi istorii," in idem, *Est li u Rossii buduschee?* (Moscow 1991).

3. Many authors cite information collected by Andrei Dikii about the number of Jews in the Soviet government: A. Dikii, *Evrei v Rossii i v SSSR* (Novosibirsk 1994). See also *Soblasn sotsialisma. Revolutsiia v Rossii i evrei,* ed. A. Solzhenitsin (Paris and Moscow 1995).

4. A. Gerrits, "Antisemitism and Anti-Communism: The Myth of "Judeo-Communism" in Eastern Europe," *Eastern European Jewish Affairs,* 25, no. 1 (1995): 54.

5. The decree for suppression of the "antisemitic movement" issued by the Soviet of People's Commissars on 27 July 1918 is often cited as evidence of the "Jewish" character of the Revolution.

6. Some Neo-Slavophile critics of Bolshevism consider Vladimir Lenin a "Jewish member" of the Bolshevik party. In the recent survey, 2.5% of the respondents named Lenin "the Jew, who has most harmed the Russian people and other people of the former Soviet Union." See L. Gudkov "Antisemitizm v postsovetskoi Rossii," in *Neterpimost' v Rossii. Starie I novie fobii* (Moscow 1999), 85. In reality, only Lenin's maternal grandfather, Alexander (Israil') Blank, a physician, was Jewish. He converted to Christianity when he entered the Medical-Surgical Academy in St. Petersburg in 1820. In the official histories of the Ulyanov family, Lenin's maternal grandfather was described as a Ukranian *(maloross)*. Documents indicating his grandfather's conversion were unearthed in 1965 in the Central State Historical Archive (TsGIA), and later on other documents were found in the archives of the Medical-Surgical Academy. The Central Committee of the Communist Party forbade research in this area or any publication about the matter. Two people who discovered documents about the Blank family genealogy were fired from the local historical archive in the town of Zhitomir, in the province of which *(Volinskaia guberniia)* Lenin's grandfather was born. In the 1920s, Anna Ulyanova, a sister of Lenin, prepared for publication some documents disclosing the Jewish origins of her family in order "to help the fight against rising anti-Semitism in Russia," but Stalin did not allow her to publish the documents. These findings in the archives, however, became known to many people due to the efforts of a Soviet writer Marietta Shaginian; it became widely known, however, only after the collapse of the Soviet Union. See M. Stein "Dorisovannii portret," *Moskovskie novosti,* no. 15 (2000).

7. See A. Dikii, *The Jews in Russia and in the USSR* (New York 1967); V. Gladkii, *Zhidi* (Moscow 1993).

8. S. Naumov, *Zhertvi i palachi. Golod 1932–1933 godov* (Magadan 1992); excerpts were published in *Russkii vestnik*, no. 3 (1993). See also Gladkii, *Zhidi*, 66–70.

9. For more details about Yaroslavsky see A. Nezhny, "Protokoli kremlevskikh mudretsov," *Ogoniok*, no. 31–33 (1992): 8–11 (Engl. tr., "Protocols from Meetings of the Kremlin Wise Men," *Russian Social Science Review*, 35, no. 2 (1994).

10. In his interview with the poet Felix Chuev, Lazar Kaganovich attributed this decision to Stalin. He claims that Stalin accepted this suggestion from the Union of Architects. See V. Backrevsky, "Ispoved' Kaganovicha," *Pravda*, 28 May 1993.

11. S. Naumov, "Palachi. K 60-letiiu okonchaniia stroitelstva Belomorsko-Baltiiskogo kanala," *Russkii vestnik*, no. 44–46 (1993).

12. See, for instance, G. Mosalov, "Terror Sverdlova v deistvii" *Russkii vestnik*, no. 14 (1993).

13. The word "Holocaust" is used to express the uniqueness of the Jewish experience during the Second World War. It is acknowledged that the Nazis also killed, often through starvation and brutality, other non-Jewish groups. However, as Yehuda Bauer points out, the purpose of these crimes was different. The Nazis were trying to denationalize Eastern European nations, to absorb the "Nordic" elements into the Germanic race, to murder the intelligentsia, and to turn the rest of the people into slaves. This is not a policy of genocide and it is very different from the planned and systematic murder of every member of a community. Bauer demonstrates that there never was a Nazi policy to apply the measures used against the Jews to other national communities; only the Jews were singled out for complete physical annihilation. See Y. Bauer, *The Holocaust in Historical Perspective* (Seattle 1978), 32.

14. "Forum: Judaica" (editorial), *Den'*, no. 18 (1992).

15. I. Shafarevich, "Rusophobia: desiat' let spustia," *Nash sovremennik*, no. 11 (1991): 138.

16. V. Bondarenko, "Otvetstvennost' natsii," *Den'*, no. 18 (1992).

17. A. Yudin, "Legendi i fakti. Statia Marksa 'K evreiskomu voprosu' i vokrug nee," *Moscow*, no. 8 (1994): 144.

18. S. Kuniaev, "Etot vozdukh pust' budet svidetelem," *Den'*, no. 37 (1993).

19. Kazintsev, A., "Bluzhdaiiuschie ogon'ki," *Nash sovremennik*, no. 3 (1995): 184–85.

20. Ibid., 185.

21. See also A. Vasil'chikov, "Obschina protiv kommunizma," *Nash sovremennik*, no. 7 (1994).

22. Kazintsev, "Bluzhdaiiuschie ogon'ki," 185.

23. Y. Borodai, "Komu bit' vladel'tsem zemli?," *Nash sovremennik,* no. 3 (1990): 105–107.

24. See, for instance, R. Wistrich, *Revolutionary Jews From Marx to Trotsky* (London 1976); R. Brym, *The Jewish Intelligentsia and Russian Marxism. A Sociological Study of Intellectual Radicalism and Ideological Divergence* (London and Basingstoke 1978); D. Rubinstein, *The Left, the Right, and the Jews* (London and Canberra 1982); L. Volovici, "Antisemitism in Post-Communist Eastern Europe: A Marginal or Central Issue?" (Vidal Sassoon International Center for the Study of Antisemitism, Hebrew University of Jerusalem, ACTA series, no. 5, 1994), 16–17; A. Gerrits, "Antisemitism and Anti-Communism: The Myth of 'Judeo-Communism' in Eastern Europe," *Eastern European Jewish Affairs,* 25, no. 1 (1995).

25. Students of Russian Jewry note a lack of reliable and complete quantitative information about Jewish involvement in the Left. However, some available data (e.g., analysis of the ethnic composition of political prisoners) strongly suggest that Jews were over-represented in Left political parties. See A. Noemi, "Politicheskie prestupleniia i evrei," in *Soblasn sotsialisma. Revolutsiia v Rossii i evrei,* ed. by Alexander Solzhenitsin (Paris and Moscow 1995), 460–65. Noemi cites the political crimes statistics from the official report in the *Journal of the Ministry of Justice,* which covered only three years: 1901, 1902, 1903.

26. Vladimir Burtsev, author of "The Jews and Bolshevism," cites data about the ethnic structure of the St. Petersburg organization of the Russian Communist Party of Bolsheviks (RKPb). Jews represented 2.6% of the RKPb members, and were 1.8% of the city population. Russian members constituted 74.2%, and were 92.6% of the city population. Letts were by 10.6% of the Party membership; 0.7% of the city population. These numbers, Burtsev says, "should dispose of the widespread legends about the overwhelming number of the Jews in Bolshevik organizations." V. Burtsev, "Evrei i bolshevism," *Obschee delo* (an émigré newspaper published in Paris), no. 61 (1919). Zvi Gitelman cites data from the 1922 Party census, according to which "there were only 958 Jewish members of the Communist Party who had joined before 1917, while the total party membership in January 1917 was 23,600. Less than 5 percent of Jewish Party members in 1922 had been Bolsheviks before 1917." Z. Gitelman, *Jewish Nationality and Soviet Politics* (Princeton, N.J. 1972), 105.

27. Volovici, "Antisemitism in Post-Communist Eastern Europe," 16.

28. C. Gassenschmidt, *Jewish Liberal Politics in Tsarist Russia* (London 1995), has shown that "Jewish politics" in Russia was mostly associated with the activity of Jewish members of the Constitutional Democratic Party. Leaders of this party (lawyer Maxim Vinaver and G. Sliozberg) along with Bramson and Krol (leaders of the "Trudoviki" liberal party) lobbied for Jewish emancipation. They [initiated the establishment of the Union for the Attainment of Full Equality for the Jewish People

in Russia. Jewish Bolsheviks and other radical socialists did not play any serious role in "Jewish politics" and lobbying for Jewish rights.

29. Most Jewish social democrats were members of the Bund (General League of Jewish Workingmen in Lithuania, Poland and Russia). Many of them were Mensheviks (whose most conspicuous leaders — Deutsch, Martov, and Axelrod — were Jewish). Only a small minority of the Bolsheviks was Jewish. Joseph Stalin's tasteless joke, made in 1905, is illuminating: "The Mensheviks were a Jewish faction while the Bolsheviks were truly Russian, and hence it would not be amiss for us Bolsheviks to instigate a pogrom in the Party," quoted in L. Trotsky, *Stalin: An Appraisal of the Man and His Influence* (New York 1967), 152. At the Russian Social Democratic Labor Party Congress in 1907 there were almost 100 Jewish delegates (one-third of the total). Of these, fifty-seven delegates were Bundists and one-fifth of the Menshevik delegates were Jewish. Z. Gitelman, *Jewish Nationality and Soviet Politics: The Jewish Sections of the CPSU, 1917–1930* (Princeton, N.J. 1972), 105; L. Shapiro, "The Role of the Jews in the Russian Revolutionary Movement," *Slavonic and Eastern European Review,* 40 (1961).

30. Boris Brutskus, "Evreiskoe naselenie pod evreiskoi vlastiiu," *Sovremennie zapiski,* no. 36 (1928), has shown that in economic terms, Soviet rule (especially with the elimination of private property) was detrimental to the majority of Jews. The well-known Jewish economist concluded, "the interests of the Jewish population radically and implacably contradict the very foundations of the economic and social politics of communism." Norman Cohn, *Warrant for Genocide* (Ann Arbor, Mich. 1981), 122, points out that since the Jews were mostly small shopkeepers and self-employed artisans, they were, from the Leninist point of view, class-enemies. Because of this, "under the Soviet régime...in the 1920s more than a third of the Jewish population was without civil rights, as compared with 5–6 per cent of the non-Jewish population."

To give two examples, Vladimir Gringmut, founder of the Russian Monarchical Party (later transformed into the Black Hundred), was Jewish. He was editor of the main mouthpiece of the Black Hundreds, the newspaper *Moskovskie vedomosti.* Historian Vladlen Sirotkin reports that there was a special Jewish section of the Union of Archangel Michael, and that "in Odessa the authorities have registered the Jewish society which prayed to God for the Tsar." V. Sirotkin, *Vekhi otechestvennoi istorii* (Moscow 1991), 50.

32. "Cheka" is the abbreviation of the full name of the early Soviet "All-Russian Special Commission for Combating Counter-Revolution and Sabotage."

33. See A. Vaksberg, *Stalin Against the Jews* (New York 1994), especially the chapters "Jews Against Jews" and "Brother Jews."

34. Z. Gitelman, *Jewish Nationality and Soviet Politics* (Princeton, N.J. 1972), 105.

35. T. Deutscher, ed., *The Non-Jewish Jew and Other Essays* (Oxford 1968).

36. It does not mean, however, that Jewishness did not constitute a problem for the Bolsheviks of Jewish extraction. For instance, Trotsky refused to take over the Commissariat of the Interior in 1917 and one can speculate that he refused to sign the Brest Peace Treaty because of this problem. "Was it worthwhile to put into our enemies' hands such an additional weapon as my Jewish origin?," he writes in his memoirs; cited in Gerrits, "Antisemitism and Anti-communism: The Myth of 'Judeo-Communism' in Eastern Europe," *Eastern European Jewish Affairs,* 25, no. 1 (1995): 65.

37. Bakunin, the founder of anarchism, claims that "the whole Jewish world, forming a single sect of exploiters, a kind of human leech, a collective devouring parasite, organized not only across state frontiers, but even across all political divisions, this world is in fact, for the most part at least, at the disposal of Marx, on one side, and Rothschild, on the other.... What can there be in common between socialism and high finance? Well, it is the fact that authoritarian socialism, Marx's communism, wants central power for the state, and wherever there is state centralization, there must necessarily be a state central bank, and where there exists such a bank, the Jews are always sure not to die of cold or hunger." Bakunin believed that the Jewish Marxists were trying to seize the bourgeois state with the help of Rothschild money in order to serve Jewish interests. See A. Mendel, *Michael Bakunin: Roots of Apocalypse* (New York 1981), 382.

38. On the reception of this Russian theory by the Nazis, see W. Laqueur, *Russia and Germany: Hitler's Mentors* (Washington 1991).

39. For the historical account of his life see Z. Z. B. Zeman and W. B. Scharlan, *The Merchant of Revolution. The Life of Alexander Israel Helphand (Parvus), 1867–1924* (New York 1965).

40. For more details, see the excellent discussion of the antisemitic implications of the novel in Alexander Yanov, *The Russian Idea and the Year 2000* (Oxford 1987). It could well be that Solzhenitsin never meant to articulate the sinister antisemitic implications of his novel. It is true that Parvus was both a revolutionary and a banker. However, Solzhenitsin's interpretation of his activity and his role seem to be very tendentious. It is also wrong to take Parvus as a representative figure of the Jew in the Russian revolution as Solzhenitsin apparently does. The message of the novel is quite clear as well as the identification of Parvus with the devil. It seems that Solzhenitsin was driven by the logic of the antisemitic narrative that did not allow him to exercise full control over the image which he created.

41. Mikhail Nazarov (b. 1948) is a prolific nationalist writer living in Germany. He can be categorized as both a neo-Slavophile and representative of National Orthodoxy. His perspective on the "Jewish question" fits both paradigms.

42. Many Jewish bankers made the availability of funds to the Russian government dependent on relaxing its policy towards its Jewish citizens. As a result of Louis

Marshall's campaign, the United States did not extend the Russian-American trade agreement in 1911.

43. I. Dobra, "Podlinnik!" *Molodaiia gvardiia,* no. 11–12 (1993): 145.

44. A. Sutton, *Wall Street and the Bolshevik Revolution* (New York 1974).

45. M. Nazarov, *Zagovor protiv Rossii. Belie piatna drami XX veka* (Potsdam 1993), 57.

46. Nazarov claims that Jacob Schiff, of Kuhn, Loeb, and Co., made no secret of his support for the Russian revolution. Nazarov refers to H. Coston, *La haute finance et le revolution* (Paris 1963). The "Bolshevik banker" Olof Ashberg, an owner of Nya Banken in Stockholm, funnelled funds from the German government to Russian revolutionaries.

47. Nazarov, *Zagovor protiv Rossii,* 29–30.

48. Ibid., 57–61.

49. Z. Borodai, "Tretii put'," *Nash sovremennik,* no. 9 (1991): 133.

50. Ibid.

51. T. Fritsch, *Handbuch zur Judenfrage. Die wichtigsten Tatsachen zur Beurteilung des jüdischen Volkes* (Leipzig 1941), 537.

52. Y. Borodai,"Komu bit' vladel'tsem zemli?," *Nash sovremennik,* no. 3 (1990): 109.

53. Ibid., 110.

54. Ibid., 112.

55. Ibid., 112.

56. Bogrov was a double agent for the secret police and the Socialist Revolutionary Party, whose motivation was, of course, much more sophisticated than in Borodai's account. Bogrov was not connected in any way with the bankers. Alexander Solzhenitsin tried to reproduce the psychological world of Bogrov in his novel *August 1914* (New York 1989). On the antisemitic connotations of the book see L. Navrozov, "Solzhenitsin's World History: *August 1914* as a New Protocols of the Elders of Zion," *Midstream,* 6 (1985); L. Navrozov, "Solzhenitsin: The Ayatolla of Russia?," *Midstream,* 9 (1994).

57 T. von Laue, *Sergei Witte and the Industrialization of Russia* (New York 1969), 78.

58. See S. Morozova, *Savva Morozov* (Moscow 1998).

59. Y. Borodai, "Totalitarism. Khronika i likhoradochnii krisis," *Nash sovremennik,* no. 7 (1992): 121.

60. Y. Borodai, "Tretii put'," *Nash sovremennik,* no. 9 (1991): 131.

61. Ibid.

62. Borodai, "Totalitarism: khronika i likhoradochnii krisis," 121.

63. Borodai, "Tretii put'," 133–34.

64. Y. Borodai, and F. Shipunov, "Krest narodnogo kormiltsa," *Socium,* no. 1 (1991): 25. The idea that Stalin put into practice many of Trotsky's ideas is plausible and is shared by a number of historians. See D. Volkogonov, *Trotsky: The Eternal Revolutionary* (New York 1996). Borodai and other nationalist ideologists, however, imply that Trotsky was more responsible for the crimes and repression than Stalin.

65. Y. Borodai, "Pochemu pravoslavnim ne goditsia protestantskii kapitalism?," *Nash sovremennik,* no. 10 (1990): 6–7.

66. Ibid., 10–13.

67. Y. Borodai, "Mif i kultura," in *Literaturno-filosofskii ezhegodnik,* edited by Y. Borodai (Moscow 1990), 186.

68. Y. Borodai, "Pochemu pravoslavnim," 14. By "Judeo-Protestant temples" he means Reform (Progressive) Judaism and some Christian fundamentalist trends, in reference to Kozhinov's paper in which he speaks of the tendency of Protestantism and Judaism to converge. V. Kozhinov, "Sionism Mikhaila Agurskogo i mezhdunarodnii sionism," *Nash sovremennik,* no. 6 (1990): 144.

69. Borodai, "Mif i kultura," 182–83.

70. Borodai, "Tretii put'," 139; Y. Borodai, "Rossiia i Zapad: vzaimodeistvie kultur," *Voprosi filosofii,* no. 6 (1992): 3–49.

71. Borodai, "Tretii put'," 138–39.

72. Ibid, 124.

73. Borodai, "Totalitarism," 124.

74. A. Kazintsev, "Samoubiistvo pod kontrolem," *Nash sovremennik,* no. 9 (1993): 151–52.

75. On Shafarevich's activities and the background of his nationalist theories see J. Dunlop, "The 'Sad Case' of Igor Shafarevich," *East European Jewish Affairs,* 24, no. 1 (1994).

76. Remarkably, *Russophobia* was written as early as 1981, but was only widely circulated and discussed after glasnost in 1987. It was originally published in the magazine *Kuban',* nos. 5, 6, and 7 (1989); and *Nash sovremennik,* nos. 6 and 11 (1989).

77. The expression *maly narod* was translated by some as "small nation" or "lesser people" as well.

78. A. Cochin, *Les Societés de pensée et la democratie* (Paris 1921); idem, *Les Societés de pensée et Révolution en Bretagne (1788–89)* (Paris 1925).

79. I. Shafarevich, *Est' li u Rossii buduschee?* (Moscow 1991), 392–93.

80. Shafarevich's position has much in common with German revisionist historian Ernst Nolte, who holds that German history after the Second World War was written from the standpoint of the victors and thus became a "negative myth" ("imagine a picture of Israel presented by a victorious PLO after the total destruction of Israel"). Nolte implies that the standpoint of the victors is the Jewish standpoint. See J.

Habermas, "Apologetic Tendencies," in idem, *New Conservatism* (Cambridge 1989), 221. Mikhail Nazarov, another neo-Slavophile author, is more explicit: he believes that both German and Russian histories were distorted by Jewish historical "revisionism" and that Russia and Germany should unite to oppose the attempts of the victors to taint the glorious past of the two nations. He claims that "Germany was made a scapegoat for the two World Wars, while the real initiators and victors — the Jewish and Masonic circles — remained in the shadow. They provoked a conflict between the most powerful European monarchies and caused their mutual annihilation to increase their own power; it was the democratic ideology of the First World War.... They provoked the Second World War to eliminate the national reactions to their first victory.... The victors gave their own interpretation to everything. The history of the 20th century is distorted both in Russian and Western historiography. The unity of Russia and Germany should be based on their common interest in the exposure of these distortions," in "Rossiia ili Germaniia?... The Conversation between Vladimir Bondarenko and Mikhail Nazarov," *Zavtra,* no. 16 (1994).

81. Ironically, in the Soviet era Shafarevich was a founder of the Committee for the Defense of Human Rights, responsible for documenting abuses of psychiatry and exposing cases of religious persecution.

82. Shafarevich, *Est' li u Rossii buduschee?,* 445.

83. Ibid., 440–41.

84. Ibid., 445–46.

85. Ibid., 437.

86. Ibid., 474.

87. Ibid., 475.

88. A. Kazintsev, "Eres' zhidovstvuiuschikh," *Nash sovremennik,* no. 9 (1992): 173.

89. I. Shafarevich, "Russophobia: desiat' let spustia," *Nash sovremennik,* no. 12 (1991); Dunlop, "The 'Sad Case' of Igor Shafarefich."

90. To mention only a few: D. Shturman, "Natsionalnie fobii," *Dvadtsat' dva* (Israel), no. 68 (1989); S. Stratanovsky, "Chto zhe takoe russofobiia?," *Zvezda,* no. 4 (1990); A. Shmelev, "Po zakonam parodii? (Shafarevich i ego 'Russophobia')," *Znamia,* no. 6 (1990); B. Kushner, "Otkritoe pis'mo Shafarevichu," *Dvadtsat' dva,* no. 64 (1989); Z. Krakhmalnikova, "Rusophobia, Khristianstvo, Antisemitism," *Neva,* no. 8 (1990) (Engl. trans., *Religion, State and Society,* 20, no. 1 (1992).

91. D. Rancour-Laferriere, *The Slave Soul of Russia. Moral Masochism and the Cult of Suffering* (New York and London 1995).

92. L. Nikitinsky, "Griadeot pobeda pravosudiia," *Moskovskie novosti,* no. 38 (1996).

93. Originally the idea was intimated in Abbé Barruel's five-volume *Mémoires pour servir à l'histoire du Jacobinisme* (1797). See also Norman Cohn, *Warrant for*

Genocide. The Myth of the Jewish World Conspiracy and the Protocols of the Elders of Zion (London 1967), 25–30.

94. Oleg Platonov and Andrei Putilov are among the most conspicuous champions of the conspiracy theories.

95. See Y. Gessen, *Evrei v masonstve* (The Jews in Masonry) (St. Petersburg 1903); J. Katz, *Jews and Freemasons in Europe 1723–1939* (Cambridge, England 1970).

96. Nazarov, *Zagovor protiv Rossii,* 27.

97. Ibid., 33–34.

98. Nazarov, "Mir, v kotorom okazalas' emigratsiia, ili Chego boialis' pravie," *Nash sovremennik,* no. 12 (192): 151.

99. Ibid., 152.

100. Nazarov, *Zagovor protiv Rossii,* 16.

101. See A. Nachimovsky, *Russian-Jewish Literature and Identity* (Baltimore 1992).

102. A. Belyi, "Shtempeliovannaia kultura," *Nash sovremennik,* no. 8 (1990): 185–86 (originally published in 1909 in the magazine *Vesi*). [Some critics attribute the essay to the influence of Emilii Medtner, one of the key figures in early 20th century European culture. He was a theoretician of Symbolism and a friend and colleague of Carl Jung. Belyi may have been influenced by Emilii Medtner, a key figure in early twentieth-century Symbolism and colleague of Carl Jung. Medtner's essay on Judaism characterized the Jews as "horrible masked individuals, entirely devoid of creativity yet with an amazing aptitude for usurping the role of leaders and organizers of intellectual life." See M. Ljunggren, *The Russian Mephisto. A Study of the Life and Work of Emilii Medtner* (Stockholm 1994), 47, 67.

103. Jews are accused of inventing Esperanto in order to deprive ethnicities of their authentic native languages and identity. Interestingly enough, Esperanto advocates suggest that its use would help preserve native languages! Valery Yemelyanov refers to Belyi's essay in his attack on the Russian-Jewish physician Lazarus Ludwig Zamenhof, who wrote the pioneering pamphlet describing the grammar of a new international language in 1887. "The members of the Pharisaical Judaic sects, especially Chasidists, have laid the foundations for a global primitive language for the gentiles.... [The Chasidists] realize the functions of spiritual Inquisition: they emasculate the history of the gentiles; they distort their intellectual and cultural heritage, trying to make it cosmopolitan and deprive it of the best national traditions. It is a crystal dream of Chasidism to deprive the gentiles of their main spiritual heritage, their national languages. They try to replace all these by the unified primitive universal gentile language, the language of the bipedal working cattle...." V. Yemelyanov, *Desionisatsiia* (Moscow 1995), 116–18. The primitive international

language, he claims, would be very accessible to the Jews, while their own language (Hebrew) would be incomprehensible for the gentiles.

104. See, for instance, speeches given at the board meeting of the Writers' Union, in which concern was voiced about the ubiquity of crypto-Jews and "Russian-speaking writers" in the Union: "Zasedanie Soiuza pisatelei," *Ogoniok*, no. 48 (1989).

105. E. Zderev, "Korroziia kulturi," *Russkii vestnik*, no. 32–35 (1994).

106. The "Odessa school" was prominent after the revolution of 1917 and in the interwar period. The majority of its writers were Jewish, the best-known being Sasha Chornii, Isaac Babel, Yurii Olesha, Ilf and Petrov, Eduard Bagritsky, Margarita Aliger, Kornei Chukovsky. Odessa style is distinguished by a specific use of language, sense of humor, and special subject matter, all of which are believed to result from the substantial presence of Jews in Odessa.

107. M. Lobanov, "Liberal'naiia nenavist'," *Zavtra*, no. 17 (1996).

108. A.M.A., "Ne uchite detei idishu," *Russkaiia pravda*, no. 5 (1995).

109. K. Parthé, "The Empire Strikes Back: How Right-Wing Nationalists Tried to Recapture Russian Literature," *Nationalities Papers*, 24, no. 4 (1996): 616.

110. K. Parthé "Chto delaet pisatelia russkim (Rusifikatsiia russkoi literaturi posle 1985 goda)," *Voprosi literaturi*, no. 1 (1996).

111. See G. Murikov "Igor' Talkov: khronika ubiistva," *Nash sovremennik*, no. 12 (1993).

112. A.Tsiganov, "Prorvat'sia v buduschuiu Rossiiu", *Literaturnaiia Rossiia*, August 6, 1999.

113. V. Kuznetsov, "Svet Esenina i Chernii chelovek," *Zavtra*, no. 38 (1995).

114. S. Kuniaev, *Sergei Esenin* (Moscow 1995). A special commission investigating the death of Sergei Esenin found no evidence suggesting he was assassinated; rather, it appears that he committed suicide. See Yuri Prokushev, et al, eds., *Smert' Sergeia Esenina: Dokumenti, fakti, versii* (Moscow 1996).

115. Gachev (b. 1929) is a doctor of philology and member of the Union of the Writers of Russia. He worked in many academic institutions, including the Institute of World Literature, Institute of History of Natural Sciences and Technology, and the Institute of Slavic and Baltic Studies (Academy of Sciences of the USSR).

116. G. Gachev, talk presented at the "Free Word," club, *Suschestvuet li v Rossii 'evreiskii vopros'?* (Moscow 1994), 46.

117. Ibid.

118. A. Goldstein, "Natsionalnie obrazi Gacheva," interview, *Okna* (Tel Aviv), 6–12 July 1995.

119. Gachev, "Free Word" club talk, 45–46.

120. Goldstein, "Natzionalnie obrazi Gacheva."

121. Ibid.

122. G. Gachev, "Rus', kuda zh neseot tebia?" *Nezavisimaiia gazeta,* 23 March 1992.

123. Goldstein, "Natsionalnie obrazi Gacheva."

124. Ibid.

125. Gachev claims that the "Father principle" was brought into the world and is maintained by the Jews, and was reinforced with the advent of Christianity. "The Oedipus complex — son murders his father and marries his mother — is specific for Western Europe. The New Testament is the first powerful articulation of the Oedipus complex. To be sure, Christ and Mary have overshadowed the God-Father.... The Jews keep their loyalty to the Lord, while Christianity is loyal to Christ and the Virgin with some respect for God who has dwindled." Quoted in Goldstein, "Natzionalnie obrazi Gacheva."

CHAPTER 5

National Orthodoxy:
"Two Millennia of Religious War"

In the late 1980s the emerging ideological vacuum left by the collapse of communism set the stage for an eruption of interest in the doctrines and practices of the Russian Orthodox Church. Under Mikhail Gorbachev, restrictions on religious practice eased and the Church emerged from its long and painful subjugation to the state as a serious social and political force. The years of official Soviet atheism gave way to a new relation between religion and the state.

James Billington, an authority on contemporary Russian religious life, distinguished two factions in the Orthodox Church during the perestroika period —nationalist hard-liners, and new-style believers. "One [group] sees the Russian Church providing a unifying national identity for a rejuvenated traditional state. The other sees the Church as providing the moral basis for building a responsible society independent of state structures."[1] Nationalist hard-liners seek authoritarian discipline, and disseminate and reinforce the old medieval anti-Jewish stereotypes; while new-style believers attempt to reform Orthodoxy from within.

In the first years of perestroika the new-style believers were more visible. The widespread emphasis on universal human values in Russian society, in particular, were similar to Christian ideals, especially those of the Orthodox dissenters (who had opposed both the Soviet state and the official Church hierarchy) who had become the new Orthodox leaders. These former dissenters took an active part in public debates. The charismatic liberal Orthodox priests Alexander Menn and Gleb Yakunin were emblematic of a significant trend within the Orthodox revival. The position taken by the official leaders of the Church also greatly contributed to the new image of Orthodoxy. They tried to dissociate themselves and the new post-communist Church from both its connivance with state and party authorities, and from the xenophobic ideology of the Black Hundreds. Patriarch Alexii II, for example, denounced antisemitism. In his address to Jewish rabbis in New York and on other occasions, he emphasized the common biblical heritage and spiritual bonds of Christianity and Judaism, and also pointed to a tradition of Orthodox anti-antisemitism.[2]

Thus the public visibility of the Church's new leaders has overshadowed the nationalist trend within Orthodoxy that more recently has seriously challenged the liberal faction. Perhaps, due to the situation in the first years of glasnost, some observers of contemporary Russian nationalism either exonerated or disparaged the antisemitic undercurrents of the Orthodox revival as expressed by Orthodox nationalists. As Theodor Friedgut pointed out:

> It is important to note that the revival of public religious activity in Russia has not been accompanied by Church propagation of antisemitism. The newly emergent religious establishment has concentrated on re-creating its material and moral domain.... While various "national-patriotic" groups have raised the issue of Jewish culpability in the destruction of churches and the repression of the Russian Orthodox religion under communism, Church authorities have totally eschewed this debate, looking forward rather than back.[3]

This idyllic picture of the Orthodox revival is far from adequate. Religious anti-Jewish arguments in fact figure prominently in the agenda of many nationalist Orthodox ideologists.

It should be acknowledged that Orthodox values and standards appeal to many different groups of nationalists. In fact, few members of these groups would admit aloud if they are *not* Orthodox believers. National Orthodoxy should be discussed as a separate trend in Russian nationalism due to the weight attributed to religious considerations in the discussion of various questions. The nationalist spokesmen for Orthodoxy advocate their own ideological position with respect to the Jewish question and Judaism and suggest their own program for resolving Jewish issues.

Before pursuing the issue of the revival of contemporary Orthodox antisemitism, it is necessary to review the historical background and contexts in which the Jewish question was raised in the Orthodox tradition.

THE RUSSIAN ORTHODOX CHURCH AND THE JEWS

The "patriotic" trend in Orthodoxy follows a centuries-old tradition traceable to some teachings of the early Church. The major prerequisites and ideological sources of Orthodox hostility to Judaism are the same as those of other Christian confessions. Two basic themes found in Christianity underlie the hostility towards the Jews: the crime of "deicide" attributes collective responsibility to the Jews for the passion and death of Jesus. The Jews were viewed as cursed by God, since they rejected the Messiah and brought about his death.

The second teaching focused on the Jews as "Chosen People," asserting that the Christian Church has superseded the Jewish people and become the "new" or "true Israel" because of the Jews' spiritual blindness and refusal to recognize Jesus as the messiah.

Although these beliefs do not necessarily imply a violent attitude towards the Jews, they have inspired and fueled persecution and physical violence against the Jews from the time of the early Church and continue to influence the perception of Jews in significant segments of the Christian world.

The Russian Orthodox Church shared these teachings with other mainstream Christian churches, albeit with its own modifications and accents. Christianity was brought to Russia in the ninth century by missionaries from Byzantium. Thus the Russian Church's theology, liturgy, and culture are derived from Eastern, rather than Western Christianity.

The Orthodox Church claims to preserve the teachings of the early Church and puts great emphasis on the writings of the Church Fathers, who are regarded as the authentic interpreters of the faith. It was crucial for these ecclesiastical writers of the Roman period to emphasize the differences between Christianity and Judaism. First of all, they wished to clarify the tenets of the Church, which was making its first steps as an institution. Second, it wished to express its opposition to elements of Judaic doctrine that still survived in the Church. One of the most popular genres of Orthodox theological writing was the anti-Jewish polemical treatise.[4] The criticism of Judaism by the Church Fathers left its stamp on the whole theological tradition of the Eastern Orthodox Church, for the diatribes against the Jews became a model for theological discussion. Steven Bowman, a historian of the Byzantian Jews, points out that the majority of the polemical treatises and homilies against the Jews were "literary theological exercises rather than records of actual confrontations." In Byzantium, "heretics were called 'Jews' regardless of the presence of the Judaizing tendencies in their ideology or ritual practices. Newer heresies, such as Bogomil, were best combated through the traditional arguments, forged over generations, against Jews."[5] This tradition of theological hostility was bequeathed to Russian Orthodoxy. The first Russian theological work, the "Sermon on Law and Grace" delivered by Mitropolitan Hillarion of Kiev (11th century) is a polemical anti-Judaic treatise which addresses the relation between Jewish Law and Christian Grace. The stigmatization of Judaism as an inferior religion and the implacable opposition to the real and imagined Judaizing heresies came to be permanent and persistent ingredients of the Orthodox theological tradition.[6]

There are other peculiar facets of Orthodox theology and its historical setting that shaped the attitude of the Orthodox Church towards the Jews.

In Byzantium, church and state were united under imperial leadership. The emperor could appoint and depose patriarchs at will. Byzantine caesaropapism spread from the Byzantine Empire to all its dependencies, including Russia. Whereas in Western Europe the Catholic Church enjoyed autonomy from the state and offered a counterweight to the secular authorities, the Eastern Orthodox Church traditionally acted in "symphony" with the government (autocracy). In practice this "symphony" meant the subjugation of the patriarchs and the Church to the Emperor.[7] Because of its dependency upon the state, the Russian Church adopted and carried out state policies of the tsars and government. The very structure of power had determined the predominantly conservative orientation of the Russian Orthodox Church and its hostility to the "fundamentalist" Christian ideology that held that religion was inherently superior to the state, as noted by Agursky. Byzantine caesaropapism determined some important aspects of the attitude of the Church to Jewish matters. Very few representatives of the Orthodox Church opposed the antisemitic policies of the Russian Empire or took a stand on behalf of the social movement for the promotion of constitutionalism, civil emancipation, and human rights. In his study of the link between religion and nationalism, the American Jewish historian Salo Wittmayer Baron aptly points out:

> Unlike Western Europe, where the clergy was found in the front ranks of fighters for social justice, the number of progressive priests in the Orthodox Church was always small; of those supporting the revolutionary movements practically nil. Nor was the absence of an organized Christian Socialist Movement due solely to governmental repressions. The first flush of the Revolution of 1905 produced a few progressive clerical deputies to the First and Second Dumas. But forty-four and forty-three priests serving in the Third and Fourth Dumas, respectively, belonged for the most part to the staunchest supporters of the reaction. Many were known to be leaders of the notorious "Black Hundreds."[8]

The other specific aspect of Orthodox theology which shaped its attitude to the Jews was a special emphasis on the theology of replacement, or what William Nichols calls a "theology of supersession."[9] Attempts to reexamine the concept of the Chosen People, and the concomitant idea of the special missions of different kingdoms in the eschatological process and in the context of the Russian historical experience is also closely connected with the Oriental fusion of religion and state. After the fall of Constantinople (1453) and the subjection of all other Greek Orthodox peoples to the rule of Turkey, the Russian Church (which had become autocephalous in 1448) stood as the sole independent champion of Orthodoxy. The rise of the Moskovite grand prince to the position of tsar lent great luster to the Russian Church.[10] The monk Philotheus (Filofei), in his epistle to Ivan III written between 1514 and 1521, was the first to introduce a concept that envisaged Moscow as the "third Rome" destined to supplant the previous Romes on the Tiber and the Bosporus.. "For two Romes fell and the third stands, and a fourth there will not be." Originally the concept had an eschatological rather than political meaning, presupposing that after the fall of Byzantium the Russian Orthodox Church was the sole custodian of the true faith in the world, which prevented the coming of the Antichrist.[11] This status made the Russian Orthodox Church the only legitimate claimant to the title of the "new Israel."[12] The Russian Orthodox state thus took over the mission of the old Chosen People that had failed to be faithful to its election. Whereas the second Rome (Constantinople) fell physically, Jerusalem and the first Rome fell spiritually.[13]

After Philotheus, some clerics and statesmen tried to appropriate the designation "Jerusalem" for the traditional Russian religious centers. Shortly after Moscow asserted itself as the third Rome, the ancient capital of Kiev claimed to be the "second Jerusalem."[14] In the seventeenth century, Patriarch Nikon built the Resurrection Monastery as the "New Jerusalem" near Moscow, and designed to replicate the topology of the Holy City. In Moscow, Boris Godunov planned to pull down all the buildings of the Kremlin, including the most sacred sites (e.g., the Cathedral of the Assumption) and to build Jerusalem in the very heart of the Russian capital.[15] The title of "second Jerusalem" was applied even to St. Petersburg, where the emperor Pavel I erected the Mikhailovsky Castle at the turn of the eighteenth century, whose design was meant to duplicate the First Temple of Jerusalem.[16] According to architecture historian Grigorii Kaganov, the inspiration for this project derived from the emperor's membership in the Masonic lodge, where the idea of a second Jerusalem also played a role.[17] However, its indigenous inspiration should not be underestimated, as it indicates the appeal of the idea of the Third Rome for Russians, as well as the long-held desire to establish the "new Jerusalem" in one of Russia's cultural centers, endowed with its special mission.

One might consider it odd to designate Moscow as both "Rome" and "Jerusalem." However, in the minds of the theologians, Russia became the third Rome precisely *because* it was already the second Jerusalem: historical Rome had taken over the mission of Jerusalem, for in Rome, Christianity had become the universal faith. In this sense, — and this is exactly what Russian theologians meant — Rome was only the "second" Jerusalem. In the time of Philotheus in the fifteenth century, Moscow in its religious and imperial aspect took over the mission. Because of the inseparable unity of religion and state, Russia was better equipped to preserve and transfer the divine truth that first was revealed to Jerusalem. The very strength of the Russian empire was a sign of God's favor and of itself justification for Moscow's spiritual pretensions. Attempts to "nationalize" the Christian ideal resumed in the nineteenth century when many clerics and Orthodox writers proclaimed that Orthodoxy and the Russian people were the bearers of the supreme religious truth and had a special eschatological mission in world history. The concept of Russian religious "election" challenged the Hebraic idea of the "chosen people," and created a breeding ground for religiously-grounded jealousy of the Jews, and fueled anti-Jewish sentiment.

The other ideological source of antisemitism is a traditional Russian Orthodox demonology and a specific version of apocalypse. In many examples of religious writing, Satan or Antichrist has been portrayed as a Judean Prince who, as Antichrist, would attempt to imitate Jesus Christ, subverting Christianity with terror and false teaching. He would also attempt to rebuild the Temple of Solomon, and in this theological narrative the Jews play the role of the main supporters of Antichrist, since having rejected Jesus, they are vulnerable to the influence of demonic forces.[18] This pattern of demonology survived through the centuries and is still effectively used by the post-perestroika generation of Orthodox nationalists:

> The Jews did not accept Christ, the real Messiah, who came in the name of God the Father. They are waiting for their own Messiah, Antichrist, who will come in his own name.... In spite of the temptations to which Antichrist will subject people — he will give peace, he will feed the poor and miserable and will establish the social justice and will assume the title of the tsar — he is still an Antichrist who will ruin the world.[19]

This theological image was also utilized in the discussion of political issues.[20] Walter Laqueur has pointed out that the Devil was perceived in Orthodoxy not as a metaphor or allegory, but as a real power associated with actual political forces:

> The belief in Satan and demons...has persisted longer and more strongly in Russia than elsewhere and it has taken on pronounced political overtones over the last hundred and fifty years.... In recent years many elements of demonology...have been resurrected in the doctrine of the Russian far right not just in the abstract, but with reference to concrete political enemies....[21]

Under these circumstances the struggle against the satanic forces associated with the Jews was considered normative for all true Orthodox believers.

In the nineteenth and beginning of the twentieth centuries these structural and doctrinal peculiarities of Orthodoxy predetermined the conservative and inimical position of the Church toward the Jews. The majority of Orthodox clerics joined reactionary political forces and opposed the civil rights and constitutional movements. Many Orthodox writers associated democracy and liberalism with the intrigues of the Jews and called for joint efforts by the state and Church against the "common foe" of both Christianity and monarchical order. They condemned not only the activity of the revolutionary parties but also the ideas of the Enlightenment and the advent of modernity. Many directly supported the activities of the Union of Russian People and other reactionary and antisemitic organizations. [Orthodox leaders were indubitably guilty of instigating widespread massacres of Jews in 1881, 1903, and 1905 — all of which were also promoted by governmental organs. The Holy Synod, placed in charge of state censorship, allowed the publication of a flood of antisemitic literature. Not surprisingly, the famous antisemitic forgery, the *Protocols of the Elders of Zion* was disseminated largely in the Orthodox milieu. The manuscript of *It is Near, At the Door* (1917) which contained the *Protocols* was printed by the Sviato-Troitsky Monastery. Nikon (Rozhdestvensky), the archbishop of Arkhangelsk and Vologda, and the Orthodox writer Bronzov publicly defended the authenticity of the *Protocols.* Some clerics even instigated pogroms (e.g., the celibate priest Iliodor Trufanov), and reinforced and popularized the medieval blood libel (Bishop Porfirii Uspenskii), especially during the Beilis affair (Archpriest and Professor T. I. Butkevich).[22] Father John (Ioann) of Kronstadt (considered a saint of the Russian Orthodox Church) condemned the pogrom in Kishinev but blessed the banner of the Union of Russian People and enjoyed honorary membership in this organization.[23]

In listing these examples, I do not suggest that Orthodoxy's attitudes and actions toward the Jews was somehow "worse" than that found in Western Christianity, for one cannot really compare the two. My intent here is simply to highlight some lines of thought prevalent in Russian Orthodox thinking that laid the foundation for religious animosity.

A number of Orthodox priests condemned the Christian use of antisemitic rhetoric and involvement in pogroms. In 1882, Metropolitan Makarii (Bulgakov) of Moscow and Kolomna defended the Jews in a speech delivered in the Kremlin Cathedral of the Assumption asserting that the Christian faith is incompatible with involvement in antisemitic manifestations. In 1884, Archbishop Makarii (Miroliubov) of Nizhnii

Novgorod and Arsamas appealed to the citizens to end the pogrom in the city. In 1886, Archbishop Nikanor (Brovkovich) of Kherson and Odessa addressed a special appeal to those who count themselves Orthodox believers and at the same time express anti-Jewish sentiment. He emphasized the congruity and close historical ties between Christianity and Judaism and claimed that Christian moral perfection presupposes care and concern not only for the co-religionists but also for the representatives of other religious confessions. Orthodox clerics Ivan Troitskii (a professor at the St. Petersburg Spiritual Academy) and Archpriest Alexander Glagolev (a professor of the Kiev Spiritual Academy) defended Mendel Beilis during his trial and denounced the blood libel as a medieval prejudice.

The most interesting attempt to address the "Jewish question" in terms of Christianity and to reexamine the traditional Christian attitudes to the Jews was undertaken by Russian religious philosophers of the Silver Age.

THE RUSSIAN RELIGIO-PHILOSOPHICAL RENAISSANCE

The ideas of Russian religious philosophers are significant not only as an intriguing part of Russian intellectual history but also as a living ingredient of the cultural and political debates in present-day Russia. The rediscovery of the Silver Age religious philosophers is an important part of the Orthodox revival. In many public debates their names are invoked as undisputed authorities, and their discussion of the "mystery of Israel" is extremely important for understanding contemporary discussions. Theosophy also played an important role in the religio-philosophy of the Silver Age, although it did not quite follow the Orthodox doctrines.

Many Orthodox thinkers of the period came to the Church after years of dramatic spiritual quest and after suffering disappointment in the most influential political ideologies of the age. Some advocated reform in the Russian Orthodox Church. The search for a "new religious consciousness," along with new mystical and esoteric dimensions of religion with a specific emphasis on the apocalypse were typical of the fin-de-siècle Russian intellectual climate.[24] Whereas some tried to restore what they believed to be a more authentic Christian truth overshadowed by the legacy of historical Christianity, others tried to "smuggle" into the Church their own philosophical and religious ideas and introduce them as the genuine teaching of Russian Orthodoxy.

Remarkably, all the prominent Russian philosophers addressed the "Jewish question" and the "mystery of Israel" from a predominantly religious and theological point of view. However, the discussion was no mere exercise in theological hermeneutics, but rather, addressed the topical problems of the age.[25]

A complete discussion of the varying perspectives on the Jews is beyond the scope of this volume, so I shall focus on the ideas of two groups of the Orthodox thinkers with some additional attention to the early theosophists, whose esoteric notions also influenced those Christians who sought an esoteric mysticism. Representatives of one group were opposed to antisemitism and tried to distance themselves from antisemitic stereotypes (especially those circulated in the Orthodox milieu) by appealing to the authority of Holy Scripture especially the gospel of Luke and the Pauline epistles. Because all of them fell under the spell of philosemitic attitudes originally introduced by the great Russian religious thinker, Vladimir Soloviev, I shall refer to them as "Solovievites." This group included Fr. Sergii Bulgakov, Nikolai Berdiaev, Fr. Vasily Zenkovsky, Georgii Fedotov, and Semyon Frank. All were strongly influenced by Soloviev, although they did not necessarily share his philosophical insights. It is also noteworthy that the members of this group advocated liberal Orthodoxy and tried to incorporate some individualistic elements into traditional Orthodox theology.

The second group as well was characterized by a modification of traditional Orthodox doctrine. However, very few of them would be willing to admit that there was a spirit of innovation to be found in their works. These enlightened Judeophobes developed new antisemitic notions and often tried to introduce them as an esoteric truth of Christianity.

Since the theories of both the philosemites and the Judeophobes are little known among English speakers, I will introduce their thought before comparing the two groups to show that the differences between them are not so radical as some students of Russian intellectual history tend to think. In fact, they share many assumptions about the Jews and their role in modern history. The distinction between the Judeophobes and the Judophiles in the context of the Silver Age is not as sharp as some students of Russian intellectual history suggest. In many cases the difference is one of degree rather than kind. In particular, some elements of Judeophobia can already be found in the patterns of argument characteristic of classical philosemitism.

Judeophobia of the Silver Age: The Paradox of Discontinuity
The Orthodox renaissance of the Silver Age generated some intense manifestations of ideological antisemitism. Certainly, government provocations were not the only source for this, for to a great extent, antisemitic ideas and myths were reinforced by the intellectual climate of that time. Symbolism — the master code of the Silver Age — stimulated the

search for that "other reality" behind mere appearances. This interest triggered a common passion for mysticism and for conspiracy theories. Historical and political realities were understood as symbols of transcendental religious forces, and ideas about esoteric traditions and a "secret language" figured at the very center of intellectual debates. Symbolism was also closely connected to the development of a special apocalyptic mentality.[26] Many intellectuals of the time believed in the special role of ritual in social life; this was often coupled with attempts to galvanize the ritual dimension of life. Such thinking was a breeding ground for discussion of mysterious, supposedly secret Jewish rituals. All this found its way into the realms of politics and social theories, where it became dangerous and inflammable.[27]

Many saw themselves in opposition to the "profane" Orthodox religious tradition, whereas they themselves advocated a special mystical and esoteric Christianity, an "authentic" Church, which they believed had been forgotten or suppressed during its long history. Their intellectual constructions, however, contained new forms of old antisemitic prejudices.

These philosophers consistently emphasized the discontinuity between the historical experiences of Judaism and Christianity. The two religions were not only different but seemingly opposites. However, they also sought to expose differences between Christianity and Judaism outside traditional Church teaching in the esoteric features that were understood only by "initiates." Hence, their interpretations of both Christian and Jewish teaching differed radically from the conventional images of these religions. I shall discuss four of these intellectuals — the philosophers Nikolai Fedorov and Vasily Rozanov; the founder of the theosophical movement, Elena Blavatsky; and the Orthodox theologian Sergii Nilus. Although they appear to be quite different in terms of their interests and intellectual pursuits, we shall see that they share antisemitic prejudices inherited from some trends of the Orthodox tradition.

Nikolai Fedorov (1828–1903) identified the essence of any true religion with the ancestor cult, and argued that the true meaning of Christianity is found in the veneration of ancestors. He described Orthodoxy as a religion of son- and daughter-ship. It is a moral obligation and a "common task" of the people to "resurrect" their fathers. Christ himself restored life to Lazarus and himself returned from the dead. By so doing, he pointed the way to salvation and promised humanity that at some point everyone will be resurrected. Fedorov considered Christianity to be flawed, in that it had not attempted to carry out the task of "resurrection-patrification" of the ancestors. This task is allegedly prescribed by Jesus and by the Christian amendment to the fifth commandment of the Old Testament ("Honor your father and mother and love your neighbor as yourself"). Humanity has thus far failed to realize true brotherly relations and to act according to the idea of universal son-ship suggested by the "original" Christian teaching.

Christianity and Confucianism — whose principles lead to "patrification" — were contrasted with the Semitic religions, which are blind to ideas about brotherly love. Fedorov distinguished two ideas in the Semitic religions that would make it impossible to realize the resurrection of the dead: (1) The Hebrews supposedly rely on God rather than their own efforts to overcome evil in the world. Fedorov argued that the Jewish Sabbath was a day of passivity, as opposed to the active Christian Sunday.[28] (2) Only a minimal understanding of the concept of universal brotherhood — crucial for the realization of the "common task" of mankind — can be found in Judaism. In addition, Fedorov blamed the Semites (i.e., Jews, Phoenicians, and Arabs) for developing the capitalist system. Its cruelty and ruthlessness he attributed specifically to the Jewish religion.

The value of family ties were also exalted by Vasily Rozanov (1856–1919). In contrast to Fedorov, he saw in Judaism an emphasis on this primary value, equally applicable to the Russians. However, later on during the Beilis affair, he published a book in which he expressed his belief in the existence of special bloody rituals of the synagogue that have survived since the very ancient period.[29] Students of Rozanov's writings point to his movement from a philosemitic to an antisemitic stance, but in fact there is a continuity between the two phases. In fact, his later development demonstrated that his ambivalent attitude toward the Jews harbored more hatred than love.

Rozanov's 1903 book, *Judaism,* was commonly described as philosemitic. Yet its subject is the "secret cult" of the Jewish religion behind the conventional interpretation of its teachings and rituals. Rozanov wrote that unlike Christianity, Judaism is a religion of sexual joy and sacred eroticism, the origins of which could be found in ancient fertility cults and phallus worship. The Jews' religion merely disguised elements of the archaic mysteries of Egypt, Babylon, and Phoenicia.

Rozanov suggests that those interpretations of Judaic rituals, which the Jews are willing to share with outsiders are misleading. All of them, in fact, sanctify sexuality and family life. The celebration of the Sabbath is identical with the worship of the Middle Eastern fertility goddess Ashtoreth, hence the Sabbath has a secret sexual meaning.[30] The Jews describe the Sabbath as a Queen, and the Jew as a groom. It is a day of hierogamy — the sacred marriage of God and "Queen Sabbath." The ancient equivalents of the groom and Queen Sabbath are the god Bel (identified with the phallus) and

Ashtoreth.[31] "The Sabbath is a means and method for the resolution of the great and universal sexual problem." Immersion in the ritual bath (mikveh) by men and women, according to Rozanov, is a ritual that sanctifies sexual intercourse. The rite of circumcision is a sanctification of the organ of procreation that is identified with God, since Yahve himself was originally conceived as a god of procreation and conception. Circumcision, Rozanov contended, plays the same role in Judaism as the cross plays in Christianity. In short, marriage is at the center of Jewish religious life. "The Jewish theism is sacredly sexual, sacredly matrimonial, male-female in its most profound and suprahuman foundations."[32]

The only difference between the archaic religions and Judaism is the secretive nature of the Jewish religious beliefs, since other archaic religions, in contrast, make no secret out of their sexual nature. Rozanov attributes the vitality and the potency of the Jewish people to the sexual nature of their religion and contrasts this attitude with that of Christianity, which does not sanctify the sexual and family life: "In the most important moments of one's life the Aryan lives only physiologically, *modus animalium,* not in the sacred manner."[33] This failure of Christianity to address the sexual problem in a religious way leads to weakness and degeneration. This drawback was crystallized in a "worship of death," that transformed Christianity into a religion of suffering and asceticism. The revitalization of Christianity requires an accommodation to the life-affirming sexual aspects of Judaism, since the connection of sex with God is greater than that of mind or conscience.

In 1914, in the course of the Beilis trial, Rozanov published another book on the Jewish issues. This time it was a book on the Jewish "olfactory and tactile attitude to blood." The book surprised many members of the intelligentsia, who saw it as a transition to antisemitism. However, the shift in his ideas about Judaism is not as radical as is often suggested. His notions about the Jews' relationship to blood is perfectly in line with his previous writings about a Judaism that embraces a secret blood cult in addition to a cult of sexual prowess. Rozanov retained the idea of the Jews' special materialism, and the purely sensual nature of their perception of the divine. In both cases, the Jews are depicted as animalistic creatures. They have "big noses and fleshy lips" as opposed to the idealistic and spiritual Aryan. Rozanov emphasized the sensuality of the Jews by referring to the image of their God, identified with the phallus and said to love bloody sacrifices.[34]

Claims about the sexual nature of the Jewish religion can also be found in *The Secret Doctrine* (1888), by Helena Petrovna Blavatsky, a foundress of the theosophical movement.[35] It is unlikely that Rozanov ever read the book, whose first Russian translation appeared only in 1937. More likely is that Rozanov was familiar with reviews of the book and the works of the numerous Russian theosophists which appeared in the Russian Theosophical Society's journals and other periodicals. Though we cannot know how familiar Rozanov was with the theosophical movement, there is no doubt that he would have found Helena Blavatsky's ideas on the sexual nature of Judaism to be very congenial.

Of course, Blavatsky was extremely critical of the Orthodox Church and of historical Christianity in general, claiming that her doctrine represented an "authentic" esoteric Christianity that was never understood by the "profane" clergy. Her teachings provided a conceptual key to this esoteric Christianity, through a universal tradition that provided a grand synthesis of science, philosophy, and the ancient wisdom of different religions.[36] Though she represents a distinctly anti-Orthodox voice, her views are important in view of the Silver Age search for "authentic" Christian mysticism, as mentioned above.

Blavatsky believed that the "Aryans" and "Semites" provided two opposing interpretations of the same universal esoteric symbolism. She challenged the common view that Christianity was founded on a Semitic base, asserting that the Jews borrowed their most important religious symbols from the Aryans — particularly those of India and Egypt — yet were unable to adequately grasp the meaning of this symbolism.

Regarding her belief in the strongly sexual foundation of Jewish religious life, she held that the most sacred universal sexual symbols were interpreted metaphorically by the Aryans as symbols of cosmic creative forces. The Jews, however, retained a literal interpretation as the symbols of coitus. In the second volume of *The Secret Doctrine* she examined the symbolism of the Ark of the Covenant (synonymous with the Holy of Holies/*Sanctum Sanctorum*). Blavatsky concluded that such rites were of Aryan origin. [She claimed that the solar and lunar symbols which represent male and female principles, the creative forces of nature, are central for the Sanctum Sanctorum. The High Priest – the "initiated" — who entered the Ark/Holy of Holies symbolized the "male" sun, while the Ark itself is the female lunar kteic symbol. However, these symbols of creation and spiritual transformation (regeneration) were interpreted by the materialistic Jews in a purely physiological sense.[37] The Jews dismissed the metaphysical and psychological meaning of these sacred symbols and associated them with their androgynous God (YHVH), the God of coitus and procreation.[38] Jews interpreted the Ark as an image of the womb. Blavatsky pointed out that the most sacred symbols of Jewish culture are lunar because of the connection between the position of the moon and the physiological cycles of conception and procreation.

> The abyss which separates Aryan and Semitic religious thought is the abyss between two opposite poles, sincerity and secrecy. For the Brahmans who never associated the natural reproductive forces with the element of original sin it is a sacred obligation to have a son. After his mission as a human agent was over, a Brahman used to go to the jungle and spent the rest of his days in religious contemplation. He carried out his duties to nature as a mortal and as an associate.... In the case of the Semite it was different. He comprised the temptation of the flesh in the garden of Paradise and presented his God...as someone who curses for ever the action which was logically a part of the program of this Nature. But this is an esoteric approach.... However, esoterically he saw the supposed sin and the fall as so sacred that he chose the organ of the culprit of the original sin as the most pertinent and the most sacred symbol of the same God for whom the performance of its function was disobedience and eternal sin.[39]

In the ancient mystery religions, birth symbolized initiation (spiritual rebirth) and the transformation of matter into spirit, that is to say, "the divorce of Spirit from Matter." The Aryans elevated and spiritualized these images. In the Jewish religion, symbols of the mystery of spiritual transformation became merely the images of physical conception ("generation"), "a wedlock of Spiritual Man and Material Female Nature." Blavatsky contended that the phallic worship of the Jews and their preoccupation with physical conception are the result of spiritual degradation. She believed that Jews had lost "the keys to the inner meaning of the universal religious symbols" and emphasized the "idiosyncratic defects that characterize many of the Jews to this day — gross realism, selfishness and sensuality."[40] "Being based exclusively on phallic worship," Blavatsky argued, "contemporary Judaism in terms of theology turned into a religion of hate and malice toward everyone and everything outside itself."[41] Blavatsky especially emphasized the reasons for the Jewish rise to power in the modern age: it was not surprising that in an age when human monads had completed their descent into matter and humanity had come to the end of this particular cycle, the Jews came to be "the 'Masters' and 'Lords' of the European potencies."[42]

Blavatsky and Rozanov are quite different in their assessment of sexuality in religion. While Blavatsky condemns the materialistic contamination of religion with sex, Rozanov unequivocally valorizes the sexual nature of religion. Blavatsky believes that this contamination is a sign of vulgarity and degradation, while Rozanov sees the sacralization of sex as a people's only source of vitality. However, they defend a number of premises in similar ways. Their discussions blend the central issues of the Silver Age — problems of sexuality, the Jewish issue, and questions on the nature of political power. Both held that Judaism is (1) a secret religion; (2) a religion of sex; that (3) the sexual nature of Jewish religion is determined by the special sensual and materialistic character of the Jews as opposed to the idealistic Aryan character and religion; and (4) the Jewish religion is a relic of ancient Oriental fertility cults and phallic worship. Remarkably, both Rozanov and Blavatsky link the economic and political power of the Jews, that is, their dedication to Mammon, to their sexual power and prowess.[43]

The antisemitic leanings of the early theosophists were not confined to the theoretical constructions: several members of the Theosophical Society were directly involved in propagating theories of a Jewish conspiracy, and disseminating antisemitic pamphlets.[44] Some of Madame Blavatsky's doctrines were confluent with racist ideology in Europe in the early twentieth century. In this respect her concept of the series of successive races each embodying a different spirit or stage of evolution, is especially important. Blavatsky believed that the process of history is a process of "spiritualization" determined by the alterations of seven root races. She associated the current period with domination by the fifth — Aryan —root race. In her doctrine a special role was reserved for Russians. Maria Carlson, a historian of the Russian Theosophical movement, summarized Blavatsky's views on the role of the Slavs:

> The Slavs are the seventh sub-race (i.e., the youngest branch) of the Aryan race; their cosmic duty or mission (dharma), based on the Slavic folk soul's ability to conceptualize and to receive the contents of other cultures, is to assist in the realization of a more spiritualized humanity that will be achieved with the sixth root race.[45]

Blavatsky believed that the Jewish race is a mixture of the archaic fourth race of Mongol-Turanians and the fifth race of Indo-Europeans.[46] Thus, the Jewish race has been outdated by the historical process, and in any event, the most valuable parts of its spiritual legacy had been borrowed from the Aryan race.

Blavatsky never advocated a biological concept of race as later conceived by the Nazis. However, her concept of successive races was both attractive and congenial to the national myth put forward by Nazi ideologists. It is no coincidence that their German Aryosophe precursors admired Blavatsky and tried to integrate the historiosophical ingredients of theosophy into their doctrine.[47]

Sergii Nilus (1862–1929) is another thinker whose ideas were characteristic of the Orthodox Judeophobia of the Silver Age. In many accounts of Russian intellectual history, Nilus acquired dubious fame as the first publisher of the *Protocols of the Elders of Zion*. However, it must be emphasized that the *Protocols* first appeared merely as an appendix to his book *The Great in the Little* (1905). Nilus is rarely discussed in the context of the Russian religious and philosophical renaissance, although one can discover some striking similarities in his lunatic ideas and the cultural climate of the Silver Age. His antisemitism went beyond a mere reproduction of old Orthodox stereotypes, for many of his theological ideas were quite original and innovative. His social and intellectual background, and the story of his spiritual experience is reminiscent of the background and intellectual biographies of many well-known Russian philosophers of his generation. Nilus had graduated from the Law Department of Moscow University. He admired Nietzsche and the radical political trends in European thought.[48] However, he rediscovered the Orthodox tradition and underwent a spiritual crisis that moved him toward mysticism. He acquired a special interest in Orthodox folklore and Orthodox moral wisdom, and published several moral homilies collected when he wandered from one monastery to another after his return from France.

It was no accident that the Tsarist Secret Police chose him for the mission to disseminate the *Protocols*. Nilus was totally committed to what he believed to be the true teaching of the authentic Orthodoxy. His religious inspiration and bigotry blinded him to any possible evidence that the *Protocols* were fake. He believed that even if so, they were still a sign of God's providence and that God could teach people about coming danger even through "the ass of Balaam."[49]

Nilus not only published the *Protocols,* but provided his own interpretation that was extremely important in shaping their perceptions for many Russian readers. The *Protocols* supposedly provided evidence for his philosophy of history espoused in *The Great and the Little* and *It is Near, At the Door,* both of which focused on the apocalypse. Nilus associated the end of history with the contemporary craving for pleasure and forgetting of God. This worldliness dominated social life in Europe and America, and thus Russia was the only hope for the world. The arrival of Antichrist, Nilus believed, would be preceded by the activity of certain international organizations (later identified with the League of Nations) ruled by the "Learned Elders of Zion." Nilus associated the "peaceful invasion of the world" with the "symbolic snake" of a world government controlled by the Jews. A century after Adam Smith, he focused on the mechanism of operation of the "invisible hand," meaning, not Smith's concept of the mechanism of the open market, but world government. At the end of history, the Jews would serve as blind instruments of the Antichrist, who would be a Judean king. Nilus emphasized this political dimension in the subtitle of *The Great in the Little: Antichrist Considered as an Imminent Political Possibility.*

Nilus's image of the coming apocalypse owed a lot to Soloviev and Merezhkovsky. Savva Dudakov, a student of the story of the Protocols, showed that some Nilus's religious works bear remarkable similarity to Soloviev's ideas from his last book, the *Three Conversations Concerning War, Progress, and the End of History.*[50]

Interestingly, some central concepts of the *Protocols* could have had their origin in theosophical doctrines. The idea of an evil "Jewish world government" is the inversion of the idea of the "world government" by a group of Eastern adepts and sages of Tibet. According to some of the early theosophists, the Tibetan sages rule the world from their mysterious region of "Shambhala" in the Himalayas. It seems plausible that the "Elders of Tibet" who were the spirit guides of Helena Blavatsky became the prototypes for the "Elders of Zion" in the forgery disseminated by Sergii Nilus. Students of the history of the *Protocols* seem to have neglected so far the importance of theosophy as an inspiration for its writers. I believe that the involvement of the theosophists in the dissemination of this forgery is more than a coincidence. Examination of the document demonstrates the close affinity between the philosophies of history espoused in the *Protocols* and the theosophical doctrine, in spite of other serious differences.

The Silver Age generated not only the antisemitic ideology of neo-Orthodoxy but also a strong opposition to the proliferation of Judeophobic ideas. Yet there are serious limitations in their condemnation of antisemitism, often overlooked by students of Russian intellectual history.

The Paradox of Orthodox Philosemitism: "The Axis of World History"

The tradition of philosemitism in Russian religious philosophy began with Vladimir Soloviev. He laid the foundations for discussion of the "mystery of Israel" in Russian philosophy. At the end of the nineteenth century, his speeches and papers on antisemitism had a great influence on both intellectuals and the general public.[51] His essay, "Jewry and the Christian Question" (1884) is his most significant contribution to the discussion of the historical fate of the Jewish people and the lessons that can be learned by Christians.

Soloviev distinguished three peculiar characteristics of the Jewish people which determined the idiosyncratic features of their history and their election: (1) profound religious devotion; (2) a strong sense of individuality and self-consciousness, and (3) materialism. These features, Soloviev claims, are not as incompatible as they seem to be at first blush, and their combination in Jewry is perfectly natural. The interaction and dialogue with God (the absolute personality) requires people with a strong sense of personhood. By the same token, the materialism of the Jews does not contradict their religious convictions, for it is by its nature religious rather than practical or scientific. Even the extreme materialism of the Jewish financial elite is inspired by the intention to glorify Israel not by the desire to gain profit. It is not merely because of their Jewishness that Jews exploit the peasants, but rather because Jews posses special skill and a vocation for financial dealings. It is not the Jews who are responsible for the separation of economics from the religious and moral sphere; rather, Europeans themselves established the [present] godless and inhumane economic principles.[52] Moreover, the materialism of the Jews is motivated by an aspiration to bring the divine ideals into reality and to transform everyday practice in accordance with these ideals.

While the appropriate balance and ordering of the three features of the Jewish psyche determined their election, an improper balance has led at various times in history to great disasters and misfortunes. For example, when the religious foundation of the Jewish character collapses, the strong sense of individuality will degenerate into national egotism and hostility toward others, while materialism will turn into a mercenary and cynical realism.

Soloviev emphasized the original unity and continuity of the religious experience of Judaism and Christianity. Both religions dreamed of an incarnation of transcendent ideals in the reality of this world, through a theocratic government. The kingdom of God is not only spiritual but also this-worldly. The political dimension of the Jewish concept of the messiah, Soloviev argued, is not completely alien to Christianity: Judaism and Christianity disagree only over the means of realizing the theocratic ideal. Whereas Christianity chose the "way of the cross," Judaism wishes to achieve the ideal through following the literal instructions of its ancient covenant.

[The Jews] did not want to understand and accept the way of the cross which does not bring the kingdom from the outside but facilitates its adoption from within. They did not want to accept Christ's cross and, [consequently] they have been carrying their own heavy cross for eighteen centuries.[53]

Christianity elaborated and perfected the Jewish ideals of theocracy and God-manhood. The Christian theocracy presupposes a threefold divine-human union, namely the "priestly," "royal," and "prophetic" unions. Soloviev believed that each mode of this threefold union could be abused. Catholicism, for example, is prone to the abuse of religious power and interference into state affairs. Eastern Orthodoxy emphasized and developed the "royal aspect," which occasionally degenerated and led to state interference in religious affairs. Conversely, Protestants and Jews overemphasized the prophetic aspect of theocracy at the expense of priestly and royal authorities. Soloviev found Judaism closer to the proper combination of the three modes. Jews had never denied the authority of the priests and kings, and never placed faith and deeds in opposition to one another. In addition, the Jews never made Holy Scripture into nothing more than the subject of scholastic exercises and criticism, as happened in Christianity and led to the development of atheism.

Today, Soloviev went on to argue, messianism and the theocratic ideal are especially present among Russians and Poles, even taking into account certain distortions. It is no coincidence that a majority of Jews — who originally developed these ideas — live in those countries.[54] The religious development of these three "theocratic people" is a prerequisite for the realization of the ideal of God-manhood.

Realization of the theocratic ideal and an internal transformation of Orthodox and Catholic institutions — beginning with a change in the Christian attitude to the Jews — will eventually lead to the conversion of the Jews. "We are separated from the Jews because we fail to fully embrace Christianity and they separate themselves from us because they still have not fully embraced Judaism."[55] The majority of Jews will join with Christians to establish a theocracy, and all of Israel will be saved. Moreover, a sphere of activity in the Christian theocracy is reserved especially for the Jews. The sphere of economic relations is in need of Jewish talent, so that it will serve not the selfish greed of individuals, but rather, will foster the humanization of material life and nature. "The Israel of the future will become the active mediator in the humanization of the material life and nature, just as the pick of Jewry had served the embodiment of the Divine."[56]

Other Orthodox philosemites continued to rely on Soloviev's ideas, but they discussed Jewish issues in a quite different historical and intellectual context shaped by two epochal events — the Russian Revolution and the Second World War — as well as their experiences as emigrants. Their essays were published in the aftermath of the Nazi persecution of the Jews in the

1930s and 1940s, along with the spread of antisemitism in some Russian émigré circles.

Nikolai Berdiaev (1874–1948) follows Soloviev in insisting that antisemitism is essentially a "Christian problem." His most famous work on this issue was *Christianity and Antisemitism* (1938).[57] Berdiaev considered Christian antisemitism (as distinct from economic and racist antisemitism) to be especially persistent and dangerous. Christian antisemitism is paradoxical since the principles of the Christian faith deny any inequality between various races.[58] However, "in the past antisemitism was generated first of all by the Christians," and Berdiaev attributes to them a special responsibility for the historical injustice against the Jews. Nevertheless, he himself was not completely emancipated from Christian antisemitism.

Berdiaev believed that the Jews committed the crime of deicide *(bogoubiistvo)* because they expected the messiah to be a powerful earthly king and failed to recognize the Savior in the crucified and suffering Jesus. Even so, the crime of deicide committed by the Jews does not justify hostility towards them. Berdiaev also argued that the Jews continued to play a positive role in the development of Christian civilization even after their mission as the forerunner of Christianity was accomplished. The goals of Christianity, he wrote, are twofold, transcendent and this-worldly.[59] The Jews have always yearned to transform society in accordance with their ideals of social justice, whereas Christians have often been more concerned with individual sanctity and failed to address social issues. Berdiaev also had misgivings about the Jewish preoccupation with this-worldly affairs. He thought that the Jewish vision which often favors human perspective might ultimately be in conflict with the Divine plan. Communist and socialist doctrines were degraded and secularized incarnations of religiously-inspired Jewish ideals of social justice and messianism. Russian-Jewish communists, and even Karl Marx himself, were insufficiently aware of the Jewish roots of their social ideals and activity.[60] Christians need to demonstrate to the skeptical Jews the feasibility of implementing Christian ideals of social justice.

Berdiaev believed that only at the end of time would the Jewish question be resolved. The Jews would voluntarily convert to Christianity as a prelude to the return of Christ and final salvation. For these events to emerge, Christianity must first be transformed, and Jews must overcome their own negative features — their racial arrogance and particularism, opposition to God, preoccupation with themselves as an ethnic group at the expense of the Christian sense of personhood and individual freedom, and their attraction to secularized religious ideals such as socialism and Marxism. With these changes, Jews would then be able to appreciate Christian doctrines such as the immortality of the soul, the sense of individual freedom, and personal responsibility.

Fr. Sergii Bulgakov (1871–1944) also followed Soloviev in his views on Jewish issues. His last paper, *Persecutions of Israel* (1942) summarized his earlier works on the subject.[61] Bulgakov's central thesis was that the coming of Jesus did not abolish God's covenant with the Jewish people, and he agreed with Berdiaev that the Jewish fate was the "axis of the world history." This axial role results from their special genealogical relation to the messiah as presented in the gospels of Matthew and Luke, which suggest the universality of the Jewish mission. God's "peculiar people" — the Jews — were chosen for the universal mission as the vessel for the human incarnation of Christ.

However, Bulgakov argued, the Jews betrayed their universal mission by their rejection of the messiah, and the Jewish national consciousness became corrupted by racism and ethnic idolatry. In this sense Bulgakov argues that "German racism is only a jealous parody" of this Jewish ethnic idolatry. In addition, the Jews expose themselves as secret or overt persecutors of Christ. They occupy the throne of the Prince of this world and worship Mammon, the god of money, the golden calf. They initiated the pseudo-messianic and godless teaching of socialism. Bulgakov argues that "Israel came to be the laboratory of all spiritual banes which poison the world."[62] All these misdeeds indicate that the Jewish people "still wander in the desert in search of the Promised Land, in search of Christ in the struggle against Him and ignorance about Him."[63]

In spite of individual and collective lapses, the covenant and the "election" of Israel cannot be revoked and invalidated, "gift and calling of God are irrevocable" (Rom. 11:29). The potential for Jewish conversion and the continuity of the covenant can be seen in the following scriptures: "There is a remnant according the election of grace" (Rom. 11:5) through which "all Israel shall be saved" (Rom. 11:26). Blindness only temporarily "happened to Israel" (Rom. 11:25). The messiah himself dreams of gathering the children of Israel as "a hen gathereth its chicks" (Matt. 23:37; cf. Luke 13:34). The Jews suffered for Christ and with Christ without being aware of the meaning of their suffering, like the firstborn [*sic*] murdered by King Herod (Matt. 2:16).[64] The "righteous remnant" of Israel, which was not very visible and was overshadowed by the misdeeds of the Jews, carries two crosses — that of Israel and that of Jesus. "The persecutors of Israel persecute Christ himself in it just like the Jews themselves fight against Christ, resisting their own election."[65]

The Jewish mission and fate is inextricably intertwined with that of the Church. Unless the Jews recognize and accept Christ as their messiah, they will be unable to complete their calling. At the same time, Christianity can find completion only with the addition of the Jewish people as converts, in the same unity evident in the early Church of the Apostles.[66] Bulgakov understood the future conversion of the Jewish people as inevitable.

Vasily Zenkovsky (1881–1962), an Orthodox priest and well-known historian of Russian philosophy argued that Jewish history could never be properly understood in terms of conventional historical concepts, nor could Jewish problems be settled through the promotion of liberalism. The very survival of the Jewish people in history and their earthly fate testifies to the suprahistorical mission of Israel. A secular interpretation of Jewish history is "tragically non-sensical."[67] Only Christian eschatology and the perspective of final salvation can provide the key for understanding the Jewish fate, which is only conceivable in terms of Christ's advent — "the grandest event in the history of Israel." "The relationship between Jews and Christians," Zenkovsky contended, "is the most important one both for the Jewry and for Christianity. Without any exaggeration it is the central issue of history."[68] The mission of Israel in the process of ultimate salvation, he wrote, is to "provoke the jealousy of the Gentiles" by teaching Christians a lesson in humility. The temporary "blindness" of the Jews is in fact, providential.[69]

Semyon Frank (1877–1950), a professor of philosophy at Moscow University, had no particular commitment to Soloviev's ideas. He had been baptized in the Orthodox Church in 1912, and his perspective on Jewish matters can be interpreted in the context of Soloviev's writings, and more broadly as part of the Russian religious renaissance. Like the Solovievites, Frank regarded Christianity as a natural and advanced outgrowth of Judaism. In "The Religious Tragedy of the Jews" (1934), he wrote that to any impartial observer, God's greatest revelation in the history of Judaism was in the person of Christ.[70] Jews had a negative attitude toward the church because it had persecuted them when it came into power. The individual Jew — like Frank himself — faced the dilemma of betraying the Jewish people by giving up his nationality in order to benefit from conversion, or else denying God's greatest revelation in the Messiah.[71]

Like Bulgakov and Berdiaev, Frank associated Judaism with socialism, which both share the "denial of the past and the real for the sake of the purity of a dream," and both "transfer the immanence of God to the future." Jewish morality, he thought, was more transcendent, since it derived from a sense of external duty; Christian morality, by contrast, was immanent, as it comes from the heart. By the same token, socialism imposes a sense of duty, which lacks immanent ontological roots in the human heart and human nature.[72] In contrast to Berdiaev and Bulgakov, Frank associates socialism not with the corrupt and degraded secularized Judaism but rather with Orthodox Judaism.

The Solovievites share the following assumptions about the role of the Jews in world history, and the meaning of the Jewish experience for the Christian world.

(1) All of them were skeptical of the ability of political, legal, and social means to resolve Jewish problems. Most were sympathetic to Zionism, but still maintained that only the eschatological perspective held any final answers for the Jewish people.[73]

(2) Positivist and materialist accounts of history fail to explain the "mystery" of Jewish history. Only the Christian historical narrative can make it clear.

(3) The "Jewish question" is essentially a Christian question, for two reasons. First, the fate of the Jewish people is inconceivable apart from the "grand narrative" of the coming of the Messiah. The Jews retain their status as the "Chosen People" even after the coming of Christ, and they are the "axis of human history," since their crucial role in the eschatological drama remains to be played out. The Solovievites did not fully accept the common theological premise that Christianity had superseded Judaism. Second, the Solovievites considered the Christian attitude toward the Jews to be a special test for Christians. Those throughout the Christian world who truly embraced Christianity must also make a radical shift in their attitude toward the Jews.

(4) Christianity and Judaism are not separate religions but rather, two phases of the same religion of God-manhood. They share not only a common historical origin, but also the same historical perspective on the salvation of mankind.

These common points allow some observations about the nature of Orthodox philosemitism and its limitations. In spite of the generally favorable, indeed almost apologetic assessment of the Jewish role in history, and probably contrary to their own intentions, the Solovievites' writings still contain antisemitic images and in different degrees reinforce Jew-baiting clichés. A few examples:

(a) Statements about Jewish control of European and world financial life are quite common. Even the most radical Russian philosemite, Soloviev himself, contended that

> Judaism is not only tolerated; it has managed to occupy a position of domination in the most progressive nations.... The financial sphere and the majority of the periodicals are controlled by the Jews....

Judaism makes both money and Europe devoted to it to serve its own cause.[74]

(b) The writings of Berdiaev and Bulgakov hint at a Jewish-Bolshevik conspiracy. Bulgakov reproached the Jews for their enthusiastic participation in the revolution and for the persecution of Christianity in Soviet Russia. He held the Jews collectively responsible, and expected them to declare to Russians their repentance. His ideas about the Jewish origins of German Nazism and racism in general are problematic, not only in terms of historical accuracy, but especially given that they were voiced during the Second World War. In this context, his description of Israel as the "laboratory of all spiritual banes" in the modern world is especially provocative. In general, Soloviev's followers tend to stigmatize actual Jewry while praising the benign Jewry of the past and future.

(c) All the philosophers of the religious renaissance held that the Christian "grand narrative" was the sole basis for understanding history and the Jews' part in it. The Jews suffer and "carry their cross" unaware of the true meaning of their suffering. Yet this narrative deprives Judaism of its own vision of world history. Soloviev and the others believed that not only the Old Testament, but the whole of Jewish post-biblical history should witness to the ultimate truth of Christianity. They overlooked the possibility of a dialogue between the two independent traditions in interpreting Holy Scripture, believing that all the vital aspects of the Jewish tradition were already embraced by Christianity. The only "dialogue" they could anticipate was one with a thoroughly Christian agenda.

(d) Though the Solovievites did not subscribe to the explanation for the persecution of the Jews as God's just punishment, their account of Jewish history did suggest that persecution of the Jews is part of the process of redemption. Of course, they never tried to vindicate persecution in moral terms on the basis of this historical perspective. However, even if this theological premise does not legitimate the persecutions, it exonerates in some sense the guilt of the persecutors, who were seen as merely instruments for the realization of the original divine plan.

(e) All the philosophers of the religious renaissance employ — or at least intimate — the paradigm of the "fallen angel," though it is never mentioned directly in their discussions of Jewish matters. In the apocryphal legend, Lucifer was the archangel cast from heaven after leading an angelic revolt against God. This idea of the fallen angel is better articulated in the contemporary ideology of national Orthodoxy to be discussed below. This interpretation of the Solovievites (also found in National Orthodoxy) suggests that the "angelic" qualities of the Jews in the early stages of their religious development (the "chosen people" stage) turned sinister at a later stage, and were transformed even further into a superhuman power of evil, from which they may be released by God at the end of the time. Even in the favorable views of the Solovievites, the Jews are seen as a challenge to Christianity and, like Lucifer, subject Christians to special temptation.

(f) Almost all of these philosophers generally accepted the traditional caricature of post-biblical Judaism as a dead and fossilized religion lacking the spiritual vitality and dynamism of early Judaism.

As we see, both philosemites and judeophobes of the Silver Age have much in common despite their differing conclusions. In particular, we may note the similarity between the views of Nilus and Soloviev, the central figures in the two camps. Both were obsessed with the "Jewish question" and attributed to the Jews a special role in the final drama of the apocalypse. Both believed that the Jews dominated European finance and had introduced the cult of the "golden calf." Both theologians identified the Jews with the fallen angel (Nilus explicitly and Soloviev implicitly). Yet, notwithstanding his active propagation of the *Protocols,* Sergii Nilus opposed the pogroms, and even prayed for the Jewish people, insisting that they were only "blind instruments" in the hands of the Antichrist. Nilus had pointed out that only the leaders of the Jewish community should be held responsible for the crimes of the Jews:

> I pray and ask my reader not to give vent to their anger on the temporary blind Chosen People, the great people in their faith and in their misfortune. Its blindness is our eternal salvation and their conversion is the resurrection of the dead. It is necessary to know and to remember that through Israel God punishes us for our treason toward him.... When we persecute Israel and shed the blood of the descendants of the patriarchs, we bring more of God's rage upon ourselves. It is not God's people that is responsible for the satanic spirit of iconoclasm, but its secret Sanhedrin who are hidden from our fury by the bayonets and cannon-balls of the world army....[75]

The philosemites' views on the temporary blindness of the Jews, the responsibility of the Jewish financial elite or the leaders of the revolution for the wrong path of development of the Jewish people do not differ substantially from those of Nilus, who, after all, counted himself a student of Soloviev.

It would be wrong to identify Soloviev's position and his courageous public defense of the Jews with that of Nilus and kindred spirits who instigated Judeophobic campaigns. The philosemites and Judeophobes constitute quite distinct groups, yet one must be aware of the limitations of Orthodox philosemitism.

Beyond the differences in their public stances, the other significant difference is the emphasis on the "angelic" possibilities of the Jewish people and the employment of the paradigm of the prodigal son. Whereas the most radical religious antisemites were obsessed only with the satanic power of the Jews and unequivocally identified the Jews with the kingdom of darkness, the Judeophiles believed that the "blindness of Israel" was not irrevocable and they articulated the mechanism through which the Jews would redeem themselves from their misdeeds in the purgatory of the historical process. This would be realized through the "great return" of the "prodigal son" to the only possible truth, that of Christianity. The Orthodox antisemites, on the other hand, tended to view the Jews as the eternal enemies of Christ and do not allow for the re-angelization of "Lucifer."

However, even the more positive paradigm of the prodigal son's return is problematic as a basis for dialogue between the two religious traditions, for it denies the Jewish people their own independent religious development. Of course, this paradigm does grant a "happy ending" to the story through the Jews' eventual conversion. For the philosemites, all that remained was the possible timing of the Jews' realization of the insufficiency of their religious ideas and institutions.

In sum, even the most sympathetic Orthodox religious philosophers never considered the prospect of a full-fledged dialogue between Judaism and Christianity, and believed the conversion of the Jews to be a prerequisite for full mutual understanding.

Contemporary Orthodox Hard-liners: "The Mystery of Iniquity" in Action

The advent of perestroika brought to the surface the legacy of Orthodox anti-Judaism, which persisted underground for seventy years. The number of militant Orthodox groups, which express an extremely hostile attitude toward Judaism and are involved in systematic overt antisemitic propaganda mushroomed in the early 1990s. The Orthodox-Monarchist Alliance, the Union of Orthodox Brotherhoods, and the revived Black Hundred are the most conspicuous.[76] It is noteworthy that the Union of Orthodox Brotherhoods (led by Konstantin Dushenov and Archimandrite Kirill) has a great influence on the educational programs of the Moscow Spiritual Seminary (MDS) and the Moscow Spiritual Academy, two major centers of specialized Orthodox education in Russia. The Union issues a bulletin,

Vestnik Soiiuza Bratstv. Individual divisions of the Union, the St. Sergius Brotherhood, the Union of Christian Regeneration (led by Vladimir Osipov), and the Dmitrii Rostovsky Brotherhood (led by Sergii Razumtsev), acquired notoriety as strongholds of radical nationalism. Another organization closely connected with the Orthodox Church, is the Committee for the Moral Renassance of the Fatherland, well-known for its defamatory comments on Judaism. It is headed by Archpriest Alexander Shargunov and publishes a bulletin entitled *Anti-Christ in Moscow.*

Representatives of these groups oppose the liberal Orthodox priests and express dissatisfaction with the attitude of the Church and the patriarch to the Jews, blaming him for "pro-Zionist leanings" in the belief that Judaism is the center of all the destructive anti-Christian forces which dominate the modern world.

Notable publications that offer the National Orthodox point of view include the monthly magazine *Moskva,* the weekly *Russkii vestnik,* and the daily *Sovetskaya Rossiia.*[77] Other articles advocating this position appear in the neo-Slavophile *Nash sovremennik.* Although none of these periodicals are issued by the Russian Orthodox Church and none of them appeal specifically to the Orthodox audience, they profess to express the Orthodox ideological position and purport to educate readers in the spirit of national Orthodoxy.

The late Ioann (Ivan Snichev, 1927-1995), Metropolitan of St. Petersburg and Ladoga, spiritual leader of the second-largest Russian city, was the most conspicuous figure in national Orthodoxy. Ioann wrote a great number of articles and gave interviews to various nationalist periodicals, ranging from the national Bolshevik *Sovetskaia Rossiia* to the elitist *Elementi.* Here, I shall focus on his papers and books.

Ioann considered the "Jewish question" to be a religious question, and he did not refer to Jewishness in terms of ethnicity. His concept of human history hinged on the idea of total religious war between Judaism and Christianity. Ioann believed that differences in religious doctrine underlie all other differences in culture, moral ideals, and historical fate, and thus all conflicts of human history could be described as religious conflicts. The central and most serious is the 2000-year-old war of Judaism against Christianity.

> In bitterness of struggle, in scale and in outcome, none of the clashes [in human history — V.R.] could be compared with the religious war which was persistently and uninterruptedly carried out by Judaism against the Church of Christ for two millennia. The spiritual foundations of the two parties are absolutely opposite and irreconcilable. In terms of Christianity, Judaism lacks any positive

content. Being the only people in the world to whom God revealed that Christ will come to save mankind from sins, the Jews did not accept him with love and reverence as they were supposed to, and crucified the Messiah, God's Son, Jesus Christ. Since that moment anti-Christianity came to be the keystone of Judaism.[78]

Metropolitan Ioann argued that after the destruction of Israel and Judea, the Jews "misinterpreted" the Holy Scriptures by linking the restoration of their state to the coming of the Messiah. Christ demonstrated the mistakes of the Jewish prophets and undermined the myth of the "Chosen People," which was associated with the idea of world domination. Outraged, the Jews decided to crucify Jesus, becoming the "God-killer people." The further history of the Jewish people is the history of moral and religious degradation. An examination of Talmudic religious principles demonstrates the lack of moral consideration for gentiles.[79]

Lacking political power, the Jews were compelled to find secretive means with which to confront Christianity. In Western Europe, Christianity was destroyed through social upheavals, culminating in the bourgeois revolutions of the nineteenth century.

Revolutionary convulsions, which took place all over the continent, were too similar to be coincidental, too perfectly coordinated to be spontaneous and had too pronounced an anti-Christian character to be hidden.[80]

Ioann believed that the novels of the English prime minister, Benjamin Disraeli, revealed the subversive, anti-Christian character of Jewish activity. Ioann saw an important Jewish role in the organization of secret societies in Europe.[81]

Not surprisingly, Ioann believed Russia to be the primary target for sinister Jewish attacks, since Russia is the guardian of the pure Christian faith in a world of apostasy, and has a special eschatological role to play. Russia is destined to carry out the mission that the Hebrews and Hellenes failed to accomplish. Ioann's writings focused on the theology of replacement. He saw abundant evidence of Jewish subversion throughout Russian history, and subscribed to Gumilev's notion of the "Khazarian Yoke." For Ioann, the Judaizing heresy of the fifteenth century was yet another political intrigue of the Jews, and contended that they tried to weaken and then occupy the Russian throne during the "Time of Troubles" (1598–1613). He believed that the imposter, Pseudo-Dmitrii II, to be a "crafty adventurer of Jewish origin" who tried to promote Jewish interests.[82]

The destructive anti-Orthodox and anti-Russian activities of the Jews culminated in the twentieth century: Ioann did not see any serious economic or political causes for the two Russian revolutions, but rather a Jewish conspiracy targeting this most faithful Christian country. Jewish bankers subsidized revolutionary propaganda, and the nature of the revolution was anti-Christian rather than anti-capitalist. The "class struggle" was merely an ideological invention of the Jews.

> The revolution-makers had centuries-old experience of organizing anti-Christian social cataclysms. They knew that each people was a child. It is especially true about the Russian people, a gullible, credulous and simple-hearted child. They deceived the Russian people with tales about "democracy," "universal equality" and "class justice" and put the faith of Russia under a terrifying, bloody and fiery trial.[83]

Underlying Ioann's narrative of history is the notion that the Russian people are re-enacting the story of Jesus Christ.

The Second Crucifixion: Russia = Jesus

Ioann was not alone among the Orthodox nationalists to offer a narrative based on the conception of Russia as the elect guardian of the true Christian faith. Russia was also a metaphor of the passion and mission of Christ, and national history is sometimes recounted as that of "St. Russia." Father Dmitrii Dudko may have been the first to introduce the idea of Russia suffering for universal salvation in his 1979 *samizdat* essay, "From the Russian Golgotha."[84] Today, the image of Russia crucified by its enemies haunts the imagination of many Orthodox hard-liners. The appeal and persistence of this metaphor can be seen in the agenda of several nationalist forums (e.g., the first World Russian Sobor that took place in May 1993).[85]

Crucial episodes recorded in the gospel — Christ's baptism, temptations, betrayal, crucifixion by his enemies, resurrection, and the future salvation of mankind —parallel events of Russian history.[86] Metropolitan Ioann made only insignificant qualifications to the metaphor of Russian history formulated by Alexander Prokhanov: "Different periods of Russian history are the icons in the iconostasis of the hagiography of Jesus." The Orthodox historian, guided by the hermeneutic code and the narrative of sacred history, needs only to select appropriate events to find a one-to-one symbolic correspondence between the New Testament story (prefiguration) and Russian history (fulfillment).

This reading of Russian history employs a medieval hermeneutic introduced by Christian theologians who saw New Testament events prefigured in the Old Testament. However, the new scheme of Orthodox nationalists is even more radical and provocative, for it sees Russian history itself as an update of the New Testament. The historical Jesus is himself only a prefiguration of Russia and its earthly fate.

The Russian Revolution thus correlates with the crucifixion, and leads to the conclusion that the Jews, "God-killers" and implacable enemies of Holy Russia, found it natural to crucify again the incarnation of Jesus [i.e., Russia].[87] Ioann described the Bolshevik ascent to power as a Judaic attack on Christianity and the divine, elect Christian state. The Bolshevik revolution consisted of a series of ritual murders and symbolic crucifixions perpetrated by the Jews, including the murder of the anointed Russian sovereign, the tsar, as well as Russian Orthodox priests and believers, and White Army officers.

Revolutionaries of Russian descent are portrayed in Ioann's writings as self-deluded and indoctrinated, "gullible children" who followed the instructions of perfidious Jewish leaders. The Revolution was an outburst of satanic Jewish forces attempting to realize the "centuries-old dream of world supremacy." Even ordinary Bolsheviks are described as members of a satanic sect of religious bigots. The internationalist communist doctrines only disguised the real goal of the revolutionaries "to annihilate the Christian population."

Ioann dilated on the atrocities perpetrated by the "Judaist revolutionaries" including mass murders by Cheka officials accompanied by sadistic cruelty. The most brutal tortures were perpetrated by Jewish members of the CheKa, in particular, "comrade Vera" and Rosa Schwarz, who were particularly brutal toward Russian victims who wore crosses.[88] Ioann claimed that the bodies of White Army soldiers carried the marks of ritual murder. The Bolshevik satanists symbolically reproduced the terrifying crime of deicide when they tortured and humiliated their victims.[89] Examples can be found in the memoirs of Prince Nikolai Zhevakhov, vice-Procurator *(tovarisch glavnogo Prokurora)* of the Holy Synod in 1916–17; he was obsessed with the Jewish conspiracy theory. Thus, the "crucifixion of Russia" is not only a metaphor but also reflects known historical incidents.

What makes Russians the elect "God-bearing" people? In what sense do they replicate the earthly fate of Jesus Christ ? Is it only a coincidence that the Jews have performed the role of executioner of the Russian people? First of all, it seems that Russian election is determined and confirmed by the amount of suffering endured by the Russians throughout their history, and by the country's "sacrificial" role. In the thirteenth century, Russia saved Europe from the Tatar invasion. The French-Russian war of 1812 is counted as a deadly struggle against the Antichrist — Napoleon. The Russian victory over fascist Germany saved Europe from barbarism. Some authors even described the Soviet political experiment as a kind of Russian sacrifice, since it gave the West a practical knowledge of communism.[90] The Russian national character is sacrificial, as contrasted with that of the Jews. Whereas the Jewish idea of "election" is manifested in the obsession for world domination, Ioann argued, the Russian election is closely connected with sacrifice and special service to one's neighbors — Russian character traits include selflessness, self-abnegation, love of one's neighbor. The Old Testament maxim to love one's neighbor, he wrote, was considered by the Jews as applicable only to one's *Jewish* neighbor, and hence could not be considered universal.

Christ's admonition to love one's enemy, (Matt. 5:44; Luke 6:27), Ioann insisted, could not be extended to the Jews who betrayed Christ. The Christian maxim, he claims, implies only personal enemies, whereas the Jews are "God-killers" and the enemies of God, Jesus Christ.[91] Ioann called for a militant Christianity, claiming that "pacifist" misinterpretations of the New Testament had been imposed on believers by the enemies of Christ. Christianity is not a religion of humility. There can be no compromise or shared values with the degraded apostate partisans of contemporary anti-Christian civilization.

Not surprisingly, many within National Orthodoxy believe in a Judeo-Masonic conspiracy, and in the authenticity of the *Protocols of the Elders of Zion.* Metropolitan Ioann also supported the idea:

> It does not matter who wrote the "Protocols." What is important is that the whole history of the 20th century reproduces with terrifying precision the ambitions, which were expressed in this document.[92]

He referred to the work of Yurii Begunov of the Russian Academy of Sciences, a well-known antisemite, who supposedly discredited the resolutions of the international commission in Berne (May 14, 1936). Begunov claimed that the *Protocols* was not a forgery by the Russian secret police, but an accurate account of the Jewish conspiracy.[93] Ioann contended that the "hypothesis about the fabrication of the document today could not be taken seriously because of all the nonsensical assumptions on which it is based."[94] It should be observed that among the National Orthodox, the Jewish conspiracy and its goals are described in purely religious terms.

The "Heresy of Heresies":
The Judaizing Heresy within the Orthodox Church and Beyond

Orthodox nationalists attribute the religious decline of the modern world to the spread of the Judaizing heresy that arose within the Orthodox Church in the fifteenth century.[95] The heresy is viewed as a universal factor encompassing and affecting every dimension of political, social, and cultural life throughout the world. A persistent religio-political phenomenon never completely defeated in the course of Christian history, it is a kind of ideological monster which always revives and constantly assumes new forms, even with all the efforts of true Christians to destroy it. It is the destructive force behind the political and social tendencies of the contemporary world of apostasy, and is the tool with which the Judaists set out to control the world —not one heresy among many others, but the "heresy of heresies."[96] Manifestations of it are found both in religion (in Catholicism, Orthodoxy, and among Protestants) and in ideologies (liberalism and the Russian perestroika).

(1) Doctrinal differences between Orthodoxy and Western Christianity are explained as an outcome of the infiltration of the Judaizers into the very heart of the Western Church. Both Catholicism and Protestantism are described as two expressions, different in degree rather than in kind, of the same Judaizing heresy. The largely Protestant World Council of Churches is considered the ideological center of the heresy, for Protestantism is hardly discernable from Judaism, having inherited the concept of the "chosen people" in a Judaic interpretation, along with many other concepts of the Old Testament. It is more difficult to expose Judaizing strains in the ideology and practice of the Catholic Church, although Catholicism was initially more resistant to the heresy. Eventually, it could not escape the pervasive influence of this spiritual poison and its official ideology was contaminated.

Looking back to the historical divisions in the early Church over questions of authority and jurisdiction, the National Orthodox accuse the Catholic Church of "an appalling distortion of Christianity" by claiming that the bishop of Rome (the Pope) is *deus in terra* — the only deputy of Christ on earth. The Catholic hierarchy, they explain, is based on the Jewish "order of Aaron," and has abandoned the original Christian "order of Melchisedek" (Heb. 7:11). Christ himself is "high priest after the order of Melchisedek," the "high priest of the good things to come" (Heb. 5:10, 9:11). The Catholic pope, in fact, attempts to displace "the only high priest of the New Testament and pave the way for the Antichrist who will put himself in the position of Christ."[97]

Twentieth-century Catholic documents and declarations about the Church's relations with the Jews provide ample ammunition for national Orthodox assertions that the Western Church has fallen victim to the Judaizing heresy: Pope Pius XI declared that Christians are "Semites in spirit," and Pope John Paul II, addressing Jewish rabbis, said, "You are our elder brothers." The Second Vatican Council document, "Nostra aetate" declared that the Jewish people as a whole are not responsible for the death of

Christ, and the Church is further accused of teaching that the Jews did not lose their "election" after the coming of Christ; and has conflated the Jewish expectations of the messiah with the Christian's awaiting the second coming. In addition, the Catholic Church has participated in the ecumenical movement through its participation in the World Council of Churches, along with Jewish representatives.[98]

It is no accident, Orthodox nationalists argue, that Cardinal Lustiger, the leader of French Catholics, and minister of European affairs at the Vatican, is Jewish. Cardinal Lustiger does not conceal his Jewish origins and even asserts that his Jewish origins are reinforced rather than abolished by his Christianity. Not surprisingly, he is considered the top agent of the Judaizers in Catholicism. The possibility that Lustiger could be elected pope inflames apocalyptic visions in which the Jewish Antichrist seizes power and, pretending to be Jesus, disseminates false teaching. One polemicist argues that Lustiger perfectly fits the descriptions of the Antichrist in Russian apocalyptic writings, and his name can be phonetically associated with Lucifer.[99] Orthodox nationalists further hold that the real target of Catholic anti-communist activity (culminating in a secret pact of "Holy Union" signed by the Vatican and Washington) was Russia and the Orthodox Church — the most significant enemies of the Judaizers.[100]

(2) Orthodox nationalists insist that the Judaizing heresy persists within the Orthodox Church, represented today by liberal priests as well as those within the Orthodox hierarchy. Their crimes against true Orthodoxy are numerous, including attempts to disarm the militant Orthodox by imposing upon Christianity the concept of "blind love" of one's neighbors. They advocate reconciliation with heretics, blur the differences with other religious confessions, and compromise with the sinister and godless secular humanistic concepts at the expense of doctrine. The ecumenical efforts of liberal priests expose them as traitors to the Orthodox cause.

Oleg Soloviev offered his own peculiar list of features of the Judaizing heresy, which included: a pseudo-academic interpretation and attitude to the Bible; justification of ancient and present-day witchcraft; and defining the purpose of Christian life in terms of reconciliation with world Jewry rather than communion with the Holy Spirit.[101]

Judaizers smuggle sinister racist concepts into Orthodoxy, such as describing Jesus and the Holy Family as Jewish. One of them, Yurii Tabak, claimed that "Jesus Christ has all the features of a concrete human being, including the ethnic ones."[102] Responding to Tabak, Vladimir Gubanov argued that it is blasphemous even to talk about the Jewishness of Jesus — who was a God-Man rather than "God-Jew" — who had nothing to do with the rabbis, and whose mission was to reject Judaic teaching. The Gospels mention the genealogy of Jesus from Abraham and David "only allowing for human weaknesses."[103] "Human weaknesses" appears to refer to the interest in genealogies and ethnic origins.

Orthodox nationalists are also prone to exaggerating the number of Jews who have been baptized (and are therefore perceived as potential Judaizers). Vladimir Osipov, speaking at the Third Congress of the Christian Regeneration Union held in May 1995 lamented that 15–25 percent of those admitted to Orthodox seminaries are Jewish. In his paper, "The Church under Siege," he admitted that "there is no Jew and no Hellene" in the Church, yet claimed that only one of every ten or twenty Jewish believers "come to the Church without any other side motivation."

> The majority of them introduce the spirit of innovation, modernism, and reformation, despise the canons, and undermine the centuries-old traditions of the Church. It is not a big deal for these people to change the order of the liturgy, to render Church Slavonic into modern jargon,[104] and to disparage the "unacceptable" saints of the Church and even "inconvenient" parts of the faith. The priests of Jewish extraction normally are indifferent to Russia, Russian people and to our national self-consciousness. These clerics create a special cosmopolitan atmosphere in the Church. Did they feel sorry about the disintegration of the motherland in 1991? Did they grieve about the horrifying tragedy, the transfer of 25 million Russians to the newly organized ethnocratic regimes? The ordinary laymen often complain that it is difficult for them to go to confession to a Jewish priest. They have a very different psychology.... Because of this many good Russian people leave the Church and switch to paganism.[105]

The danger of the Jewish presence in the Orthodox Church, Osipov goes on to argue, is constituted by the "special ideological persuasions" of the Jews and by their "aversion to historical Orthodoxy":

> They stigmatize this canonical Christianity as the Black Hundred leaning.... Orthodoxy is the soul of the Russian people. Therefore, the infiltration of this anti-canonical trend amounts to a penetration into the very soul of the nation. I don't mind the presence of some individual Jewish priests who are completely devoted to Orthodoxy and identify themselves with Holy Russia. However, we cannot be unmindful of the mass of these priests, of their real invasion to the very cloister of St. Sergii of Radonezh and Joseph Volotsky, Patriarch Germogen and John of Kronstadt.[106]

This line of argument is quite common among nationalist religious leaders. In a similar vein, Metropolitan Ioann argues that although it is against the spirit of Christianity "to blame someone for his nationality," one should not underestimate the "reviving Judaizing heresy which is introduced to the Church by the priests of Jewish extraction." Ioann notes that "in the Foreign Chapter of the Church this problem is much more serious and painful."[107]

The late Archpriest Alexander Menn (1935–1990) is villified as the one primarily responsible for the revival of the Judaizing heresy, and a spiritual father to the Judaizers. Fr. Menn came to be quite well known during the first years of perestroika. The Orthodox nationalists objected to his Jewish origins, which he did not try to hide. They also objected to his denunciation of chauvinism and open advocacy of ecumenism. He was hated for his popularity among the Russian Jewish intelligentsia, and for baptizing many of them into the Church. Many of his books were published in the West. Menn believed that Jews did not need to abandon their traditions and holy days in order to be converted to Christianity. In an interview, "The Jews and Christianity," published in the British magazine, *The Jews in the USSR,* he said:

> A Jewish Christian does not stop being a Jew. Moreover, he starts to understand even better the spiritual calling of his people.... Every Christian people has its own national holidays besides the religious ones. For instance, the holidays which are reminiscent of the miraculous liberation from enemy invasions. Why should not the Jewish Christians count the day of victory of the Maccabees as their holiday?[108]

Menn also had ideas about establishing a special Jewish Christian Church in Israel to be governed by the National Council of Jewish Christians of Israel.

Menn is also accused of attempting to reestablish an Orthodox Christian tradition of biblical criticism, but also drawing on liberal Protestant theology. Inspired by the writings of Vladimir Soloviev, Menn thought it would be possible to reconcile the various Christian confessions, and thus aligned himself with the ecumenical movement. Hence, the Archpriest Antiminsov and Oleg Soloviev see a direct manifestation of the Judaizing heresy, including the use of historical and archeological data, and interpretation of the biblical text independent of the Orthodox tradition.[109] Soloviev wrote:

> If we take into account that Alexander Menn, a favorite of our cosmopolitan intelligentsia, advocated the decanonization of Russian saints "tortured by the Jews" and identified the miracles of Russian Christian devotees with the witchcraft of the pagan magicians, we have in front of us all the ingredients of the Judaizing heresy.[110]

The Union of Orthodox Brotherhoods warn that although Alexander Menn is dead, his cause and his poisonous spiritual seeds are not.[111] According to the Brotherhoods' publications, the Alexander Menn Open Orthodox University in Moscow is the stronghold of Russian Judaizers, as is the Catechetical School of Father Georgii Kochetkov and his parish in Moscow. Kochetkov was a student and champion of Menn and his ideas in contemporary Russia. Father Kochetkov is involved in missionary activities and it is noteworthy that many of his parishioners are Jewish. Moreover, he uses vernacular Russian for the liturgy — just as the historical Judaizers attempted to translate the Bible into colloquial Russian to make it accessible to ordinary people.[112] This is regarded by national Orthodox polemicists as a sacrilege against the language of the liturgy.[113]

Leontii Saveliev recounts the history of Russian philosophy from an Orthodox perspective that seeks evidence of the Judaizing heresy. Saveliev believes that the positions of different thinkers are shaped by their religious views, and he contrasts Western philosophy — focused on logic — to that of the Russian Orthodox, which relies upon intuition. Western philosophers, he claims, learned logic and other philosophical disciplines from Jewish teachers who smuggled sinister Judaic concepts into their courses, while mainstream Russian philosophers happily escaped the harmful influence of logic and rationalism on their spirituality. Both in the middle ages and Enlightenment, they could enjoy the purely intuitive grasp of reality.[114] However, some corrupting ideas have still managed to infiltrate into Russian spiritual life, therefore it is important to discuss Russian philosophy in terms of the struggle between the patriotic trend and the cosmopolitan or Russian-Judaist trend. Two millennia of Christian history, especially that of the Russian people, go under the sign of struggle between the two powers — Christ and Antichrist, Evil and Good, patriotic and cosmopolitan forces, forces of the "Great People" and of the "Little People" — the parasites who use [up] the material and spiritual resources of the "Great People."[115]

Saveliev uses the distinction that recalls Engels' idea about the struggle of the "line of Plato" (idealism) and the "line of Democritus" (materialism) in the history of philosophy, which was so persistent in the Soviet period. The Judaizing trend is represented by Vladimir Soloviev, Nikolai Berdiaev, Lev Shestov, Sergii Bulgakov, Vasilii Zenkovskii, and other famous Russian philosophers of the Silver Age. The patriotic trend is represented by truly Orthodox thinkers such as Nikolai Gogol, Feodor Dostoevsky, and the Russian Slavophiles and pagan thinkers. The pagan thinkers, however, failed to realize the difference between Judaism and Christianity, and attributed Jewish features to Christianity. "It is not Christianity itself but rather its

Judaic side that carries the seeds of death and destruction...for the whole life on the Earth."[116] Both Judaism and paganism are "dead religions," unlike Orthodoxy. Judaism is "the most petrified, distorted and hypocritical religion in the world."[117]

(3) Religious war continues under the guise of political and social conflicts. Concepts like the "new world order" and "world government," the spread of democratic ideals and liberalism in Eastern Europe and the former Soviet Union are by-products of the Judaizing heresy. Perestroika is described as an intervention of satanic forces into the socio-political life of Russia. There is a continuity between perestroika and the subversive revolutionary activity of the first part of the century. In both cases the Jews played an important role in the historical events and in both cases — in spite of differences in implementation — the social transformation was accompanied by an anti-Christian policy.

> International democratic ideology and perestroika are supposed to replace the doctrines of international communism, which exhausted their destructive potential, and to complete the breakdown of historical Russia, which was already started under the leadership of Trotsky and Kaganovich.[118]

Metropolitan Ioann claimed that the recent changes in Russian society had been planned by Americans and Zionists who set out to annihilate as many Russians as possible and then use Russian natural resources.[119] Plans for occupying Russia were elaborated many years ago, and "today the Judeo-Protestant heresy, relying upon the atheistic and materialistic American order, finishes the first preliminary stage of the breakdown of Russia."[120] Not surprisingly, he went on, that social and political intervention is accompanied by a spiritual aggression against the Russian people and the Orthodox Church that involves the restoration of Russian Freemason lodges and the dissemination of literature on kabbalah, astrology, witchcraft, and occultism, all of which undermine the Orthodox Church.[121]

In sum, champions of national Orthodoxy conceive the Judaizing heresy as a tendency within world history, not just a local sect that was part of the history of the Orthodox Church. The Judaizing heresy is linked to the idea of a Jewish-Masonic conspiracy. Historical "realities" which testify to the worldwide plot organized by the Jews and Judaizers are often borrowed from the *Protocols of the Elders of Zion*.

The New Life for Old Myths: Deicide, Regicide, Infanticide

A remarkable development with the nationalist Orthodox faction is their restoration of the blood libel charge and medieval allegations of ritual murder by Jews. These sacrificial killings of children and other Christians are allegedly committed for mere sacrilege, to obtain blood to make matzah (unleavened bread used in the Passover seder), and as other bloody rituals necessary for the celebration of religious holy days. These rites are supposedly symbolic reproductions of the crucifixion of Jesus. Metropolitan Ioann claimed that the "martyrology of the Christians, tortured to death by the Jews, has persistently grown with time."[122] Orthodox nationalists have also tried to restore the medieval tradition of canonizing Christians "martyred by Jews."[123]

In this context, the murder of the tsar and his family is counted as a symbolic ritual murder carried out by the Jews. Orthodox nationalists and some Church officials are obsessed with the symbolic meaning of this act, minimizing or ignoring the political context of the event as merely the insignificant frame in which the religious drama occurred. The political and historical circumstances only served to highlight the eternal metaphysical tragedy. The fact that the Jews who killed the tsar's family were members of the Bolshevik party plays a secondary role.[124] The symbolic dimension of the murder is considered its sole, true meaning — a means of humiliating the Russian empire and the Orthodox religion. The Jewish executioners (Yakov Yurovsky, Isaac Goloschekin, Pavel Voikov, and Yakov Sverdlov)[125] are accused of employing ancient Jewish ritual techniques. The mysterious circumstances of the murder attracted enormous media attention during the perestroika period and still provoke fantastic speculations coupled with scurrilous antisemitic remarks by Orthodox hardliners.

Elena Prudnikova's 1993 article in the "Orthodox Perspective on Russian History" section of *Sovietskaiia Rossiia* provides a curious example of such speculations. It's title, "Golgotha," is symptomatic. She dwells on the executioners' concealment of the bodies of their victims: "It [the execution] was a mystical act, in the course of which something terrible happened to the bodies, something that needed to be concealed by all means." She tells the reader that "the city where the 'red tsar' mated the 'white tsar' [Ekaterinburg, where the emperor's family was slaughtered — V.R.] was renamed Sverdlovsk" — for Iakov Sverdlov, director of the operation and the first chairman of the Central Executive Committee of the Soviet Union. The murder was committed in the Ipatiev House, and the Romanov dynasty had been declared tsars in the Ipatiev Monastery. Burning the victims' remains is an archaic magical ritual that is an element part of many esoteric rites; and the princess's dead dog was left at the burial site ("in the places where Christians were murdered, those whom God himself called the 'children of the devil' often put a dead dog"). The date of the murder coincided with the

Orthodox commemoration of Prince Andrei Bogoliubsky, a saint who was also ritually murdered. The "kabbalistic inscription" on the wall of the Ipatiev House is a cryptogram of a secret society. "It follows from all these facts," Prudnikova concludes, "that in the dark basement they killed not merely Nicholas Romanov but Orthodox Russia, the power which had 'preserved" the world from the universal evil which could overflow the entire world."[126] Lastly, the reader was told that Yurovsky was born in Cainsk (city of Cain) — another clue to the metaphysical and symbolic nature of the crime.

Regicide in this context *(tsareubiistvo)* is really deicide, for in neo-Byzantine culture the tsar was a religious figure central to Caesaro-papism. The émigré general Yurii Larikov, writing under the pen name "Ushkuinik," asserted that human sacrifice was common in Khazaria; in particular the idea of emperor sacrifice had been secretly preserved during the centuries of the Jewish Khazars' life in Europe, and this was clear when the Jewish Bolsheviks murdered the tsar.

> It is quite plain that the crime in Ekaterinburg is a deliberate ritual murder which was planned a long time before the event and was accomplished exclusively by the Judaists, Sverdlov, Goloschekin and Yurovsky. An Eastern Jew and a "tsadik," Yurovsky conducted the sacrifice of the Emperor of the greatest Christian empire and its successor by his own hand.[127]

However, the most intriguing aspect of the story of the regicide is the persistent motif of the identification of Nicholas II with Jesus Christ as savior.[128] For instance, in some versions of the story of the tsar's death, he takes away the sins of Russia and prays for his murderers. A fragment from Michael Nazarov's account is a good example:

> Both the remarkable obduracy of the tsar (e.g., his attitude to the Jewish question) and his lack of willpower in the days of the abdication could be explained by his knowledge of the painful fate of the tsar's family, about the revolutions and misfortunes of Russia and the possibility of the subsequent repentance and revival which he learned from many preachers.... In March 1917 the tsar looked at his milieu and realized that only a spiritual feat could save Russia.... The leaders of the Church overlooked the cross of the tsar and the meaning of the events. In a similar vein, the followers of Jesus could not understand his sacrifice.[129]

Thus, the murder of Nicholas II amounts to a symbolic crucifixion of Russia. Metropolitan Ioann expanded on the system of symbolic correlations and correspondences. His symbolic system sheds light on what he considered to be the real targets and meaning of the murder.

> When they killed the Russian Orthodox tsar, they symbolically killed the legitimate Christian national power. When they killed the heir, they killed the future of Russia. When they killed the servants of the sovereign family, they killed the all-people unity of estates which the Russians were always so willing to achieve.[130]

Pavel Tiurin, an "Orthodox psychologist," discusses the symbolic meaning of the regicide in his paper "The Tsar and the Icon." He argues that in Orthodox tradition the tsar is identical with the icon, since both represent the divine presence on the earth: "The tsar is the icon of God" and "the incarnation of the Celestial Tsar." The identity of tsar and icon implies the identity of iconoclasm and regicide, confirmed by the hostility of the Jews to the tsar and to religious images:

> One can find in iconoclasm and in the struggle against Christ, the archetypal opposition between Cain and Abel. It is opposition both to the earthly incarnation of Christ and to God himself. Cain and Abel are brothers.... One of them is the adversary of Christ, while the second is his loyal son.... Cain talks about the principles of subordination and insists on his superiority and election.... The murder of Abel is only the beginning of an unrealized prospect, namely,... desire for the death of the Father.... Cain kills Abel, the icon of God.... He cannot kill God himself.... The Cainites do not need a Savior, let alone the redemption of all mankind, since election is the only thing that is important for them.... First they kill Abel,... then they kill Jesus Christ. The Jews are stateless people living under theocratic rule.... It could be their lack of acknowledgment of the futility of human efforts in the absence of the immediate rule of God.... As a result they reject the tsar and the icon as insufficiently supernatural and not entirely divine.[131]

In August 2000 the synodal Commission on Canonization approved the "glorification" of several hundred clerical and lay martyrs of the twentieth century.[132] Tsar Nicholas II and his immediate family were canonized as "passion bearers" rather than as martyrs, for at the time of their deaths, they had not been asked to renounce their faith, but humbly accepted their destiny *(kenosis)*. Although Nicholas II was canonized as a private citizen rather than as tsar, the tsardom itself was seen by many as an important criterion for sainthood. Michael Cherniavsky has pointed out that:

in Russian popular tradition and in Russian political theology, all princes were seen as saints, through actions or in their being, mediators between God and their people in life and in death, and in that sense the true images of Christ.[133]

Although the calls for the canonization of Nicholas II need not be associated with antisemitism, the fact remains that for many, his death is categorized with other "martyrs of the Jews." He is portrayed as a martyr opposed to the new Jewish world order. Supposedly he read the *Protocols* before his death, and hence understood the meaning of his death, and was willing to sacrifice himself as Jesus did. His death at the hands of Jews is testimony to his special mission.[134]

In a sense the Orthodox hard-liners are right in taking the execution of Nicholas II and his family as a "ritual murder."[135] However, they misidentify the major actors of the drama and confuse the metaphorical sense of a ritual murder with a literal one. The murder of Nicholas II can be better understood against the background of the scapegoat theory elaborated by the French literary critic René Girard, who considered regicide to be one of the most primitive and archaic manifestations of the scapegoat mechanism that pertains to all cultures. In a system of divine royalty, the universe (identified with the body of the tsar), is renewed by his ritual murder, which marks the beginning of a new cycle of history.[136] The Bolsheviks — not the Jews — attempted to renew the universe and sacrificed Nicholas II, the incarnation of a malfunctioning cosmic order, as a scapegoat. Thus, the murder of Nicholas Romanov, committed by a group of people, can be viewed on a symbolic level as a kind of reenactment of the archaic drama which was incorporated into the normal cultural mechanism.

Other transformations of the narratives of regicide and crucifixion are taking place today. The new Orthodox-Bolshevik myth keeps the structural components of the previous ones and projects them onto the new Soviet realities. The new plot I refer to deals with the tsardom and divinity of Iosif Stalin. Victor Pichuzhkin, a deacon, compares the hagiographies of two "saints," Christ and Stalin, and finds many common "precepts" in their thinking. Stalin, of course, was the Soviet substitute for the tsar. Pichuzhkin's story of Stalin's life and death not only exposes the mystical identity of Jesus and Stalin but also demonstrates that the role played in their fate by the Jews was similar:

> Did not Stalin repeat the life of Jesus Christ? Is it not true that both of them were martyrs? However, whereas Christ was a martyr in his life, Stalin bore his crown of thorns even after his death.... In his life the Leader, the Father, the Teacher and the Liberator of Europe.... After

his death the same people who devoted their odes to him started to yell: "The butcher! The paranoiac! The criminal!" And they attributed to him responsibility for their own crimes and the crimes of their fathers and idols, for all misdeeds and malicious actions…. Today the descendants of those who have crucified the Son of God many centuries ago, crucify Stalin on the cross of lies and malice. Together with him they crucify our earth, our souls, the souls of our children and grandchildren, plunging us into death and destruction.[137]

Thus, the same mythological plot survives in the new symbiotic Orthodox-Communist ideology which borrows and reproduces the archetypes of the old religious sources.[138]

Debates about the possible restoration of the Russian monarchy —quite prominent in the Orthodox milieu — are also tainted with antisemitic undercurrents.[139] Some champions of national Orthodoxy argue that the Romanov dynasty is unsuited for the Russian throne not only because of "genealogical (morganatic marriages), moral and juridical considerations," but also because of the Jewish blood of the pretender Georgii Romanov, a grandson of the Grand Prince Kirill, the brother of Nicholas II. Articles in national Orthodox periodicals expose Georgii Romanov's connections with Jews and other foreign entities. Some of the characteristic arguments against his claims to the throne were given by Michael Nazarov, an expert in this area.[140] Georgii Romanov belongs to a branch of the dynasty contaminated by his grandmother, Leonida Georgievna Bagration-Mukhranelli, the wife of Vladimir Kirillovich. She was a member of the family of the Georgian and Armenian Bagratuni princes.[141] With this in mind, Georgii's possible ascent to the throne takes an apocalyptic slant, in which he becomes identified with the Antichrist. Two features distinguish the Antichrist: he will be a Jew from the tribe of Dan, and he will resemble Jesus and be identified by his Christ-like features. George Romanov will have both of these features. An impostor, he is identified with the Antichrist-Emperor, a mirror image of Christ. Nazarov contends that if the impostor succeeds, the idea of the Orthodox monarchy will be discredited. In this case the revival of the Russian monarchy will become a guise for apostasy (as with other present-day monarchies), rather than a sign of the continuation of the tradition of the Third Rome.[142] Some partisans of national Orthodoxy suggest that the resolution of the crisis — this "trap of pseudo-monarchy" organized by enemies of Russia — can be found in the election of the new people's tsar.

Returning to the charges of ritual murder that have been made, we find that they also include the murder of clerics and others. Three monks in the famous monastery of Optina Pustin' were murdered by a mentally ill person, yet this was interpreted by some national Orthodox writers as a ritual murder for which the Judaists were responsible. V. Shumsky notes that "666" was incised on the dagger of the murderer, and takes this as evidence of Jewish involvement in the crime. He speculates about the meaning of "666":

> The Judaic-Zionist star has six ends. It is the image of Satan, his synagogue and the seal of Antichrist. The star consists of two triangles. Each triangle has three sides, three angles and three tops; consequently two triangles have six sides, six angles and six tops. This is the origin of the sign of the Beast and Satan — 666. It is noteworthy that Satan depends on the Jewish deity Yahweh and realizes his will....
> The monsters direct the hand of the murderer, trying to destroy Russia by undermining its eternal Orthodox roots.[143]

Shumsky also claims that the same kind of ritual murder happened in Jerusalem — a young Jewish Zionist killed two Orthodox nuns — and that the Israeli court discharged the murderer as a person suffering from a nervous disorder. The Antichrist, he goes on to argue, was already born in Israel. He generates the specific satanic influences in the world and his destructive activity is concentrated on Russia.

In the language of Orthodox nationalists the concept of deicide is co-extensive with regicide, genocide, clericide, and infanticide. All these most sacred beings (infant-tsar-God-cleric-people-Russia) symbolically represent each other and refer to each other. The central element of the narrative structure which governs the whole historiosophical myth of the ideologists of national Orthodoxy is that of the crucifixion of the "divine" *X* by the Jew. The whole process of history which they envision is shaped by the "root metaphor" of crucifixion (ritual murder), and historical reality is less important and less authentic than the mythological plot. The mythologems of nationalist Orthodox antisemitic folklore reveals their paranoia and the stereotypes immune to rational arguments. In a sense, the national Orthodox are not true ideologists, since they have no control over the images and mythological structures which govern and dominate their perception of the world.

The Talmud vs. The Gospels: Religion of Love, Religion of Hate

Another primary element in the ideological subculture of Orthodox antisemitism is the abhorrence of the Talmud and other essential Jewish texts. The Talmud and Shulchan Aruch (an important code of Jewish religious and civil law) are described in opposition to the Gospels — a "law of hatred" as opposed to the Christian "law of love." Jews are said to be forbidden to accept a humane and compassionate way of life. They are said to be encouraged to observe a fanatical formalism and dishonest business practices, becoming narrow and bigoted. Judaism's period of inspiration was solely in the days of Moses and the prophets.

I will focus on only one of the anti-Talmudists, not because of his intellectual virtues and originality, but because his writings are typical. In "The Fateful Question," Mikhail Ustinov contends that the Talmud presupposes a double system of morality: "gentiles and akums (i.e., star-worshippers, or idol worshippers generally)" cannot be considered neighbors or even human beings, and Jews are taught to ignore moral obligations towards other ethnicities.[144] Ustinov claims that the Jewish sense of racial superiority is derived from the Talmud, which teaches them to regard themselves as the chosen people by right of birth. The words "Jew" and "divine" are synonyms in the Talmud.[145] Discrimination between good and evil makes no sense to Jews, since evil is the "throne of good":

> Today the idea [Judaic religious doctrine — V.R.], that exhausted its historical potential two thousand years ago, has only a chimerical existence. Interfering in the course of history, it destroys the life at the expense of which it lives.... The arms of Christ are still open to everybody. But why do they regard the cross as a wall? Why do they isolate themselves, pushing away the merciful hands that are stretched out to them?... Maybe it could be the way to solve the fateful question. Is it not in the sincere conversion to Christ that the tale of the prodigal son will become true?[146]

This passage invokes the old motif of the "prodigal son," the importance and implications of which I emphasized earlier. For Ustinov, the Talmud has made Jews insensitive to the voice of love adopted by Christians.

Denigrating the Talmud and asserting its opposition to the Gospels is not unique to Russian religious antisemitism, but one feature makes it especially popular.[147] Even short excerpts from Jewish texts are uncommon, and since Jewish studies were strongly discouraged by the Soviet government, little is known of actual Jewish culture and teaching. Not surprisingly, demonization of the Talmud often follows examples found in pre-revolutionary sources. Outside the former Soviet Union, progress in academic biblical and Jewish studies has shown how outdated are the medieval views still to be found among some Russian Orthodox clerics. In the West, for example, most Christians accept that Jesus belonged to the rabbinical tradition, and that his departure from what is known of Pharisaic teaching may have reflected internal disputes within the Jewish community rather than an outright rejection of Judaism per se.[148] Yet many Russian Orthodox writers continue to emphasize only the discontinuity of the religious experience of Judaism and Christianity, and contrast the Talmud to the Gospels as incompatible moral doctrines having nothing in common. Orthodox nationalists quote the Talmud and Shulchan Aruch in translations found in the works of pre-revolutionary antisemites like Alexei Shmakov and Hippolitus Liutostansky.[149] Thus, part of the problem is simply the lack of good resource material. Hopefully, the ambitious project of Rabbi Adin Steinsalz to translate the Talmud and other religious texts into Russian, already begun, can contribute to eliminating the phobias of the irrational hate-laden religion espoused in the writings of those bigots to be found among Orthodox Christians.

CONCLUSION

Antisemitic leanings and Judeophobia are still prominent in the Orthodox Church. Priests who advocate the nationalist position still constitute a significant segment of the clergy. The fusion of ultranationalists with Judophobic clergy is especially dangerous, for the priests give violence a divine sanction. Even those considered to be philosemitic or sympathetic to Judaism, often reiterate or reinforce the old clichés found among Christian antisemites, and seldom go beyond the positions taken by philosemites of the Silver Age. Serious efforts must be made in order to overcome this sinister legacy. The success of any such efforts would depend on the ability of the society at large to adopt religious tolerance and to create a serious dialogue with differing religious traditions, independent of the Christian master narrative of world history.

Opposing views on the position of the Orthodox Church vis-à-vis the Jews have emerged in the post-communist criticism. One side is represented by Sergei Lezov, a historian of Christianity and Orthodox believer. The other view is that of Vladimir Borzenko and Zoya Krakhmalnikova.

Lezov has argued that the Orthodox Church is substantially more hostile to Jews than Protestant churches or the Catholic Church. He is skeptical of possibilities for changing attitudes within the Orthodox Church, given the prominent antisemitism, along with a general lack of understanding of the Holocaust in Orthodox theology.

In his paper "The National Idea and Christianity," Lezov elaborated this view, stating that, in contrast to the Western religious tradition, Orthodox theology *(bogoslovie)* has not perceived the Holocaust as a religious event that challenges the faith of all Christians. Though some Protestant churches (and the Roman Catholic Church) have formally acknowledged the role of Christianity in laying the foundation for the Holocaust, articulating it in a "post-Auschwitz" theology, nothing similar, not even a "post-Gulag" theology has yet emerged in the Orthodox tradition. Among the prominent Protestant theologians who addressed the issue are Paul Tillich, Iohannes Metz, Juergen Moltmann. Lezov argues that the Silver Age theologians, like Berdiaev, also failed to articulate the significance of the Holocaust for Christians. They shared many traditional antisemitic stereotypes derived from the Christian doctrines "unshaken by the Holocaust."[150]

Vladimir Borzenko and Zoya Krakhmalnikova argue in a partisan manner that the position of the Orthodox Church is most favorable for the Jews and is incompatible with antisemitism — a position in contradiction to historical Orthodox positions. Both Borzenko and Krakhmalnikova deny that antisemites are truly Orthodox members of the Church. For instance, Borzenko disqualifies the Black Hundreds as Orthodox, for they only "called themselves the champions of Orthodoxy" and only "used [*sic!*] Orthodox phraseology and symbols." Borzenko's sociological survey reveals negative correlation between Orthodox religious affiliation and the expression of antisemitic positions.[151] Other studies, such as that by Gudkov and Levenson, however, found the opposite to be the case.[152]

Lezov's position, that there is a special hostility of the Orthodox Church to the Jews seems to be overstated, since the antisemitic legacy of Catholic and Protestant churches is no less significant than that of the Orthodox. It is true that the Orthodox Church has not addressed the Holocaust as a topic requiring special moral awareness for the believing Christian, but under Soviet rule, there could have been no independent Orthodox theology, and there was no scope for discussing controversial issues.[153] In addition, during the Soviet era, few people had access to information about the Holocaust — even professional historians could not discuss the topic.[154]

Lezov also fails to mention some positive developments within Orthodoxy, such as recent attempts by Orthodox intellectuals to foster discussion of the Holocaust.[155] Gleb Yakunin and Valery Borschov, leaders of the Christian-Democratic Union, and articles in *Vestnik khristianskogo dvizheniia, Russkaiia misl', and Voprosi filosofii* discuss it in the context of Christian religious history. In addition, the antisemitic declarations of Metropolitan Ioann and the Orthodox Brotherhoods have been harshly criticized by the priest Gleb Yakunin in an open letter to former president Boris Yeltsin.[156] A number of Orthodox believers have also spoken out against Orthodox antisemites in Russian periodicals, on television programs, and in radio broadcasts (e.g., Christian Church-Public Channel). Two other priests who have spoken against antisemitic currents in the Orthodox Church were Ioann Sviridov and Georgii Chistiakov.[157] The Black Hundreds were disavowed by some upper-level clergy, and Patriarch Alexei II has dissociated the antisemitic posture of Metropolitan Ioann from that of the Russian Orthodox Church.[158]

It might be argued that protests against antisemitism often emerge from quite marginal circles of the Church and that these protests are individual rather than official. Protests have been issued, for example, by the Russian Orthodox Church Abroad (ROCA) and by the members of the Russian intelligentsia who are outside the Orthodox hierarchy. It has also been argued that criticism of antisemitism by members of the Orthodox hierarchy are insufficient and too often assume the nature of a political gesture. It appears that antisemitic ideology within the Church is not considered a serious danger; letters protesting Orthodox fascism never resulted in lawsuits or even disciplinary measures. However, even a marginal resistance to antisemitism is an important sign of the changes taking place in the Orthodox mentality.[159]

In spite of all the optimistic signs, however, the antisemitic currents within the Orthodox Church cannot be discounted as marginal or insignificant.

Although Lezov's points are somewhat exaggerated, the position of the Orthodox apologists who claim that Orthodoxy is free from Judeophobia, is historically inaccurate, for as we see, antisemitism in several forms figures prominently in the historical background and intellectual legacy of the Church, including the participation of priests in the pogroms; the forcible conversion to Orthodoxy of Jewish boys *(kantonisti)* kidnapped into the Russian army; antisemitic elements in the liturgy; and the dissemination of antisemitic stereotypes. These antisemitic "undercurrents" cannot be dissociated from the history of the Orthodox Church.

NOTES

1. J. Billington, "The Case for Orthodoxy," *New Republic,* 30 May 1994, 26.

2. Alexii II, "Dorogie bratiia, shalom vam," *Moskovskie novosti,* 26 January 1992, speech delivered in New York, November 1991.

3. Th. Friedgut, "Antisemitism and Its Opponents: Reflections in the Russian Press," ACTA Occasional Papers, no. 3 (Vidal Sassoon International Center for the Study of Antisemitism, Hebrew University of Jerusalem) (1994), 9.

4. These tracts of the Church Fathers include the *Epistle of Barnabas,* Tertullian, *Adversus Iudaeos*; Cyprian of Carthage, *De iudaica incredulitate*; Augustine of Hippo, *Sermon Against the Jews*; Novatian, *De cibis iudaicis*; Hippolytus of Rome, *Contra Judaeos*; Jacob of Serugh, seven *Sermons Against the Jews*; Justin Martyr, *Epistle of Diognetos, Dialogue with Trypho*; and certain tracts of Eusebias of Caesarea and Cyril of Alexandria. All these works were important in Western

Christianity, and even more so for Eastern Christianity. C. Diehl, a historian of Byzantium, wrote: "After a period of creative activity inspired by the Fathers of the Church, from the ninth century onwards respect for tradition precluded all originality and freedom of thought in this great theological movement.... men relied on the authority of bygone divines.... Discussion was by quoted passages, and the main arguments were simply the affirmation of the Fathers." C. Diehl, *Byzantium. Greatness and Decline* (New Brunswick, N.J. 1957), 244–46. Not surprisingly, the anti-Judaism polemic of the early Church, outdated in the West, remained a living part of Byzantine theology for many centuries.

5. S. Bowman, *The Jews of Byzantium 1204–1453* (Birmingham, Ala. 1985), 30, 34; idem., "Two Late Byzantine Dialogues with the Jews," *Greek Orthodox Theological Review*, 25, no. 1 (1980).

6. Four examples of the Judaizing heresies are Sabellianism and Monarchianism (fourth century, stressed the monarchy of God the Father and thus undermined the doctrine of the Trinity); the iconoclast controversy (eighth and ninth centuries); the Judaizing heresy in Russia (fifteenth century); and the onomatodoxist controversy (1912–1914: "glorifiers of the name" *[imiaslavtsi]* and "wrestlers with the name" *[imiabortsi]*). On the latter, see W. Heitmuller, *In Namen Jesu, eine sprach- und religionsgeschichte Untersuchung zum Neuen Testament* (Göttingen 1903); A. Losev, "Imiaslovie," *Voprosi filosofii*, no. 9 (1993): 52–60. On the connection between onomatodoxy and the Beilis Affair see L. Katzis, "'Delo Beilisa' v kontekste 'serebrianogo veka'," *Vestnik Evreiskogo Universiteta v Moskve*, no. 4 (1993): 134–35. Similar controversies occurred in Western religious history, but in Orthodoxy they were pervasive throughout social life and more intense.

7. Peter the Great completed the Byzantine tendency toward subjugating the Church. He abolished the institute of the Patriarchy and ensured the acquiescence of the Church by transforming the Church into an instrument of the state. The chief ecclesiastical authority became the Holy Synod, whose activities were overseen by the law procurator of the Synod. From then on the tsar was empowered to interfere in the traditional structure of the Church, and came to be an autocrat of both Church and State.

8. S. Baron, *Modern Nationalism and Religion* (New York and Philadelphia 1960), 199.

9. W. Nichols, *Christian Antisemitism. A History of Hate* (Northvale, N.J. and London 1993), 172.

10. Ivan III claimed to be the direct successor of the Eastern Roman Emperors after his marriage to the niece of the last Byzantine Emperor.

11. The chief biblical reference for this concept is Daniel 2:44: the last kingdom is described as that "which shall never be destroyed: and the kingdom shall not be left to

other people, but it shall break in pieces and consume all these kingdoms, and it shall stand for ever."

12. Daniel Rowland convincingly argues that in the Moscovite sources the idea of Russia as a "new Israel" was "overwhelmingly better represented in the source base than the Third Rome idea." It "outnumbered references to Moscow as a parallel to Rome by many hundreds, if not thousands of times." Moreover, he argues that this idea was important far beyond Church circles and that "Moscow's self-image as a New Israel did have important effects both in generating internal support for the regime and its political power and perhaps in influencing some foreign policy decisions." D. Rowland, "Moscow — The Third Rome or the New Israel?" *Russian Review,* no. 2 (1996): 591, 593, 595. Older research on the prominence of the concept of "New Israel" in Russian history, N. I. Efimov, *Rus' — novyi Israil: teokraticheskaiia ideologiia svoezemnago Pravoslaviia v do-Petrovskoi pismennosti* (Kazan 1912).

13. Some contemporary clerics claim that the physical fall was caused by the spiritual failure, namely, by the attempts to unite with Catholicism. Metropolitan Ioann, *Odolenie smuti* (St. Petersburg 1995), 231.

14. For more details see R. Stupperich, "Kiev — das zweite Jerusalem," *Zeitschrift für slavische Philologie,* 12 (1935): 332–54.

15. P. Novikov, "Spor mezhdu Moskvoi i Konstantinopolem," *Russkaia misl,* 21–27 March 1996.

16. This is surprising because of the bad reputation of St. Petersburg in Russian popular Orthodox tradition; the city was associated with pernicious Western influence and Old Believers identified it with the "Fourth Rome" and death.

17. G. Kaganov, "St.Petersburg and Jerusalem," talk presented at the Center for Eastern European and Eurasian Studies, University of Texas, Austin, 25 February 1996.

18. N. Bulgakov and A. Yakovlev-Kosirev, "Sim pobedishi," *Den',* no. 29 (1992).

19. S. Karpov, "Eres eresei," *Russkii vestnik,* no. 29–30 (1993).

20. A tradition that Antichrist will be a Jew from the tribe of Dan arose in the second century. In the aftermath of Peter the Great's Church reform, Old Believers saw him as the personification of Antichrist. Some Orthodox theologians believed that, during his European travels, a Judean prince of Dan was substituted for the young Russian tsar. It was he who imprisoned the tsarina, killed the prince, and introduced anti-Christian reforms, pretending to be a god. A. Melnikov-Pecherskii, *O raskolnikakh pri imperatorakh Nikolae I i Aleksandre I* (Leipzig 1872), 73; M. Cherniavsky, "Old Believers and the New Religion," in *Structure of Russian History. Interpretive Essays,* ed. by M.Cherniavsky (New York 1970), 166–70.

21. W. Laqueur, *Black Hundred* (New York 1993), 56–57.

22. T. I. Butkevich, "O smisle i znachenii krovavikh zhertvoprinoshenii v dokhristianskom mire i o tak nasivaemikh ritualnikh ubiistvakh," in *Krov' v verovaniiakh i sueveriiakh chelovechestva*, ed. by V. F. Boikov (St. Petersburg 1995), 229–368; his extensive study of the question was originally published in *Vera i razum* (Faith and Reason) (Kharkov), no. 21 (1913): 281–99; *Vera i razum*, no. 22 (n.d.): 413–37; *Vera i razum*, no. 23 (n.d.): 554–608; *Vera i razum*, no. 24 (n.d.): 723–68. Butkevich contends that the bloody sacrifices of the Temple were supplanted in the post-biblical age by ritual murder (p. 267 of the book). Butkevich is heavily indebted to the pamphlet of the monk Neofit, a convert from Judaism: *Christian Blood in the Rituals of the Present-Day Sinogogue* (1803; it first appeared in Romanian and later in Greek, Arabic, and Russian). The pamphlet was used by the prosecution as evidence in the trial, and in the report of Vladimir Dahl (1801–1872), a Russian writer and lexicologist, to the Russian Minister of Internal Affairs, *Research on Murder the Christian Babies and Use of their Blood by the Jews* (1844). Both Butkevich and bishop Porfirii believed that only some Jewish sects — Chasidists — were involved in the ritual murder of the Christian children.

23. "Pravoslavie," *Evreiskaiia entsiklopediia,* 6 (Jerusalem 1992), 6:739.

24. For more on the apocalyptic mentality and images of Antichrist in fin-de-siècle Russia, see A. Grishin and I. Isupov, eds., *Antikhrist* (Moscow 1995).

25. Four central, and linked, questions marked the Silver Age: the "Jewish question," the sexual question, the family question, and questions about the legitimacy of political power. See A. Etkind, *Sodom i Psikheia: ocherki intellectualnoi istorii serebrianogo veka* (Moscow 1996), where he lists the questions as those of the interest in the esoteric, nationalism, eroticism, and political radicalism.

26. On the association of apocalyptic thinking, antisemitism, and violence, see M. Ostow, *Myth and Madness* (New Brunswick, N.J. 1996), 164–66.

27. See L. Katzis, "Delo Beilisa v kontekste Serebrianogo veka," *Vestnik evreiskogo universiteta v Moskve,* no. 4 (1993). I'm indebted to Sidney Monas, Professor of History, University of Texas at Austin, for his work on the connection between the Silver Age and antisemitism, "Russian Jews and Jewish Russians," lecture presented at University of Texas, Austin, March 1996.

28. The Russian word *voskresenie* — Sunday — means "resurrection."

29. V. Rozanov, *The Jews' Olfactory and Tactile Relationship to Blood* (1914). On the Beilis trial, see M. Samuel, *Blood Accusation* (New York 1966).

30. Ashtoreth (Astarte) is a Semitic goddess of sexual activity, fertility, maternity, love, and war; the Bible refers to her as the goddess of the Sidonians. See I Samuel 7:3; 12:10, and Judges 2:13; 10:6.

31. V. Rosanov, "Yudaism," *Taina Israilia* (St. Petersburg 1992), 187.

32. Ibid., 154.

33. Ibid., 153.

34. V. Rosanov, "Ob osiazatelnom i oboniatelnom otnoshenii evreev k krovi," *Taina Israilia* (St. Petersburg 1992), 244–45.

35. The Theosophical Society was founded in New York in 1875, by Helena Blavatsky and others. Theosophical thought was strongly influenced by Indian esoteric doctrines and Buddhism, and the movement aimed to stem the tide of materialism and agnosticism in European thought. It attracted a number of prominent European artists and poets, such as William Butler Yeats, Piet Mondrian, and Vassily Kandinsky.

36. On theosophy's impact, see M. Carlson, *"No Religion Higher Than Truth." A History of the Theosophical Movement in Russia, 1875–1922* (Princeton, N.J. 1993).See H. Blavatsky, *Esoteric Character of the Gospels* (Bombay 1952). Blavatsky claimed that Christianity is an Aryan religion in origin and inspiration; and that Christ was not Jewish but Aryan, and that Christianity was Judaized later by the Church. E. Blavatskaiia, *Tainaiia doktrina* (Riga 1937), 720–21.

37. To be fair, Blavatsky admitted that some Jewish kabbalists were aware of the metaphysical meaning of these symbols.

38. Blavatsky interprets YHVH as symbolic of the interwoven male and female principles, a Jewish "Trinity" in which male and female aspects are united by the Shekhina. The numerical meaning of the name revealed in the occult symbol of Tetragrammaton (10 points in the triangle) suggests that it embraces the whole universe. Blavatskaiia, *Tainaiia doktrina,* 1:774.

39. E. Blavatskaiia, *Tainaiia doktrina,* Tr. by Helena Roerich, vol. 1 (Riga 1937), 473.

40. H. Blavatsky, *The Secret Doctrine*, vol. 4, parts 2 and 3 (Wheaton, Il. 1946), 38–39; reprinted in *Nauka i religiia,* no. 2 (1989): 40.

41. Ibid., 39.

42. Ibid., 38.

43. In general their discourse merges the "four questions" of the Silver Age: the sexual question, the family question, the question of political legitimacy, and that of the Jews.

44. James Webb, a historian of occultism, mentions two cases: in 1888 Richard Hart reprinted the antisemitic pamphlet, *The Hebrew Talisman* in the London Theosophical Society's journal. Yuliana Glinka, a secret agent of the Russian Political Police and member of the Theosophical Society, brought the first text of the *Protocols of the Elders of Zion,* and *The Secret of the Jew* (which she herself may have written) to Russia. See J. Webb, *The Occult Establishment* (La Salle, Ill. 1976), 230–45.

45. M. Carlson, *"No Religion Higher Than Truth,"* 118.

46. Blavatskaiia, *Tainaiia doktrina,* 393, 385. Blavatsky also associates the Jews with the Chandal tribe that was expelled from India where they could have learned the principles and symbols of ancient symbolism.

47. Blavatsky's racial doctrines significantly influenced Lanz von Liebensfels (1874–1954), the founder of Aryosophy. The idea of an occult destiny for each particular race and the doctrine of racial supremacy appeal greatly to the early German race ideologists. *The Secret Doctrine* was published in German a year before Liebensfels's "masterpiece" *Theozoologie* (1904). See J. Webb, *The Occult Establishment*, 281.

48. Count A. M. du Chayla, "Nilus and the Protocols," in *The Truth About "The Protocols of Zion,"* ed. by H. Bernstein (New York 1935), 361.

49. Du Chayla wrote: "The will of God is accomplished through human weakness," he said. "Let us admit that the Protocols are false but is it not possible that God should make use of them in order to expose the iniquity which is approaching? Did not the ass of Balaam utter prophesy?... Cannot God transform the bones of a dog into sacred miracles? If He can do these things, He can also make the announcement of truth come from the mouth of a liar," quoted in H. Bernstein, *The Truth About "The Protocols of the Elders of Zion,"* 366.

50. See S. Dudakov, "Vladimir Soloviev i Sergei Nilus," *Russian Literature and History,* ed. by Wolf Moskovich et al. (Jerusalem 1989).

51. For more on Soloviev's public activity about antisemitism, see F. B. Getz, *Ob otnoshenii Vladimira Solovieva k evreiskomu voprosu* (Moscow 1902); V. Stroev, "Vladimir Soloviev i evreistvo," *Rassvet* (Paris), no. 49 (1925); V. Speranskii, "Vladimir Soloviev o evreiskom voprose," *Rassvet* (Paris) no. 6 (1929).

52. V. Soloviev, "Evreistvo i khristianskii vopros," in *Taina Israilia* (St. Petersburg 1992), 78.

53. Ibid., 52.

54. The idea of the providential encounter of Russians and Jews was quite common during the Silver Age. For one example, see Lou Andreas-Salome, "Russische Philosophie und Semitische Geist," *Die Zeit,* 15 January 1898: 236, n. 172. Salome's ideas about the special role of Russians and Jews in future European history may be traced to Friedrich Nietzsche, who wrote in *Beyond Good and Evil* (1886) that "a thinker who has the development of Europe of his conscience will, in all his projects for this future, take into account the Jews as well as the Russians as the provisionally surest and most probable factors in the great play and fight of forces." F. Nietzsche, *Beyond Good and Evil* (New York: Vintage, 1966), 188.

55. Soloviev, "Evreistvo i khristianskii vopros," in *Taina Israilia*, 35.

56. Ibid., 80.

57. N. Berdiaev, "Khristianstvo i antisemitism," *Taina Israilia* (St. Petersburg 1992), 325–42, originally published in *Put'* (Paris) (May–June 1938); Engl. tr. *Christianity and Anti-Semitism* (1954). The text is based on a lecture given in Paris in 1938 at one of the public meetings of the Académie Religieuse et Philosophique Russe, of which Berdiaev was president.

58. See Gal. 3:26–29.

59. Berdiaev draws on the French Catholic philosophers Jacques Maritain and Léon Bloy; see J. Maritain, *Antisemitism* (London 1939).

60. N. Berdiaev, "Sud'ba evreistva," *Taina Israilia* (St. Petersburg 1992), 314; this is a chapter from Berdiaev's *The Meaning of History* (1923).

61. Sergii Bulgakov's works on Jewish issues include: "Zion" (1915); "Sud'ba Israilia kak krest Bogomateri" (1941); "Rasism i khristianstvo" (1941–42); "Goneniia na Israil (Dogmaticheskii ocherk)" (1942); and "Karl Marx kak religioznii tip" (1906), collected by Nikita Struve in S. Bulgakov, *Khristianstvo i evreiskii vopros* (Paris 1991).

62. Bulgakov, "Sud'ba Israilia kak krest Bogomateri", 71–72.

63. Ibid., 72.

64. Ibid., 68.

65. S. Bulgakov, "Goniteli Israilia," in S. Bulgakov, in *Khristianstvo i evreiskii vopros*, 75.

66. Ibid., 71.

67. V. Zenkovsky, "Na temi istoriosofii," in *Taina Israilia* (St. Petersburg 1992), 439, 441, originally published in *Sovremenniie zapiski*, no. 69 (1939): 280–89.

68. Ibid.

69. Ibid., 443.

70. S. Frank, "Die religiöse Tragädie des Judentums," *Eine heilige Kirche* (April–June 1934): 128–33.

71. P. Boobbyer, *S. L. Frank. The Life and Work of A Russian Philosopher* (Athens, Ohio 1995), 77.

72. Ibid., 76.

73. Soloviev was impressed with Theodor Herzl's *Judenstadt,* but he associated the revival of the Jewish state with the realization of the theocratic ideal and rule of the anointed king of the House of David (or, alternatively, a community ruled by the High Priest and Sanhedrin). S. Dudakov, "Vladimir Soloviev i Sergei Nilus," *Russian Literature and History* (Jerusalem 1989), 164. Soloviev believed that the last revolt against Antichrist would take place in Israel. In a similar vein, Bulgakov believed in the prophecies that the Jewish people would return to Palestine, which would be accompanied by a Jewish religious revival that would pave the way for a complete spiritual transformation and conversion; see S. Bulgakov, "Sion," *Khristianstvo i evreiskii vopros* (Paris) (1991): 7–12.

74. Soloviev, "Evreistvo i khristianskii vopros," 32–33.

75. See V. Brachev, "'Postigshii tainu bezzakoniia,'" *Molodaiia gvardiia,* no. 8 (1992): 275.

76. The present day "Black Hundred" is an Orthodox group led by Alexander Shtilmark who is also editor-in-chief of the newspaper, *Black Hundred.* According to

one explanation, originally the word referred to Orthodox monks dressed in their traditional black garments who ran in front of the military detachments of the Russian army during the battles against the invaders. See E. Chinyaeva, "Russian Orthodox Church Forges a New Role" *Transition,* 2, no. 7 (1996): 17–18; A Krasikov, "Natsional-pravoslavie protiv pravoslaviia," *Russkaiia mysl,* 26 September–1 October 1996.

77. My analysis does not include official publications of the Orthodox Church, such as the *Journal of the Moscow Patriarchate, Moskovskii Tserkovni Vestnik,* and *Veche,* since these circulate in Church circles only and have little effect on public discourse.

78. Ioann, "Torzhestvo pravoslaviia (Ocherki russkogo samosoznaniia)," *Nash sovremennik,* no. 9 (1993): 121. The first part of this essay, entitled "The Cataclysm Makers" was originally published in *Sovetskaiia Rossiia* (22 March 1993).

79. Ioann, "Torzhestvo pravoslaviia," *Nash sovremennik,* no. 9 (1993): 122; Ioann, "Torzhestvo pravoslaviia," *Nash sovremennik,* no. 4 (1993): 11; Ioann, "Torzhestvo pravoslaviia," *Nash sovremennik,* no. 9 (1993): 129.

80. Ioann, "Torzhestvo pravoslaviia," *Nash sovremennik,* no. 9 (1993): 123.

81. Disraeli's most "conspirological" work is his novel *Coningsby* (1944). A central character is Sidonia, a Jew of unlimited wealth, super-human intellectual powers, and universal knowledge, whose words reflect Disraeli's own ideas about the superiority of the Jewish race. Sidonia held that the power of Jewish capitalists could unleash or stop a war. Baron de Rothschild is believed to be the prototype of Sidonia; see R. W. Stewart, ed., *Disraeli's Novels Reviewed, 1926–1968* (Metuchen, N.J. 1975), 201–204.

82. Ioann, "Samoderzhavie dukha," *Nash sovremennik,* no. 9 (1993): 122. Pseudo-Dmitry II *(Tushinskii vor)* claimed to be a son of Ivan the Terrible, but he never tried to promote any Jewish interests, being a protégé of Lithvonia. He was chosen by the Polish nobility because of his physical similarity to the tsar pseudo-Dmitry I. There is no direct evidence that pseudo-Dmitry was Jewish, although it was rumored that he was the baptized Jew, Bogdan, a scribe for pseudo-Dmitry I. See R. Skrinnikov, *Smuta v Rossii v nachale 17 veka* (Leningrad 1988). Various other versions of his origins are cited in F. Kandel, *Ocherki vremion i sobitii* (Jerusalem 1988), 247.

83. Ioann, "Torzhestvo pravoslaviia," *Nash sovremennik,* no. 9 (1993): 127.

84. See D. Dudko, "S russkoi golgofi," *Volnoe slovo. Posev,* no. 33 (1979).

85. F. Orekhanova, "Rossiiu raspiali, Rossiia voskresnet! K itogam Pervogo Vsemirnogo russkogo sobora," *Sovetskaiia Rossiia,* 1 June 1993.

86. See Ioann, "Roditsia russkim est dar sluzheniia," in idem, *Odolenie smuti* (St. Petersburg 1995), 227–29, originally published in *Zavtra,* no. 10 (1994), as "Rossiia — Podnozhie prestola Gospodnia." See also "Pokaiannoe slovo" (interview with monk Philadelph), *Den',* no. 33 (1992).

87. See D. Dudko, "O derzhave pravoslavnoi," *Zavtra,* no. 18 (1996). Fr. Dudko claims that it was not Russians who killed their tsar, destroyed churches, or were responsible for the repressions. Even if they occasionally took part in such activities, the original plan was devised by Jews.

88. Ioann, "Torzhestvo pravoslaviia," *Nash sovremennik,* no. 9 (1993): 128–29.

89. Ibid., 130.

90. L. Borodin, "O russkoi intelligentsii," *Grani,* no. 96 (1975): 248.

91. Ioann, "Derzhavnoe stroitel'stvo," *Sovetskaiia Rossiia,* 14 November 1992. Ioann refers to John Chrysostom, who tried to prevent the misinterpretation of the phrase. The German philosopher and geo-politician Carl Schmitt also argued against this misinterpretation pointing to the distinction in Greek between public *(polimios)* and private *(ekstros)* enemies, and contended that the biblical phrase does not refer to the public friends, that is, enemies of one's own people. C. Schmitt, *Concept of the Political* (New Brunswick, N.J. 1976), 28–29.

92. Ioann, "Ya ne politik, ya — pastyr," *Sovetskaia Rossia,* 11 June 1993. See also Ioann, *Samoderzhavie dukha. Ocherki russkogo samosoznaniia* (St. Petersburg 1995), 268.

93. See Y. Begunov, "Bil li Nilus avtorom 'Protokolov sionskikh mudretsov'?," *Russkii vestnik,* no. 7 (1993). Begunov's arguments are beyond the scope of this volume. In brief, he argues that the *Protocols* existed long before the date suggested by those who claim it was a fabrication, and cites dubious claims of having read the book or encountered its key ideas ten or more years before its Russian publicatoin.

94. Ioann, "Ya ne politik, ya — pastir," *Sovetskaya Rossiia,* 11 June 1993.

95. The Judaizing heresy first appeared in Novgorod during the reign of Grand Duke Ivan Vasilyevich III in the second half of the fifteenth century, and then spread to Pskov and Moscow. Its first propagator was the influential Jew Zecharia of Kiev, who arrived in Novgorod as the commercial agent for Prince Michael Olelkovich. He converted many clergymen into his faith, which asserted there is only one God — Jesus — and the Trinity is not divine. God has not yet appeared, but when he does, he will not appear as the son of God in substance, but through his benefactors, like Moses and the prophets. Judaizers followed some rationalistic traditions of ancient and medieval thought, especially those of Maimonides and Immanuel ben Yakov. They condemned icons and monasticism, and translated some parts of the Bible into the vernacular. The heresy was denounced in 1487, and in 1490 the Church council passed a resolution against the heretics, many of whom were tortured to death. In 1504 the leaders of Judaizers were condemned to death and were burned. See "Judaizing Heresy" in Isaac Singer, ed., *Jewish Encyclopedia* (New York 1904), 7:369–70. Some scholars consider the Russian Judaizers as forerunners of the Reformation in Europe, similar to the British religious reformer of the fourteenth century, John Wycliffe, and the Bohemian religious reformers led by Jan Hus.

96. S. Karpov, "Eres' eresei," *Russkii vestnik,* no. 29–30 (1993).

97. Anon., "Papstvo i iudaism," *Russkii vestnik,* no. 6 (1993). The article was written by an unnamed monk of the holy mountain of Afon.

98. Ibid.

99. On the Antichrist as a Judean Prince in contemporary works, see Father Superior Isaiah, "Rossiia pered vtorim prishestviem," *Russkii vestnik,* no. 33 (1993); Monk Moses (Bogoliubov), *Sbornik o predkonechnikh vremenakh i nekotorikh putiakh preodoleniia iskushenii* (Izhevsk 1994); S. Karpov, "Eres' eresei," *Russkii vestnik,* no. 29–30 (1993).

100. N. Doroshenko, "'Gorbi' iz Vatikana," *Nash sovremennik,* no. 6 (1993); D. Kalaich, "Vatikan," *Literaturnaiia Rossiia,* no. 5 (1993).

101. O. Soloviev, "Eres zhidovstvuiuschikh," *Russkii vestnik,* no. 21–23 (1993).

102. Y. Tabak, "Iisus i piataiia grafa," *Argumenti i fakti,* no. 17 (1993).

103. V. Gubanov, "Iisus — Bogochelovek," *Russkii vestnik,* no. 17 (1993).

104. Osipov refers to the use of modern Russian rather than Old Church Slavonic in the liturgy. See A. Kirlezhaev, "Ponimaet li Bog po russki. Spor o iazike bogosluzheniia," *Nezavisimaiia gazeta,* 21 April 1994.

105. V. Osipov, "Tserkov' v osade," *Zavtra,* no. 40 (1995).

106. Ibid.

107. Ioann, "Drevo poznaeotsia po plodam," *Sovetskaiia Rossiia,* 27 February 1993.

108. For more details, S. Lezov, "Obrazi khristianstva," *Inoe. Rossiia kak ideiia* (Moscow 1995), 262–70.

109. S. Antiminsov "Protoerei Alexander Menn kak kommentator Biblii," *Moskva,* no. 1 and no. 7–8 (1992); O. Soloviev, "Eres zhidovstvuiuschikh."

110. Soloviev, "Eres zhidovstvuiuschikh."

111. Menn's assassination in 1990 may have been carried out by members of a ultranationalist organization such as Pamyat'; the murderers are still unknown. He had received threatening letters before his death. Nationalists claim that he was killed by Zionists who hated him for converting many Russian Jews. See C. O'Clery, "Darkness at Dawn," *New Republic,* 22 October 1990.

112. See D. Pospelovsky, "Nekotorie problemi sovremennoi russkoi pravoslavnoi tzerkvi," *Vestnik russkogo khristianskogo dvizheniia* (Paris, New York, and Moscow), no. 172 (1995).

113. V. Demin, "O eresi zhidovstvuiuschikh i Zaiiavlenie 4-go siezda Soiiuza Pravoslavnikh bratstsv," *Vestnik Soiiuza Pravoslavnikh Bratstv,* no. 43 (May 1993): 15–29.

114. L. Saveliev, "Zapiski po russkoi filosofii," *Moskva,* no. 2 (1993): 178.

115. L. Saveliev, "Zapiski po russkoi filosofii," *Moskva,* no. 5 (1993): 166.

116. Ibid., 176.

117. Ibid., 181.

118. Ioann, "Sviaschennoe i strashnoe delo — vlast'," *Sovetskaiia Rossiia,* no. 8 (1993); reprinted in *Molodaiia gvardiia,* no. 3 (1994).

119. Ioann, "Vozrozhdenie pravoslaviia," *Russkii sobor,* no. 6 (1993).

120. Ioann, "Pravoslavnaiia revolutsiia protiv sovremennogo mira," *Elementi,* no. 4 (1993): 19.

121. Ioann, "Vo ostavlenie grekhov," *Den',* no. 7 (1993).

122. Ioann, "Torzhestvo pravoslaviia," *Nash sovremennik,* no. 4 (1993): 11. Leontii Saveliev mentions two Russian saints who were canonized because they were "martyred by Jews." On the day of Passover in 1096, Jews supposedly tortured and crucified the Russian monk Evstratii Postnik, and in 1690, the Jews "ritually murdered" the child Gavriil. L. Saveliev, "Zapiski po russkoi filosofii," *Moskva,* no. 2 (1993): 182.

123. Alan Dundes, professor of anthropology and folklore at the University of California, Berkley, claims that the legend is a part of the belief system that Christians developed about the Jews. Among other explanations Dundes explains the legend by what he calls the "projective inversion," or need for a scapegoat: A (Christians) accuse B (the Jews) of carrying out an action which A really wishes to carry out him/herself. Dundes refers to numerous Christian rituals associated with blood. A. Dundes, "The Ritual Murder or Blood Libel Legend: A Study of Anti-Semitic Victimization Through Projective Inversion." in *The Blood Libel Legend: A Casebook in Anti-Semitic Folklore,* ed. by Alan Dundes (Madison, Wisc. 1991).

124. The reviewer of Eduard Radzinsky's *The Last Tsar* (review published in the Orthodox newspaper *Tserkovnie novosti*) laments that although "Radzinsky by no means can avoid mentioning the fact that Yurovsky who put a bullet in the tsar was Jewish, fails to admit that the other organizers of the cruel murder of the tsar's family — Beloborodov, Goloschekin, Sverdlov — were also Jewish.... Radzinsky also claims that the tsar did not believe in the authenticity of the 'Protocols of the Elders of Zion'.... However, in the note which was made by the tsar three months before the murder...we read: 'Yesterday I started to read Nilus's book about the Antichrist which is complemented by the "Protocols" of the Jews and Masons. This reading is very topical.'" See Anon., "Kniga Radsinskogo," *Nasha strana* (Buenos Aires), 30 January 1993.

125. Sverdlov issued the order; Yurovsky was personally responsible for its execution; Beloborodov (Weisbart) was Chairman of the local Soviet; and Goloschekin had supervised the process in Ekaterinburg. See I. Shafarevich, *Est' li u Rossii buduschee?* (Moscow 1991), 457.

126. E. Prudnikova, "Golgotha. Russkaiia istoriia: Vzgliad pravoslavnogo," *Sovetskaiia Rossiia,* 15 July 1993.

127. V. Ushkuinik, *Pamiatka russkomu cheloveku* (Moscow 1993), 23–24. The search for symbolic and historical connections between regicide and the Jews is very pervasive. Yurii Vorobiovsky claims that the murder of the French king Louis XVI was accomplished as a revenge of the dynasty of the Merovingians against the dynasty of the Carolingians. According to the medieval legend, the early French dynasty of the Merovingians descended from the Judean king David. The murder of Loius XVI, the last Carolingian king, with which the French Revolution started, was supposedly a ritual murder and revenge against the Sacred Roman Empire and the Pope for the betrayal of the Merovigians. This regicide opened a new era for the Masons and for the Jews. The Masons supposedly tried to restore the Merovigian dynasty and Merovigian rule in the whole of Europe. See Y. Vorobievsky, "Visit ritsaria mesti," *Moskva,* no. 8 (1997).

128. One Russian theologian defined the tsar as a "Christ of the Lord" *(Khrist Gospoden').*

129. M. Nazarov, "Istoriia 'Kirillova' podloga," *Moskva,* no. 4 (1996): 114.

130. Ioann, "Shestvie razrushitelia," *Odolenie smuti* (St. Petersburg 1995), 24.

131. P. Tiurin, "Ikona i tsar'," 163.

132. V. Klikov, V. Trostnikov, V. Rasputin, et al. "Ot lukavogo...," no. 12 (1996). The tsar's family was canonized by the Russian Orthodox Church Abroad in 1981. Archbishop Melkizedek, a member of the special Canonization Committee of the Russian Orthodox Church, was the first to insist on local honoring of the members of the tsar's family. "Nicholas II to be canonized," *Russian Life,* December 1996, 8.

133. M. Cherniavsky, *Tsar and People. Studies in Russian Myths* (New York 1969), 32. Cherniavsky reports that "a list of Russian saints up to the 18th century shows that out of some eight hundred, over one hundred were princes and princesses" (p. 6). Some were regarded as saints for ecclesiastical reasons, while others were secular saints sanctified for their labors for Russia.

134. In his response to the opponents of canonization (Metropolitan Yuvenalii), priest Timofei claims that they do not understand the meaning of hagiography, the creation of the icon of the saint which provides a better picture of the life of the saint than any historical account of his life. The tsar's death was a ritual murder, he argues, and blames Yuvenalii for being afraid of the Jewish people who would look with great disfavor on the canonization. Timofei, "Vetvi lozi bozhestvennie (Pamiati sviatikh novomuchennikov Rossiiskikh)," *Russkii vestnik,* no. 8–10 (1995).

135. In 1997, the Russian Orthodox Church asked a government commission to investigate the ritual murder charge. The commission concluded there was no ritual murder, noting that only one Jew took part in the execution, although the decision to execute the tsar was made by eleven people, of which three were Jewish, and none of them members of religious organizations. See "Poriadok kazni vyrabatyvalsia kollegial'no," *Moskovskie novosti,* no. 8 (1998).

136. See, for instance, M. Yamaguchi, "Towards a Poetics of the Scapegoat," in *Violence and Truth. On the Work of René Gerard,* ed. by Paul Dumouchel (Stanford, Calif. 1988), 179–82.

137. V. Pichuzhkin, "Khristos i Stalin," *Al-Quds,* no. 2 (1995).

138. Some nationalists add a missing element which complements the structure of the mythological plot offered by deacon Pichuzhkin. The story of the murder of Stalin by the Jews recounted by Chichkin, develops the mythological plot and makes the metaphorical "crucifixion on the cross of lies and malice" more literal and physical. Some return to the "doctors' plot" against Stalin. Others offer more sophisticated versions of the murder. See A. Chichkin, "V marte 53go... Zagadka smerti Stalina," *Molodaiia gvardiia,* no. 10 (1992).

139. Not all Orthodox nationalists are monarchists. However, all monarchists are Orthodox nationalists, for the link between the monarchy and Orthodoxy is connected with Caesaro-Papism. A Russian tsardom is impossible unless the tsar is Orthodox. The monarchy represents not only a specific type of social organization, but the restoration of the world order ruined in the course of the Soviet experiment. The tsar is warrant for the restoration of the lost social harmony and of Orthodoxy ("there are four patriarchs and there is only one tsar"). Therefore, they always talk about the Orthodox monarchy.

140. See M. Nazarov, *Kto Naslednik Rossiiskogo Prestola?* (Moscow 1996).

141. According to legend, the founder of the Bagration (Bagratuni or Bagrat) dynasty was the Judean prince Shambat, taken captive by Nebuchadrezzar. Leonida Georgievna's mother was I. S. Zlotnitskaya, descended from a Jewish family in Tiflis. The first husband of Leonida Georgievna Bagration-Mukhranilly was the Jew Kirby, and through her sister-in-law Helen Kirby she "keeps the connections with the richest Jewish and masonic circles of the USA including those families which have subsidized the Russian revolution." See M. Nazarov, "Istoriia 'Kirillovskogo' podloga, *Moskva,* no. 4 (1996): 108; "Zapadnia monarkhii. Zaiavlenie postoiannogo soveta obiedineonnikh dvorianskikh obschestv v Rossii," *Zavtra,* no. 25 (1994); G. Knupffer, *Osvedomlennoe soobschenie* (London 1970).

142. M. Nazarov, "Istoriia 'Kirillovskogo' podloga," 112.

143. V. Shumsky, "Pechat' Antikhrista (po povodu ubiistva v Optinoi pustini)," *Den',* no. 16 (1993).

144. M. Ustinov, "Rokovoi vopros," *Nash sovremennik,* no. 4 (1993): 178–79.

145. This picture of the Talmud and other Jewish texts is false. In fact, moral obligations toward non-Jews are often particularly emphasized. For instance, to cheat a non-Jew was seen as a double crime: an act of robbery, and a profanation of God's holiness. "A Jew sins more against God by cheating and robbing a Christian than when he cheats and robs a Jew, because, though both acts are dishonest and criminal, in the case of a Christian the Jew offends not only against moral law, but profanes the

sacred name of God," (*Sefer Chassidim*, 12th century). The *Shulchan Aruch* (Jewish law code, 16th century) says: "A thief is a thief, though he steal a trifle, be the defrauded person Jew or be he Gentile." See I. Abrahams, *Jewish Life in the Middle Ages* (London 1932), 122–25.

146. Ustinov, "Rokovoi vopros," 180.

147. Vladimir Soloviev wrote "Talmud i noveishaiia polemicheskaiia literatura o nem v Avstrii i Germanii – Evrei I ikh uchenie I nravouchenie" (Talmud and the newest polemic literature about it in Austria and Germany – Jews, their doctrines and moral teaching) on the antisemitic interpretations of the Talmud found in Austria and Germany that were utilized by pre-revolutionary Russian antisemites, *Sobranie Soch.* (Collected Works), vol. 2 (Berlin 1925).

148. See, e.g., the pioneering work of Emil Schürer, *The Literature of the Jewish People in the Time of Jesus* (1874; reprint New York 1972). On the similarity between the rabbinical teaching and the doctrines of Jesus, see D. Cohn-Sherbok, *The Jew Crucified* (London 1992), 225–26.

149. I. Liutostansky, *Talmud i evrei. Kompiliatsiia iz rasnikh talmudov i kommentariev,* vols. 1–7 (St. Petersburg 1902–1909); A. Shmakov, *Svoboda i evrei. Predislovie. ''vreiskoe zertsalo' — sto zakonov 'Shulchan Arucha' (sokraschennogo Talmuda)* (Moscow 1906).

150. S. Lezov, "Natsionalnaiia ideiia i khristianstvo," *Russkaiia ideiia i evrei. Rokovoi spor,* ed. by Zoya Krakhmalnikova (Moscow 1994), 99–126 Engl. tr. "National Idea and Christianity," *Religion, State and Society,* 20, no. 1 (1992).

151. V. Borzenko, *Pravoslavie i evrei* (Moscow 1995). See in Engl. tr. in *Religion, State and Society,* 23, no. 1 (1995). Other studies suggest the opposite picture.

152. According to the Gudkov and Levenson survey, "the respondents who declared that they are Orthodox believers, demonstrated more severe and aggressive reaction of hostility toward Jews in comparison with those who do not belong to Orthodoxy." L. Gudkov and A. Levenson, "Evrei kak fenomen sovetskogo soz-naniia," *Teatr,* no. 7 (1992): 144.

153. See M. Agursky, "Fundamentalist Christian Anti-antisemitism in Modern Russia," *Religion, State and Society,* 20, no. 1 (1992).

154. The Soviet Union imposed a wall of silence on the Holocaust, and even if the fate of the Jews during World War II was mentioned, it was not allowed to attain any unique status, and there was no academic study of the Holocaust. The few exceptions to this include the poem "Babii Yar" by Evgenii Evtushenko, articles by Ilya Erenburg and Vasily Grossman (their *Black Book* was never published); and the novel *Babii Yar* by Victor Kuznetsov.

155. Zoya Krakhmalnikova discounts Christian guilt for the Holocaust and criticizes Lezov's attempts to align antisemitism with controversial statements from the New Testament. She claims that "in spite of Hitler's own claims, there is no

connection whatsoever between Nazism and Christianity." Z. Krakhmalnikova, "Zachem escho raz ubivat Boga? On vsio ravno voskresnet," *Russkaiia ideiia i evrei. Rokovoi spor* (Moscow 1994), 188–89. See also idem, "Russophobia. Antisemitism. Khristianstvo" (in Russian) *Neva,* no. 8 (1990).

156. G. Yakunin, "Otkritoe pis'mo presidentu Yeltsinu," *Russkaiia misl',* 14–20 April 1994.

157. I. Ilovaiskaiia, "Gazeta 'Pravda' protiv Patriarkha Aleksiia," *Russkaiia misl',* 5–10 January 1996.

158. T. Zamiatina, "Sviateishii patriarkh prizivaet otmetit' Pervomai krestnimi khodami...", *Izvestiia,* 29 March 1994.

159. Participants at the congress of Jewish religious communities and organizations, 24 February 1993, declared their intention to apply to Patriarch Alexei to take measures against Ioann for his writings "imbued with pronounced antisemitism." They referred to Ioann's article, "Fight for Russia" published in *Sovetskaiia Rossiia,* 20 February 1993. Metropolitan Ioann's spokesman called the Congress declaration a "malicious violation of racial and national equality and propaganda aimed to foment racial and national animosity." See "Ot press-sluzhbi Mitropolita Ioanna," *Sovetskaiia Rossiia,* 27 February 1993. The Council of the Union of Orthodox Brotherhoods issued a letter to Ponomarev, Procurator of Moscow, in which they castigated the Congress, demanding that proceedings be instituted against the Congress participants under Article 74 of Russia's Criminal Code, "in order to defend the honor and dignity of Ioann, other Orthodox Christians, and patriots of Russia, including Jewish Orthodox believers, whose feelings have been especially insulted," "Sovet Soiuza Pravoslavnikh Bratstv. Bez kresta," *Den',* no. 13 (1993). Gleb Yakunin was also stigmatized as anti-Russian and anti-Christian, and the Paleiia Publishing House (owned by nationalists) has issued a slanderous book about him which insists that he is a Jew and not an Orthodox priest. See A. Gridnev, *Kto takoi Yakunin?* (Moscow 1995). Yakunin was defrocked by the Russian Orthodox Church for involvement in political activity, however he is still acknowledged as a priest by the Kiev Patriarchate and the Russian Orthodox Church Abroad.

CHAPTER 6

Community of Blood:
The Aryan Myth Modernized

The racist trend is less prominent than other trends in Russian nationalism, and indeed, has never been a major aspect of Russian cultural and intellectual history.[1] Even in the period between the two World Wars, the émigré Russian fascist groups in Germany, France, China, and the United States did not subscribe to the Nazi racist doctrines.[2] Today, the popularity of racist ideologies remains quite low. Political analysts estimate that the electorate of the parties that advocate racist doctrines does not exceed 1–1.5 percent. Two main factors explain this lack of appeal. Russia is a very heterogeneous country in terms of its racial composition, and thus, the use of racist rhetoric can compromise even the most well-established political parties. In addition, the historical memory of the Second World War makes citizens of the former Soviet Union hostile to any fascist ideology, so it is no accident that the mainstream groups of Russian nationalists disavow racist concepts and resort to much more sophisticated arguments to back up their xenophobic postures.

Despite this, no student of Russian nationalism can ignore the emergence of new fascist groups that mushroomed in Russia in the aftermath of the collapse of the USSR. A racist component can be found in the arguments of various other trends in Russian nationalism; racism is the most consistent means of advocating anti-Jewish bias. Quite often, racist arguments — strikingly poor in their intellectual appeal — tell us more about the reasons for hatred of the Jews than the civilized discourse of the "enlightened" antisemites. One should not underestimate the political possibilities of racist ideology. Despite the abovementioned natural limitations on the proliferation of fascist discourse, there is a clear tendency for fascist groups to grow at a faster rate than other nationalistic organizations, and more young people are attracted to such groups. Memories of the Second World War are not a vital part of the historical memory of those who grew up in the post-Soviet era. In addition they tend to be less sensitive to the "Eurasian" component that was part of the living world of the former Soviet Union.

Valery Solovei, a political analyst for the Gorbachev Foundation, examined the transformation of Russian fascism "from a marginal phenomenon to that of a full-fledged political subject." Solovei distinguished three periods in the development of fascist parties.

In the 1987–1990 period "fascist ideology was upheld by individuals or by small groups of similarly-minded people. The organizations were quite amorphous. Some members belonged to different groups at once."[3]

The second period (1990–1993) was marked by the organization of political parties, and the establishment of contacts with other branches of political opposition and with powerful officials in the Russian government — both of whom planned to use the fascists for their own political purposes.

From 1994 to the present, Russian fascist groups have become independent political actors pursuing their own political goals. Solovei argues that the 1993 participation of fascists in the fights in front of the White House was the episode which changed their image, creating a "heroic myth" that contributed to their popularity.[4] One group, Alexander Barkashov's Russian National Unity *(Russkoe natsionalnoe edinstvo)*, has demonstrated its willingness to fight what its members believe to be anti-Russian forces, and have shown themselves willing to make sacrifices for their cause. Such a strong commitment to the nationalist cause has attracted the young generation, and has also allowed the Barkashovites to penetrate the workers' movement.[5]

Numerous other racist groups operate throughout the country, including the Russian Party (St. Petersburg, led by Nikolai Bondarik), the National-Socialist Union (Moscow, headed by Victor Yakushev), the National-Republican Party of Russia (St. Petersburg, led by Yurii Beliaev), the National-Revolutionary Action Front (Moscow, led by Ilya Lasorenko), the "Werewolves" (Moscow), the People's National Party (Moscow, led by Alexander Ivanov-Sukharevsky), the Party of Russian Nationalists (Moscow, led by Viktor Fedorov), the People's Socialist Party of Russia (Novosibirsk), the People's Socialist Party (Irkutsk), the National Front (Moscow), the Russian Front (St. Petersburg, led by Alexander Malikov), the Right Radical Party (Moscow, led by Sergei Zharikov), the Russian National Union (Moscow, led by Aleksei Vdovin and Konstantin Kasimovskii), the Union of Venedi (St. Petersburg, led by Victor Bezverkhii), the National-Democratic Party (St. Petersburg), the Russian National Resistance Center (Yekaterinburg).[6] The spokesmen of these groups express their views and propagate their racist ideas in many newspapers and periodicals. Among them we find *Nashe Otechestvo* (St. Petersburg), *Russkoe delo* (St. Petersburg),[7] *Narodnoe delo* (St. Petersburg), *Russkoe soprotivlenie* (St. Petersburg),[8] *Primorskie novosti* (St. Petersburg), *Rech'* (St. Petersburg), *Russkaia pravda* (Moscow), *Natzionalnaiia gazeta* (Moscow), *Russkii poriadok* (Moscow), *Russkie vedomosti* (Moscow), *Era Rossii* (Moscow), *Russkoe voskresenie* (Moscow), *Nash marsh* (Moscow),[9] *Shturmovik,*[10] *Za Rus'* (Novorossiisk), *Russkii vzgliad* (Orenburg), *Nakanune* (Zlatoust), *Kolokol* (Volgograd), *Primorskaiia pravda, Pamyat'* (Novosibirsk), *Rus' baltiiskaiia* (Kaliningrad). Magazine which advocate a racist position include *Ataka, Rusich, Natsiia* and *Volkhv.*[11] Although most of these periodicals do not have a very high circulation, the sheer number of them is impressive.

The diverse fascist groups have different strategy and tactics, patterns of organization, and ideas about the social incarnation of their ideal state. Here, I will emphasize aspects of their ideology with important implications for Jewish matters. The differences encompass the following areas:

(1) the attitude toward the Russian Orthodox Church and Christianity in general. Some racist parties adopt what they believe to be Russian pre-Christian paganism. They believe that pagan cultural values are more authentic than the legacy of "Judaized" Christian culture. They insist there was a primordial unity of Indo-European pre-Christian beliefs, superior to the Semitic monotheistic religions. However, not all of them are pagans, and the term is often used in the polemic of their opponents, especially Orthodox critics.

(2) the type of future Russian state envisaged (mono-ethnic or poly-ethnic), and the status of this state (Russian republic or empire);

(3) the means of political engagement (endorsement of legal or illegal political involvement);

(4) their attitude toward the "fraternal" Western European fascist movements and Nazism. Some Russian fascists (e.g., the Right-Radical Party of Sergei Zharikov) declare the unity of the "White Race" in opposition to all other inferior races — Yellow, Black, and the Jews. Others — like Russian Unity — dissociate themselves from foreign racist organizations and downplay "international" and global ambitions of the movement, emphasizing the central importance of Russian ethnicity.

(5) methods of struggle against "Jewish contagion," ranging from the encouragement of Jewish emigration, "national-proportional representation"[12] in parliament and government service, and disfranchisement, to "deportation of the Zionists," expatriation, terrorism against the alien race, and even the "Final Solution."

In spite of all these differences the racist groups are united by their agreement on the source of Russia's social problems. The core doctrine of racism is a belief in the essential role of racial characteristics in the development of society and the relations between its members. Ideologists of racism advocate and elaborate a particular concept of human community —

defined in terms of blood and racial characteristics. They hold that blood bonds transcend all conventional ties between human beings, and that the interests of race and nationality are far more important than those of the state, ideology, and religion. Cultural, religious, and linguistic allegiances are significant only as manifestations of the particular racial entities and structures.

The ideologists of race can be differentiated from other nationalists by characteristics such as the obsession with Jewish matters, as seen in some of their periodicals. They like to expose the "Jewish" views of their political, cultural, and social opponents and other prominent individuals. Ironically, they frequently blame fellow nationalists and other racist groups (Eurasians, neo-Slavophiles, etc.) for "Judaizing" the country.[13] They are often willing to use the terms "fascism" or "Nazism" as self-denominations, and they make use of Nazi symbols like the swastika and the salute. They are proud to admit their strong commitment to historic fascism, especially with regard to the "Jewish Question." Hitler and other prominent members of the Nazi party are openly admired. They consistently apply their racial anthropology to various ethnic groups of the former Soviet Union, and not only Jews but other minorities are castigated.[14]

The fascist groups are distinguished by the attempt to "aesthetisize" and romanticize their political programs. They believe it necessary to establish an "iron order" to replace the flabbiness of the conventional political parties in the face of national decline and internal subversion. They propose to reinforce social discipline in a way that would halt the current decay in political and economic life. This new Russian order would put an end to the centuries-long "Judeo-liberal yoke." In their national mythology, the "New Russians" are described as a class of warriors who will make possible the "new Russian world order."[15] The next millennium will be the "era of Russia."[16]

I have selected for my analysis several periodicals representative of Russian fascism among those having the largest circulations. The newspapers include *Russkii poriadok* (Russian order), of the Russian National Unity party; *Russkie vedomosti,* edited by Victor Korchagin; *Nashe otechestvo,* edited by Evgenii Schekotikhin; and *Russkoe delo,* edited by Evgenii Krilov, and a few articles published in *Ataka.*

IN SEARCH OF FORGOTTEN ANCESTORS:
HYPERBOREA VERSUS ATLANTIS

Fascist ideologists believe that two "Jewish" ideologies — Christianity and Communism — oppressed and poisoned the original Russian spirituality, which they wish to revive. The conventional history of Russia — that of academic historians — they assert, is preoccupied with Christianity and Communism. Russia's real history has been concealed by misleading historical narratives deliberately fabricated by cunning Jewish historians. The genealogies of Russian ethnicity which the fascists have "rediscovered" go back to the earliest roots of human civilization, while the Jews, they hold, are much more primitive. Many of these newly emerging histories employ a variant of the old Aryan myth.[17]

Members of the Union of Venedi (which publishes the journal *Volkhv* and has its headquarters in St. Petersburg), hold that Russians are descendants of the Venedi (Venethi), the Latin name for the tribe that populated the area to the east of the Vistula River in antiquity.[18] Some other groups trace Russian history back to the Etruscans and Cimmerians.[19] Regardless of the ancestral details, many ideologists suggest that Russians form a superior ethnicity within the Aryans. Alexander Barkashov, for example, claims that "Russians are the purest genetic and cultural descendants of the Etruscan-Rassen-Aryans," since they continuously occupied the original center of all Aryans — South Siberia and the valley between Caspi, Aral, and Azov).[20] Some ideologists support the idea of Russian superiority by citing para-scientific linguistic and historical theories.[21]

Many of the "histories" constructed by the fascist ideologists hinge upon the opposition between the Semitic "Atlantis" and the Aryan "Hyperborea" — two civilizations said to have determined the course of human history. Atlantis is supposedly the motherland of the red race, while Hyperborea is described as the original land of the white race.

Barkashov saw a critical difference between Atlantis and Hyperborea in the organization of labor. The Atlantean economy, he claims, was based on the use of the mass slave labor in agriculture and crafts, while the Aryan civilization did not employ slaves nor tolerate slavery. When Atlantis drowned, part of its population escaped to the Middle East, where they organized "post-Atlantean" civilizations such as those of Sumer and Egypt, with their descendants making up the ruling class. This elite provoked wars against the peoples to the North. Barkashov asserts that Russians are descended from the most courageous of these Nordic people, the Etruscans. In ancient times the Etruscans supposedly halted an Atlantean attack on

Europe and Asia. The appearance of the Jews on the historical scene resulted from the insidious efforts of the Egyptian elite:

> Finally Egypt was defeated by Greeks and Romans. Egyptian priests realized that it was impossible to win in the open fights against Aryan people and decided...to create a new tribe of people which was supposed to destroy and corrupt them from inside and to be a buffer between Egypt and people of the North. The priests carried out an artificial assimilation of the two races, the Hamites (Negroes) and the Semites (Arabs) whom they held as slaves in Southern Egypt. They did it to weaken and to exterminate their genetic peculiarities and their genetic memory. They also designed a special behavior program for the new tribe and instilled into the minds of the members of the new tribe the idea of "election." All these actions took 400 years of the so-called "Egyptian captivity." After that the new tribe led by the Levites, Egyptian priests, and by Moses, invaded Canaan....[22]

Later on, this artificially-created tribe penetrated other Aryan and Semitic civilizations and changed their spiritual foundations. The introduction of the "Asiatic" or Atlantean mode of production, which included slavery, was the most important of these changes. Barkashov claims there exists a functional and genetic continuity between the civilization of Atlantis and the contemporary neo-colonial civilization of North America and Western Europe. By contrast, Russia is said to be the last stronghold of the Aryan spirit; it was Russians who prevented the expansion of the Atlantean civilization ruled by the Jews. The Jews aim to undermine genetic memory and to create a melting pot of different nationalities that would result in a new "grey race" similar to themselves.[23] In this myth, Jews are accomplices in the hands of the Atlanteans, and are described as bio-robots, not full-fledged human beings.[24]

Sergei Zharikov, editor-in-chief of *Ataka,*[25] advocates a more radical version of the bio-robot theory. He denounces ideas about a Jewish conspiracy and Jewish omnipotence, contending that the Jews are contemptible creatures to be feared only by primitive people. Zharikov argues that the Jews cannot be identified with religion, race, or nationality. All the "Jewish" characteristics — language, culture, symbols, genes — are actually borrowed from other ethnicities. The Jews "lack any connection with any ethno-racial archetype" indispensable for any race, and thus have only a chimerical existence. Antisemitism is the only evidence there is for the existence of the Jews. Therefore, Zharikov argues, it is only natural for those who identify themselves with the Jews to promote antisemitic feelings and doctrines.

Denying that Jews have any "vital connection with the archetype," Zharikov says that they bring with themselves the "virus of robotization," and he identifies them with bio-robots and golems.[26] Despite his dismissal of the Jews, Zharikov still maintain that they have infected the Soviet Union and the United States — the two most important countries of the twentieth century — with robotization. The new Russian order (Golden Age), he believes, will eventually displace the Jewish civilization of the Iron Age.[27]

The racial ideologists' "historical" narratives are specifically designed to dehumanize the enemy. For both Barkashov and Zharikov membership in a race is a virtue of itself; to accept Jews as a race would be to grant them human status. The conflict between Russians and Jews is not the conflict of two races in which the strongest will win, but rather a conflict of machines — bio-robots — against human beings. Thus, no "moral" standards apply, for the Jews are inferior in a more fundamental sense than any other inferior races. The only difference between Barkashov and Zharikov is that the first demonizes the Jews, while the second belittles them; for both, dehumanization of the Jews is the critical factor.

Ironically, the idealized "person" for these racists is very similar to their "bio-robot." Both believe that racial characteristics are immanent in the actions of individuals.

BIOPOLITICS OF RACE:
JEWISH INTRIGUES AGAINST THE RUSSIAN GENETIC POOL

The racist press focuses on the practical implications of their theories of Jewish inferiority, and thus one finds articles on eugenics, race selection, mongrelization, and the differences between degraded and healthy ethnicities. One finds almost nothing original in their writings, which merely repeat classic Nazi propaganda.

The fascist theorists suggest various "scientific" political policies to foster an increase in the ethnic Russian birth rate, initiate a reform of physical and moral education, and isolate alien ethnicities. They have a particular interest in medical and biological "discoveries" on which they base their policy recommendations.

For example, they claim that a racial element exists in medical and psychological defects — the Jews being especially prone to various sexual and genetic disorders, including AIDS, Tay-Sachs, dysautonomia, Bloom syndrome, and dystonia, all of which point to a degeneration of the Jewish race.[28] Some claim the Jews are essentially defective to begin with, while others ascribe it to a tradition of inbreeding in Jewish families.

Some publications deal primarily with psychological disorders and mental defects among the Jews. Many articles refer to data collected by Cesare Lombroso, the Jewish-Italian psychiatrist and founding father of modern criminology, published in his well-known book, *The Man of Genius.*[29] In the book's fifth chapter, Lombroso connects madness, race, and heredity, claiming that the Jews are more susceptible to madness than any other ethnic group. He supports this thesis with data on the ratio of insane and normal people among Catholics, Protestants, and Jews in different regions.

However, the fascists suggest that Lombroso's data points to the innate intellectual superiority of Aryans over the Semitic race. V. Barabash, for example, argues:

> The myth about the genius of the Jewish people aims to conceal the symptoms of their degeneration, on the one hand, and to pave the way for their domination over the world, on the other. The Jewish professor Lombroso is not alone. Many scholars [of Jewish descent — V.R.] concur in the view of the degenerate nature of their people.[30]

Lombroso, however, did not explain the Jewish proclivity for madness (especially neurasthenia) by reference to any biological defect. Rather, he believed that it was a "residual effect of persecution."[31] Lombroso did not consider madness a sign of intellectual deficiency; he believed that it contributed to creativity. Today, many scholars treat nineteenth-century medical research — including that of Lombroso — with caution. Sander Gilman, an expert on racist discourse of fin-de-siècle Europe, offers another perspective:

> The statistics, used over and over by mental-health practitioners during this period, probably reflect the higher incidence of hospitalization of Jews for mental illness due to their concentration in urban areas, which, unlike rural ones, are not so tolerant of the presence of the mentally ill in society. Also, urban Jews have developed a better network for the identification and treatment of illness, including mental illness. The overt social pressures that were mounting against the Jews, which were often repressed by acculturated Jews anxious about their status in European society, may well have increased the amount of psychic pain these individuals had to bear. It is also quite possible that some Jews in Western European urban areas, especially those who were displaced from Eastern Europe and forced to flee westward, evidenced the traumatic results of their flight.[32]

The fascist ideologists ignore the problematic nature of the statistics and insist that special social policies be implemented to protect the "healthy" ethnicities:

"The state that ignores the data of psychiatry [i.e., Lombroso's data — V.R.] will experience a rise in the crime rate, moral corruption, a rise in the number of sexually perverse people, a fall in the level of culture and economics and the generation of the population.[33]

The fascist newspapers present Nazi social policies as an appropriate model for Russia, including sterilization of the mentally defective, isolation of sexual minorities, and extermination of "racially alien elements."[34]

The danger of the degenerative "Jewish virus" explains the interest in serology. The newspaper *Rech'*, put out by Victor Bezverkhii's Russian Party of St. Petersburg, publishes a *Methodology of Distinguishing Races by Blood*.[35] Bezverkhii, the "father of the Venedi," displays test tubes of various blood types at his headquarters. Various fascist newspapers publish advertisements for *Blood in the Beliefs and Superstitions of Mankind*, a book on ritual murder and other exciting bloody rituals.

In racist discourse, blood stands for a people's identity. The purity of blood has an almost religious meaning, since it allows people to connect with their primordial roots. Ultimately, blood is identical with race, since it is a sacred substance that reveals the secret vitality of a race. "The voice of blood is not just a nice figure of speech," asserts Roman Perin of *Za russkoe delo*.[36] "Blood is everything," Ivanov-Sukharevsky of the People's National Party and the ideologist of "Rusism," echoes. Bonds of blood are much stronger than any other human bonds:

Blood contains the qualities which constitute the Spirit. It is also a soul.... The purer the blood, the gentler the man.... The power of the golden calf will be destroyed by the pure Blood.... Human blood is more valuable than the abstract schemes of inhumane humanism.... Miscegenation is obnoxious, because it is an attempt to destroy God.... Blood unites, while faith separates.[37]

Many pages of the fascist periodicals are occupied with discussing the biochemical structure of the blood and internal organs of different races and ethnicities, since these supposedly determine psychological and emotional characteristics, among other things.

Much emphasis is placed on the dangers of miscegenation, that would weaken the genetic pool of the Russians. The author of "Your Blood Type" in *Za russkoe delo* claims that the "best" type — group 1 — is more resistant to viruses and is typical of Russians. Some publications suggest that promoting mixed marriages is a deliberate policy of the Jews, who "try to marry and procreate with the bearers of the best blood group.... In the course of universal miscegenation the best blood group will be lost for civilization."[38] In a similar vein, Roman Perin claims that

> Nature made clear boundaries between races for their well-being to prevent the miscegenation. Racial miscegenation produces bastards with biological defects and sick psyches, and that poses a question of self-identification.[39]

In the article, "How Is Sex Used in Politics?," Doctor Barabash alleges that although Jewish law disapproves of marriages with non-Jewish women, the *seduction* of gentile women by the Jewish male is perfectly compatible with Jewish law and even directly prescribed. Barabash identifies sexual relations between a Jew and a non-Jewish woman as "genetic murder." He warns:

> Even a one-night stand with the representative of a "Little People" (even if this affair took place several years before the pregnancy) can lead to the birth of a baby with the features of degeneration. One night is enough to give a baby a bad genetic heritage.[40]

Russian fascists recommend that eugenics should become an indispensable constituent of the government's domestic policy, with special legislation and educational programs to safeguard the "Russian genetic code."

ARYAN SCIENCE AND SEMITIC SCIENCE

The racial ideologists treat intellectual and spiritual spheres as branches of racial biology, and thus, articles in fascist periodicals contrast ingenious Russian scholars with "degenerate" Jewish scholars. Seeing the racial element as crucial in assessing the cultural achievements of various peoples, their approach is reminiscent of Nazi propaganda that distinguished "Aryan" science from "Jewish" science.

Albert Einstein is one of the favorite targets of the antisemites. It is claimed that his theories were previously known to Aryan scholars, whose minds were of a higher caliber than Einstein's Semitic mind. Other champions of Aryan science claim that the theory of relativity is nonsense, of a kind that could be only produced by the "flattened mind" of a Jew. The theory's worldwide fame merely results from the biased coverage by the mass media, controlled by the Jews; the "Einstein phenomenon" is merely a creation of Jewish journalists.[41]

Race counts, not only in science, but also in fields like chess and music. An article in *Nash marsh* glorified the ingenious insights of Russian chess grandmaster and world champion, Alexander Alekhin (1892–1946), who "wrote a wonderful essay on Jewishness in chess-playing in which he proved the superiority of the Aryan mind, and supported the National-Socialist Party of Germany."[42] Alekhin contrasted the Jewish "positional" and Aryan "combinatorial" styles.[43]

Wagner's essay, "Judaism in music" is not forgotten. Rock music is said to have originated within the inferior Jewish music decried by Wagner. Sergei Zharikov contends, under the heading of *Den' Rock Music: Russian Resistance:*

> By today the development of rock music in Russia and in the world has assumed an Atlanticist character. But gradually this music is transformed by the cultures in which it is practiced. A typical example of the Atlanticist model is the blues.... It is the music of slaves.... Russian rock, on the other hand, acquires a mystic and sacred character.... In contrast, Jewish rock is a profanation. It is only a device for making money and for demoralization and the inculcation of Negroism.... It is not an accident that, on ancient Egyptian frescoes, Jews were always depicted as Niggers. Jewish culture is a culture of African origin. It is a culture of omphalos and ass....[44]

Jews and the Blacks share the same kind of music, unnerving and unclear in its tone. Russian rock has a clear march tone that inspires action and induces the influx of energy.[45]

CHRISTIAN, ALL TOO CHRISTIAN:
JEWISH CHRISTIANITY VERSUS RUSSIAN PAGANISM

Religions, too, are viewed as manifestations of the racial essence. The fascist ideologists are especially preoccupied with the history and origins of Christianity, and one finds two quite different contemporary attitudes toward Christianity. One group does not see Christianity as having a unified and homogeneous doctrine, and they draw a line between the Judeo-Christianity of the West and the Orthodox Christianity of Russia. Orthodoxy is said to be the true Aryan religion, in contrast to other Christian confessions. Champions of this view allege that Jesus Christ was Aryan, not Jewish,[46] and that true Christianity was later Judaized, distorting its original Aryan message. Christian symbols and rituals are described as remnants of ancient "Aryan knowledge" (occasionally called "Vedantic knowledge"). This view is typical of Russian Unity, whose members make use of Orthodox symbols and take part in some important celebrations of the Orthodox Church. While denouncing historical Christianity, they associate Orthodoxy with elements of old "Aryan" beliefs which supposedly supplanted the venomous spirit of Judaism.

The second attitude to Christianity is typical of the more radical fascist groups, who view religions as forces for group unity that may compete with racial identity for human allegiance. All religions have some racial entity as its source. Christianity is perceived as even more dangerous than Judaism; the acceptance of Christianity was the gravest and most tragic mistake in all Russian history. Although all fascists, in varying degrees, acknowledge Jewish features within Christianity, they see the connection between the Jews and Christianity primarily in two different ways.

According to the "Trojan horse" view, Christianity is a secret tool framed by the Jews to indoctrinate gentiles and to achieve world conquest. Christian morality weakens its followers by inculcating principles alien to all healthy ethnicities, and it undermines their authentic instincts and vitality. Christianity is characterized as a "grand ideological diversion" and "export version of Judaism."[47] Through Christianity, the Jews hoped to avenge themselves against their Roman conquerors and Gentiles generally, yet they themselves sacrificed Jesus, the very means of this revenge. The Trojan horse idea clearly derives from Nietzsche.

The second interpretation — the "climax" argument — suggests that Christianity represents the climax of Jewish development. Moreover, Christianity supposedly preserves the most "authentic" Jewish message and the "true" spirit of Judaism that was lost to the Jews themselves. Christianity is said to reveal the very mystery of the corrupt Jewish soul concealed in Judaism, and reveals the lack of vitality, weakness and degradation of the Jewish race. All the old Nietzschean anti-Christian arguments are rediscovered and applied to the Jews, who are said to be the most passionate proponents of Christianity. Christian morality is a further development of Judaic principles.

Sergei Zharikov's arguments perfectly illustrate the point. The Jews, he says, are, by their very nature and by their own free choice, victims. Zharikov undertakes to prove this via etymology. In Sanskrit, the word "Yahwe," he contends, means the "sovereign of the victim," and the "victim" should be identified with Israel, that is, the Jews. Jesus Christ is the best symbol of the victim. "The true god of the Jews is Jesus Christ, the resurrected victim."[48] By contrast, the Aryan spirit is the spirit of the hero. The Aryan himself is divine. Zharikov contends that the proposals by German Nazi thinkers like Chamberlain and Rosenberg to "Aryanize" Christianity are futile. Like others before him, he identifies the Jews with a feminine, submissive element: "Jewry is the feminine pole of the universe" and the symbol of degradation of the male system. The Jews are so miserable that they don't even deserve hatred. Nevertheless, they are a necessary element in the cosmogonic process in which they perform their feminine destructive mission.[49]

Some Russian fascists consider Jews for Jesus (a San Francisco-based organization that encourages Jews to convert to Christianity) to be the most authentic expression of the Jewish mentality.[50] Members of this organization, they believe, preserve the slavishness, envy and resentment, and lack of noble and aristocratic virtues that are essential to the Jewish character.

Differences between the Trojan horse and climax arguments are important but should not be exaggerated. Both lines of thought suggest that the overall influence of Christianity on Russian history has been negative, and the Jews are blamed for this. Whatever the founders of Christianity may have intended, the Jews have succeeded in indoctrinating humankind with ideas favorable to themselves. In both arguments, the Jews corrupt others by promoting a morality detrimental to the vitality and the virility of those people. Ultimately, it matters little whether the Jews are perceived as imposing their own corrupt morality on others or merely use Christianity as a destructive tool. The Trojan horse line of argument is more popular, persistent, and consistent with other conceptual ingredients and the general appeal of the mainstream fascist ideology. The climactic argument is quite marginal, since the weak and impotent Christian Jew can be dismissed as an enemy who poses no threat to the heroic "blond beasts." Champions of the Trojan horse view take the Jews much more seriously. The book *Christianity* by Anatolii Ivanov articulates quite well many points made in other publications on the topic.

The discourse about Christianity can be better understood in the context of the Orthodox restoration. By exposing the "Jewishness" of Christianity, the fascists attempt to warn Orthodox believers — especially Orthodox nationalists — against adapting Jewish tenets embedded in the Christianity's structure and thought, for with it, they assert, Jewishness is being disseminated from the very heart of what is supposed to be Russian spirituality. A "Jewish message" is conveyed by the very authorities of the Russian Orthodox Church, and thus, the Orthodox restoration, is only a disguised Judaization of Russia.

To prove this, Russian fascists examine the genealogy of Christianity. The most common accusations against Christianity include:

(1) The historical background of Christianity presupposes a commitment to overt Judeo-centrism. Since Christians believe in the sacred nature of the Bible, they must also acknowledge the concept of the "Chosen People." Even

with qualifications and interpretations of this idea, it remains indispensable for the true Christian.

Christians are obliged to acknowledge the God of the Old Testament as their own. However, this God is not universal, but merely a tribal "God of Abraham, Isaac, and Jacob." This God privileges the Jewish people over all others. Even if Christians assume that they inherited the status of "chosen," they must still believe in the original mission of the Jewish people, opposed to all other peoples. Ironically, Christians even refer to other people as pagans, the [incorrect] translation given of the Hebrew word "goyim" (gentiles). By so doing they imitate the Jews and identify themselves with the Jews:

> The term paganism is a Slavic calque of the Jewish curse "gentile" (goi).... The Jews call others "goyim," and Russian Christians sitting on the footboard of the Jewish carriage, cast the same word, with disgust and with the servile pride on the "mediocrities" who do not understand what makes Christians so happy about wearing Jewish livery.[51]

Jesus made no secret of his real mission when he said that he "was sent unto the lost sheep of the house of Israel" (Matt. 15:24) and when he claimed that he came not to destroy but to fulfill the law (Matt. 5:17). Therefore, Jesus himself was a "Judeophile," "Zionist," and "Jewish racist."[52]

The fact that Jesus proclaimed himself "son of God" also proves his loyalty to Judaism, since all Jews are "sons of God" (John 8:41). Russian partisans of paganism emphasize the Jewishness of Jesus, the Holy Family, and the disciples. Therefore it is not surprising that Jewish names, symbols, and stories — alien to everything Russian — are deeply ingrained in the thinking of the Orthodox Church and its rituals. Ivanov contends that Jesus' opposition to Judaism is not demonstrated by the fact that the Jews crucified him. Ivanov draws an analogy between the crucifixion of Jesus and the prosecution and murder of Leon Trotsky:

> Communists also rejected and killed Trotsky but it does not mean that Trotskyism is significantly different from communism. It also does not mean that Trotskyism provides a positive alternative to communism.[53]

The crucifixion of Jesus by the Jews was merely part of their original plan of revenge. The crucifixion enabled them to dissociate Jesus from everything Jewish and thereby allowed them smuggle elements of Jewish spirituality into the new "international teaching" as if it was ethnically neutral. Ivanov contends that the crucifixion can be explained as a ritual murder of the tribal chief for the sake of the tribe as a whole.[54]

(2) In spite of its Jewish spirit, Christianity at the same time pretends to be cosmopolitan. This Christian cosmopolitanism undermines the original belief systems of other ethnicities. The process of Christianization therefore represents a Jewish subversion of the unique foundations of particular cultures. Christianity deprives these ethnicities of their natural self-protective mechanisms. Nikolai Bogdanov sardonically warns the Russian Christians:

> In the 20th century Russian Christians already held up enough cheeks to the Jews to humiliate and to render lifeless their native land and the Russian people.... Maybe it would be better if they directly held up their ass to the kick, and their head to the ax?[55]

(3) Christianity's intolerance can be traced to its Jewish origins. Manifestations of Jewish intolerance include the very concept of being the Chosen People, the prohibition of mixed marriages, the idea of sacred religious war, double standards in morality, dogmatism. Jewish monotheism was purely political, since it is can be used to justify a totalitarian state. Jewish intolerance has had a pernicious, lasting affect on the Christian church up to the present, for all these ingredients can be found in Christianity. Jewish-Christian intolerance is contrasted with the tolerant attitudes of the Aryan Indians and Iranians, who were infinitely generous, liberal, and broad-minded.

(4) The linear concept of time is ascribed to Judeo-Christians. Avdeev calls this concept of time "hopeless" and "desperate," and "eschatological nonsense," since it deprives people of present happiness for the sake of an envisioned future happiness.[56] Pagan religions, by contrast, are optimistic and life-asserting.[57]

> The old Slavonic pagan festivals (they are almost identical with the holidays of all other Aryan people) reproduced the natural cycle of life of the Russian people. Christian holidays from the beginning were alien to the temporal structure of the Russian agricultural cycle. The most ridiculous Russian Christian holiday is the New Year, since it is not clear why Russians should "celebrate the circumcision of one Jewish male."[58]

(6) Communist ideology is only a transformation and modification of the old Judeo-Christian ideals. The Christian spiritual legacy, in fact, prepared Europeans to accept communism, and should be held responsible for the devastating effects of communist rule in Russia and elsewhere. Both Christianity and Communism are messianic; the Judeo-Christian linear

concept of time is a prerequisite for the Marxist theory of history. The Judeo-Christian legacy of ideological intolerance was well preserved in the theory and practice of communist regimes, as seen in the suppression of dissent. This tradition was common both in the communist parties and in the Orthodox patriarchy.[59] The communists received the baton of violence from the Christians. Moreover, the number of victims of the "spiritual epidemic" of Christianity is much higher than that of the communist regime. Therefore, acceptance of Christianity is the key to understanding Russia's historical misfortunes, the price paid for betrayal of the Aryan gods, who are now taking vengeance for Russia's infidelity.

Returning to the worship of nature and the old Slavic gods is not the only alternative to Christianity. Some fascists claim that any religion restricts on the development of Russian ethnicity and the Aryan race in general. Sergei Zharikov, on the other hand, claims that religion should be immanent to the very being of a given ethnicity. Russian fascists take up Oswald Spengler's idea that a specific cultural entity should produce its own religious language and emancipate itself from foreign forms of religion used to suppress authentic spirituality. Christianity — Jewish in origin — has imprisoned and constrained the authentic magma-like substance of the Russian race.

> Russians never called themselves pagans. They called themselves Russians.... My faith is immanent in me and my religion consists of a sacred communion with my archetype. The religion of the race is the race.... Nazism is a religion without rivals because it is immanent to the nation and the state.[60]

Thus, authentic religion is a projection of the condition of the Russian race rather than an independently valuable true system of beliefs. The divine is identified with the very being of the nation.

JEWS AT THE ROOT OF SOCIAL PROBLEMS

Virtually any manifestation of political or social crisis is linked to the Jews — the collapse of the empire, the nuclear facility explosion in Chernobyl, ethnic conflicts, the demographic crisis, alcoholism, and the pauperization of the population. The racists, however, pay a price for the simplistic accusation that the Jews are responsible for every disaster. Their explanations sound ridiculous to anybody who is not a partisan of this ideology. A few examples follow.

Alcoholism is a vexing social issue in Russia, and Jews have been accused of using alcohol as a weapon in their struggle against the Russian ethnicity. Surprisingly, this element of the Jewish conspiracy idea has even found some support among members of the medical establishment. Feodor Uglov of the Academy of Medical Sciences of Russia has written prolifically about the Russian drinking problem, and his lobbying for a prohibition law is highly regarded by many people. In his book, *The Prisoners of Illusions,* Uglov blames the Jews for the spread of alcoholism in Russia, claiming that alcoholism was not a serious problem before the nineteenth century. Jewish tavern keepers *(shinkari)* entered the liquor trade in order to corrupt the strong traditional Russian character.[61]

Backed with Uglov's authority as a member of the Academy of Sciences, the fascist press goes on to make further accusations against the Jews. One writer complains that the Jews sold vodka to the peasants in exchange for their personal possessions and a promise to pay from their future harvest: "The Shtetl tavern — and shop-keepers deliberately seduced the people among whom they lived to drink, the people who were strangers to them."[62] He finds a continuity between the policy of the "alcoholization of Russia" promoted by the tavern-keepers, and the policy of the political leaders of perestroika, whom he refers to as the "grandsons of the Shtetl tavern-keepers." Today they import into Russia a huge amount of Western alcoholic beverages. In a similar vein, Professor Boris Vladimirov blames Leon Trotsky, "the Zionist who is known to the whole world," for the abolition of prohibition. In the period of perestroika, he argues, "alcoholism has contributed to the numerical decline of the population" and helped to "simplify the rule over people who ruin themselves by drinking."[63]

Perhaps, nothing in recent history is more painful and serious in the magnitude of its ramifications than the tragedy of Chernobyl. The fascists speculate that the explosion in the nuclear facility was no accident, but a "diversion" planned by the Jews. Jewish scientists, they argue, invented the type of atomic reactor built at Chernobyl, expecting the catastrophe to be "the first stage in the destruction of the Slavic people." The reactor's safety devices failed because Jews working in the plant switched them off. The Jewish organizers of the crime supposedly informed their brethren about the coming accident through specially-encoded messages, such as the picture of a rectangle containing circles that was published in the local Novosibirsk newspaper.[64] "Two days before the tragedy the most prominent families of the 'Little People' started to leave Kiev and other cities of Ukraine and Belorussia.... The Slavs had no idea about the disaster, enjoying the May holidays."[65]

Denial of the Holocaust is another common preoccupation. Two explanations for the Holocaust appear in their writings. The first asserts that the Holocaust was organized by the Jewish establishment in order to get rid of the "dry branches" of the Jewish race,[66] while the second suggests that the Holocaust was invented by efforts of Jewish scholars and journalists to soften the hearts of the gentiles in the face of Jewish tragedy and to instill a guilt complex in the European nations.[67] The Jews "invented" the Holocaust as an additional weapon in their war against Aryans. Valentin Prussakov, a prominent Russian fascist, argues: "The journalists of the West keep writing of the 'terrible experiments of Doctor Mengele'; nobody dares to say that Leiba Trotsky conducted very similar experiments on a much larger scale. He is even admired by the most 'progressive' circles in Europe."[68] Prussakov's argument is an example of a common tactic used by deniers which involves making unwarranted comparisons that deflect from the Jewish tragedy or minimize it.

Russian fascists opened discussion on the "myth of the Holocaust" in connection with the screening of Steven Spielberg's film, *Schindler's List*. In his review, Alexander Aratov, editor-in-chief of *Russkaiia pravda,* argues that the counter-Holocaust of the Slavic people in the period of economic reforms numbered more victims than the "mythical" Jewish Holocaust:

> It is a blasphemy to talk about the six million victims of the Holocaust when in reality the Europeans murdered only three hundred thousand of the "chosen people." It is especially strange to discuss this issue when in a relatively peaceful time more than one million Slavs died because of the genocide organized by the same parasitic tribe. This ethnicity is not dying now, in contrast to ethnic Russians.[69]

The irrational, paranoid thinking evident in these excerpts shows that the racist discourse will not appeal to other trends of Russian nationalism and does not really fit into a discussion of intellectual antisemitism. It only preserves popular all-encompassing stereotypes of the Jew found in grass-roots antisemitism.

In closing, I would like to touch upon one issue which might be puzzling for readers unfamiliar with legal practices in post-Soviet Russia. One might imagine that the racist periodicals could scarcely proliferate when the Federal Criminal Code makes it a crime to provoke ethnic conflict and incitement to racial or ethnic hatred. A number of organizations and individuals have sued the fascist periodicals and their editors more than once, yet taking legal action has had only limited success.[70] Many factors are at play in such cases: the lack of conventional legal definitions for the most basic concepts of Article 74 of the Criminal Code,[71] along with a lack of experience in applying the Article; the climate of tolerance for antisemitism, which the public and prosecutors do not consider very serious, especially in the face of a general massive crime wave. The Moscow Anti-fascist Center prepared a special collection of documents, *The Prosecution and the Problem of National Dissension,* which contains a number of items that confirm that prosecutors tend to downplay the danger of fascism, and are reluctant to take seriously charges made against political extremists.[72] However, the main reason for unsuccessful court cases against extremists seems to be the public's high degree of acceptance of many stereotypes propagated by the most radical antisemites, and the lack of any institutional opposition to antisemitism. The climate of tolerance for racist antisemitism indicates that civil society in post-communist Russia has not yet advanced significantly.

CONCLUSION

The doctrines of the racists combine a modernized Aryan myth with biological pseudo-science. World history is portrayed as a struggle between the Aryan and Semitic races, and the period of reform in Russia merely represents a new stage in this ancient and eternal struggle. The fascist periodicals promote a social agenda in accord with the racist grand narrative that governs their vision of society, politics, and history.

Racist ideology appeals to a younger generation of Russian nationalists because it provides simplistic answers to historical and social questions and offers an attractive national myth in contrast to the pitiful social and economic realities of post-communist Russia. It consoles the people by suggesting that in some other dimension and from some other standpoint they are superior to those who appear to be so successful, and who have lost their identity in the course of social reconstruction. Racism also appeals to people due to the comprehensive nature of its explanations of the reality. It becomes not only "science" and history, but in many cases a new religion.

NOTES

1. Some scholars of nationalism have tried to draw a sharp line between nationalism and racism. Benedict Anderson, for example, suggests that the two phenomena have little in common. He traces the genealogy of racist ideology back to that of class struggle: "The dreams of racism actually have their origin in ideologies of class rather than in those of nation: above all in claims to divinity among rulers and to 'blue' and 'white' blood and 'breeding' among aristocracies." See B. Anderson, *Imagined Communities* (New York 1994), 136. I believe this distinction is overstated, and that historically speaking, George Mosse's position seems more plausible. Mosse claimed that although "racism was never an indispensable element of nationalism," "racism and nationalism seem to belong together... Racism gave new dimensions to the idea of rootedness...providing clear and unambiguous distinctions between them

[nations — V.R.]." G. Mosse, "Racism and Nationalism," in *Nations and Nationalism,* vol. 1, no. 2 (1995): 163.

2. See J. Stephan, *The Russian Fascists: Tragedy and Farce in Exile 1925–1945* (New York, San Francisco, and London 1978).

3. V. Solovei, "Rossiia ne obrechena na fashism, no uzhe ne zastrakhovana ot nego," *Nezavisimaiia gazeta,* 29 March 1995.

4. Ibid.

5. In 1994 they established very close political ties with the Confederation of Free Trade Unions of Russia led by Alexander Alekseev, Chairman of the Confederation, and the Chairman of the Russian National-Socialist Workers' Party. See G. Kovalskaiia, "Natsionalnaiia ideia vkhodit v modu," *Ogoniok,* no. 14 (1995).

6. For more details about the structure of Russian fascist organizations see L. Dadiani, "Nazis and Their 'Fellow-Travellers'," *New Times,* (September 1994): 26–29.

7. The new name of the newspaper is *Za russkoe delo.*

8. It is the official publication of the National-Republican Party.

9. *Nash marsh* and *Russkoe voskresenie* have ceased publication.

10. It is the mouthpiece of Russian National Union.

11. *Ataka* is an organ of the Right Radical Party; *Volkhv* is from Victor Bezverkhii's Party of Venedi. *Rusich* purports to synthesize Orthodoxy and racism.

12. Many nationalist groups advocate "national-proportional representation." The fascists often quote Mikhail Gorbachev on the prominence of Jews in Russian politics and culture. In an interview, he claimed that "the Jewish people comprising only 0.69 percent of the total population is represented by no less than 10–20 percent in the political and cultural life of the country." Smirnov-Ostashvili, the first and probably the only person who received a prison term for incitement of ethnic hatred and violation of Article 74 of the Criminal Code, was chairman of the Union for National Proportional Representation.

13. See, for instance, the curious critique of the "Judaized" Russian nationalist establishment written by V. Shumsky, *Trupnie piatna ozhidovleniia* (Moscow 1994).

14. One group of Russian racists, led by Nikolai Lisenko, "flatters" the Jews by including them in the fraternity of the white races. Lisenko is the former Chairman of the National Republican Party. Lisenko claims that the white race, particularly the Russian ethnicity are endangered by the rise of the Third world Negroid and Mongoloid races. Muslims and the people of the Caucasus are far more dangerous than the Jews, since they occupy Russian markets and organize networks of ethnic Mafia on Russian territory. The Jews, as part of the white race, and a "complementary" ethnicity, could become Russia's allies both in economics and trade and in military operations against the Muslim South. Lisenko sees a danger only with the assimilated Jews who propagate universal values. Traditional Jews — especially Jewish nationalists — are natural allies in resisting the expansionist Muslim, Arab,

and Turkish worlds. Lisenko criticizes the tendency to stigmatize Israel as the "concentration of world evil," claiming that Israel is a victim of Third World aggression. Israel tries to preserve traditional values and opposes the assimilationalist tendencies of the United States, just as Russia does. N. Lisenko, "Otkrovennii razgovor o druziakh, vragakh i korennikh interesakh russkoi natsii," *Nash sovremennik*, no. 7 (1993): 158. Lisenko's position is probably unique. Almost all Russian fascists consider the Jews an inferior race and the paradigmatic enemy in the racial war, so it is not surprising that Lisenko was replaced as chairman of the National Republican Party by Yurii Beliaev.

15. A. Lobkov, "Mif tretego tisiacheletiia," *Natsionalnaiia gazeta*, no. 1 (1995).

16. A. Ivanov-Sukharevskii, "Moiia vera — rusism," *Era Rossii*, no. 24 (1997).

17. See Leon Poliakov, *The Aryan Myth: A History of Racist and Nationalist Ideas in Europe* (New York 1977).

18. In the first century A.D., the name Venedi was extended to the Slavic people (who never described themselves by this name). Johannes Irmscher and Renate Johne, eds., *Lexikon Der Antike* (Leipzig 1987).

19. Cimmerians were first described in Homer's *Odyssey* as dwelling beyond the ocean-stream, in thickest gloom, unvisited by Helios. "The sum of our certain knowledge respecting this people is that they seem to have been the chief occupants of the Tauric Chersonesus (the Crimea), where they had a large city." "Cimmerians," *Encyclopedia Americana* (Danbury, Conn., 1985), 6:678.

20. A. Barkashov, "Usnaiuschii proshloe — vidit buduschee," *Russkii poriadok*, 20 March 1993.

21. See, e.g., the insistence on the primacy of Russian civilization over Greek, Sumer, and others. Oreshkin and Grinevich in their pseudo-scientific books try to demonstrate the historical primacy of the so-called "para-Slavonic scripture" and alphabet, etc. See S. Grinevich, *Praslavianskaiia pismennost. Resultati deshifrovki* (Moscow 1993).

22. A. Barkashov, "Rasoblachonnaia doktrina," *Russkii poriadok*, 20 August 1993.

23. Ibid.

24. Barkashov seems to be recounting in his own interpretation the story which was constructed by the notorious antisemite Valery Emelyanov. See V. Emelyanov, *Desionizatsiia* (Moscow 1995), 30–36.

25. Formerly, this was a newspaper, *K toporu* (To the axe), also edited by Zharikov, who would have been named Minister of Culture if a Zhirinovsky government had come to power.

26. In medieval Jewish folklore, the golem is an artificially-created human being endowed with life by supernatural means. For many Russian right-wing intellectuals, the figure of the golem indicates that the Jews are obsessed with robotization and opposed to everything natural.

27. S. Zharikov, "Lenin — eto Stalin segodnia. Informatsionnii musor kak orudie natsionalnoi kontrrevolutsii," *Ataka,* no. 7 (1995): 27, 29.

28. "Virodki. Bolezni virozhdeniia u zhidov," *Russkoe voskresenie,* no. 8 (1992). The article makes reference to an American Georgian racist newspaper, *The Truth at Last,* and to Richard Goodman's book, *Genetic Disorders Among the Jewish People.*

29. Cesare Lombroso, *The Man of Genius* (London 1891).

30. V. Barabash, "Kak v politike ispolzuetsia seks," *Primorskie novosti,* no. 8 (1992).

31. In the context of fin-de-siècle science and against this background, Lombroso's ideas on the implications of the psychopathology of the Jews sound actually anti-antisemitic. In his book *Anti-Semitism and the Jews in the Light of Modern Science* (1893) Lombroso sharply criticized biologically-based forms of antisemitism. Remarkably, he did not believe that the Jews comprise a single race. However, some of his arguments, especially his attacks on the singularity of the Jews and their cultural practices, lend themselves to antisemitic interpretation. See N. Harrowitz, "Lombroso and the Logic of Intolerance," in *Tainted Greatness. Antisemitism and Cultural Heroes* (New York 1994). The idea of a Jewish proclivity for madness was quite common in the medical science of the latter nineteenth century. Jean-Martin Charcot, one of Freud's teachers, held that Jews were prone to such illness due to an inbred weakness of their nervous system, while Krafft-Ebing attributed this loss of nerve to inbreeding. Krafft-Ebing also believed that these Jewish diseases could explain religious fanaticism and an intensified sensuousness. Both Charcot and Krafft-Ebing, however, referred only to a tendency rather than an absolute and immutable characteristic of the Jewish race. See G. Mosse, *Nationalism and Sexuality. Respectability and Abnormal Sexuality in Modern Europe* (New York 1985), 142–43. The important differences between the various doctors lies in the explanation of the etiology of the mental diseases. Whereas some saw the source of Jewish degeneration in specific racial features, others attributed them to the practice of intermarriage, the specific intellectual occupations of the Jews, and the transition from the closed world of the ghetto to the competitive world of modern urban society. See S. Gilman, *Freud, Race, and Gender* (Princeton, N.J. 1993), 93–31.

32. S. Gilman, *Freud, Race and Gender,* 93–94.

33. "Otveti na pisma chitatelei," *Russkii poriadok,* no. 9–1 (1993–1994).

34. B. R., "Evgenicheskie meropriiatiia — norma zhisni zdorovogo obschestva," *Narodnoe delo,* no. 2 (1992).

35. E. Maneilov, "Metodika razlicheniia ras po krovi," *Rech',* no. 1 (1993). The article focuses on the difference between Russian and Jewish blood.

36. R. Perin, "Rasism neizbezhen," *Za russkoe delo,* no. 7 (1995).

37. A. Ivanov-Sukharevsky, "Moiia vera rusism," *Era Rossii,* no. 1 (1997).

38. "Vasha gruppa krovi," *Za russkoe delo,* no. 7 (1995).

39. R. Perin, "Rasism neizbezhen," *Za russkoe delo,* no. 7 (1995).

40. V. Barabash, "Kak v politike ispolzuetsia seks."

41. L. Moiseev, "Pripliusnutii mir (Navstrechu 115-letiia so dnia rozhdeniia Alberta Einsteina)," *Ataka,* no. 33 (1995). Yurii Brovko discusses the "real" physicists associated with the great discoveries of Einstein in physics. Y. Brovko, "Einsteinianstvo — agenturnaiia set' mirovogo kapitala," *Molodaiia gvardiia,* no. 8 (1995).

42. "Natsionalnie dati," *Nash marsh,* no. 2 (1992).

43. A. Alekhin, "Evreiskie i ariiskie shakhmati," *Pariser Zeitung,* March 1941; reprinted in *Deutsche Schachezeitung* and *Deutche Zeitung in den Niederlanden.* See S. Dudakov, "Ob 'ariiskikh' i 'neariiskikh' shakhmatakh," in *Evrei v kulture russkogo zarubezhiia. Sbornik statei, publikatsii, memuarov i esse,* ed. Mikhail Parkhomovskii, (Jerusalem 1992), 1:447–62. Reflecting Wagner, Alekhin's paper claimed that the Jewish strategy is based on purely quantitative calculations, while Aryan strategy is based on the Romantic sacrifice of chess-pieces. While a Jewish chess-player tries to acquire numerical superiority of pawns, the Aryan is looking for artistic combinations. Boris Spassky, another Russian Grand Master, recently approved this racist theory of chess playing in an interview in *Den':* "Mne nravitsia delat' igru rukami," *Den',* no. 10 (1993).

44. "Rok i sudba Rossii," *Den',* no. 10 (1993).

45. Ibid.

46. "Volkhvi, nas zastavliaiiut stat osvoboditeliia mi mira," *Rossiianin,* no. 2 (1993). Some fascist ideologists Aryanize and Russify the Bible.

47. See, e.g., A. Ivanov, *Khristianstvo kak ono est* (Moscow 1994), 9.

48. S. Zharikov, "Vladiki zhertvi," *Ataka,* no. 33 (n.d.), 29.

49. Ibid., 31.

50. In May 1994, the fascist "Werewolf" group made a (failed) bombing attempt at the Olimpiiskii sport complex in Moscow where Jews for Jesus were sponsoring a festival. See A. Chelnokov, "Podmoskovnii fashism ne proshel," *Izvestiia,* 14 March 1994.

51. Ivanov, *Khristianstvo kak ono est,* 7.

52. Ibid., 7–8.

53. Ibid., 9.

54. Ibid.

55. N. Bogdanov, "Khristianstvo v voprosakh i otvetakh," in *Khristianstvo kak ono est,* 68.

56. V. Avdeev, *Preodolenie khristianstva* (Moscow 1994), 65, 160.

57. Ibid., 89.

58. Bogdanov, "Khristianstvo v voprosakh i otvetakh," 66. The January 1 New Year is more important than Christmas for Russians; for Christians, it commemorates the circumcision of Jesus Christ.

59. Avdeev, *Preodolenie khristianstva,* 65.

60. Zharikov, "Lenin — eto Stalin segodnia," 29–30.

61. F. Uglov, *V plenu illusii* (Leningrad 1986). See also "Piteinoe delo rastet," *Za Rus!,* no. 5 (1993).

62. B. Vasiliev, " 'Roiial' ot demoshinkarei," *Za russkoe delo,* no. 5 (1995). In 1896 the government introduced the liquor monopoly. Despite the fine talk about preventing drunkenness and concern for the spiritual and material welfare of the population, it was merely designed to increase government revenues, and had no effect on the level of alcoholism. The displacement of the "Jewish tavern keepers" only deprived certain local administrative bodies of their previous revenue derived from licensing the taverns. See Th. von Laue, *Sergei Witte and the Industrialization of Russia* (New York 1969), 280–81.

63. B. Vladimirov, "Budet li vveden sukhoi zakon?," *Primorskie novosti,* no. 8 (1992).

64. V. Barabash, "Chernobil' — diversiia Gorbachevskoi kliki," *Nashe Otechestvo,* no. 54 (1996). The "secret causes" of the Chernobyl accident were disclosed in many fascist publications. See V. Volokhov, "Vlastelini 'vremeni'," *Nashe otechestvo,* no. 42 (1995); *Russkii vestnik,* no. 41–44 (1992).

65. V. Barabash and V. Pavlov, "Neobiiavlennaiia iadernaiia voina," *Za russkoe delo,* no. 6 (1996).

66. F. Krasavtsev, "Stanet li Zhirinovskii 'russkim Gitlerom'," *Russkii vzgliad,* no. 3–4 (1996).

67. Champions of the second interpretation borrow their arguments from the "historians" of the American Institute for Historical Review. See, e.g., "Kholokost — mif XX veka," *Russkoe voskreseniie,* no. 8/16 (1992); the authors refer to R. Faurisson, "The Problem of the Gas Chambers," in *The Truth at Last,* no. 343 (n.d.).

68. V. Prusskakov, "Internatsionalka pasporiadilas'," *Den',* no. 20 (1992).

69. A. Aratov, "Spisok shizika," *Russkaia pravda,* no. 4 (1995).

70. Those put on trial include: Alexander Andreev, editor of *Narodnoe delo* (1993); Victor Korchagin, editor of *Russkie vedomosti* and director of the publishing house, Vitiaz (1995); Victor Bezverkhii, leader of the Union of Venedi (1995); the magazine *Rusich* and its editor-in-chief Evgenii Pashnin; the newspaper *Nashe otechestvo* and its editor-in-chief Evgenii Schekotikhin (1995–1996).

71. In the courts the fascists and their lawyers often try to mislead the jury and spectators by redefining basic terms (e.g., fascism, Nazism, antisemitism, Jews, Zionism). Some of the most common rhetorical arguments: (1) "Antisemitism" is really the Israeli hatred of the Palestinians; the term "antisemitism" is not related to the Jews, since they are really descendants of Turkish Khazars; (2) the fascists are criticizing *Zionism,* not the Jews in general, and this should not be taken as insults against the Jews; (3) the word *zhid* (yid) has no pejorative connotations; it is a kind of

literary norm with Ukrainian flavor; (4) the Jews interpret the reaction of Russian people against Russophobia as an expression of antisemitism.

72. O. Latzis, "Fashistam v Rossii boiiatsia nechego," *Izvestiia,* 2 December 1994.

CHAPTER 7

Conclusion
The Invisible Hand and the Secret Hand

I have focused on the ways in which the ideologists of antisemitism articulate their positions, and have depicted the vigor of intellectual antisemitism in post-Soviet Russia, distinguishing five groups of Russian nationalists, and exposing some of the mythological constructions which govern their social vision. Nationalist intellectuals reinforce and embellish the old antisemitic stereotypes and also create new ones. Many arguments of the intellectual antisemites are quite sophisticated and call for a serious critique, both historical and philosophical.

The obsession with Jewish matters masks concern about much more serious issues relating to community and collective identity which the antisemites fail to state more directly. Following the collapse of the USSR, nationalist ideologists have tried to compensate for the lost sense of identity by "imagining" a new, more authentic, and durable community to offset the loss and heal the trauma. The five ideological positions explored in this book suggest five models of identity (geopolitical, religious, social, racial, cultural) for citizens of the post-Soviet states. The antisemitic ideologists have created the mythical Jew as a foil against which to define their ideal community, saying in effect not so much what the members of that community *are*, but what they are *not*.[1] The image of a Jew becomes invested with concepts essential to the self-definition of the post-Soviet community in ways suggested by different groups of intellectual antisemitism. The imaginary character of the "Jews" in antisemitic ideology can be confirmed by the lack of correlation between the physical presence of the Jews in the countries of the former Soviet bloc and the scale of proliferation of antisemitic discourse. The Jews have traditionally functioned in the Christian societies of Europe as classical "others" and this "otherness" was reinforced by political antisemitism in the Soviet period. This explains why the nationalist intellectuals employ the old antisemitic clichés in the construction of the enemy of the new "imagined communities."

The five trends continue some traditions in Russian thought and, in a broader sense, have their foundations in the political philosophy of the

Counter-Enlightenment. I especially wish to emphasize the influence of the Weimar conservative revolutionaries in laying the foundations of a political philosophy which played an important role in the formation of xenophobic ideology. Post-communist antisemitism, however, offers some features unique in the history of antisemitism — geopolitical antisemitism, and the specific religious-political development within Russian Orthodoxy.

The evidence suggests that antisemitic ideology has its source not only in deliberate falsifications of history and forgery of documents. The most troublesome aspect of antisemitism lies not in pragmatic politics of the Russian government, but rather, in genuinely held beliefs in the negative role of the Jews in world history — beliefs shared by many prominent intellectuals. Therefore, it is especially important to examine some assumptions that seem to facilitate the development of these beliefs. These assumptions do not necessarily convert people who share them to an antisemitic "faith"; however, they are extremely conducive to the advancement of antisemitic beliefs. Students of antisemitism often neglect, or fail to take a critical view of these normative assumptions, even though they govern the social vision of the intellectual antisemites and can shed light on the origin of their antisemitism.

ASSUMPTIONS IN POLITICAL PHILOSOPHY

(a) Ideologists of antisemitism construct a false dichotomy between the values of the cultural community versus "universal" values. They believe that membership should be restricted to those having true allegiance to the community's moral standards. This premise of itself presents no problem, but their interpretation of the causes of social problems imply that any commitment to liberalism necessarily destroys the collective identity or uniqueness of the community and the common forms of cultural life preserved in the unique habits, history, and arts of a particular community. They also believe that political liberalism is incompatible with any allegiance to the communal values. Such assumptions do not stand up to serious criticism. A commitment to liberalism certainly does not require the denial of the value of cultural membership.

Although they claim to be advocates of community in opposition to cosmopolitan liberals, the communitarian nationalists actually advocate a homogeneous or "organic" community, whose members must posses a declared set of character traits, values, and virtues. They offer little free choice to their ideal community members, who may wish for something different from the "shared ends and meanings sustained by the community" or who may evolve untraditional practices and values. The community is constricted in space and extended in time through the inclusion of gods and cultural heroes.

Nationalist communitarians attribute challenging new tendencies to real and imagined "Jews." As a result, not only the Jews, but also the non-Jewish imagined Jews whose commitments and social ideals are different from the "imagined" ones are stigmatized and excluded. It is important to realize the real purpose of this theory of community: it is used to protect the particular preferred vision of the community. Many communitarian critics of liberalism discuss the concept of the so-called "organic community" which presupposes a type of the social consensus incompatible with the exercise of personal rights, not as their own concept of community, but as the normative and only possible definition of the community.[2]

Among the "imagined" Jews are included the "New Russians" who exhibit "Jewish" traits in their economic and political behavior, and hence are traitors to Russian civilization. It is important to bear in mind the real purpose of this theory of community — to protect the particular preferred vision of the community. Many communitarian critics of liberalism refer to the concept of an "organic community" which presupposes a type of social consensus incompatible with the exercise of personal rights. Their actual concept of the community — they assert or imply that it is a historical or descriptive concept — is in fact a normative concept. In other words, the ideologists of xenophobia often suggest their own vision of what this ideal Russian community should be and imply that this is what the Russian community is historically and politically.

(b) Communal identity need not contradict universal identity. The ideologists of nationalism suggest that the Jews should be excommunicated because they do not share the fundamental moral beliefs of the cultural community in which they find themselves. However, even if Jews do not share or understand these beliefs (and this is not a very plausible assumption), communication and understanding between the "Jews" and "Russians" should still be possible. Communitarian assume that human beings must be members of a single moral community to be able to understand each other. Human beings have multiple identities, and are members of their local cultural communities as well as members of the universal moral community. The political community, for example, often balances the interests of various cultural communities that compose the whole of the state. "Jewish" and "Russian" values may be in competition, but there is no need to condemn either.[3] One can also observe that the "local standards" in fact have ranging degrees of locality, and some nationalists tacitly assume the existence of universal cultural and moral standards. For instance, standards of the "Eurasian community" will be the universal standards — not those of particular locales — from the standpoint of the multiple cultural communities which constitute the "Eurasian" whole.

(c) The antisemitic ideologists assume that people are irrational and unable to think out political issues. Liberal systems, they assert, merely camouflage secret masters, and any country lacking a nationalist ideology may easily fall prey to these international secret forces, identified with the "Secret Hand of the Jews" (although they can have many different political manifestations).[4] Such a belief has its psychological and intellectual roots in the critique of modernity that was advanced on behalf of antiquity by the most conservative sectors of society. Often cited is the British philosopher Mandeville, who ironically claimed that the new social system required the vices of greed and avarice, rather than virtues for the maintenance of public order and to generate more benefits for the society. Nationalist intellectuals suspected that the anonymous Invisible Hand of the new social order is in fact a Secret Hand. The old prejudice against the Jews merged with the new animus against the "anonymous" social order, and the institutions of the modern liberal ideology were associated with the Jews, many of whom gained prominence in distinctly modern spheres. Thus, the social forces behind these institutions came to be identified with the "Elders of Zion," Jewish bankers, and with a supposed joint conspiracy of revolutionaries and bankers. The contemporary apostles of antisemitism share the sense of social despair with communitarian and post-modern critics of liberalism. It is important to remember that although Jews benefited from the new freedoms gained in the course of the Enlightenment, this does not mean that they directed the course of European history after the French Revolution and created the liberal system.

(d) Many identify the advent of liberalism with the triumph of the "Jewish principle." A supposed Jewish genealogy of liberalism figures prominently in many accounts of the history of liberalism.[5] This view can be criticized on both historical and philosophical accounts.

Historically, there is little connection between Judaism and liberalism. The traditional Jewish community was oligarchic and conservative, and in fact, resisted modernity and liberalism with the same passion as representatives of other traditional cultures.

Second, even if the genealogy of liberalism suggested by the enemies of the "open society" were true, it still does not give grounds to disregard and disqualify liberal ideals. Liberal values might indeed originate out of the interests of a particular group (the "Jews") and yet still have universal appeal.

The idea of liberty, for instance, grew out of the struggle of the aristocracy against absolute monarchy, yet became universally accepted quite independently of its class origins. By the same token, the "Jewish" liberal ideas — even if we grant the unlikely conjunction — may have universal appeal regardless of its origin The specific point of origin cannot discredit the universal character of an idea by itself.

ASSUMPTIONS ABOUT HISTORY

Throughout the narratives of the five ideologies discussed, one finds certain assumptions about the crucial role of Russia in history, in opposition to that of the Jews.[6]

(a) Nationalist ideologists proclaim that there is "significance" or "meaning" in historical events, that is not captured in the studies by conventional historians. Only a person initiated into a particular type of nationalist ideology — neo-Eurasianism, neo-Slavophilism, National Bolshevism, National Orthodoxy, or Aryanism — can understand the mystery of world history. In reality, however, the very mind-set that is seeking the meaning of history tends to "create" the crimes of the Jews in the process of "observation." The antisemitic ideologists cite facts that supposedly attest to the narrative that predicted the appearance of the facts.

The representatives of each of the five trends attribute to the "imagined" Jews quite different characteristics, depending on the national myth that governs its particular social vision. Each group sees in the Jew a personification of what it dreads or hates the most. For National Bolsheviks, the Jew personifies heartless capital; to neo-Slavophiles, the rootless and rabid communists with devastating global ambitions; they haunt the imagination of the neo-Eurasians as messengers of the Anglo-American "maritime" civilization; to the champions of National Orthodoxy, they appear as destructive and formalist servants of the cruel Old Testament "Law." The outburst of ideological antisemitism in Russia marks the growing need to provide a narrative of a powerful "enemy" to act as a counter to the "authentic" community. Such a narrative affirms the boundaries between the community and the outside world.

Not all of the antisemitic ideas are mere constructions; only some of them clearly belong to the domain of pure fantasy (e.g., human sacrifice, the meeting of the Elders of Zion in Basel, the creation of an anti-Christian coalition). What makes the antisemitic ideologies so potent is the reliance on the slim basis of fact that provides the basis for the meta-narrative of human history. Many people of Jewish origin are indeed successful in business, and it may even be true that the religious principles of Judaism are more conducive to the development of capitalism. Some Jews belong to Masonic lodges. Many Jews occupied prominent positions in the Soviet government, and it cannot be denied that several people of Jewish descent were involved in the decision to execute the last Russian emperor. Bogrov, a baptized Jew who was a police double agent assassinated Russian Minister of the Interior Stolypin. Yet all these facts hardly give any credence to the accusations of collective responsibility of "the Jews" for these crimes and misdeeds. Such examples cannot validate a theory of Jewish conspiracy and the picture of human history as a struggle between the Semitic and Aryan races. What is wrong with the dissemination of these accounts by antisemitic ideologists is not the facts themselves, but the conclusions and assumptions on which such accounts are based. Clearly, there is a gap between "the abundance of empirical evidence" and the sweeping generalizations made about the pattern of human history and its meaning, said to be revealed in large part through an analysis of the fate of the Jews.

(b) Father Zenkovsky, we will recall, asserted that the history of the Jews becomes "incomprehensible" and "tragically nonsensical" without the Christian narrative of world history. In fact, the nationalists' accounts suggest that world history itself is incomprehensible without Jewish history, for the status of the Jews and their "crimes" serves them as an indicator of the stages of world history. The historical mission of Russia itself is derived from the failure of the Jews to carry out their own mission and the loss of their "election." It seems plain that even the secularized grand narratives of neo-Eurasianism, neo-Slavophilism, racism, and National Bolshevism have inherited the association between the Jews and the meaning of history from the Judeo-Christian tradition. Christianity suggests that the Jews will play an important role as history comes to an end. The secularized narratives of the nationalist intellectuals detach this idea from God but preserve the old connection. Ideas about the end of history presuppose some radical change in the position of the Jews, and thus, one can supposedly read history through observation of the Jews.

ASSUMPTIONS IN MORAL PHILOSOPHY

(a) The ideologists assume that commercial activity or any involvement in trade is intrinsically bad and morally corrupt. While commerce is described as socially detrimental, the moral and social background of the nationalist ideologists force them to accept the intrinsic value of occupations like agriculture. Some theoreticians, e.g., Dugin, even consider merchants to be the aliens in the Indo-European world, although in most cases, such assumptions are rarely spelled out, and the ideologists fail to examine this assumption critically.

The negative attitude to commerce is grounded in agrarian society, in which engaging in trade was viewed as shameful, since it appeared that the merchant's gain inevitably meant his customer's loss.[7] This belief is grounded in another primitive belief, that of "real value." Many students of European modernity have observed that the change in the attitude to commercial activity, specifically the shift from realism to nominalism in understanding economic values, greatly contributed to the development of Western capitalism. The concept of a sphere of morally neutral action, e.g., the pursuit of self-interest in economic activity, provided support for economic and political reforms. Antisemitic ideologists, however, did not accept such a notion, and condemned the Jews as engaging in "parasitic" occupations.

One can agree that trade can present moral problems under certain conditions. For instance, one party might be so limited in its range of options that it would be forced to enter into a commercial contract against its will, blocking it from the exercise of free choice, or the pursuit of its own interests. However, such a situation is not a necessary condition for commercial activity. Western capitalism has demonstrated the possibility of socially responsible commercial activity which does not involve economic coercion. The antisemitic ideologists fail to recognize this basic idea and assume that the only purpose is the generation of profit, ignoring the importance of trade to the society as a whole and the potential benefits.

Let me emphasize again that all these assumptions of themselves do not commit a person to antisemitism. Nevertheless, it would be difficult or impossible to advocate many antisemitic arguments without these assumptions.

My analysis of intellectual antisemitism in general does not suggest that Russian Jews are in danger. The majority of Russians simply do not share the views and assumptions of the antisemitic ideologists. However, one shouldn't disregard the dangers of intellectual antisemitism. Many of the intellectuals discussed in this study are not marginal figures, and there is a widespread sense among Russians that their views should be taken seriously.

The antisemitic arguments embody a comprehensive anti-liberal vision of social development. The "Jewish topic" allows the nationalist theoreticians to provide false explanations of social and economic processes. Both their diagnosis of the situations and the cures they suggest are inadequate to resolve the serious questions which they raise about the cultural and social identity of the people, the new types of integration of the post-Soviet states, international ethics, status and membership in different cultural and political communities, the efficient use of resources, among other problems. The nationalist ideologists mystify these real problems by their speculations about the "Jews." The paradigm of discussion they suggest does a disservice to the nation. The most important question seems to be the possibility of reconciling the maintenance of a distinct cultural identity with the universal and cosmopolitan character of the political and economic transformations. It is liberal theoreticians who provide a more adequate way of addressing this matter. One can also look to Asian countries such as Japan, Taiwan, and Singapore, to find examples of the combination of Confucian social ideals and moral values with liberalism. Thus, a uniquely "Eurasian" type of capitalist civilization might arise in Russia in the future. Understanding and resolving these problems may therefore displace the necessity of defining some "imagined enemy."

NOTES

1. The production of the image of the "other" and the "stranger" are studied in the new sociological field of ksen-iconology. Some sociologists and political scientists argue that many self-defined communities depend for their existence and reproduction on an excluded, objected Other. See A. Norton, *Reflections on Political Identity* (Baltimore 1988). Zygmund Bauman describes the type of community that constructs its identity on the basis of opposition to the Other: "Such a community lives under the condition of constant anxiety and thus shows a sinister and but thinly masked tendency to aggression and intolerance.... [It is] therefore, bound to remain endemically precarious and hence bellicose and intolerant, neurotic about matters of security and paranoic about the hostility and ill intentions of the environment." Z. Bauman, *Intimations of Post-Modernity* (London 1992), 235.

2. A critical response to this view can be found in W. Kymlicka, *Liberalism, Community, and Culture* (Oxford 1989).

3. The theory of value-pluralism was elaborated by Isaiah Berlin; see J. Gray, *Isaiah Berlin* (Princeton, N.J. 1996), 38–105.

4. It is no coincidence that the ideas of the Elders of Zion in the *Protocols,* rediscovered after perestroika, present a Machiavellian position. One of the primary sources of the *Protocols* is the Maurice Joly's 1864 liberal pamphlet against Napoleon III, *Dialogue aux enfers entre Montesquieu et Machiavel.* The "Jewish plot" is taken almost literally from the words Joly ascribes to Macchiavelli.

5. Two points of supposed similarity between Judaism and liberalism are especially important. The nationalists believe that the liberal's concern for human

rights is actually a disguised concern for trade and profit. The other similarity which they find is the supposed indifference of the capitalists ("Jews") to the members of the larger community. The members of the community become strangers to each other. The communitarian nationalists deduce the liberal idea of the abstract self from the disregard for the communal attachments and the prominence of the strangers ("the Jews") in society. They believe that the liberals (and the capitalists) assume a "Jewish" attitude towards other members of the society.

6. The fantastic narratives of world history in Russia have much in common with the speculative philosophy of history prominent in nineteenth-century Germany. In a sense the philosophy of history espoused in the *Protocols* is a caricature of this speculative philosophy. The Serpent of Zion circling the globe described by Sergii Nilus (who was very well versed in nineteenth-century German philosophy) is reminiscent of the Hegelian spiral of world history.

7. Maria Ossowska, in *The Knight and the Bourgeois. Studies in the Sociology of Morals,* observes that the Jews were very suitable for the role of middlemen because they emancipated both sides of trade from the shame originally associated with exchange. The Jews allowed "de-personalization of the exchange" since they were outsiders in the community, and absorbed the shame associated with commerce. See M. Ossowska, *Ritsar i Burzhua* (Moscow 1987), 353. The French sociologist Marcel Mauss contrasted the patterns of exchange in traditional societies and modern societies — the gift exchange and the commodity exchange. While gift exchange was considered sacred; commodity exchange was profane. The assumptions underlying the arguments of antisemites can be viewed as a relic of the archaic mentality of primitive societies. Mauss demonstrated that the gift exchange in ancient societies is "in theory voluntary, disinterested and spontaneous"; but, "in fact it is obligatory and interested." M. Mauss, *The Gift: Forms and Functions of Exchange in Archaic Societies* (Glencoe 1954).

Selected Bibliography

Anon. "Doli antisemitism — orudie reaktsii" (Down with antisemitism — the weapon of reactionary forces). *Spartacist* no. 3 (1992).

Anon. "Evrasiistvo: za i protiv, vchera i segodnia" (Eurasianism: Pro and con, yesterday and today [the round-table discussion]). *Voprosi filosofii* no. 6 (1995).

Anon. "Holocaust in Palestine," *Al-Quds* no. 13 (1994).

Anon. "Jewish Bankers and Chechen Bazookas" (in Russian) *Zavtra* no. 48 (1996).

Anon. "Zasedanie soiuza pisatelei" (The meeting of the Writers Union). *Ogoniok* no. 48 (1989).

Agursky, M. *The Third Rome: National Bolshevism in the USSR.* Boulder, Colo.: Westview Press, 1985.

Anderson, B. *Imagined Communities: Reflection on the Origins and Spread of Nationalism.* London: Verso, 1983.

Andreas-Solome, L. "Russische Philosophie und Semitische Geist." *Die Zeit* n.172.236 (1898).

Andreski, Stanislav, ed. *Max Weber on Capitalism, Bureaucracy and Religion.* London and Boston: Allen and Unwin, 1983.

Bakrevsky, V. "The Confessions of Kaganovich." *Pravda,* 28 May 1993.

Barkashov, A. *Azbuka russkogo natsionalista* (The alphabet of Russian nationalists). Moscow: Slovo-1, 1994.

————. *Era Rossii* (The era of Russia). Moscow: Russkoe natsionalnoe edinstvo, 1991.

Baron, S., and Kahan, A. *Economic History of the Jews.* Ed. N. Gross. New York: Schocken Books, 1975.

Baron, S. *Modern Nationalism and Religion.* New York and Philadelphia: Meridian Books, 1960.

Bauman, Z. "Exit Visas and Entry Tickets: Paradoxes of Jewish Assimilation," *Telos* no. 77 (1988).

Bauer, Y. *The Holocaust in Historical Perspective.* Seattle: University of Washington Press, 1978.

Belianchikova, M. "Dostanetsia li zemlia faraonu" (Will the land go to the pharaoh?). *Nash sovremennik* no. 4 (1995).

Belov, Y. "Sheilok i Kuz'ma. Evreistvo na fone russkikh problem" (Shylock and Kuz'ma. Jewry against the background of Russian problems). *Sovetskaiia Rossiia,* 21 October 1995.

Belyi, A. "Shtempeleovannaia kultura" (The rubber-stamp culture). *Nash sovremennik* no. 8 (1990).

Berdiaev, N. *Christianity and Anti-Semitism.* Trans. by Alan Spears and Victor Kanter. Aldington, Kent: Hand & Flower Press, 1952.

Bernstein, H. *The Truth About 'The Protocols of Zion.'* New York: Covoci Friede Publishers, 1935.

Bikerman, ed. *Rossiia i evrei* (Russia and the Jews). Paris: YMCA Press, 1978 (Originally published in Berlin, 1923).

Birmingham, S. *Our Crowd. The Great Jewish Families of New York.* New York: Harper & Row, 1967.

Blavatsky, H. *The Secret Doctrine.* Wheaton, Ill.: Theosophical Press, 1946.

———.*Esoteric Character of the Gospels; A Study of Occultism.* Adyar: Theosophical Publishing House, 1952.

Boikov, V. ed. *Krov' v verovaniiakh i sueveriiakh chelovechestva* (Blood in the religions and superstitions of mankind). St. Petersburg, CIS: Sofiia, 1995.

Boikov V., ed. *Taina Izrailia. 'Evreiskii vopros' v russkoi religioznoi misli kontsa 19 - nachala 20 veka* (The mystery of Israel. The "Jewish Question" in Russian religious thought at the end of the 19th and in the first part of the 20th century). St.-Petersburg: Sofiia, 1993.

Bondarenko, V. "The Responsibility of the Nation" (in Russian). *Den'* no. 18 (1992).

Borodai, Y. (1991) "Tretii put'" (The third way). *Nash sovremennik* no. 9, (1991).

———. (1992) "Totalitarism: khronika I likhoradochnii krisis" Totalitarianism: the chronicle and the crisis). *Nash sovremennik* no. 7, 1992.

———. (1990) "Pochemu pravoslavnim ne goditsia protestantskii kapitalism" (Why Protestant capitalism is not good for Orthodox believers). *Nash sovremennik,* no. 10 (1990).

Bowman, S. "Two Late Byzantine Dialogues with the Jews." *Greek Orthodox Theological Review* 25, no. 1 (1980).

Brafman, J. *Kniga kagala: mirovoi evreiskii vopros* (The book of kahal: the world Jewish question). St. Petersburg: S. Dobrodeev, 1888.

Britanitskaya, A. *Pyotr Suvchinsky i ego vremia* (Peter Suvchinsky and his times). Moscow: Kompozitor, 1999.

Bromberg, J. "O neobkhodimosti peresmotra evreiskogo voprosa" (On the necessity of reconsidering the Jewish question), *Evrasiiskii sbornik.* Book 6. 1929.

Brym, R. *Jewish Intelligentsia and Russian Marxism.* London: MacMillan, 1978.

———. *The Jews of Moscow, Kiev and Minsk. Identity, Antisemitism, Emigration.* London: MacMillan, 1994.

Brym, R. "Russian Attitudes Towards Jews: An Update." *East European Jewish Affairs,* 26, no. 1 (1996).

Bogoliubov [Moisei], Bulgakov, N., and Yakovlev-Kozirev, A. *Pravoslavie, armiia, gosudarstvo* (Orthodoxy, army, state). Moscow: Russkii Vestnik, 1993.

Bulgakov, S. *Khristianstvo I evreiskii vopros* (Christianity and the Jewish question). Paris: YMCA-Press, 1991.

Burtsev, V. *V pogone za provokatorami; 'Protokoli sionskikh mudretsov' — dokazannii podlog* (Pursuing the provocateurs: the Protocols of the Elders of Zion is a Proven Forgery). Moscow, 1991.

———. "Evrei I bol'shevism" (The Jews and Bolshevism). *Obschee delo.* no. 61 (1991).

———. *Suschestvuet li evreiskii vopros v Rossii?* (Does the "Jewish Question" exist in Russia? The meeting of the theoretical club "The Free Word"). Moscow, 1994.

Carlson, M. *"No Religion Higher Than Truth": A History of the Theosophical Movement in Russia, 1875–1922.* Princeton, N.J.: Princeton University Press, 1993.

Cherniavsky, M. *The Tsar and the People. Studies in Russian Myths.* New York: Random House, 1969.

Cohn, N. *Warrant for Genocide. The Myth of the Jewish World Conspiracy and the Protocols of the Elders of Zion.* Chico, Calif.: Scholars Press, 1967.

Dahl, G., "Will the Other God Fail Again? On the Possible Return of the Conservative Revolution." *Theory, Culture and Society* 13, no. 1 (1996).

Delevsky, Y. *Protokoli sionskikh mudretsov. Istoriia odnogo podloga* (The Protocols of the Elders of Zion. The history of a forgery). Berlin, 1923.

Deutscher, I. *The Non-Jewish Jew and Other Essays.* New York: Oxford University Press, 1968.

Diehl, C. *Byzantium. Greatness and Decline.* New Brunswick, N.J.: Rutgers University Press, 1957.

Dikii, A. (1994) *Evrei v Rossii i SSR* (The Jews in Russia and in the USSR: Historical sketch). Novosibirsk: Blagovest, 1994.

————. *The Jews in Russia and the USSR: Historical Sketch.* Ottawa: L. Volovikoff, 1967.

Dobra, I. "Podlinnik!" (The original!). *Molodaiia gvardiia* no. 11–12 (1993).

Dreizin, F. *The Russian Soul and the Jews.* New York: University Press of America, 1990.

Dudakov, S. "O ariiskikh I evreiskikh shakhmatakh" (On Aryan and Jewish chess-playing) in *The Jews in Russian Culture Abroad.* Ed. Mikhail Parkhomovsky. Jerusalem, 1992.

————. (1989) "Vladimir Soloviov I Sergei Nilus" (Vladimir Soloviov and Sergei Nilus) in *Russian Literature and History.* Ed. Wolf Moscovich. Jerusalem: Hebrew University of Jerusalem, 1989.

Dugin, A. "Apokalipsis stikhii" (The apocalypse of the elements). *Elementi* no. 8 (1997).

————.*Konservativnaiia revolutsiia* (Conservative Revolution). Moscow: Arktogeya, 1994.

————.*Konspirologiia* (Conspirology). Moscow: Arktogeya, 1993.

————.*Osnovi geopolitiki* (The foundations of geopolitics). Moscow: Arktogeya, 1996.

————. *Tseli i zadachi nashei revolutsii* (The goals and tasks of our revolution). Moscow: Fravarti, 1995.

————. *Misterii Evrasii* (The mysteries of Eurasia). Moscow: Arktogeya, 1996.

————.*Tamplieri proletariata* (The Templars of the proletariat). Moscow: Arktogeya, 1997.

————. "We Russians are the New Israel" (In Russian). Interview by Abraham Shmulevich. *Vesti,* 21 January 2001.

Dumouchel, Paul, ed. *Violence and Truth. On the Work of Rene Gerard.* Stanford: Stanford University Press, 1988.

Dundes, A. *The Blood Libel Legend: A Casebook in Antisemitic Folklore.* Madison: University of Wisconsin Press, 1991.

Efimov, N. *Rossiia—novii Izrail: teokraticheskaiia ideologiia sovremennogo pravoslaviia v dopetrovskikh istochnikakh* (Russia—the new Israel: The theocratic ideology of contemporary Orthodoxy in the pre-petrian sources) Kazan, 1912.

Emelyanov, V. *Desionizatsiia* (De-Zionization). Moscow: Vitiaz, 1995.

Etkind, A. *Sodom i Psikheiia: Ocherki po intellektual'noi istorii serebrianogo veka* (Sodom and Psyche: Essays on the intellectual history of the Silver Age). Moscow: ITs-Garant, 1996.

Frank, S. "Die religiöse Tragödie des Judentums." *Eine heilige Kierche* (Apr.–June 1934).

Friedgut, T. "Antisemitism and its Opponents: Reflections in the Russian Press." ACTA Occasional Papers. no. 3. Vidal Sassoon International Center for the Study of Antisemitism, The Hebrew University of Jerusalem. 1994.

Furman, D. "The Mass Consciousness of Russian Jews and Anti-Semitism." *Russian Social Science Review* 36, no. 5 (1995).

Gassenschmidt, C. *Jewish Liberal Politics in Tsarist Russia, 1900–14.* London: MacMillan, 1995.

Gellner, E. *Nations and Nationalism.* Ithaca, N.Y.: Cornell University Press, 1983.

Gerrits, A. "Antisemitism and Anti-Communism: the Myth of 'Judeo-Communism' in Eastern Europe." *Eastern European Jewish Affairs* 25, no. 1 (1995).

Gibson, J. "The Misunderstanding of Anti-Semitism in Russia: An Analysis of the Politics of anti-Jewish Attitudes." *Slavic Review* no. 53 (1994).

Gilman, S. *Freud, Race, and Gender.* Princeton, N.J.: Princeton University Press, 1993.

———. *Jewish Self-Hatred: Anti-Semitism and the Hidden Language of the Jews.* Baltimore & London: Johns Hopkins University Press, 1986.

Gitelman, Z. *Jewish Nationality and Soviet Politics: The Jewish Sections of the CPSU, 1917–1930.* Princeton, N.J.: Princeton University Press, 1972.

Gladkii, B. *Zhidi* (The Yids). Moscow: Vitiaz', 1993.

Goldstein, A. "Natsional'nie obrazi Gacheva" (Gachev's national images), *Okna,* 6–12 July 1995.

Gray, J. *Isaiah Berlin.* Princeton, N.J.: Princeton University Press, 1996.

Gumilev, L. *Drevniia Rus' i velikaiia step'* (Ancient Russian and the Great Steppe). Moscow: Nauka, 1989.

———. *Etnogenez I biosfera Zemli* (Ethnogenesis and the biosphere of Earth). Leningrad: Izdatelstvo Leningradskogo universiteta, 1989.

———.*Otkritie Khazarii. Ocherk istorii I etnografii* (The discovery of Khazaria. A study in history and ethnography). Moscow: Nauka, 1966.

———.*Ot Rusi k Rossii. Ocherki etnicheskoi istorii* (From Rus' to Russia. Essays in ethnic history). Moscow: Ekopros, 1992.

———. *Tisiacheletie vokrug Kaspiia* (A millenium in the area of the Caspian Sea). Moscow: Michel and Co. 1993.

Nancy Harrowitz and B. Hyams, eds. *Jews and Gender.* Philadelphia: Temple University Press, 1995.

Harrowitz, Nancy, ed. *Tainted Greatness. Antisemitism and Cultural Heroes.* Philadelphia: Temple University Press, 1994.

Hertzberg, A. *The French Enlightenment and the Jews.* New York: Columbia University Press, 1968.

Holmes, S. *Anatomy of Antiliberalism.* Cambridge, Mass.: MIT Press, 1993.

Ioann (Metropolitan). *Samoderzhavie dukha. Ocherki russkogo samosoznaniia* (The autocracy of spirit. Essays on Russian self-consciousness). St. Petersburg: Tsarskoe delo, 1995.

————. *Odolenie smuti. Obraschenie k russkomu narodu* (How to overcome discord? Address to the Russian people). St. Petersburg: Tsarskoe delo, 1995.

Ivanov, A. *Khristianstvo kak ono est'* (Christianity). Moscow: Vitiaz, 1994.

Jaspers, K. *The Question of German Guilt.* New York: Capricorn Books, 1961.

Kandel, F. *Ocherki vremen i sobitii. Iz istorii russkikh evreev do vtoroi polovini 18 veka* (Essays on the life and times of Russian Jews before the second part of the 18th century). Jerusalem: Mili-Tarbut, 1988.

Kara-Murza, S. "Po sledam Menelaiia" (Following the tracks of Menelaus). *Sovetskaiia Rossiia,* 26 January 1995.

————. "Mifotvortsi" (The mythmakers). *Sovetskaiia Rossiia,* 6 January 1995.

————. "Novie russkie i Iskhod" (The new Russians and Exodus). *Pravda,* 27 June 1994.

————."Tainaiia ideologiia perestroiki" (The secret ideology of perestroika." *Nash sovremennik,* no. 3 (1994).

Katz, J. *Jews and Freemasons in Europe 1723–1939.* Tr. from Hebrew by Leonard Oschry. Cambridge, Mass.: Harvard University Press, 1970.

Katzis, L. "Delo Beilisa v kontekste russkogo serebrianogo veka" (The Beilis Affair in the context of the Russian Silver Age). *Vestnik evreiskogo universiteta v Moskve* no. 4 (1993).

Kazintsev, A. "Samoubiistvo pod kontrolem" (The controlled suicide). *Nash sovremennik* no. 9 (1993).

————. "Eres' zhidovstvuiuschikh" (The Judaizing heresy), *Nash sovremennik* no. 9 (1992).

————. (1995) "Bluzhdaiuschie ogon'ki" (The wandering lights). *Nash sovremennik* no. 3 (1995).

Kei, L. *Mirovoi zagovor* (The world conspiracy). Moscow and New York. 1975.

Khlebnikov, P. *Godfather of the Kremlin. Boris Berezovsky and the Looting of Russia.* N.p.: Harcourt, 2000.

Klimov, A., *Iadovitie ribi. Sionisti I masoni v Iaponii* (Venomous fish. Zionists and Masons in Japan). Moscow, 1992.

Kliuchnikov, Sergei, ed. *Russkii uzel evraziistva* (The Russian knot of Eurasianism). Moscow: Belovodie, 1997.

Korey, W. *Russian Antisemitism, Pamyat, and the Demonology of Zionism.* Chur, Switzerland: Harwood Academic Press, 1995.

Kozhinov, V. "Istoriia Rusi I russkogo slova" (The history of Russia and the Russian word). *Nash sovremennik* no. 10–11 (1992).

————. *Tainstvennie stranitsi istorii 20 veka: chernosotentsi I revoliutsiia* (The mysterious pages of the history of the 20th century: The Black Hundreds and the revolution). Moscow: Prima B, 1995.

————. "Zhertvi nasiliia. Nashi realnie zhertvi mezhdu 1917 I 1941 godami" (The victims of violence. Our real losses between 1917 and 1941). *Moskva* no. 6 (1994).

————. "Sionism Mikhaila Agurskogo i mezhdunarodnii sionism" (The Zionism of Michael Agursky and International Zionism). *Nash sovremennik* no. 6 (1990).

Krakhmalnikova, Zoya, ed. *Russkaiia ideia I evrei. Khristianstvo. Antisemitism. Natsionalism* (The Russian idea and the Jews. Christianity. Antisemitism. Nationalism). Moscow: Nauka, 1994.

Krefetz, G. *Jews and Money. The Myth and Reality.* New Haven and New York: Ticknor and Fields, 1982.

Kuniaev, S. "Etot vozdukh pust' budet svidetelem" (Let this air be a witness…). *Den'* no. 37 (1993).

Kuzmich, A. *Zagovor mirovogo pravitel'stva. Rossiia I zolotoi milliard* (The conspiracy of the world government. Russia and the golden billion). Moscow, 1994.

Kymlicka, W. *Liberalism, Community and Culture.* Oxford: Clarendon Press, 1991.

Laruelle, Marlène. "Lev Nikolaevich Gumilev (1912–1992): Biologisme et Eurasisme dans la pensée Russe." *Revue des Études Slaves* 72, nos. 1–2 (2000): 163–89.

————. "Politique et culture dans l'émigration russe: les débats entre l'eurasisme et ses oppenents." *La Revue Russe* 17 (2000): 35–46.

————. Pereosmislenie imperii v post-sovetskom prostranstve: novaya evraziiskaia ideologiia." *Vestnik Evrazii—Acta Asiatica* (Moscow) no. 1 (8) (2000): 5–18.

Laqueur, W. *The Black Hundreds. The Rise of Extreme Right in Russia.* New York: Harper Collins, 1993.

————. *Rossiia i Germaniia: nastavniki Gitlera* (Russia and Germany: Hitler's mentors). Tr. by Vadim Meniker. Washington, D.C.: Problemy Vostochnoi Evropy, 1991.

Laue, Th. von. *Sergei Witte and the Industrialization of Russia.* New York: Atheneum, 1969.

Levine, H. *Economic Origins of Antisemitism.* New Haven and London: Yale University Press, 1991.

Lezov, S. "The National Idea and Christianity." *Religion, State and Society* 20, no. 1 (1992).

Liuks, L., "Evrasiistvo" (Eurasianism). *Voprosi filosofii* no. 6 (1993).

————. "Evrasiistvo i konservativnaiia revolutsiia" (Eurasianism and conservative revolution). *Voprosi filosofii* no. 3 (1996).

Löwe, H.-D. *The Tsars and the Jews.* Hamburg: Harwood Academic Publishers, 1993.

McGinn, B. *Antichrist. The Two Thousand Years of the Human Fascination with Evil.* San Francisco: Harper, 1994.

Mohler, A. *Die Conservative Revolution in Deutschland 1918–1932: Ein Handbuch.* 3rd ed. Darmstadt, 1989.

Moore, G. "Racism and Nationalism." *Nations and Nationalism* 1, no. 2 (1995).

Moskvitianin, S. "Tainaiia diplomatiia Dzhorzha Sorosa" (The secret diplomacy of George Soros). *Molodaiia gvardiia* no. 2 (1994).

Mosse, G. *Nationalism and Sexuality. Respectability and Abnormal Sexuality in Modern Europe.* New York: Howard Fertig, 1985.

Nazarov, G. "Bolsheviks Are Different" (in Russian). *Molodaiia gvardiia* no. 5–6 (1992).

Nazarov, M. *Zagovor protiv Rossii* (The conspiracy against Russia). Potsdam: Gelikon, 1993.

Naumov, S. *Zhertvi i palachi. Golod 1932–1933 goda* (The victims and the butchers: The famine of 1932–1933). Magadan, 1992.

————. *Spisok palachei Rossii* (List of the butchers of Russia, 1936–1939). Magadan, 1989.

Nechvolodov, A. *L'Empereur Nicolas II et les juifs. Essais sur la revolution russe dans ses rapports avec l'activité universelle du judaïsme contemporain.* Paris: Etienne Chiron, 1924.

Nezhny, A. "Protokoli kremliovskikh mudretsov" (Protocols from meetings of the Kremlin wise men." *Ogoniok* no. 31–33 (1992).

Nichols, W. *Christian Antisemitism. A History of Hate.* Northvale, N.J., 1993.

Nilus, S. (1917) *Az esm pri dveriakh* (It is near, at the door). Moscow: Sviato-Troitzky Monastery Press, 1917.

————. (1919) "Velikoe v malom" (The great in the small). *The Ray of Light* no. 4 (August 1919).

Novikova, L. and I. Sizemskaiia, eds. *Mir Rossii—Evraziia* (The world of Russia—Eurasia). Moscow: Viscshaiia shkola, 1995.

Obukhov, V. "Sionism kak mezhdunarodnii fashism" (Zionism as International Fascism). *Molodaiia gvardiia* no. 8 (1994).

Ostretsov, V. *Chernie sotni i krasnie sotni* (Black Hundreds and red hundreds). Moscow: Voennoe izdatelstvo Otechestvo, 1991.

Parthé, K. "The Empire Strikes Back: How Right-Wing Nationalists Tried to Recapture Russian Literature." *Nationalities Papers* 24, no. 4 (1996).

Platonov, O. *Tsar' Nikolai II* (Tsar Nicholas II). Moscow: Informexpress, 1992.

———. "Evreiskii vopros v russkom gosudarstve" (The Jewish Question in the Russian State). *Al-Quds* no. 2 (1995).

Poliakov, L. *The Aryan Myth. The History of Racist and Nationalist Ideas in Europe.* Tr. from French by Edward Howard. New York: Basic Books, 1974.

———. *The History of Anti-Semitism.* Tr. from French by Miriam Kochan. London: Routledge Kegan Paul, 1975.

Radzikovsky, L. "Evreiskoe schast'e" (Jewish happiness). *Novoe russkoe slovo,* 17 January 1996.

Rancour-Laferrière, D. *The Slave Soul of Russia. Moral Masochism and the Cult of Suffering.* New York: New York University Press, 1995.

Rose, P. *Revolutionary Antisemitism in Germany from Kant to Wagner.* Princeton, N.J.: Princeton University Press, 1990.

Rostikov, E. "Russian People Suffer From 'Russian' TV." *Pravda,* 26 December 1996.

Rotenstreich, N. *Jews and German Philosophy: The Polemics of Emancipation.* New York: Schocken Books, 1984.

Rowland, D. "Moscow—The Third Rome or the New Israel?" *Russian Review* no. 2 (1996).

Saveliev, L. "Ocherki po russkoi filosofii" (Essays on Russian philosophy). *Moskva* no. 1–3 (1996).

Selianiniv, A. *Evrei v Rossii* (The Jews in Russia). Moscow: Vitiaz, 1995.

Shafarevich, I. *Est' li u Rossii buduschee?* (Does Russia have a future?). Moscow: Sovetskii pisatel, 1991.

———. "Rossiia i mirovaiia katastrofa" (Russia and the world catastrophe). *Nash sovremennik* no. 1 (1993).

———. "Rusofobiia: desiat' let spustia" (Russophobia ten years after). *Nash sovremennik* no. 11 (1991).

Shimanov, G. "Kto bol'she vsego zainteresovan v mirazhakh I utopiiakh?" (Who is most interested in the mirages and utopias?). *Molodaiia gvardiia* no. 4 (1994).

———."O tainoi prirode kapitalisma" (On the secret nature of capitalism). *Molodaiia gvardiia* no. 11–12 (1993).

Simanovich, A. *Rasputin i evrei. Vospominaniia lichnogo sekretaria Grigoriia Rasputina* (Rasputin and the Jews. The memoirs of the personal secretary of Grigorii Rasputin). Moscow: Sovetskii pisatel, 1989.

Shapiro, L. "The Role of the Jews in the Russian Revolutionary Movement" *Slavonic and East European Review* 40 (1961).

Shevtsov, I. "Fascism and Zionism are the Twins" (in Russian). *Molodaiia gvardiia* no. 9 (1995).

Shmakov, A. *Svoboda i evrei* (Freedom and the Jews). Moscow: Moskovskaya gorodskaya tipografia, 1906.

Solzhenitsin, Alexander, ed. *Soblazn sotsialisma. Revolutsiia v Rossii I evrei* (The temptation of socialism. The revolution in Russia and the Jews). Paris and Moscow: YMCA-Press. 1995.

Stephan, J. *The Russian Fascists. Tragedy and Farce in Exile 1925–1945.* New York, San Francisco, and London: Harper and Row, 1978.

Steopin, V. *Suschnost' sionizma* (The essence of Zionism). Moscow: Vitiaz, 1994.

Stravinsky, I. *Russian Correspondence.* In Russian. 3 vols. Edited by Victor Varuntz. Moscow: Kompozitor, 1998–2000.

Sviatopolk-Mirsky, D. "Narodnosti SSSR. Evrei" (Ethnicities of the USSR. The Jews). *Evrasiia* no. 26 (1929).

Sutton, A. *Wall Street and the Bolshevik Revolution.* New Rochelle, N.Y., 1974.

Tuirin, P. "Ikona i tsar'" (Ikon and tsar). *Moscow* no. 3 (1997).

Turoverov, N. "The Doctor-Murderers: Truth and Fiction." *Al-Quds* no. 9 (1993).

Toporov, V. "'Spor' ili 'druzhba'"? ("Argument" or "friendship"?). In *Aequinox.* Edited by I. Vishnevetsky and E. Rabinovich. Moscow: Carte Blanche, 1991.

Trotsky, L. "Termidor i antisemitism. Antisemitism kak orudie Stalina v ego bor'be s levoi oppozitsiei" (Termidor and antisemitism. Antisemitism as Stalin's weapon in his struggle against the Left opposition. Trotsky's archives from Harvard University. Rpt., *Spartacist* no. 3 (1992).

Trubetskoi, N. "O rasisme" (On racism). *Neva* no. 7 (1992).

Trushkov, V. "Geroi kapitalisticheskogo truda" (Heroes of capitalist labor). *Pravda,* 20 February 1996.

Uglov, F. *Iz plena illuzii* (From the prison of illusions). Leningrad: Lenizdat, 1986.

Vaksberg, A. *Stalin Against the Jews.* New York: Knopf, 1994.

Vlasov, Y. "Zionists Against Jews and Russians" (in Russian). *Zavtra* no. 37 (1995).

Volkogonov, D. *Trotsky: The Eternal Revolutionary.* New York: Free Press, 1996.

Volokhov, A. "Zolotoiskateli ot sionisma" (Zionist gold-diggers). *Al-Quds* no. 13 (1994).

Volovici, L. "Antisemitism in Post-Communist Eastern Europe: A Marginal or Central Issue?" ACTA Occasional Papers, no. 4. Vidal Sassoon International Center for the Study of Antisemitism, Hebrew University of Jerusalem, 1994.

Webb, J. *The Occult Establishment.* La Salle, Ill: Open Court, 1976.

Wistrich, R. *Revolutionary Jews From Marx to Trotsky.* New York: Barnes and Noble, 1976.

Woll, J. "Russians and Russophobes: Antisemitism on the Russian Literary Scene." *Soviet Jewish Affairs* 19, no. 3 (1989).

Yanov, A. *The Russian Idea and the Year 2000.* Oxford: Oxford University Press, 1987.

Young, G. *Nikolai Feodorov: An Introduction.* Belmont: Norland Publishing House, 1979.

Yudin, A. "Legendi i fakti. Statiia Marksa 'K evreiskomu voprosu' i vokrug neio" (Legends and facts. The discussion of Marx's "On the Jewish Question"). *Moskva* no. 8 (1994).

Vasil'chikov, A. "Obschina protiv kommunisma" (The community against communism). *Nash sovremennik* no. 7 (1994).

Ziuganov, G. *Za gorizontom* (Beyond the horizon). Moscow: Informpechat, 1995.

Ziuganov, G. "Empire of the US: 200 Years of American Dream" (in Russian). *Nash sovremennik* no. 8 (1994).

Websites

http://www.compromat.ru
http://arktogaia.ru
http://jeffsarchive.com

Index